Subversive Sounds

Subversive Sounds

*Race and the Birth of Jazz in
New Orleans*

CHARLES HERSCH

The University of Chicago Press   Chicago and London

CHARLES HERSCH is associate professor of political science at Cleveland State University. He is the author of *Democratic Artworks: Politics and the Arts from Trilling to Dylan*.

The University of Chicago Press, Chicago 60637
The University of Chicago Press, Ltd., London
© 2007 by The University of Chicago
All rights reserved. Published 2007
Printed in the United States of America

16 15 14 13 12 11 10 09 08 07   1 2 3 4 5
ISBN-13: 978-0-226-32867-6 (cloth)
ISBN-10: 0-226-32867-8 (cloth)

Library of Congress Cataloging-in-Publication Data

Hersch, Charles, 1956–
    Subversive sounds : race and the birth of jazz in New Orleans /
Charles Hersch.
        p.   cm.
    Includes bibliographical references (p.), discography (p.), and index.
    ISBN-13: 978-0-226-32867-6 (cloth : alk. paper)
    ISBN-10: 0-226-32867-8 (cloth : alk. paper)   1. Jazz—Louisiana—
New Orleans—History and criticism.   2. Music—Social aspects—
Louisiana—New Orleans—History.   3. Music and race.   I. Title.
    ML3508.8.N48H47   2007
    781.65′20976335—dc22
                                                                    2007017404

♾ The paper used in this publication meets the minimum requirements of the American National Standard for Information Sciences— Permanence of Paper for Printed Library Materials, ANSI Z39.48-1992.

To my sons
Max and Gabriel

Contents

Acknowledgments

Writing is a solitary activity, but this book would not have been possible without the help of many people. I am particularly grateful for the support of Douglas Mitchell, executive editor at the University of Chicago Press. Bruce Boyd Raeburn, the tireless curator of the William Ransom Hogan Archive of New Orleans Jazz at Tulane University, guided me through a forbidding array of oral histories, clippings, scrawled notes, and reprints of obscure publications. He also generously shared his vast knowledge of New Orleans jazz. Lynn Abbott of the Hogan Jazz Archive cheerfully helped me access information and availed me of his intimate familiarity with the Crescent City's musical history. The staff of the Williams Research Center of the Historic New Orleans Collection, particularly Siva Blake, also provided invaluable assistance. Christine Day and Steve Schmitt welcomed me into their home during my several trips to New Orleans, and I am grateful for their friendship.

Two readers for the University of Chicago Press, William Howland Kenney and John Gennari, provided a wealth of insightful comments that were indispensable in revising the manuscript. Tim McGovern, editorial associate, and Ruth Goring, manuscript editor, also helped me in the publication process.

Brian Weiner, Joshua Miller, Jason Earle, Jeneen Hobby, Dan Malachuk, Jefferey Lewis, and Peter Meiksins offered helpful suggestions on various parts of the book. Three important scholars in jazz studies provided encouragement and advice: Sherrie Tucker, William Howland Kenney, and Robin D. G. Kelley.

Thanks to Ajay Heble of the annual Guelph Jazz Festival and Colloquium for giving me a forum to present my ideas as they were being developed. Neil McLaughlin provided a place to stay and great conversations while I was presenting papers at Guelph. Wayne Everard of the New Orleans Public Library helped me locate police records for the period. Donald Marquis, author of the indispensable *In Search of Buddy Bolden*, also assisted me with those documents. William J. Shafer provided me with copies of John Robichaux's scores to "High Society." Tom Lanham at the Louisiana State Museum and Lynn Abbott of the Hogan Jazz Archive helped me acquire the photographs in this book. I am also grateful for Laura Walker's extraordinarily careful proofreading of the manuscript.

Shahin Afnan created the maps of New Orleans, with the assistance of James Wyles and Sita Lambden.

I would like to thank my colleagues at Cleveland State University for their support, particularly my chair, David Elkins. Virginia Varaljay provided valuable secretarial help, cheerfully photocopying hundreds of pages.

For their friendship (and occasional advice) I would like to thank David Shutkin, Connie Friedman, Jason Earle, Marquita Rodgers, Josh Miller, Brian Weiner, and Garnette Cadogan. Members of my family provided crucial support: my sister Julie Hersch, my father Robert Hersch, and Joanne Hersch. The energy and creativity of my sons Max and Gabriel are a continuing inspiration to me, and they showed remarkable patience when I had to check over my endnotes instead of playing catch on the front lawn.

Lastly, I want to thank my wife, Shahin Afnan, for her love, companionship, and insight as well as her research assistance.

Portions of chapter 5 were previously published in *Polity* 34, no. 3 (Spring 2002): 371–92. I am grateful to the publisher for permission to reprint them.

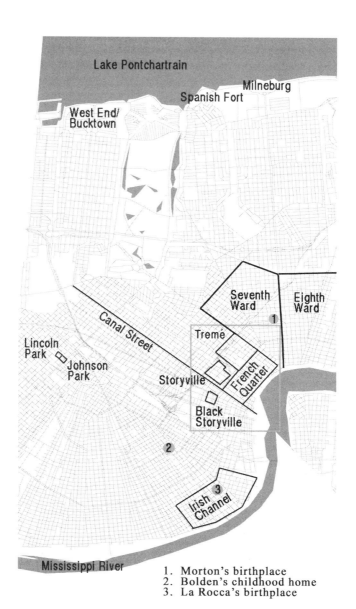

1. Morton's birthplace
2. Bolden's childhood home
3. La Rocca's birthplace

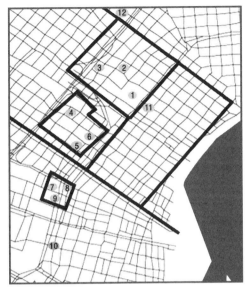

1. Congo Square
2. Economy Hall
3. Jeunes Amis Hall
4. The Frenchman's
5. The Big 25
6. The 101 Ranch
7. Funky Butt Hall
8. Armstrong's birthplace
9. Spano's
10. The Red Onion
11. Homer Plessy's shoemaker's shop
12. Artisan Hall

Opening Riff: Jelly Roll Morton's Stars and Stripes

Recalling his youth in early-twentieth-century New Orleans, Ferdinand Lamothe sits down at the piano to play that most American of marches, John Philip Sousa's "The Stars and Stripes Forever."[1] Lamothe is a mixed-race, Afro-French Creole of Color, though he has abandoned his Gallic surname in favor of Morton, he claims "for business reasons."[2] Like many in the underworld of the red light district—Sheep Bite, Toodlums, Gyp the Blood, Boar Hog, Dirty Dog, Sore Dick, Steel Arm Johnny, Willie the Pleaser, Okey Poke, Chicken Dick, Greasy, Knock-on-the wall, and Black Dude—the sometime pimp Morton has a nickname: Jelly Roll. Adopting such a nickname created a new identity that placed one beyond the role whites had assigned people of color, like Railroad Bill, the "conjure man" who could change his appearance whenever the law was after him. Such "bad men" frequented the "disrespectable" saloons and honky-tonks from which jazz emerged.[3]

Jelly Roll Morton, playing "Stars and Stripes": Creole by birth, black thanks to Jim Crow, playing a "white" song straight out of Americana. One can only imagine what it meant to Morton at the height of America's love affair with racial segregation to celebrate his country in song. Or was it his country? If he plays the song, is he accepting America's rejection of his claim to citizenship or even his humanity? Should he refuse to play it, insisting, with Frederick Douglass, that "this Fourth [of] July is *yours*, not *mine*"?[4]

Figure 3. Jelly Roll Morton at the piano with his Red Hot Peppers, including Kid Ory on trombone and Johnny St. Cyr on banjo. (Photo courtesy of the William Ransom Hogan Archive, Tulane University.)

Morton takes a different path. Rather than either refusing to play the song or playing it in a reverent, patriotic style, Morton "signifies" upon it, transforms it using African-based musical devices. Morton was a master at signifying, satirical and otherwise, singing countless lewd variations of popular songs.[5] His most obvious transformation of "Stars and Stripes" is rhythmic. Morton syncopates the melody, moving the emphasis to the offbeats (2 and 4), and shifts the time signature from 2/4 to 4/4. His alterations loosen and lighten the tune, converting stately march music into something more African and yet more American. Sousa could not fully break away from the European models; it takes the Creole Morton to truly reclaim the music for the New World.

Morton also transforms the piece melodically through "call and response," the most dialogic of African American musical devices. In the first chorus of "The Stars and Stripes Forever," Morton plays jazzy responses to the written melody in the empty spaces, and in the second he adds another voice to the conversation by playing a descending bass line to accompany his "responses" to the melody. Rather than substituting a monolithic, African-based response to Sousa, Morton with these complex layers creates a dialogue that refuses to foreclose continued interaction among the strains that make up America. In short, Morton sets up a multilayered musical conversation with his country, taking a traditional American march and turning it into jazz. Transforming the piece for people of color, Morton inserts them into mainstream American culture and simultaneously changes that culture. Morton's "Stars and Stripes" thus exemplifies jazz's Africanization of American music, a process that had begun with ragtime and, with rock and hip-hop, continues to this day.

Introduction

In New Orleans, on a summer's day in 1892, a shoemaker boarded a "white" railroad car and was arrested. Four years later, the United States Supreme Court took up the case of this man, Homer Plessy, described in the opinion of the Court as "a citizen of the United States and a resident of the state of Louisiana, of mixed descent, in proportion of seven-eighths Caucasian and one-eighth African blood [such] that the mixture of colored blood was not discernible in him."[1] In a landmark decision, the Court ruled against Plessy, placing a constitutional seal of approval on a series of Jim Crow laws meant to preserve the purity of the white race.

Plessy confronted racial purity spatially, as it were, by placing his "colored" body in a "white" space, threatening it with impurity. More fundamentally, he challenged racial purity through his very identity: though Plessy is remembered as a "black" man fighting for civil rights, he was in fact a Creole of Color, of French and African descent. He argued that since a conductor would not be able to tell that he was black, the classification into black and white train cars was unworkable. In making this argument, he called into question the binary division between the races that is still taken for granted by many today, challenging uniformity with multiplicity, purity with impurity.

New Orleans in the 1890s also saw the birth of a new music, designated "ratty" or, later, "jazz," that was also viewed as a threat to racial purity. Early attacks on jazz centered on its association with African Americans and claimed the music would produce national impurity and degeneration. As early as 1890, the *New Orleans Mascot* criticized a "nigger band" in the tenderloin district for encouraging racial boundary cross-ings: "Here male and female, black and yellow, and even white, meet on terms of equality and abandon themselves to the extreme limit of ob-scenity and lasciviousness." Other "undesirable" ethnic and immigrant groups involved in jazz were thought to similarly taint the music, mak-ing it dangerous to "real" Americans. In a 1918 essay, Daniel Gregory Mason argued that ragtime could never really represent America because many of its composers, like Irving Berlin, were Jewish.[2] (He was clearly speaking of popular derivations of ragtime rather than the music of Scott Joplin and his associates.)

Jazz's opponents heard racial and ethnic mixing in the music itself, European harmonies sullied by African rhythmic and tonal devices. An 1894 *New Orleans Daily Picayune* editorial, comparing the new music to classical works, said that "it is to be regretted that something which is in itself pure and beautiful, and which is capable of inspiring the profound-est sentiments and inciting to the noblest acts, has ever been associated with that which is frivolace [sic], demoralizing and degrading. The union is wholly forced and unnatural." In short, the integrity of American cul-ture was dependent upon ethnic purity, and keeping America ethnically pure meant protecting music from impure influences. Mason argued that just as expressions like "I reckon" pervert the English language, ragtime threatens the integrity of music. In a kind of displacement of racial is-sues onto musical ones, another author associated jazz with "primitive people and savages" like Chinese and Arabs and with bad grammar, con-tending that jazz violinists' use of the glissando muddied the cleanliness of standard pitch.[3] Jazz was musical miscegenation.

In this book I argue that jazz did in fact subvert racial segregation, mu-sically enacting and abetting Plessy's assault on white purity. At a time when racial boundaries in America were rigidifying, jazz arose out of and encouraged racial boundary crossings by creating racially mixed spaces and racially impure music, both of which altered the racial identities of musicians and listeners.

Jazz subverted sexual purity as well, for according to the *Mascot*'s edi-torial when jazz causes the races to mix, they "abandon themselves . . . to obscenity and lasciviousness." To its critics, jazz represented an attack on traditional moral values. Newspapers and "reformers" charged that in place of hard work and sexual restraint, jazz encouraged promiscuity and hedonism. For opponents of the music, jazz embodied what Bakhtin calls the carnivalesque, the transgressing of bodily boundaries, an ele-vating of "lower" (literally and morally) bodily functions over "higher" ones.[4] The music had such associations for some enthusiasts as well, creating the opportunity to stretch their identities beyond acceptable boundaries. Thus did jazz bring together the threats of race mixing, musical defilement, and moral degeneration.

In telling the history of jazz's subversion of racial and, to a lesser degree, moral boundaries, I ask a number of questions. What are some of the ways jazz resisted or accepted Jim Crow? How did relations among blacks, whites, and Creoles of Color affect the development of jazz? How did the musicians' racial identity affect the music that they played? How did the racial composition of the audience influence musicians and their music? The book also raises larger questions, mostly reserved for the conclusion, about music, race, and politics: What is the best way to talk about race's role in music? What is music's effect on racial identity? How can music act as a vehicle for political change?

Drawing on oral histories, newspaper editorials, police reports, and musical performances, I foreground the struggles of musicians to negotiate a complex, changing political landscape. The growing push for racial purity in New Orleans limited the ability of musicians to pursue their craft and grow as artists, circumscribing who could play with whom, where and what they could play, and for which audiences. Musicians sometimes found ways to transgress or evade such boundaries, and those transgressions, as well as the boundaries themselves, influenced the development of the music. In the shadow of Jim Crow, the complex interactions among musicians, the music's opponents, and its audiences shaped jazz and its political meaning.

"Pancultural Bouillabaisse": The Melting-Pot Model of Jazz and Its Limitations

This book arose in part out of my dissatisfaction with previous accounts of early jazz. Jazz historians like Sherrie Tucker, Scott DeVeaux, Eric Porter, and David Ake have insightfully analyzed the myriad ways race and social and economic conditions have affected the identities and practices, musical and occupational, of jazz musicians. Yet although a number of short essays regarding New Orleans have come out of "the New Jazz Studies," there has been only one book highlighting race in New Orleans jazz, and its focus on Louis Armstrong and the "black vernacular" is very different from mine.[5] Popular histories of early jazz have increasingly considered racial issues, but in a way that does not do justice to the complexity of race, particularly in New Orleans, and thus they miss much of what is important about the music.

The earliest accounts of jazz attributed the music either to whites or to naïve blacks expressing a primitive racial essence. Thus, according to *Jazzmen* (1939), blacks had an "innate power of invention"; the New Orleans musician played "only what he *felt*," "having no teacher to show him the supposed limitations of his instrument," free "from any restraining tradition and supervision" (emphasis in original). Deriving in part from a Popular Front leftism that saw African Americans as a "folk" akin to the proletariat, this picture of blacks as "natural" musicians combines admiration with racism.[6] Proponents of this point of view sought to preserve what they saw as pure jazz against outside influences, particularly commercial ones, even viewing swing music as a perversion of jazz's black essence.

Later accounts also saw jazz as "black music," but from a black nationalist perspective, and considered white musicians to be at best foreign-language speakers. Thus in his influential *Blues People* (1963), Amiri Baraka compares the "natural" expression of African Americans with the "tendency" of white jazz musicians to play music that is a kind of "artifact" removed from themselves. Wynton Marsalis draws on this tradition when he laments how the "white musician learns how to play and gets to a certain degree of proficiency, not as good as the black musician that they've learned from," yet are celebrated as masters in the media.[7] For Marsalis, jazz is completely "'outside' of European conventions of instrumental technique and performance," and the mixing of black and white musical cultures represents an unnatural union, "like having sex with your daughter," that destroys each of them.[8]

More recent general histories retell what I call the jazz melting-pot narrative in which black, Creole, and white influences melted into something "American." ("Creole" in this book refers to Creoles of Color, unless noted otherwise.) According to Ted Gioia's *History of Jazz* (1997), nineteenth-century New Orleans culture was an "exotic mixture of European, Caribbean, African, and American elements," "perhaps the most seething ethnic melting pot that the nineteenth-century world could produce." Evoking exotic jungle stereotypes, Gioia attributes this "cultural gumbo" to New Orleans's "laissez-faire environment," a "warm, moist atmosphere" where "sharp delineations between cultures gradually softened and ultimately disappeared." Culinary metaphors also loom large in Ken Burns's *Jazz*, with Wynton Marsalis invoking "gumbo" and Gary Giddins dubbing the music a "pancultural bouillabaisse" that uses "diverse ethnic spices."[9] Here popular jazz historians retell a classic narrative, in which America has slowly incorporated different races and nationalities and melted them into a homogenous "American." Thus jazz itself is a triumph of the American dream—black African-based music and white European music came together and formed jazz, which then became simply American music.

Although it is true that various elements from different cultures went into the making of jazz, the language of amalgamation, gumbo, and melting pot is problematic. Despite the appearance of trying to understand the birth of jazz in its social and political context, melting-pot narratives ultimately eliminate race, seeing racism as simply an obstacle to be overcome rather than something that affected the music itself. From this perspective, some musicians were impeded by racism, while others overcame it through sheer will: as Burns tells it, "nothing could demean Duke Ellington because he refused ever to be demeaned." Yet seeing racial boundaries as mere artifacts that sometimes inhibited the music's progress does not allow us to understand how society's racial rules, customs, expectations, and prohibitions influenced the creation and development of jazz.[10] Such narratives depoliticize a richly political story, evading race's role in jazz while evoking it, making a process that was full of dynamic, even chaotic activity appear inevitable and seamless.

The "black origins" and melting-pot models are, in fact, two sides of the same coin, both seeing racial identity as an inborn essence but disagreeing about the extent and desirability of "melting." Wynton Marsalis and his forebears Albert Murray and Stanley Crouch combine the two, arguing that jazz and blues embody an essential "omni-American" culture, the "negro" constituting "maybe the most American of Americans." Ironically, in positing a "pure" American jazz tradition, Marsalis fails to see how the music of his hometown was impure from its inception, constantly picking up traces of its influences without melting them down.[11] Jazz was never singular but always multiple, constantly overflowing the containers critics tried to force it into.

A relatively recent understanding of racial dynamics in culture that goes beyond the melting pot is "creolization." Creolists emphasize the continuous quality of interactions between the races, calling into question the idea of pure cultures of any sort. As Robert Baron and Ana C. Cara put it, "Creole forms are never static. They are at no time fully formed; their protean nature continually adjusts to their immediate interactive context, often improvising as they adjust. Creolization can thus liberate us from a notion of fixed or 'finished' products of culture to a focus on cultures in transition, allowing us to grasp the 'in-betweens,' the ambiguous spaces, where cultural boundaries blur and disappear as hierarchical categories collapse into each other." From this perspective, "creole cultural forms are often subversive social and political tools," fomenting "continuous creative exchange." In the process of creolization, "a multiplicity of codes, voices, styles, meanings, and identities" come together, creating something new.[12]

Such analyses of the encounter between African and European cultures are useful, yet in their celebration of openness they minimize the surrounding historical/political constraints. In one early example of creolist theorizing, Daniel J. Crowley argued that "a Trinidadian feels no inconsistency in being a . . . Negro in appearance, a Spaniard in name, a Roman Catholic in church, an obeah (magic) practitioner in private, a Hindu at lunch, a Chinese at dinner [and a] Portuguese at work."[13] What Crowley failed to acknowledge is that all these influences are not equally powerful, and one cannot always fully choose different identities. There is something creative and open about creolization, but the openness is bounded by power relationships. To really understand the coming together of African and American cultures, we have to look at the power dynamics attending any particular combination of cultural forms.

In this book I seek to talk about jazz's roots in the interaction of African, European, and American music in a way that pays attention to the larger social context, particularly the differing power relationships among the actors. New Orleans was "creole," but the interactions between the races were bounded by power; Gioia to the contrary, New Orleans was hardly "laissez faire" in relation to race. A relative tolerance in particular neighborhoods did help bring jazz into being, but violent racism was an undeniable part of the city's culture. Jazz was a means for those who were marginalized to have their voices heard, but it was shaped by those who fought against the music, resisting the racial impurity that it represented. This book describes jazz's formative years (roughly 1890–1915) in a way that pays attention to both the possibilities for individuals to negotiate their racial identities and the constraints on racial boundary crossings.

Beyond Racial Purity: Race as Contextual

Subversive Sounds also differs from previous accounts of New Orleans jazz in its understanding of race itself. Recent theorists see "white," "black," "Hispanic," "Asian," and so on as socially constructed rather than natural, contingent rather than fixed. Thus one's race can change depending on the context. A light-skinned African American may be "black" to white neighbors but "high yellow" to other African Americans. Racial identity can also change with one's location. When Piri Thomas, born in Puerto Rico with a mixture of Indian, African, and European ancestry, moved to the United States, he was forced to choose a single racial identity; he eventually chose black because of his dark complexion, whereas his brother, lighter in skin tone, became white. However, even within the United States, Thomas's racial identity varied; in Spanish Harlem he was Puerto Rican, in Long Island he was accused of passing for white, and in the South he was black.[14]

Racial categories have shifted over time as well. An influential book published at the time of jazz's emergence claimed that some ethnic groups we would now call white were essentially different races from northern Europeans. Thus, according to Frederick L. Hoffman, while those of "Indo-Germanic stock" can intermarry without harm, "it is an entirely different manner when Germans and Italians, English and Spaniards, Swedes and Turks intermarry and have children."[15]

Racial identity was particularly malleable in New Orleans during the period of jazz's emergence, and this malleability made jazz possible. Not only was the city known for its large mulatto population, but racial classifications were in flux, with the one-drop rule increasingly overshadowing a system based on national origin (French or "American") and color gradation. Courts struggled to define race, sometimes emphasizing color, sometimes genealogy (percentage of white ancestry) and sometimes even (as one court put it in 1910) "evidence of reputation, or social reception, and of the exercise of the privileges of a white man." Any particular individual might constitute a different combination of color, ancestry, and demeanor. One could be less African by ancestry yet darker than someone with more "African" blood. Sometimes courts said that the kinkiness of the hair was the deciding factor.[16] Which factor—color, ancestry, or demeanor—made one "black" or "white" depended on who was doing the classifying.

This inherent indeterminacy of racial classifications, particularly apparent in New Orleans, posed a problem for the implementation of Jim Crow, as Homer Plessy asserted. Segregation rests on a rigid, "pure" white identity that excludes the "nonwhite"; admitting any blackness within the white self threatens its integrity. But if race is a social construction, an individual's racial designation is open to modification, creating the possibility of a more fluid racial identity, what Ronald Radano calls "blackness in whiteness" and "whiteness in blackness."[17] This possibility in New Orleans contributed to the creation of jazz, and jazz fostered further racial malleability.

Music and Ethnic Identity

Works of art are particularly well suited to open up fissures, however small, in racially pure identities, for they can affect what Raymond Williams calls "structures of feeling"—"meanings and values as they are actively lived and felt." This is particularly true of music because of its effect on the body and through it the emotions. Music, in the words of Martin Stokes, "provides means by which people recognize identities and places, and the boundaries that separate them. . . . Musical performance, as well as the acts of listening, dancing, arguing, discussing, thinking and writing about music, provide the means by which ethnicities and identities are constructed and mobilized."[18] A dark-skinned black woman who listens to "alternative" rock may be considered "not black enough" by her hip-hop-loving friends, whereas whites who listen to or play African American music sometimes see themselves as black to various degrees. This phenomenon runs the gamut from Milton "Mezz" Mezzrow and Johnny Otis, white musicians who tried to "become black," to contemporary "wiggaz" (or "wiggers"), white youth obsessed with hip-hop culture.[19]

In its construction of ethnic identity, music can be a force for purity, shaping a rigid self that excludes the Other. Catholics in Northern Ireland try to keep their music "pure" by rejecting "English" instruments like guitar; one musician not too many years ago was assaulted with an ax because he brought a guitar to an Irish club. Protestants march through Catholic neighborhoods playing loud drums as an "assault on the ears" in which "no alternative thought is possible. The drums demand that people either march in time to them, or go away," creating a monologic Protestant public space.[20]

Yet music can also create opportunities for the thinning of racial boundaries, creating the possibility of more inclusive selves, more open to the Other, racially and otherwise. When New Orleans musicians used African musical devices to "blacken" European forms or adjusted the music they played to the race of the audience, they were facilitating such racially impure identities.

Politics and Music

I am not arguing that jazz musicians consciously thought of themselves as political actors or that their music necessarily overtly referred to political themes. Rather, I draw on Robin D. G. Kelley's insight that "politics comprises the many battles to roll back constraints and exercise some power over, or create some space within, the institutions and social relationships that dominate our lives." According to Kelley, politics cannot be separated from "issues of economic well-being, safety, pleasure, cultural expression, sexuality, freedom of mobility, and other facets of daily life. Politics is not separate from lived experience or the imaginary world of what is possible; to the contrary, politics is about these things."[21] Thus at the same time that New Orleanians of color were excluded from many professions; treated unequally in the legal system; not allowed to vote or hold office; forced to use separate streetcar compartments, water fountains, and toilets; and constantly threatened with violence, they pushed against the limits of these boundaries by playing and listening to jazz. In the process they created pockets of freedom—literally free spaces where jazz was performed for interracial audiences, as well as the existential freedom that comes from stretching one's identity beyond socially and legally imposed limits, crossing the barrier between African American and white subjectivities. Jazz musicians tried to accomplish a number of objectives—entertain, make a living, express themselves—but the music's meaning and impact went beyond what they intended and the conceptions of those listening to jazz or trying to stop it. When jazz spread beyond New Orleans, it helped create a racially "impure" American popular music that is still with us.

I am cognizant of limits to the ability of music to bridge racial gaps. It is possible to love jazz and hate African Americans. Whites expected blacks to utilize music for their entertainment and pleasure; such interchange was in many ways consistent with racial subordination, for blacks were seen as naturally rhythmic and inventive but incapable of higher thought. Musicians found ways at times to evade the strictures of segregation, but racism influenced which musicians played together, what kind of music was played before a particular audience, who listened to the music and with whom, and what the music meant to those listeners. One could not be any race at any time, but musicians exploited and expanded the fuzziness around racial boundaries that did exist. The intersection of political reality—racial categories and economic conditions—and the attitudes and practices of jazz musicians, audiences, and opponents lies at the core of this book's narrative.

My story of jazz, race, and politics in New Orleans begins with the *place* of its origins: New Orleans itself, with its traditions of music, racism, and racial mixing. More particularly, the music began in working-class black clubs, where it served to bring joy into the life of listeners who were mired in poverty and oppression, facilitating pleasure and the blurring of interpersonal boundaries—values hostile to the growing mainstream valorization of the work ethic, asceticism, and individualism (chapter 1).

The music and the values it represented did not stay confined to this lower-class milieu, however, but spread to middle-class audiences through parades, lawn parties, picnics, and other public events. "Impure" spaces allowed listeners to be exposed to the music of different races, and such exposure stretched the identities of musicians and listeners. At the same time, upholders of purity condemned the music and sought to stop its spread by confining it to certain neighborhoods (chapter 2).

The attempts to contain the music ultimately failed, and subsequent chapters analyze in more detail the means by which early jazz subverted racial boundaries. Chapter 3 focuses on the role of musicians in facilitating the circulation of the music across racial lines. In order to learn their craft and maximize their employment opportunities, musicians had to acquire a multiracial musical vocabulary, crossing racial lines by listening to, learning from, and emulating musicians of other races. The challenges to doing so differed depending on whether the musician was black, white, or Creole as well as his or her class background. These racial crossings by musicians set in motion a process by which an ever-changing array of sounds circulated throughout the city, spreading impurity.

Chapter 4 looks at the effects of such circulation on the music itself, focusing on African Americans' alteration of American and European musical sources through "signifying." *Signifying* is an African American trope, usually understood as a literary device, that draws on a source but changes it, somewhat like satire but not necessarily derisive. Jazz musicians signified upon American music using African-influenced devices like syncopation, polyphony, call and response, and blues inflections. In doing so they Africanized American culture, making more porous the boundaries between black and white.

Chapter 5 looks at the dissemination of jazz from New Orleans outward. I show how Jelly Roll Morton (Creole), Nick La Rocca (white), and Louis Armstrong (black) spread the carnivalesque values of the Crescent City, continuing the musical miscegenation that began there. With a focus on Armstrong, who thought of his music as a device for racial rapprochement, I argue that the contrasting fates of the three men was influenced by their racial identities and their relationship to those identities. Though La Rocca and the Original Dixieland Jazz Band achieved mass success and Morton created innovative and influential compositions and recordings, only Armstrong reached a wide audience for the long haul. Using African devices to transform popular songs, Armstrong and his impure, subversive sounds challenged racial boundaries for decades.

I conclude in a bit more speculative vein, drawing on the story of New Orleans jazz to briefly explore the relationship between the music, racial identity, and political reality. This music, I suggest, created the possibility of what I call racial intersubjectivity, a kind of opening of the racial self to the racial Other.

But that is at the end of this book's journey. Let us begin by taking ourselves back to New Orleans in the 1890s, immersing ourselves in the city's politics and racial and class geography and observing the freer spaces opened up by the emergence of a new kind of music. New Orleans had a unique mix of copious music tied up with everyday life, relative racial fluidity and tolerance, and virulent racism. It was this milieu, akin to the idiosyncratic mixture of amino acids that resulted in life on earth, that provided the conditions under which jazz could develop. What kind of music do we hear when Homer Plessy, civil rights pioneer, and Buddy Bolden, "the first man of jazz," jam together?

ONE

Places

"Change life!" "Change Society!" These precepts mean nothing without the production of an appropriate space.... New social relationships call for a new space. HENRI LEFEBVRE

Aurora Borealis

As the nineteenth century turned to the twentieth, New Orleans overflowed with music. For guitarist Danny Barker, music was a pied piper that could appear at any moment, causing people to drop what they were doing and follow it: "[A] bunch of us kids, playing, would suddenly hear sounds. It was like a phenomenon, like the Aurora Borealis.... The sounds of men playing would be so clear, but we wouldn't be sure where they were coming from. So we'd start trotting, start running—'It's this way!' 'It's that way!'—And, sometimes, after running for a while, you find you'd be nowhere near that music. But that music could come on you any time like that. The city was full of the sounds of music."[1] The sounds of cornetist Buddy Bolden were described in similar terms. Legend has it that Bolden would simply point his cornet in the air, "calling his children home," and crowds came running from miles away.

Music in New Orleans was part of everyday life, closer to the West African music tradition than the European concert model. The city had brass bands, singing street vendors, black string quartets playing classical European dances (schottisches, mazurkas, quadrilles) and ragtime, and a whole variety of others. Bolden, Morton, and others learned tunes

15

that some described as blues from the rag man, who blew on a tin whistle as he traveled the streets. Surrounding towns had both black and white brass bands; in addition, brass bands from the city would travel into the country. As a port city, New Orleans was exposed to music from all over the globe. One musician remembered hearing music wafting down from various ships docked in the harbor, one nation's vessel speaking to another, akin to the jazz melodies emanating simultaneously from different campsites at Milneburg, the lakefront resort.[2]

New Orleans, in short, boasted a virtual cacophony of musical styles and institutions, including a famous French opera house. At Fisk School at Franklin and Perdido, in what would become Black Storyville, students performed "singing and acting of numerous selections from the burlesque opera 'HMS Pinafore'"; alumni include Buddy Bolden and Louis Armstrong. There were also many children's bands ("spasm bands"), sometimes using homemade instruments, playing for change or food. Such children played music on cigar-box guitars and violins, tin-bucket banjos with thread and fishing-line strings, soapbox basses, or "homemade drums made by punching holes in a tin can and using chair rounds for sticks." Trombonist Edward "Kid" Ory as a young child sang in a "humming band," performing on a bridge at night for ginger cakes.[3]

Most of the music at the turn of that century we would not recognize as jazz, let alone "New Orleans jazz." Small groups with woodwind and brass instruments, though existing, were not the norm; most ensembles featured a violin or accordion as the lead instrument, with a guitar or banjo, and perhaps a mandolin, and a bass. According to Barney Bigard, "Most of the bands had a violinist as a leader. Those early bands didn't sound anything like the kind of jazz bands you hear today." When Eddie Dawson formed a band in 1902, it was, like many bands then, a "string band"—mandolin, guitar, bass, and banjo. Dawson claims brass instruments were not even allowed in Storyville until 1906, when Freddie Keppard received special permission to play cornet with the Tuxedo Band at the 101 Ranch. As late as 1910, according to some, most bass players played with the bow rather than plucking the strings.[4]

Sometime around the 1890s, however, a new music had begun to emerge in New Orleans, called "ratty," a kind of embryonic jazz. Though some recent commentators have attempted to refute what is in their view the outdated "myth" that jazz began in New Orleans, I believe the evidence shows that the Crescent City was in fact the music's birthplace. While it is true that jazz was influenced by other kinds of music, notably ragtime and black folk music (spirituals, work songs, and other precursors of the blues), those sources first combined into something new in

New Orleans. Instrumental ragtime containing elements central to jazz, most notably syncopation, sprung up around the country, but it lacked the improvisation and connection with the blues that are central to jazz itself.[5] All of the major innovators in early jazz—Buddy Bolden, Freddie Keppard, Joe "King" Oliver, Ferdinand "Jelly Roll" Morton, Sidney Bechet, and Louis Armstrong, to name only a few—were New Orleanians. In addition, the uniqueness of New Orleans jazz was constantly noted by observers at the time. Hailing from Indiana, Wilbur de Paris, who traveled with his father's family band in the early 1900s, later recalled being surprised by the unique rhythms and improvisations played by the city's musicians: "[The] music I heard in New Orleans was different from any music I had heard anywhere else.... I hadn't heard music like this even on the road, traveling all over the country."[6]

"Africanized" Culture and "Africo-American" Activism

Central to the growth of this new music was a strong black population unafraid to assert its power. The strength of the city's black community was reflected in New Orleans's "Africanized" culture: "No other American city has such a pronounced African identity." West Africa has given New Orleans a distinctive style, expressed through movement and music. The "second line" whereby children and others follow alongside a marching band, dancing, seems to have its origin in Africa, and the jazz funeral, central to New Orleans culture, shares a sensibility with African rituals, one "in which death is one stage in the longer journey of the spirit."[7]

Because of its unique history, Louisiana allowed African culture to survive longer than in other states. In the words of Gwendolyn Midlo Hall, "A free population of African descent emerged quite early in New Orleans." "In early New Orleans . . . being black did not necessarily mean being a slave. Nor was whiteness associated with prestige and power," since the whites were members of low-status groups. Another contributing factor to the preservation of African culture in Louisiana was the concentration of slaves from Senegambia, the area between the Senegal and Gambia rivers, a uniquely cohesive civilization and a crossroads where various cultures met in trade and warfare.

Despite their forcible removal to the new world, slaves maintained emotional and symbolic ties with Africa; new slaves from the same region gave updated information about the homeland and reinforced ties. Just like other immigrants or displaced populations, Africans were "active agents in reformulating their cultural and social identities in the Americas, despite the oppressive setting to which they were subjugated." They drew on their heritages to make sense of their enslaved lives in America, creating "a new social world that drew on the known African experience." For many slaves in the Americas, "Africa continued to live in their daily lives." In short, according to Hall,

French Louisiana was not a stable society controlled by a culturally and socially cohesive white elite ruling a dominated, immobilized, fractionalized, and culturally obliterated slave population. The chaotic conditions prevailing in the colony, the knowledge and skills of the African population, the size and importance of the Indian population throughout the eighteenth century, and the geography of lower Louisiana, which allowed for easy mobility along its waterways as well as escape and survival in the nearby, pervasive swamps, all contributed to an unusually cohesive and heavily Africanized culture in lower Louisiana: clearly the most Africanized slave culture in the United States.[8]

By the late nineteenth century, New Orleans, "the only real urban center" in the primarily rural deep South, had the biggest population of free African Americans in the region, a population that took to the streets to assert its rights. As early as 1865, black and white dockworkers in New Orleans launched an interracial strike, and five years later black dockworkers in the city formed the Protective Benevolent Mutual Aid Association, which went on to become one of the strongest black unions of the next fifty years. During the same period, more than thirty black and white workers' organizations combined to form the Central Trade and Labor Assembly, encompassing over fifteen thousand members. In the 1880s, large numbers of dockworkers had taken part in strikes and other activities with the Knights of Labor, and in the mid-1890s black longshoremen forced the New Orleans Cotton Exchange and shippers to give workers of all races equal job opportunities and wages.[9]

This activism was not confined to unionized workers. In the words of one historian, "Negroes in New Orleans were far more articulate, literate, and cosmopolitan than blacks in most other Southern cities.... In no Southern city did Negro leaders express their racial, social, and economic philosophies more clearly or on a more sophisticated level than in New Orleans." Blacks fought for integration and spoke out for their rights. As one black paper put it in 1872, "We will agitate, and agitate, and struggle for enjoyment of our rights at all times, under all circumstances and at every hazard."[10] In an expression of racial pride, blacks in New Orleans called themselves "Africo-American" or "African," and in 1878 there was a movement to capitalize the word *Negro*.

Partly due to this activism, Louisiana's legal codes displayed relative racial tolerance until well into the 1890s. Cities in the South in general gave more freedom to African Americans than they had in rural areas, and New Orleans was no exception. Such tolerance had existed from the city's beginnings. The Code Noir of 1724 prohibited interracial marriages but also guaranteed freed slaves "the same rights, privileges and immunities which are enjoyed by free-born persons." When the Spanish took over in 1762, they freed many slaves, resulting in an increase in the Creole of Color population. At the time of the Louisiana Purchase, the right to vote or serve in the legislature was given exclusively to whites, but anyone who "could prove descent from a French or Spanish ancestor was regarded as a white citizen," regardless of color; one of the conditions of the territory's sale to the United States was that this policy continue.[11]

Reconstruction and the activism it spurred saw further advances in racial equality. Written by an interracial group of activists, the Louisiana constitution of 1868 gave all citizens equal rights, including the right to vote; required integrated public schools; and opened public facilities "to the accommodation and patronage of all persons, without distinction or discrimination on account of race or color." During the 1870s, approximately five hundred to a thousand African American children and several thousand whites attended racially mixed schools. Even in the 1880s, New Orleanians of color were able to ride in first-class railroad cars if they desired. In 1888, half of Louisiana's registered voters were African American, and the legislature included eighteen people of color.[12] Though fast disappearing, New Orleans's relative racial tolerance, as we shall see, laid the groundwork for a music that would catapult African Americans into the center of American culture.

"All Jubileed Up"

The emergence of a music that crossed racial boundaries also required a group that itself blurred such borders—mixed-race Creoles of Color. Though some see Creoles' hybridity as "an awkward middle ground," a kind of political and social no-man's-land, Creoles in fact produced "a syncretic and mercurial culture, one whose overt expression could have only been possible during such a time of social transformation." Creoles represented "the celebration of being both, of creating a culture from what America has always believed, if not always said, was impossible." Whites said race mixing would produce weakness, but Creole culture and the principle of hybridity it represented was full of subversive strength.[13]

The very meaning of the term *Creole* was (and is) a matter of some dispute. Originally referring to a Louisiana-born person of French ancestry, the label said nothing about one's race. Both whites and people of color referred to themselves as Creole, with few conflicts arising over this. Creoles of Color were typically the offspring of French slave owners and slaves during the period of French rule (1718–68); many of the children of such unions were freed by their fathers. The *plaçage* system, begun in the Caribbean, in which French slaveholders had essentially common-law marriages with racially mixed women, helped perpetuate the Creole class. Alice Zeno, clarinetist George Lewis's mother, born in 1864, embodies the African and French mixture in New Orleans. Her grandmother knew some Senegalese and cooked African dishes, but her mother rejected the African language and spoke French and Creole; Zeno grew up speaking French, though she could understand Creole.[14]

The Caribbean, the hub of the slave trade, played a central role in the creation of Creole culture and ultimately jazz. Thomas Fiehrer has argued that the European and African musical traditions "first met and interpenetrated in the West Indies," which contained a powerful, independent mixed-race class called *afranchi*, who could own land and had more freedom than slaves but were prohibited from certain careers and even from wearing clothing associated with the white upper class.[15]

This "third race" took root in the Crescent City when, in response to the 1804 revolution in Saint-Domingue (creating the Republic of Haiti), about ten thousand Creoles, blacks, and whites came to New Orleans, and by 1815, half of the urban population hailed from the West Indies. The vast majority of New Orleans Creoles had roots in Saint-Domingue; refugees from that country were "responsible for the cultural flowering of New Orleans" and "for introducing a Gallic-African pattern into the United States."[16]

The Crescent City's Creoles of Color commonly enjoyed ties with France and the Caribbean, drawing on a "transatlantic network of prominent individuals and families—both black and white—who maintained close connections with New Orleans, and moved freely between France and America, as though the two 'colonies' constituted a single cultural realm." Musician Peter Bocage's grandfather and his violin teacher emigrated from France, while his mother came from Haiti. Many Creoles (and many musicians in particular) worked as cigar makers and in this way had connections with Haiti and Cuba. Creoles sometimes went to

France for education because of lack of opportunities (due to racism) in the United States.[17]

But although the majority of Creoles of Color had French and African ancestry, others represented different mixtures. *Creole* was in fact a catch-all term for those of mixed race, as long as the white part of the mixture was not "American." Louis and Lorenzo Tio Sr., who taught a whole generation of musicians, were born in Mexico, and their descendants had African, French, and Choctaw ancestry and spoke Spanish, English, and French.[18] When cornetist Natty Dominique was asked about the ancestry of the dark-skinned Hispanic Manuel Perez, he replied, "They called him a Creole, that's all I know." Dominique himself, like pianist and "Professor" Manuel Manetta, although considered "Creole," was of Afro-Italian heritage. Sometimes Creoles themselves could not trace their complex lineages with certitude; Louis Keppard, brother of the pioneering cornetist Freddie Keppard, described his ancestry as "all jubileed up."[19]

"Creole" as a Challenge to Racial Categories

The existence of Creoles challenged the binary racial system, and indeed the concept of race itself, in a number of ways. Race in popular consciousness and in the law is rooted in nature, as even those who challenge racial hierarchy often do so based on an essentialist or nature-based notion of race ("Black is beautiful"). From this perspective the presence of Creoles simply meant an expansion of the number of "races" from two to three; in other ways, however, it blurred racial categories in general. Ultimately, the term *Creole* exemplified a way of thinking, in decline at the time jazz emerged, that recognized gradations between black and white, resulting in a whole host of categories specifying one's exact racial mixture. These labels included *mulatto* (black and white), *griffe* (black and mulatto), *sacatro* (black and griffe), *marabon* (mulatto and griffe), *os rouge* (black and Indian), *quadroon* (white and mulatto), *tierceron* (mulatto and quadroon), and *octoroon* (white and quadroon).[20]

At some point such categories collapse due to their complexity, making it very difficult to determine one's "race." Early in the city's history, Denis Macarti, a free man of color from New Orleans, was stabbed and died within a few days. "When he was first stabbed he was a nègre libre. While being treated, he was a grif. When he was buried, he was a mulâtre." Louis Martinet, a civil rights leader, described the racial situation in the late nineteenth century in a letter to one of Homer Plessy's attorneys: "There are the strangest white people you ever saw here. Walking up & down our principal thoroughfare—Canal Street—you would [be] surprised to have persons pointed out to you, some as white & others as colored, and if not informed you would be sure to pick out the white for the colored & the colored for the white." Such race mixing created complications for some families, who might artificially divide into "white" and "black" branches. As musician Mike De Lay put it, "Everyone's colored." "Find me five pure ones . . . of anything."[21]

In addition, the existence of Creoles of Color challenged race-based thinking because it rested on culture rather than biology. As far back as Saint-Domingue, though there were ostensibly three castes (slaves, free people of color, and whites), "the prevailing ambiguities and inherent contradictions of the plantation structure continually operated to undermine rigidity and permitted vagueness, uncertainty, overlap, and social 'passing' on a limited scale." In the late 1880s, speaking of Martinique Creoles, Lafcadio Hearn observed that "it is impossible to establish any color-classification by the eye alone; and whatever line of demarcation can be drawn between castes must be social rather than ethnical." Thus rather than an innate or inherited identity, Creoleness was something one performed, for it depended not on skin color but on how one lived. Usually those who came from a well-known family and were free born, skilled workers, Catholic, mulatto, and French speaking were seen as Creole, even if dark skinned.[22]

However, though in theory Creoleness did not derive from physical appearance, dark-skinned Creoles were sometimes looked upon with suspicion by lighter Creoles who were trying to protect their unique status and avoid falling into the category "black." Clarinetist Joe Darensbourg reported, "I've seen some guys two shades blacker than your shoes call themselves Creole," but acknowledged that this assertion was not always accepted by the majority of Creoles: "You always had a little friction between the real dark race and the light-skinned Creoles." This prejudice may hark back to Saint-Domingue, where the mixed-race Creole (*afranchi*) class split into light-skinned (*milat*) and dark-skinned (*nwa*) factions. Creole, then, was a very slippery category based on assertion—one could never be sure if a person was "really" a Creole or not. As Louis Keppard put it, "When you know a person from birth, then you can tell who they is."[23]

Creoles simply did not fit into a binary racial system. Ultimately, the category "Creole of Color" was a remnant of a dichotomy between "Americans" and "Europeans" that no longer held sway, for though the term purported to name a racial category, it combined race and nationality.[24] Two individuals might have identical proportions of African blood and yet one was "black" and the other "Creole," the latter a different "race" because of French ancestry.

In short, Creoles were hybrid, encompassing what Paul Gilroy has called the "black Atlantic," a cultural system or "formation" involving the circulation of culture, ideas, and persons between Europe, Africa, and the Caribbean.[25] As living embodiments of race mixing, they were direct agents of racial circulation, musically and otherwise.

Enter Jim Crow

In the period during which the music later called "jazz" first emerged, New Orleans's tradition of relative racial tolerance was largely being destroyed by Jim Crow, with a dramatic overturning of the vestiges of equality in the city. Louisiana prohibited interracial marriage in 1894, and a new state constitution in 1898 disenfranchised blacks through a grandfather clause. The pervasive racism is evident in the governor's 1898 address to the Louisiana legislature, praising the new document: "The white supremacy for which we have so long struggled... is now crystallized into the Constitution.... The whole nation with one accord is gathering itself in a common brotherhood for the exercise of its united power." These changes, backed by violence, disenfranchised at least 120,000 African Americans between 1897 and 1900, shrinking the black share of the voting population from 44 percent to 4 percent. (That number would wither even further: in 1910 blacks represented 0.6% of the state's voters.)[26]

By 1900, any advantages New Orleanians of color had over their rural counterparts had vanished, and in 1908 the state legislature outlawed interracial concubinage (the plaçage system).[27] The deterioration of race relations in New Orleans can be seen in the Robert Charles incident in 1900, which began when Charles shot a policeman who had questioned and beat him because he was a "suspicious looking negro." Police eventually killed Charles but only after he had shot twenty-seven whites, killing seven of them (including four policemen). In the aftermath, whites marauded through town for four days, killing at least twelve New Orleanians of color, including the father of clarinetist "Big Eye" Louis Nelson Deslile, wounding many more, and destroying black-owned property, including a school.[28] New Orleans entered the Jim Crow era with a vengeance.

In addition to enduring discrimination, the African American community faced rampant poverty. In 1880, 18 percent of New Orleans males of color were unemployed, with the number reaching 25 percent in some occupations. In the Fifth District, which includes the French Quarter and part of Tremé, African American unemployment was 55 percent. A visitor to the Quarter in the 1880s would observe an "immense eyesore" featuring decomposing garbage, standing water that bred disease, and primitive wooden planks for sidewalks. The average lifespan for a black New Orleanian in 1880 was thirty-six years (forty-six years for whites), with the infant mortality rate at 45 percent; overall mortality rates were 56 percent higher than in the average American city.[29]

Matters worsened during the next decade. The years 1893 to 1897 saw the worst economic crisis of the nineteenth century, with high unemployment heightening tensions between black and white workers. Irish and German immigrants began taking over skilled trades that had been held by African Americans; in 1870, according to a city directory, 3,460 "blacks" (probably including Creoles of Color) worked as carpenters, cigar makers, painters, clerks, shoemakers, coopers, tailors, bakers, blacksmiths, and foundry hands, while by 1904, under a tenth of that number held those jobs, although the number of blacks in the city had increased by 50 percent. Formerly cooperative black and white dockworkers battled in the latter half of the 1890s in the dire economic environment, and by 1900, blacks were excluded from most trade unions.[30]

During the era of jazz's emergence, then, New Orleans was a difficult place for most African Americans. Despite the heavy African influence in New Orleans, to be black meant not having one's identity affirmed by whites and the dominant culture; in addition to discrimination, African Americans suffered the constant humiliation of rituals of subjugation (being addressed as "boy," having to lower one's eyes, and so on), backed by the constant threat of violence.[31] Poverty increased the sense of exclusion.

Ironically, a music that represented a joyous assertion of black culture reaching into the heart of white America—jazz—arose during the nadir of postbellum racial oppression in New Orleans and elsewhere. But what if this simultaneity is not ironic? What if the birth of jazz was both a response to and result of such racial politics?

Urban Villages and the Black Church's "Counter-Public Sphere"

New Orleans's citizens of color responded to these difficult conditions by asserting their pride and identity, carving out their own cultural spaces, literally and figuratively. Though heightened by segregation, New Orleans has always been divided into semiautonomous neighborhoods:

"New Orleans is less a city than a collection of urban villages." These pockets of semiautonomy allowed alternative cultures to flourish in the middle of a highly racist city. Louis Armstrong has described the camaraderie and mutual support in the "battlefield" area of the city, even amidst crime and poverty. Such was the sense of community that when Armstrong's mother initiated him into local bar hopping, no one would let them pay for their drinks. Rightfully fearful of the city's police force, such neighborhoods also policed themselves to some degree.[32]

New Orleans' Creoles of Color were particularly well organized, and after the Civil War, they became active in the fight against discrimination. By 1868, the lieutenant governor and state treasurer, as well as other high officers prominent in the state Republican party, were Creoles. Shut out by insurance companies, they formed a variety of benevolent associations that provided, among other member benefits, burials and funerals accompanied by music.[33] Creoles were central to the civil rights movement in New Orleans as well as the history of jazz.

Creole neighborhoods were held together by strong social networks, both musical and political, that centered on particular families. As one musician put it, "All the Creole families down in [the Seventh Ward]...were closely knit." Cornetist Don Albert's uncle was Natty Dominique, also a cornetist, and his second cousin was clarinetist Barney Bigard; Bigard's father ran a cigar factory that employed clarinetist and music teacher "Papa" Louis Tio.[34]

These close-knit Creole communities facilitated cultural and political activism. The social aid and pleasure clubs and benevolent (fraternal) associations of the Tremé neighborhood, home to Homer Plessy, both provided support for political activism such as Plessy's and sponsored the neighborhood's many musical events. When Creole activists formed a Comité des Citoyens in response to the segregation of railroads in 1890, it drew the majority of its funds and support from organizations like the Société Économie, Société des Artisans, and Société des Jeunes Amis, all of which had halls that figured prominently in early New Orleans jazz. Members of the committee included relatives of influential jazz musicians Sidney Bechet, Peter Bocage, George and Achille Baquet, and Armand Piron, among others. When the committee ultimately chose a New Orleanian of color to board a "white" train car in protest, it selected Creole Daniel Desdunes, who played in the Onward Brass Band, training ground for important jazz musicians like Joe "King" Oliver, and whose sister, pianist Mamie Desdunes, taught Jelly Roll Morton.[35] (Charges against Desdunes were dropped on a technicality, making the way for Plessy's subsequent challenge.)

For blacks, the church created a similar sense of cohesion. Religious services had provided an opportunity for slaves from various plantations to gather, free from the eyes of the master. In turn-of-the-century New Orleans (and elsewhere), the church remained a central institution, if not *the* central institution, in the life of African Americans. One of the few organizations not controlled by whites, it was a "counter-public sphere," "a public distinct from and in conflict with the dominant white society and its racist institutional structures," "the matrix out of which black society was to be cohesive." Through music and prayer the black church celebrated black identity in the midst of a society that at best dismissed it and at worst attempted to exterminate it. It also served as a quasi-legal dispute resolution mechanism, a means to promulgate and enforce morality, a "mutual aid and burial society," and in some cases a venue for the performing arts. Churches "sponsored revivals, excursions, fairs, camp meetings, benevolent societies, and Sunday schools."[36]

Sunday church services allowed blacks to counter the innumerable slights of Jim Crow by adorning themselves in their finest clothes, enacting and celebrating their respectability. In such displays, blacks "were repudiating white society's evaluation of the black body as an instrument of menial labor." Though conservative in the sense of honoring white society's standards of respectability, such clothes challenged white belittlement of them. Whites would sometimes complain that blacks going to church dressed better than they did, trying to show them up.[37]

The church has also served as "the chief reservoir of Africanisms that have survived in the West." Sterling Stuckey has argued that Christianity acted as a "cover" for the continuation of African rites, and this continued, in extenuated form, after emancipation. Secret religious meetings became "the principal means for transferring esoteric African knowledge to the North American colonies for the first generation of American-born African slaves," and they then passed on this knowledge to subsequent generations. Some have argued that the very secrecy required in the slave church helped preserve African culture through an Africanized version of Christianity. Retaining African culture and worldviews affirmed individuality and resisted the dehumanization of slavery.[38]

Some have made the case that the spirituals drew on specific West African songs, given the similarities in rhythm, tonal structure, and melody. According to one commentator, the spiritual "in form, content, and performance resembles the African heroic epic tradition more closely than it does the mythic traditions of the Euro-American religious song." Spirituals, as we shall see, incorporated improvisation and other African musical techniques as well.[39]

A central African feature of the black church was the ring shout, an ecstatic movement of individuals joined in a circle moving counterclockwise to the accompaniment of a song leader in dialogue with a chorus. Since dancing per se was prohibited, the feet did not cross; "they'd be shouting, it wasn't dancing, but it was so near dancing," in the words of one musician.[40] Observed in New Orleans black church services in the 1850s, the ring shout has roots in West and Central African burial ceremonies and other rituals honoring ancestors. For Africans at a funeral, the circular movement represents "togetherness and containment," and the ring shout was "the main context in which Africans recognized values common to them." Zora Neale Hurston called shouting "nothing more than a continuation of the African 'Possession' by the gods." In lieu of drums, worshipers accompanied ring shouts by stamping their feet. Congregants also stamped their feet in affirmation of a sermon, reminiscent of Bolden's injunction to listeners to stomp to his music.[41]

"A community thing," shouting helped tie African Americans together, whether in the church or at an outdoor camp meeting; according to one churchgoer, "at camp meeting there must be a ring here, a ring there, a ring over yonder, or sinners will not get converted." Yet the ring shout had an influence beyond the black church, in the movements central to New Orleans festive culture. According to Jason Berry, "In second line music, the human architecture of the ring dances at Congo Square was rearranged—dancers in long sinuous lines opened the ring, stretching it out, coursing ahead, moving the African polyrhythmic sensibility on a more linear path of melody. The joy-shouts of parade people and the groundbeat of feet on the streets surged with call-and-response patterns of the horns and woodwinds, playing off the rhythm and roll of drum syncopations."[42]

Shouting and other movements in the black church were threatening to many whites. In slave times, the dance of possession was a threat to the master's control, and later white observers also saw the frenzied movement of black churchgoers as savage and primitive, indicating a lack of emotional restraint.[43] Some "shouts" literally shook the building, leading neighbors to complain about the noise.

Wary of the power of religion in the hands of slaves, slave owners often prohibited religious meetings, so that slaves had to hold secret ring shouts late at night, with a large iron pot they hoped would capture the sound. At camp meetings, blacks often shouted in tents, away from the eyes of those religious leaders who opposed them. When blacks formed the First African Baptist Church in New Orleans in 1826, they could worship only with a police officer present. In 1853, police broke up a black baptism at Lake Pontchartrain, charging the participants with unlawful assembly. Five years later, a city ordinance prohibited all black religious organizations, but the ban proved to be ineffective, and by 1883 the state of Louisiana had five hundred black Baptist churches with more than seventy thousand members.[44]

The egalitarian, participatory nature of the black church may have scared whites but attracted blacks. The Baptist and Methodist denominations, with their populist, egalitarian creeds, had led the First Great Awakening, and they were the first to try to convert slaves to Christianity. The Baptist Church in particular gave slaves more liberty to participate or preach, and its decentralized structure allowed individual congregations much freedom. In the black folk church, everyone was expected to participate; the whole congregation constituted the choir, making a formal body of singers unnecessary. Underpinning the Baptist church is the idea of the "priesthood of all believers," according to which the Holy Spirit speaks directly to those with faith, without any intermediary. Unlike most of their white counterparts, black churches rejected a firm boundary between minister and congregation. Women in the Baptist church had a history of important roles as "church mothers," perhaps descendants of women in African secret societies who guided young men through rites of passage. New Orleans in particular had a tradition of powerful black women with spiritual powers, whom some saw as dangerous.[45]

The democratic nature of the black church derives from West African religion, which is inseparable from everyday life, the sacred intertwined with the secular. In the religions of the area from which most slaves came, divine forces inhabit everyday life; immanent rather than transcendent, invisible spirits are near at hand, within reach of the individual who needs them. Through song and dance, the worshiper becomes possessed by the god, merged to the point at which he feels he is no longer directing his own actions.

Yet unlike Christian epiphanies like Paul's on the road to Damascus, the West African spirit possession requires a collective, participatory ritual and a particular kind of music. In West African music all take part even if only by dancing and clapping; sitting rigidly and listening to someone "perform" represents bizarre, even rude behavior. Portia Maultsby speaks of the "performer-audience" as one unit, a concept that can be seen in many African American musical performances today. Slave religion and spirituals kept this emphasis on the collectively evoked, immanent, in-this-world nature of the divine spirit. After emancipation, black preaching involved a dialogical process, whereby parishioners answered the minister with a shout or a moan, the preacher in turn shaping his words and style in response to the continual feedback of the congregation, creating a kind of improvised dance.[46]

Disrespectable Spaces

Other black counterinstitutions, also centered around music, existed in opposition to the respectability of the church. Nonchurchgoing New Orleanians of color also used music to create their own spaces, but with a very different set of values. Late-nineteenth-century debates around purity and racial mixing in New Orleans centered on a series of clubs in the so-called tenderloin districts, where bands played "ratty" music for working-class, largely black audiences. One might speculate that had it not been for such "disrespectable" venues and audiences, jazz might not have developed at all. The old story that jazz emerged fully formed from the tenderloin districts is a myth—many kinds of music that went into the making of jazz were played throughout the city, at parades, picnics, parties, and elsewhere. However, there is a grain of truth to the myth in that an essential component of jazz did come from these "disrespectable" clubs. The African bluesy music that came out of these lower-class clubs, though not yet jazz per se, provided the key ingredient to convert music like ragtime, popular throughout the country, into jazz. Jazz developed in New Orleans precisely because it was only there that this essential element combined with ragtime and other forms, partly, as we shall see, through Creole musicians.

For lower-class black audiences, who had little social, political, and economic power, the pleasure of "ratty" music created a kind of counterworld to poverty and the increasing routinization of life. In clubs in seedy areas of the city, working-class and underclass blacks congregated and created communities based on an alternative set of values, enacting a carnivalesque, pleasure-seeking ethic through music and dance. As we shall see, these clubs also could be dangerous, violent places. In an era stressing self-control and the Protestant ethic, their rebellious way of life offended many whites, who loathed the music and the values it represented and tried to stop or contain it. Yet the joyous "disrespectable" music could be neither stopped nor contained—it flourished in poor neighborhoods and then burst into the city's streets and parks like a

Figure 4. Storyville, the city's red light district. (Photo courtesy of the Louisiana State Museum.)

torrent. Ironically, Jim Crow had created spaces that ultimately helped undermine racial hierarchy.

———

The "ratty" music that would become jazz was inseparable from the nightclubs and honky-tonks where New Orleanians gathered to listen and dance to it. Those musical performance spaces were each the province of a particular race and class. Although racial segregation in New Orleans clubs was readily apparent, equally important for the development of jazz was a kind of class segregation, the African American community dividing roughly into "society" or "respectable" blacks, the working class, and a criminal underclass. "Respectable" and lower-class New Orleanians of each race had particular musical venues catering to their lifestyles and featuring their favored music. According to Danny Barker, each music hall "had a class distinction based on color, family standing, money, and religion."[47] While some, especially Creole clubs, served "respectable" New Orleanians, other spaces catered to black lower-class audiences, audiences who demanded the more African-based, cutting-edge "ratty" music that would become jazz. Indeed, during its early days, jazz could be played only in disrespectable places; it was not accepted elsewhere.

The earliest reports of the music that would come to be called jazz locates it in the heart of disrespectable New Orleans: on Franklin Street, from Canal to a little below Bienville—the area that in about 1897 would become Storyville, New Orleans's red light district, called by locals simply "the District." An 1890 editorial in the *New Orleans Mascot* criticizes a black band for playing in a respectable neighborhood raucous, apparently improvised music that belonged in "the gambling hells of Franklin Street."[48] The "honky-tonk" (or simply "tonk") emerged in New Orleans as a gathering place for urban laborers, featuring gambling, prostitution, and early jazz music. Bolden himself probably played in these working-class venues, and one of the songs in his repertory is about working on the docks. In addition to the whorehouses, Storyville boasted dance halls and saloons, featuring bluesy music by small groups at late-night jam sessions after the brothels closed. Of places like the Big 25, Creole musician Manuel Manetta comments, "All wild people . . . *Ratty . . . ratty . . .* You know, *ratty.*" "Men with respect wouldn't go in them kind of places."[49]

These clubs were frequented by New Orleans's lower classes, consisting of working-class blacks as well as the "good time people," a kind of lumpenproletariat consisting of pimps, whores, and petty criminals. Pete Lala's, Billy Phillips's, the Hot Cat, the Honky Tonk, the 101 Ranch, and the Pig Ankle were not exactly elegant: their floors were sometimes littered with comatose patrons. Franklin Street barrelhouses, called "pig ankle clubs" (probably referring to "pig ankle corners," the corner of Franklin and Customhouse), had a saloon in front and a piano in back and served large plates of red beans and rice for five cents. Clubs like the Big 25 had gambling tables and a piano; typically they did not hire musicians, but people simply sat down and played.[50]

Opponents of such clubs denigrated their audiences and the music played there as "ratty," as opposed to "respectable." For most Creoles, according to Leonard Bechet, "the district was one of the worst places." The *New Orleans Item* in 1900 described one "notorious" club: "The lower floor is used as a dance hall, where the negroes commence to congregate at dark, and to the discordant music of the so-called orchestra they indulge in dancing, drinking and carousing until the light of day drives them back to their hovels. . . . The second floor . . . is occupied by the dozen black courtesan attaches of the place." By 1900 cocaine use was common among prostitutes and poor residents of the District as well as roustabouts; some Franklin Street clubs served a mixture of California Claret, water, and cocaine for a dime. Some musicians refused to work there except when they could not get work elsewhere (for example,

during Lent), and young ones who did work there risked parental disapproval.[51]

Uptown from the District stood another center of prostitution, Black
Storyville, that featured the rattiest of the ratty halls. Halls like the Masonic (Odd Fellows) at South Rampart and Perdido charged less than
"respectable" venues and thus catered to the lower classes, and Bolden,
Bunk Johnson, Armstrong, and others held forth there as well as at nearby Dago Tony's. The Red Onion, located just outside Black Storyville,
drew an equally talented roster of musicians, including Morton. It was
in this rough neighborhood that Bolden first gained a following, which
later accompanied him to the parks and other parts of the city.[52]

While the dance halls in the red light districts catered to the lower
classes, pianists at downtown brothels made huge sums of money by
performing for their wealthy white customers. At Lulu White's, Manetta
(born in 1889) remembered playing an upright piano in the parlor on the
second floor while twelve or fifteen prostitutes sat nearby, passing the
hat every three or four tunes and urging customers to "give the professor
something"; if a customer refused to give a tip, he would be asked to
leave. Sometimes houses had several parlors, and the pianist played one
for fifteen minutes and moved on to the next, collecting a steady stream
of tips when the house was busy. According to Barney Bigard, Morton's
tips from one night at Lulu White's brothel exceeded a week's earnings
elsewhere, while another musician claimed Morton made $50 in contrast
to the average musician's $1 or $1.50 a day. Morton himself claimed to
have made hundreds of dollars in one evening playing at a "sporting
house."[53]

"Professors" at a brothel sometimes accompanied a "naked dance,"
or (as one put it) "women doing freakish things to each other"—"lots of
uncultured things . . . that probably shouldn't be mentioned." Men paid
a dollar to see a woman "smoke a cigarette in her box," engage in bes-
tiality, or eat mock feces made from ginger cakes mixed with limburger
cheese and water. In the midst of such goings on, the pianist had to
keep his eyes on the keyboard; sometimes a screen was even put near
the piano to prevent him from looking, although Morton claims he cut
a hole in it.[54]

There is one account by bassist Albert Glenny of musicians' themselves apparently being paid to engage in sex acts at a brothel, though the
details are sketchy. Glenny describes a night when, after they "knocked
off" at two in the morning, he made five dollars (as opposed to the $1.25
he would get for playing) by engaging in a sexual act with a guitarist,
Jimmy Wright, whom he "know . . . too good." According to Glenny,

Figure 5. Roustabouts: waterfront and riverboat workers who frequented "ratty" dives featuring early black music. Also known for their work songs. (Photo courtesy of the Louisiana State Museum.)

wealthy men drinking champagne, "all them big ole' fellers[,] . . . got the money" and wanted "to see how a colored fellow, you know, do his business," so the two musicians performed on a mattress on the floor, making good money, including tips.[55]

Some early jazz musicians who played disrespectable clubs themselves came from (or joined) the lower classes. Armstrong described Henry Zeno as a fine drummer and a pimp popular with "the prostitutes—pimps— gamblers—hustlers and everybody"; many pianists in the District, including Morton, pimped on occasion. Armstrong said that the best blues piano players in Black Storyville "often came from the levee camps," while Pops Foster worked as a longshoreman and said many other fine musicians did so as well. Whites who played jazz, predominantly Jews and Sicilians, also tended to be from the lower classes.[56] And although not all, or even most, early jazz musicians came from the lower strata of New Orleans, most of the black audience that supported their most adventurous playing did.

"Blues-Loving, . . . Cane-Cutting People" and "People of the Fast Type"

Venues in both the downtown and seedier uptown red light districts were frequented by "the lowest of people," including roustabouts from the riverboats, "the lowest level of the black working class," who were said by newspapers and magazines to spend all their free time and money there.[57] Violently abused by ships' officers, roustabouts on their time off were reputed to be "happy-go-lucky" and rather wild, frequenting gambling houses, dives, and brothels. Leon J. Fremaux, an engineer and sketch artist, described the roustabout as "an unworried creature, sometimes a brawler, always happy"; his drawing portrays two black men with patches on their clothes and tattered shirts, one barefoot, the other wearing old shoes without laces. Situated near a bale of cotton, one whistles and taps his foot while the other dances. As early as 1876, Lafcadio Hearn had described a roustabout dive in Cincinnati featuring a black and mulatto band (bass, violin, banjo) and a racially mixed audience that included cigar-smoking, pistol-packing women and roustabouts singing folksongs and "patting juba," the latter an African-based dance involving rhythmic striking of the knees, shoulders, and hands while moving the feet and singing.[58]

As opposed to the "gentleman" Creole John Robichaux, New Orleans cornetist Chris Kelly played for (in Danny Barker's words) "those blues, cotton-picking Negroes, what they called in the old days, 'yard and field' Negroes." These were (Barker again) "blues-loving, real primitive cane-cutting people; people who worked in the fields," "hard-working people: stevedores, woodsmen, fishermen, field hands and steel-driving men. . . . The women were factory workers, washerwomen, etc." Many Creoles disliked Kelly—indeed could barely understand his accent—because he "played for what was supposed to be the bad element. When he would play a street parade . . . all the kitchen mechanics would come out on the street corner, shaking." The distrust was mutual: Barker wanted to play with him, but Kelly refused to hire him because he came from a well-known Creole family.[59]

These working-class black patrons listened to music and danced at these clubs to express pride in their community, a community rejected by "respectable" New Orleanians. As Barker paraphrased their attitude: "I work hard, make an honest living. You all look down on me and I am looking down on you all. Everybody thinks they are more than me: white folks and yellow and colored folks. You all don't want to associate with me when you all go for a good time, so I have my good time [here]." Like their churchgoing critics, club audiences expressed their pride by their sartorial care, the men sporting "box-backed suits, hats with two-colored bands on them, and shoes with two-dollar gold pieces in the toe"; though the women wore "common gingham dresses," they made sure they were "starched and iron stiff."[60]

For the underclass, the "good time people," music was a means to tolerate and transcend an increasingly difficult life lived on the margins because of racism and poverty. These "ratty" audiences idolized Bolden; according to cornetist Peter Bocage, Bolden's music spread because of the excitement it generated among the lower classes, "people of the fast type." There was something of the outlaw, the Stagolee, about Bolden. Members of his band were described as "ratty" people who refused to take their hats off and "wore their braces down and their pants half falling down."[61] Bolden himself had a swagger reminiscent of Elvis Presley and early rock musicians, an image enhanced by his subsequent madness; some of the symptoms of his insanity included practicing in the street and violating other social conventions, perhaps regarding race ("talking to the wrong people"). His outlaw image partly explains his appeal to the lower classes and women as well as the older generation's antagonism. Bolden, like Robert Charles, was a "bad nigger" like those immortalized in folk ballads.

Lower-class audiences worshiped other black musicians as well, and this adulation influenced their music. During competitions between bands, prostitutes enjoyed songs like Ory's "If You Don't Like the Way I Play, Then Kiss My Funky Ass"; according to Barney Bigard, "whichever band had the nastiest lyrics would win." "King" Joe Oliver borrowed from the songs of railroad and dockworkers and once played a benefit for whores and madams.[62]

The new "ratty" music, one of the few sources of joy and self-assertion, created freer, pleasurable spaces for lower-class blacks. For workers, on the waterfront and elsewhere, or those without jobs who struggled in New Orleans's underclass, these relatively autonomous spaces represented a haven from oppressive surroundings or even a rebellion against them, becoming what Foucault calls "heterotopias"—"counter-sites, a kind of effectively enacted utopia in which the real sites, all the other real sites that can be found within the culture, are simultaneously represented, contested, and inverted" by mixing elements normally seen as incompatible.[63] Leon Litwack has described a kind of black urban culture in the Jim Crow era based on "interior exile," a rejection of the dominant culture and its hierarchy by way of escape rather than direct confrontation: "Operating in a kind of underworld emerging in the 1890s... young blacks tested the limits of permissible dissent and misconduct, sometimes outside the law, and found alternative ways to survive and to circumvent the system.... Within their enclaves and neighborhoods, in the saloons, roadhouses, juke joints, and pool halls they frequented, they created and sustained a culture of their own."[64]

Early audiences of this music in New Orleans pursued a life built around rebellion against authority in general and the Protestant ethic in particular, instead celebrating the pursuit of pleasure. Foster describes the way the "good time people" looked and acted: "They'd dance with no coats on and their suspenders down. They'd jump around and have a bunch of fun. They wanted you to play slow blues and dirty songs so they could dance rough and dirty." Social restraints were thrown off—at times, as we shall see, to the point of chaos.

The good time people and their social world thus represented a kind of carnivalistic ethos, in which dominant values were reversed, substituting pleasure for self-denial. Celebrating "thieves, clowns, prostitutes, downs-and-outs, rogues, convicts, outlaws, and other such liminal figures who appear in everyday life only in unfortunate circumstances," carnival's "focal point is the forbidden, the illicit, the impossible, that which is outside the system or which lies in the interstices of it."[65] Nationwide, there were increasing attempts, in the name of efficiency, to keep workers from drinking on the job; bars or nightclubs became places in opposition to such values. However, even more shocking to authorities than these black enclaves, racially mixed clubs soon arose, focused on the same music.

Racial Intermingling

From its beginning, New Orleans was known for interracial encounters that mocked the rigid boundaries set by the law. One historian has called New Orleans a "permeable society and culture" in which "race mixture was common and widely accepted." To a degree unparalleled by any city in the United States, New Orleans embodied a crossroads of African, Caribbean, and European (primarily French) culture. From its founding, Louisiana was a place where "racial lines were blurred, and intimate relations among peoples of all three races flourished. . . . Hybrid race, culture, and language were created."[66] Louisiana was a "colony of deserters"— many of the whites who came there were "undesirables" who had been deported or hired as indentured servants. Furthermore, the primitive frontier conditions of colonial Louisiana required people to cooperate, especially since many Africans brought there possessed needed skills in "metalworking, shipbuilding, and river transport." In 1720 fifteen people were arrested as members of a conspiracy plot, and the group included "an eighteen-year-old Indian slave, a fifteen-year-old runaway African slave, a French sergeant of the troops, a twenty-eight-year-old Swiss soldier, and a twenty-seven-year-old French woman who had been sent to Louisiana and married against her will." The French allied with various Indian tribes against others, blacks and Indians intermarried, and such interracial couples at one point formed a network to help slaves escape. As a major port city, with a waterfront marketplace featuring traders of numerous nationalities, New Orleans was a center for ethnic mixing, arousing a fear of impurity among some.[67]

This tradition of interracial relations continued into the late nineteenth century, when jazz was beginning to develop. In 1885, Charles Dudley Warner, a friend of Mark Twain, visited in the International Exposition in New Orleans and found that "white and colored people mingled freely, talking and looking at what was of common interest," while blacks "took their full share of the parade and the honors" and both races associated "in unconscious equality of privileges." While Warner's perception of interracial intermingling was probably exaggerated, a product of naiveté and a lack of experience in the city, native New Orleanians voiced similar observations, though with very different evaluations. For example, around the same time that Warner wrote, the *New Orleans Mascot* criticized the prevalence of interracial dating: "This thing of white girls becoming enamored of Negroes is becoming too common."[68]

Racial intermixing was abetted by a series of interracial "crazy quilt" neighborhoods that brought together blacks, Creoles, and white ethnic groups like Sicilians and Jews. In fact Bolden lived in an Irish and German neighborhood, with a Jewish cemetery directly behind, on First Street between Howard and Liberty, occupying the same block as Larry Shields, later a member of the (white) Original Dixieland Jazz Band. As Jim Crow pushed the city toward a system of classification based on color rather than national origin or specific racial mixture, jazz drew on and encouraged the continuation of interethnic alliances as well as existing ethnic bonds.[69]

Impure Spaces

While many clubs catered to only one race and class, some, especially lower-class venues, drew mixed audiences. Racial mixing around music was not a new phenomenon in America. At the camp meetings of the Second Awakening (1780 to 1830) blacks and whites ecstatically sang, moved, and prayed together, provoking fears in observers. Whites who attended Methodist and Baptist camp meetings came from the lower, marginal sections of society and thus shared some affinity with the slaves.

One account has blacks and whites on opposite sides of a tabernacle, singing back and forth in African-style call and response, "the voices of the masters and veterans among the white people . . . echo[ing] back, in happy response, the jubilant shout of the rejoicing slaves." In such "echoes," much to the chagrin of observers, blacks transformed whites' religious music, teaching them the "merry chorus-manner of the southern harvest field." Like the later black and white bands holding forth at Milneburg lakefront resort in New Orleans, separation did not preclude mutual influence; camp meetings ended with a "farewell march around the encampment," initiated by blacks' knocking down the fence separating the white and black camps. As in black churches, whites during the "awakenings" of the eighteenth and nineteenth centuries gave themselves up to emotional outpourings in the midst of prayer and music; at a Kentucky revival in 1799, "many fell to the ground and lay powerless, groaning, praying, and crying for mercy.[70] The emotional power of music combined with religious fervor threatened racial boundaries.

Mixed clubs in New Orleans had a similarly long history; according to one early nineteenth-century observer, "at the corners of all the cross streets of the city are to be seen nothing but taverns, which are open at all hours. There the canaille white and black, free and slave mingled, go openly without any embarrassment, as well as without shame to revel and dance indiscriminately and for whole nights with a lot of men and women of saffron colore, or quite black, either free or slave."[71]

From its inception, New Orleans's ubiquitous dances created relatively free spaces for interactions between the races. The pleasure associated with listening to music ultimately brought diverse people together and sometimes allowed them to interact in ways forbidden by law; slaves sometimes flocked to dance halls, making owners worried about a possible revolt or the damaging of their "property" through injury or fatigue. In the antebellum era, the races mixed at some cafés and ballrooms, and small clubs held "tricolor balls" in which anyone of any race, free or slave, could attend. Masked balls in particular afforded the opportunity for boundary crossing, and during Mardi Gras disguised New Orleanians of color mingled and danced with whites, providing a thrill of the forbidden to both parties.[72] Even during non–Mardi Gras times, dances, which were held as often as two or three times a week, were sites for the blurring of racial boundaries. Racial mixing in seedy clubs had a history extending back to slavery times, throughout the South. According to C. Vann Woodward, "Every Southern city had its demimonde, and regardless of the law and the pillars of society, the two races on that level foregathered more or less openly in grog shops, mixed balls, and religious meetings. Less visibly there thrived 'a world of greater conviviality and equality.' Under cover of night, 'in this nether world blacks and whites mingled freely, the conventions of slavery were discarded,' and 'not only did the men find fellowship without regard to color in the tippling shops, back rooms, and secluded sheds, but the women of both races joined in.'"[73]

Another early "impure" public space was Congo Square, a nineteenth-century gathering spot where slaves and free people of color danced and sold goods. Unlike in the former British colonies, slaves in French-descended New Orleans were permitted to play drums, allowing mixed audiences on Sunday afternoons to see a spectacle probably unique in the United States—Afro-Caribbean dances accompanied by percussive music, sometimes using animal bones. Some have argued that by bringing together African, French, Spanish, and Native American influences, Congo Square was a critical site for the creation and preservation of the culture that eventually produced jazz.[74]

Many whites looked at Congo Square as hedonistic, childish, or barbaric, representing outcasts—the workman, the quadroon, the prostitute, the black. However, it brought together poor mulattos and blacks, creating and preserving rituals of music and dance that allowed them to momentarily escape the dominant culture. In Congo Square, disturbingly to some, Creoles from the neighboring Tremé area mingled with slaves, watching the bamboula and calinda, dances of African origin, and listening to African-based music. Yet these were not the Creole of Color elite; rather, Congo Square "attracted the lower orders from all over New Orleans to its coarse carnival, circus, and bearbaiting spectacles." One of the earliest demonstrations against segregated streetcars, beginning a movement that would ultimately be rejected in *Plessy v. Ferguson*, took place in Congo Square in 1867.[75]

Congo Square did not last. As an "impure" meeting place for slaves and free blacks, some found it threatening, and as New Orleans became Americanized and connections with Africa became more remote, the dances there ceased, somewhere around the mid-nineteenth century. But dances like the calinda continued elsewhere, and "local voodoo pockets" kept the African-Caribbean heritage alive. By 1885, Hearn reported that although "old colored folk who remember how to dance the *Congo* and the *Calinda* still chant African choruses," they no longer knew the meaning of the words.[76]

More important for the development of jazz, even with the demise of Congo Square, there continued to be impure nightclubs and dance halls where blacks, whites, and Creoles interacted and their cultures intertwined, much to the dismay of "respectable" citizens. This dismay is vividly illustrated in a *New Orleans Mascot* cover portraying a Franklin Street "gambling hell," with blacks and whites sitting at a gaming table together and a white police officer with his arms around two black women, all accompanied by a racially mixed quartet of musicians.[77] Some whites gravitated to the music, and from the beginning, "slumming...tourists" came to hear it. In addition to music and gambling, some clubs featured "ham kicking" contests whereby women were enticed into revealing their undergarments by kicking at a ham suspended from the ceiling in the hope of knocking it down and winning it.[78]

As the *Mascot* cover suggests, these clubs were concentrated in the red light districts. Jelly Roll Morton has described interracial clubs like the Frenchman's, in the heart of Storyville, where in the early twentieth century piano players congregated after they left their jobs at the brothels at 4 a.m. According to Morton, "They had every class, we had Spanish, we had colored, we had white, we had Frenchmens, we had Americans.... All the girls that could get out of the houses, they were there. There weren't any discrimination of any kind. They all sat at different tables at any place that they thought like sitting. They all mingled together as they wished to, and everyone was just one big happy family." Holding forth with blues, ragtime, and sentimental popular songs, piano players accelerated as they played, trying to outdo one another as wealthy customers shouted encouragement.[79]

The uptown district presented a scene even more alarming to the upholders of respectability and racial purity. Honky-tonks like Kaiser's, the Red Onion, and Spano's were "dirty, filthy places" that had not been swept in months with patrons who rarely bathed. Kaiser's, resembling "a huge saloon," featured "a bar on one side, a cotch game (Spanish poker) going on in the rear, and probably a game of pool in another part of the room." Yet alongside the lower-class longshoremen and screwmen from the levee sat slumming wealthy patrons from the St. Charles "millionaire's district," "nudging elbows with all the big bums."[80]

These were liminal spaces that were not easily classified as black, white, or Creole, "neither here nor there...betwixt and between the positions assigned and arrayed by law, custom, convention, and ceremonial." According to Victor Turner, those who frequent such spaces "fall in the interstices of social structure," "are on its margins, or...occupy its lowest rungs." Yet such seemingly marginal spaces evoked a larger breaking down of social boundaries and hierarchies that separate individuals, thus representing both a dangerous dissolution of society as it is and a reconstruction of a new one based on more egalitarian principles. One is reminded here of Homi Bhabha's evocation of the way "'inbetween' spaces provide the terrain for elaborating strategies of selfhood—singular or communal—that initiate new signs of identity, and innovative sites of collaboration, and contestation, in the act of defining the idea of society itself."[81]

Other descriptions call into question Morton's view of customers of various races at the clubs as "one big happy family" devoid of discrimination. According to Morton himself, prostitutes lured customers upstairs, and filthy men waited for well-dressed upper-crust customers to rob; if one wore a pair of good shoes and fell asleep, someone was likely to cut the laces off and steal them. Morton recalled that the "bums" at these clubs expected wealthier customers to buy them drinks, and if they refused, the "bum" took a louse off his body, an "educated louse," and placed it surreptitiously on the offending gentleman, hoping to inflict his own problems on him. This account, while unique and perhaps fanciful, suggests that rather than continuous interracial and interclass harmony, a kind of class warfare took place between poor customers of color and wealthier white patrons. An ex-slave's recollection of visiting clubs at Franklin and Iberville, including the Pig Ankle and the 28, reinforces this picture. Frank Moss called the Pig Ankle "'the' place" to be and recalled that "seven nights out the week niggers and white folks used to crowd in there" together. But Moss's assertion that "white folks like to died laughin'" at the drunken prostitutes and came "just to throw nickels and dimes" suggests condescension rather than solidarity.[82]

The picture, then, is a complex one. While some whites went to hear jazz at interracial venues in the spirit of appreciation relatively devoid of racism, others frequented the clubs in a condescending manner steeped in racism and class snobbery. How much of each existed is impossible to even guess. But in the emerging Jim Crow era, such venues facilitated older, freer forms of social interaction for some.

"Blues and All That Stink Music"

In addition to the clubs' interracial and disrespectable clientele, racial and sexual purity were threatened by the music played there. Musical styles in New Orleans reflected the city's social divisions. According to drummer Paul Barbarin, the close interconnection between race, class, and musical style was physically exemplified in the three bands that played at a typical picnic at the fairgrounds. Downstairs, the Excelsior or Onward brass band performed "European" quadrilles, marches, and waltzes for the "elite," but New Orleans musicians inevitably put a kind of jazz accent on it so it did not become "stiff and starchy." Upstairs another Creole band—John Robichaux or Manuel Perez—held forth for "less formal" audiences favoring "livelier music," more modern and syncopated, which to the chagrin of the older generation smacked of ragtime. Out in the field, the Eagle band played slow blues and barrelhouse music like the risqué songs of guitarist Lorenzo Staulz for "ratty" people who danced "ratty." As Barbarin put it, "It wasn't high class, it wasn't all starchy and respectable. But man, it was music!" In sum, brass bands played "dignified music," the upstairs band played popular songs and rags of the day, and the field band played "lowdown" music: in Barbarin's view, three kinds of music for three different kinds of people.[83]

Respectability, or lack thereof, thus adhered to certain sounds and rhythms, each sonic-social world associated with particular performance spaces. Musical venues ranged from the Jeunes Amis, "the most exclusive, . . . where very few jazzmen ever entered—down to the Animal Hall, where even a washboard band was welcome if they could play the blues." "Lowdown," disrespectable music filled the air in lower-class dives. Music in the uptown district—rough, unrefined sounds on broken-down pianos—especially emanated disrespectability, and the best pianists did not play there because they would have made less money than they did downtown. One white musician, John Provenzano, described the difference between the two parts of the District: Downtown, listeners heard the "sweet" sound of "the cornet augmented by the variations of the clarinet" played by Creoles like Alphonse Picou and Manuel Perez. Uptown, on the other hand, one encountered "the ear-splitting blast of a cornet, augmented by the screech of some clarinetist who was perhaps just beginning" and "the off beats of the drums with the discords of guitar and bass that actually made you jumpy." The uptown music may have been less skilled; however, it may have simply been more raw and blues based ("discords"), with "the offbeats of the drums" suggesting syncopation. Perhaps the downtown music Morton and Provenzano described more closely resembled ragtime, whereas to hear the more blues-based music, an essential ingredient in the budding jazz, one had to venture uptown.[84]

Bolden pioneered this new "ratty" music. His playing and attitude made him a kind of pop star, initially among the disrespectable and then for a wider group. Bolden on Monday nights would play "lowdown" blues for prostitutes, pimps, and madams, and the whores would dance, "dropping their drawers and teddies." According to cornetist Peter Bocage, while those in the older generation like his father played

Figure 6. Buddy Bolden, holding his cornet in the back row. This is the only known photo of the enormously influential (and unrecorded) cornetist whom many consider the first jazz musician. (Photo courtesy of the William Ransom Hogan Archive, Tulane University.)

strictly written music—European dances like quadrilles, mazurkas, and waltzes, which his father referred to as "German music"—Bolden played music his "own way," and "all those old blues and that stuff" came into his "improvisation." Bolden's brash music challenged conventions by its stentorian boldness; unlike the quiet, respectable playing of most reading bands, his playing was inevitably described as loud and sometimes as rough and unrefined by Creoles of Color. (Ory even said Bolden had "no tone.")[85] For critics, like later opponents of rock and roll, the music's volume threatened the boundaries that guard the social order.

The new music's use of blues devices made it disrespectable as well. One musician describes music in the District as "barrel house"—a slow blues "dragged out"—"bump music" or "slow drag music," while Pops Foster called it "blues and all that stink music."[86] Blues in this sense was not necessarily the twelve-measure progression we know today, but rather an African-derived approach to music making. This approach, discussed in more detail in chapter 4, encompassed a distortion of the norms of tonality and "proper" timbre by playing below the standard pitch ("blue notes") and using a variety of effects to produce unusual sounds ("growling" on wind instruments and other "bluesy" effects). The loud and bluesy music at these clubs violated European musical conventions, and such musical transgression took place in a milieu that threatened larger racial and social boundaries.

Time Recaptured

Central to the new music's transgressiveness was its assault on conventional experiences of time itself. The lateness of the hour and new ways of dancing created freer experiences of time, illustrating Foucault's assertion that heterotopias "open onto...heterochronies. The heterotopia begins to function at full capacity when men arrive at a sort of absolute break with their traditional time." At "ratty" clubs, musicians held forth late at night, when the normal routines gave way. As the midnight hours approached in small clubs in poor black neighborhoods, new patrons arrived who demanded a different kind of music reflecting a new sensibility. According to bassist Pops Foster, "The first part of the night at the Masonic Hall was supposed to be 'dicty' [upper-crust, snobbish] dancing, they played nothing but waltzes, but after midnight then they would do the blues and quadrilles, slow drag and more. That was all honky tonk. You would see all them sportin' women come in after they finished their work. . . . The sportin' women wouldn't come in till after midnight, because they never played no blues before then."

Early in the evening Bolden played "sweeter," more traditional music like waltzes for society people, and then late at night, when they had left, he improvised on "ratty" tunes, blues and slow drags, with risqué lyrics for the underclass. King Oliver played more blues as the night went on as well. The increased bluesiness of the music thus mirrored a change in the audience, as a rougher class of people—the "good time people," black ("uptown") rather than Creole—predominated in these hours. Respectable people considered this blues-oriented music, as opposed to ragtime, "trash" and refused to listen to it; the "nice people would know it was time to go home" when the "rough guys," "pimps, whores, hustlers, and that bunch" came in.[87]

Reveling into the early morning hours burst the boundary of the routinized day, creating new experiences. The good time people lived in an upside-down world, sleeping in the day, active during the late night, liminal hours where boundaries dissolve—when the hour gets late enough, it is even unclear whether it is night or morning. Such carnivalistic celebrations have roots in the West Indies, where "a celebration that can't be sustained all night is a disgrace to the performers and the community."

As early as 1790 in the United States, observers noticed the tendency of African Americans to "play" all night, which most whites considered dangerous because of what they saw as its lack of restraint, its violation of "natural" limits. The New Orleans custom of serenading exhibited a similar attitude: a few musicians played outside the window of someone who was asleep, whereupon the sleeper would awake and offer the musicians food and drink. Some musicians even reported serenading police officers.[88]

Late-night ecstasy was oppositional in another sense: In the waning hours of the day, the capitalist imperative to work and produce lessens and the perception and meaning of time changes from an opportunity to progress toward a goal to an opening to experience for its own sake. These venues created a noninstrumental, nonlinear experience of time, time as a never-ending parade of moments, like the trancelike dancing of a second line winding its way throughout the city. In this liminal state, individuals exist both "in and out of time," as if the clock were stopped as timepieces become useless or a hindrance to the flow of activities. As a contemporary jazz musician once said about the trancelike "groove" created by good jazz, "it's about feeling like time itself is pleasurable."[89]

The music also evoked "impure" bodily movements. West African music foregrounds rhythm, through the use of percussion instruments, making music inseparable from movement and dance. Like its African influences, "ratty" music engaged the body, affecting the way listeners moved and felt in a fundamental way, generating a particular experience of being.

Not just any bodily movement is central to African-based music. According to Roger D. Abrahams, African and African American movement places the "center of gravity at the hips. Movement is initiated from that area and emanates outward to the shoulders, arms, hands, and the knees and feet, which play off against the pulse established by the hip movement." This emphasis on hip movements gives African American dances a "sense of strong sexuality." It was just such movements that whites found disrespectable and had since Congo Square.[90]

Such dancing exemplified the carnivalesque celebration of "the lower bodily stratum." In classical and Enlightenment philosophy, the head rules over and is superior to the lower body, particularly the genitals and organs of excretion. For the good time people, the pleasures of the lower body took precedence, and the sensuality of their music was often commented on by critics. However, the music was also associated with excretion, called "stink music" or "dirt music," and one of the most unrespectable, "ratty" venues was nicknamed "Funky Butt," *funky* here being black slang for "smelly."[91] Ratty jazz musicians took a melody of Bolden's and wrote lyrics referring to one of his favorite venues:

Thought I heard Buddy Bolden say,
Funky butt, funky butt, take it away . . .
Thought I heard Buddy Bolden say,
Dirty, nasty stinky butt, take it away,
Dirty, nasty stinky butt, take it away,
And let Mister Bolden play . . .[92]

Tempos also carried racial and class connotations, impelling listeners to move in particular ways and evoking certain attitudes and experiences. According to one musician, whites wanted to dance only to fast music. Black lower-class audiences rejected the popular dance forms (schottisches, waltzes, mazurkas) preferred by more affluent listeners in favor of "the slow drag," a languidly paced bluesy music to which "couples would hang onto each other and just grind back and forth in one spot all night." Often the slow songs had suggestive lyrics; typical titles included "If You Don't Like My Potatoes, Why Do You Dig So Deep" and "Stick It Where You Stuck It Last Night."[93]

The quadrille in particular evoked disrespectable behavior—so much so that the man calling the dance figures also acted as a "stick" or bouncer when the "quadrille people" would "get unruly." Couples also danced newer, risqué dances like the "hooch-ma-cooch," the Eagle Rock, and the Buzzard Lope to more "raggy" music. (The Buzzard Lope, though coming out in the open at this time, has been traced back to slave times.) Dances with animal names like the turkey trot, the bunny hug, and the grizzly bear began replacing the waltz and the two-step; the dances reflected their animal names by featuring more body movement, individual improvisation, and rhythmic drive.[94]

Syncopation also altered the experience of time as musicians decentered the downbeat, emphasizing that which is normally seen as secondary (the "offbeat") and bringing the marginal to the center.[95] The analogy with the situation of African Americans is striking; the music in symbolic form seeks to assert their heretofore marginalized identity and bring it to the center. The downbeat, particularly beats 1 and 3, is a command—in the case of a march, impelling the listener militarily to put one foot in front of another. Where the downbeat represents obedience and uniformity, the upbeat, and even downbeats two and four, is a surprise, a deviation, an interruption. Suggesting flight, syncopation draws the listener away from the downbeat, pulling him or her away from the insistence of the everyday routine. This tension between up-beat and downbeat helps create the distinctive sound of jazz, and by playing with this tension, beginning and ending phrases at different points in the measure, musicians create a fluid sense of time. A new kind of time, or a new experience of time, is born, a time not anchored to the insistent, predictable rhythm of everyday routine. The experience of this sense of time invites listeners to cast off their established identities and try on new modes of being.

Musicians discovered and created a new experience of time for them-selves and listeners, and these experiences challenged social constraints. The control of time is an arena of power struggles, for "social practice is made up of rhythms" (Lefebvre). A defining feature of slavery was its near total control of the slave's time. Yet time can be reappropriated, particularly during periods of transition or upheaval.[96] Emancipation held out the promise of, so to speak, time recaptured, but sharecrop-ping and routinized industrial labor monopolized time in a particularly dehumanizing way. Improvising musicians controlled time and how it felt—for what is music but sound unfolded in time?—and created a vari-ety of experiences (rushed, languid, tense, or relaxed) with the rhythmic figures they played. Ultimately, the echoes of such rhythms reverberated beyond the confines of ratty New Orleans clubs.

In short, these clubs embodied a kind of lifeworld, a whole that was more than the sum of its parts. The new music generated new feel-ings and ways of moving the body, and as a result new sensibilities, new subjectivities, became possible, subjectivities not tied to instrumen-tal rationality. Late at night, this music was played in an atmosphere that emphasized pleasure and suspended boundaries between people and even between id and (super)ego.

This carnivalistic environment produced momentary interruptions of a hierarchical mode of being. Yet one can speculate that the experience of such interruptions carried over into customers' everyday lives. Such interruptions were not confined to working-class dives but were endemic to a certain part of New Orleans culture, including more "mainstream" audiences. As Bruce Boyd Raeburn has shown, theaters could be places of disruption; at the Dauphine, Jack Laine's Reliance Band was thrown out of an engagement at the opening of a religious film for playing a happy tune ("Oh, Mister Dream Man, Please Let Me Dream Some More") during a crucifixion scene. As Raeburn puts it, "The juxtaposition most common to New Orleans is the seedy and the sublime, and New Orleans audiences have never made a secret of their preference for the 'down and dirty.' In Papa Laine's 'inappropriate' humor at the Dauphine, we see performer and audience united in a 'low brow' conspiracy against too much propriety and refinement, and such attitudes often created favorable conditions for jazz at New Orleans theaters."[97]

"Shooting the Agate": Jazz and Gender

Despite providing respite from some kinds of domination, these sites reinforced other hierarchies, notably patriarchal ones. Descriptions of such clubs invariably focused on the display of female bodies. According to Armstrong, "To a tune like The Bucket's Got a Hole in It, some of them chicks would get way down, shake everything, slapping themselves on the cheek of their behind. Yeah! At the end of the night, they'd do the quadrille, beautiful to see, where everybody lined up, crossed over—if no fights hadn't started before that." That is, the enactment of some kinds of freedom from constraint sometimes centered on the sale of women, either directly as in the case of prostitutes or indirectly in dance halls where women danced with customers for money. The customers did not necessarily go to hear the music per se but to have a "good time," and this entailed a kind of mutual con game involving mind-altering substances. Such venues had no admission charge, but when a man came into the saloon, a woman approached him, asking him to buy her a drink; the man often complied, hoping to get her intoxicated and that much closer to his bedroom. However, the drink was in fact a nonalcoholic, faux whisky, and she retained her sobriety, the better to induce the man to buy her more drinks, as she received a cut for each one sold. But just as women got male customers drunk to make money, men used dope for the "persuasion of girls."[98]

In addition, the District had a kind of hypermasculine culture characterized by competition, fighting, and sexual conquest. District denizens lived a stylized life, dressing fashionably by, for example, letting one suspender hang down or wearing a red flannel undershirt, a fad perhaps started by Bolden and continued by other musicians like King Oliver. Morton commented on Oliver's brazen style: "His shirt bustin' open on the stand, blowing, his red undershirt showing, 'Now you'll get a chance to see my red underwear.'" According to Manetta, men in the District wore box back coats—little pleats in the side, loose and long in the back, like a preacher's coat—derby hats, expensive shoes, and diamonds.[99] (It is interesting that preachers, who were opposed to the "vice" of the District, wore coats that were similar to those of the hoodlums who frequented it.)

Although some of the clothes worn in the District reflected reigning fashions, others had a wilder, improvised style. According to Albert Glenny and Leonard Bechet, "They had a type of people . . . that would try to dress real decently. . . . But they had another type . . . that would put on expensive shirts" and shoes, but the shoes were a "funny, funny shape," turned up at the bottom. Bechet and Glenny considered the shoes "awkward" and "out of place," but to the wearers they were expressive, in the African tradition of assembling an idiosyncratic wardrobe, often by mixing apparently incompatible items.[100] Morton tells of someone who rigged a light bulb on his shoe, illuminated when he pressed a button in his pocket, hoping to win over females.

Life among musicians in the District was a kind of performance where dress, speech, and movement created a complete role. The essence of such an attitude can be seen in a description of Morton by James P. Johnson: Morton walked into a club with a big grin "so everyone would get a glance at his diamond studded tooth." Ready to perform, Morton then "would take his overcoat off. It had a special lining that would catch everybody's eye. So he would turn it inside out and, instead of folding it, he would lay it lengthwise along the top of the upright piano. He would do this very slowly, very carefully and very solemnly as if the coat was worth a fortune and had to be handled very tenderly." Still not ready to play, Morton first had to "shake out his silk handkerchief, ostentatiously dust the piano stool with it, sit down, and hit his signature chord."[101]

Even walking was stylized; sporting men imitated longshoremen by "shooting the agate," in a kind of "truckin'" stance, arms thrust out with index and middle finger extended together. Such behavior represented the embrace of a rough, working-class model of masculinity, even by men like Morton who did not come from the lower classes, and a rejection of middle-class models of manhood based on "respectable" values of hard work and renunciation of pleasure. This culture challenged society's lack of recognition of black manhood but simultaneously reaffirmed traditional gender divisions.[102]

In the midst of musicians' masculine display, certain instruments traditionally associated with women, most notably the piano, had to be regendered, as it were, sometimes by playing risqué songs. For many Creole men, playing the piano was a new experience. In more respectable Creole dance halls, there was no piano, because the band played on a raised platform far above the floor, and male pianists were viewed with suspicion. As Morton put it, "Of course, when a man played piano, the stamp was on him for life . . . the femininity stamp. And I didn't want that on. So of course, when I did start to playin' . . . the songs were kind of smutty a bit."[103] Manetta also had to convince his mother that piano was not just for "sissies." Creole pianists like Morton and Manetta adopted the masculine persona of black blues players in order to shed the suspicions regarding their sexuality; in a sense they crossed gender lines but stretched their racial identity to do so. By adopting the conventions of black music, male Creole musicians performed the equivalent of sex reassignment surgery on the piano, shoring up established gender lines. Race became an actor in a drama of gender.

New Orleans's lower-class masculine culture encouraged the denigration of women; both Armstrong and Morton could be physically abusive to women, the latter once pistol-whipping a woman onstage because she cursed him. Women were rarely allowed to express themselves musically in public as men did. Morton apparently took this attitude with him to California, erupting when Anita Gonzalez, his girlfriend, unexpectedly took the stage and sang with his band. As Anita tells it, "When I finished, there was a stack of money on the floor. Jelly was furious. He dragged me outside and made me swear to never sing or dance again." This exclusion of women was particularly perverse since the vast majority of music teachers of color were women.[104]

This ostracism was not by any means total, for there were important female musicians, usually pianists. Lizzie Miles, Mercedes Fields, Blanche Thomas, Wilhelmina Bart, Martha Boswell, and Lottie Taylor all played piano in New Orleans in the early twentieth century. Dolly Adams played with Armstrong and Oliver in her teens; Edna Mitchell with Papa Celestin and Armstrong; and Sweet Emma Barrett with Celestin, Robichaux, Sidney Desvignes, and Armand Piron and on riverboats with Armstrong. Female blues singers like Ann Cook, sometimes called "coon shouters," performed at dives like the Funky Butt; when he was asked whether Cook was tough, Manetta said, "She was as black as your shoes," referring not just to her color but to her lower-class black status. Betsy Cole was famous for lawn parties featuring jazz by well-known musicians.[105]

Many prostitutes could sing, dance, or play an instrument, but they were not widely known or heard. One musician has said that in the early twentieth century, "many hustling women could play the piano, but weren't professional . . . they played for pleasure." Manetta recalled a female entertainer and dancer at one of the houses who played piano but would play only if no customers were present. There were exceptions, however, as can be seen in Antonia Gonzalez's advertisement in the "Blue Book," a guidebook to brothels: "[Gonzalez is a] first-class Octoroon. She also has the distinction of being the only singer of opera and female cornetist in the Tenderloin. She has had offers to leave her present vocation and take to the stage, but her vast business has kept her among friends. Any person out for fun among a lot of pretty Creole damsels, here is the place to have it. For ragtime, singing, and clever dancing . . . Antonia stands in a class all alone."

The capacity of these venues to transgress traditional boundaries had its limits, then, as gender lines were, if anything, rigidified. This rigidity reaffirms Kevin Hetherington's insight that heterotopias do not just resist domination but enact their own systems of power, establishing new hierarchies or reinforcing existing ones.[106]

"The Fracas Has Begun"

The emancipatory potential of these spaces was also limited by their facilitation of violence. Customers' escape from powerlessness, asserting themselves in the face of opposition to early clubs, led to excessive displays of force, and unleashed inhibitions facilitated destructiveness as well as pleasure seeking. The violence can be seen as either revenge against oppression or an uncovering of the id when the restraints of the ego are lifted. Robert Orsi has written about the ways holidays evoke violence, and what he says is applicable more generally to the revelry accompanied by early jazz musicians: "Popular rage and frustration with the discrepancies between the world as it is said to be and the world as it is experienced at work and at home have frequently erupted during civic and religious festivals. . . . The suspension of the ordinary makes holidays potentially very dangerous times. . . . Worlds are made and unmade during holidays, and because the power of these days is so elemental, sex and violence in complex patterns of creation and destruction are inevitably a fundamental part of them."[107]

Nightclubs in general could be perilous places. Performances sometimes turned into free-for-alls when patrons extinguished the lights and started throwing beer bottles; some clubs erected chicken wire in front of the bandstand to protect musicians. At one club in Tremé, customers periodically became intoxicated and shot out the lights, leading the policeman on duty to panic and sound an alarm summoning several officers to round up the troublemakers (and sometimes others as well). According to one musician, "You'd have to fight your way through the fight to get in the street car." Chris Kelly played in rough halls like the New Hall or Artesan Hall (Tremé); the undertakers always looked forward to the balls there, because by night's end three or four bodies inevitably littered the floor. At the Tuxedo Dance Hall, formerly a brothel, a band escaped through the back door after a gunfight; two were killed and others injured. Even in the early years of the twentieth century, according to clarinetist Tony Parenti, jazz was accepted only in places like the New Lusitanos Hall, in the French Quarter, which was populated by prostitutes and their boyfriends, with frequent fights breaking out.[108]

The uptown district, or Black Storyville, was especially dangerous.[109] Particularly notorious was Kinney's Hall, popularly known as Funky Butt Hall; according to Kid Ory, "why, if you didn't have a razor or a gun, you couldn't get in there." Because of the frequent violence, Ory played there only once, but the "rougher" Bolden held forth on a number of occasions.

Other clubs represented similarly unsafe environments. The famous Animal (or Animule) Hall, in the Eighth Ward, got its name from the behavior of patrons under the influence of its cheap liquor; the owner, Joe Baggers, kept an iron pipe to whack people who got out of hand. (Baseball bats broke on some hard heads and were too expensive.) The "star attraction" was Long Head Bob's Social Orchestra, playing only blues from 8:00 in the evening until 3:00 in the morning, although things usually ended earlier with the arrival of the police. Typically fights broke out when someone danced with someone else's lover; the women sometimes fought until they were naked. Somewhere between 1:00 and 2:00 a.m., Bob starting playing the slow drag, signaling customers to find their lovers and inducing the policeman on duty, Officer Kennedy, to call the desk sergeant; he would leave the phone line open until a fight broke out, at which time he announced, "Send the wagon. The fracas has begun."[110]

Though often the quarrels involved lovers, the music itself played a role in evoking chaos. Sometimes customers became violent because they did not like the band or were upset because a previous band had been replaced. More fundamentally, the dark side of music's ability to weaken social boundaries, sometimes erotically, was its facilitation of violence, for as the night went on and the band started playing the blues, inhibitions were unleashed and the crowd started getting unruly. Late at night, using plunger mutes, Chris Kelly spat forth bluesy, vocalized riffs, influenced by the church, and when he played "Careless Love," or perhaps "DMF" (dirty motherfucker), a fight would begin, leading police to close the club. To prevent such outcomes, when the band felt things getting out of hand, they played more traditional music like waltzes to calm people down. On the other hand, sometimes musicians used the violence-provoking tendency of the music to their advantage. According to Earl Humphrey, "The band would often play certain provocative numbers about an hour before the end of the dance, in the expectation that a fight would start. The police would come in and they [the band] could go home early. We knew what was coming when we played 'Dirty M. F.'"[111]

Sometimes the musicians themselves took violent action. Ed Garland once punched Johnny Dodds, a fellow band member, in the mouth, while another musician tells a story of Kid Ory's chasing someone around with a kitchen knife.[112] Of course, sometimes the violence was defensive—Armstrong once had to defend himself from a razor wielded by his first wife, Daisy, a former prostitute.

Even the celebrated jazz funeral, now seen by many as a nostalgic cultural ritual, could become unruly. According to Hypolite Charles, when he played funerals, "we only played a few blocks outside of the graveyard because things usually got real bad with all the people by then. It was a disgrace the way some of them acted. The police would always have to be there to try and keep trouble down." Once a woman at a funeral ran up to George Lewis and snatched the clarinet from his mouth, complaining that he was playing too softly. In Kid Ory's view, such funerals were for "gamblers and hustlers." Comfortably middle-class Creoles like Lorenzo Tio Jr. rarely played funerals because they did not need the money.[113]

Parades in general sometimes bordered on the edge of chaos. Though the second line—the crowd marching and dancing alongside the band—inspired musicians at times, it could also be dangerous. Often second liners were "raggedy [sic] guys who hung around poolrooms and et cetera" (Armstrong), "belligerent" and "sarcastic" "thugs" (Barker) who annoyed the "polite Creole members" of the Onward Brass Band by dancing in the path of the musicians and threatening them at stops. Barker's uncle refused to let him second line because it was too dangerous, often culminating in a fight between Creoles and "Americans" who carried broomsticks, baseball bats, knives, shovel handles, and ax shafts and used them when they crossed from "their" territory into that of their enemies. A second liner once threw a brick at George Lewis's head, scarring him.[114]

Musicians sometimes took harsh measures to defend themselves or retaliate. If the second line got too close to the band, drummer Black Benny hit the intruder with his mallet or simply slugged him. Another musician told of playing with Jack Laine's (white) band and having a band member fend off black second liners with a billiard cue. If these efforts failed, mounted police moved the second liners back, if only because they annoyed the society members.[115]

As in the nightclubs, conflicts during parades sometimes arose over the music itself. Lower-class second liners ridiculed traditional brass bands like the Onward, calling them old fashioned and demanding that they play the newer, "rattier" music. (By most accounts due to the insistence of its leader Manuel Perez, the Onward did not play jazz or "hot" proto-jazz even though some of its members were capable of doing so.) On holidays and big occasions, the bands at the front of the parade played "heavy, serious marches for the very dignified marching of the officials," while the rattier units brought up the rear. According to Barker, "Many times the members marching to the second and third band would get annoyed at the strict serious music and tell the leader to play some barrelhouse or gutbucket music, and then the battle would be on" as second liners ran back and forth between bands, causing pandemonium.[116]

The apparent chaos of such clashes concealed complex political dynamics, for battles over the kinds of music encapsulated generational, racial, and class conflicts. An older generation of middle-class Creoles, who saw themselves as superior to blacks and tried to uphold their pre–Jim Crow era status, championed more traditional and European marches. On the other hand, the newer, more bluesy and improvisational music that would come to be called jazz was supported by the lower classes as well as Creoles who more easily identified with blacks and their music. Racial and class conflicts thus took musical form, just as they had from the city's beginning when French and Americans fought over dance styles.

TWO

Reaction

Defending Purity

From the beginnings of the African presence in New Orleans, authorities feared the potential of unsupervised black music making. As early as 1758, one Louisiana planter wrote, "Nothing is more to be dreaded than to see the Negroes assemble together on Sundays, since, under the pretence of Calinda, or the dance, they sometimes get together to the number of three or four hundred. . . . It is in those tumultuous meetings that they . . . plot their rebellions."[1] Congo Square in particular embodied disrespectability. *Paxton's Directory of New Orleans* (1822) called the square "the place where the Congo, and other negroes *dance, carouse and debauch on the Sabbath*, to the great injury of the morals of the rising generation; it is a foolish custom, that elicits the ridicule of the most respectable persons who visit the city."[2] These whites most dreaded the possibility that the disrespectable music and dance would spread to the broader population, threatening racial purity.

The same fears came to the fore during the time of jazz's birth. As we have seen, the milieu that gave birth to jazz was a compound consisting of lower-class blacks, sensual dances, and "ratty" music. These three elements together constituted a whole ethos, and defenders of purity and the Protestant ethic directed their wrath at each of them. However, in the eyes of the authorities, the most objectionable feature of these clubs was their facilitation of racial mixing.

Attacks on race mixing reached their peak during the era of jazz's birth. Under slavery, race relations had been well defined; despite much interaction between the races, the categories of master and slave created clear roles of domination and subordination. Emancipation threatened to blur the boundaries between the races both literally (through increased miscegenation) and figuratively. By enforcing segregation and denying basic rights to people of color as well as withholding citizenship from certain immigrants, the law helped construct a white, northern European national identity. The Compromise of 1876, withdrawing federal troops from the South and allowing racist Democratic state governments to rule there, cemented this identity.[3] The last decade of the nineteenth century saw the enactment of Jim Crow laws designed to keep the races separate, while prominent scientists argued that since blacks formed a separate species, miscegenation threatened the extinction of the human race: such unions would produce sterile, defective, or "effeminate" offspring.[4] The late nineteenth century also saw an increase in immigrants from southern and eastern Europe, who were often disparaged in terms similar to those used against African Americans.

The push for racial purity and respectability even pervaded the disrespectable red light district, Storyville. Despite their immoral reputations, madams like Josie Arlington cultivated respectability, decorating brothels with classical images and sculptures to create a sense of "refinement, worldliness, wealth, and sophistication." Prostitutes were prohibited from smoking, becoming intoxicated, and cursing, which might threaten their image of refinement.

People of color with light skin, though not "pure" per se, were privileged at such houses. Often brothels advertised the services of octoroons, light-skinned women with just a touch of color for exoticism. The pianists in these houses were primarily Creoles like Morton and Manetta, although there were exceptions like the black, phenomenally talented Tony Jackson and the white "Kid Ross."[5] Darker musicians were unlikely to be hired by houses of prostitution, but blacks were employed to clean up there. Prostitutes were often segregated by race (with different houses offering whites, Creoles, or blacks), and the customers were primarily white.[6]

To jazz's opponents, racial mixing at nightclubs represented a dire threat to civilization. The backdrop to such fear was a nationwide increase in the mingling of different races, classes, and ethnicities in places of public amusement, particularly "concert saloons, "disorderly spaces that encompassed a mixture of theatrical forms, ethnic and cultural antecedents, people from different social classes, and perhaps most explosive of all, men and women who flouted the rules of respectability brazenly and in public." Throughout the country, fear of contamination by immigrants helped fuel a campaign against saloons led by middle-class citizens, mostly Protestants, associated with the Progressive movement.[7]

In New Orleans, race mixing at dances had been an object of criticism since colonial times; in 1800 the Spanish attorney general had tried to close some of the city's dance halls to prevent such interactions. Authorities also periodically tried to enforce integration by requiring revelers to remove their masks before entering a ballroom, but such attempts inevitably failed.[8] By the late nineteenth century, when jazz developed, critics attacked New Orleans tenderloin clubs for their impurity, the mixing of black and white, male and female, upper and lower classes.

Opponents also saw the music itself as racially impure. Had black folk music and European forms stayed separate, newspapers and other self-styled arbiters of culture would not have objected as they did. Of course the intermixing of black and white culture had already occurred in minstrelsy, but it was a mostly Northern phenomenon confined to theatrical performances. Jazz, on the other hand, foisted itself into everyday life, in clubs, parades, picnics, and parties, and led to actual race mixing, with its supposed potential for crime and countercultural values, in a way that minstrelsy did not. Minstrelsy, whether by white or black performers, was an acceptable form of racial mixing because blacks, at least on the surface, were in an inferior position; the hierarchy became less certain during jazz performances.[9] Blacks, whites, and Creoles sometimes listened together to a music that partook of a variety of ethnic traditions.

But it was not the mixing per se of black, white, and Creole, men and women, immigrants and natives, and European- and African-based music that was objectionable. The coming together of such elements, in the eyes of jazz's opponents, would lead to dire social consequences. In a legal claim against a concert saloon in New Orleans, the city's attorney argued that the saloon's mixture of "music, wine, and women" was like "keeping gunpowder, petroleum, and nitro-glycerine in one and the same building," ready to explode.[10]

These clubs and their music represented an assault on social boundaries, particularly sexual ones. Their racial mixing also threatened a set of values—hard work, temperance, chastity for women—associated with whiteness and racial purity. The most widely cited racist tract in the South, Frederick L. Hoffman's *Race Traits and Tendencies of the American Negro* (1896), spoke of immorality as a "race trait" of African Americans, arguing that "immorality and vice are a habit of life of the vast majority" of blacks. According to a district judge in New Orleans in an opinion later printed in the local newspaper, integration "upsets the whole order

SIGHTS OF NEW ORLEANS, THE HARPERS DID NOT SEE.—The Gambling Hells of Franklin Street.

Figure 7. An early black music venue on Franklin Street through the eyes of its opponents, 1887. Notice the apparently interracial band as well as the white police officer with his arms around two black women. (Courtesy of the Louisiana State Museum.)

of society, tramples upon the usages of centuries and contains the germ of social war."[11] Early jazz thus conjured up race mixing as well as the triumph of the anti–Protestant ethic values of the "good time people" that such mixing would produce.

In many ways, attacks on jazz merely extended criticisms of ragtime songs as crude and suggestive, lowering the taste of the public, and threatening to sexual mores. Segregation aimed to protect the purity of white women, and to its critics ragtime, and later jazz, represented their defilement; in morality plays, ragtime music signified the fall of a character, typically a white woman, into degeneracy and immorality. To its critics such music recklessly unleashed the passions, especially sexual ones, threatening to make whites as uninhibited as blacks were said to be. According to one writer, ragtime symbolized "the primitive morality and perceptible moral limitations of the negro type. With the latter sexual restraint is almost unknown, and the widest latitude of moral uncertainty is conceded."[12]

Yet venues featuring jazz threatened female sexual purity more directly by generating environments conducive to immorality. The campaign against saloons and dance halls, which reached its peak in the early 1910s, centered on the clubs' apparent insulation from the law and the control of family and traditional ethnic structures, particularly in the case of women.[13] Saloons had been a male preserve, but around the beginning of the twentieth century, bars, nightclubs, and dance halls began attracting women, often from the middle rather than working class, who repudiated traditional roles and explored their sexuality. Rejecting traditional entertainments as well as arranged courtship and marriage, immigrants and working-class youth found new freedom in the dance hall. Critics described dance halls and saloons as "dens of iniquity" and "pitfalls for the unwary," citing "the breakdown of social proprieties, the ease of making acquaintances, the sensual character of the dancing which is allowed to prevail, the sale of liquor, the tendency to coarse conversation and profanity, darkness in certain portions of the building accessible to the dancers, or shadow dances, the lack of supervision, and the character of at least some of the persons in attendance." According to the *New Orleans Daily Picayune*, "The women, sloughed in the depths of degradation, frequent the halls and dance with those who happen to walk into the place." While the women who worked and caroused there were assumed to be disrespectable and sexually available, however, male patrons walked out the door with their respectability intact.[14]

Criticism of the clubs as snares for the virtue of women was a double-edged sword. Although opponents sought to protect women from exploitation, they worried only about white middle-class women and showed little if any concern about the mistreatment of women of color. Fearing only that the exploitation in tenderloin areas, presumably fueled by the spread of the new music and dance styles, would spill into white middle-class milieus, they attempted to restrict the music and its social problems to lower-class areas populated by New Orleanians of color.

However, anxiety about the clubs was not confined to the middle class. Many working-class whites also resented the new music, perhaps because they were in danger of becoming black by association. The night of the Robert Charles riots, a group of white working-class men went to the neighborhood of black dance halls along Franklin and Customhouse ("pig ankle corners," in the District) hoping to take revenge, but the saloons were closed and deserted.[15]

Jazz symbolized the evils of modernity, encompassing the liberalization of racial and sexual mores as well as a frenzied industrialization and urbanization that swept away tradition. Both critics and supporters of jazz embraced this perspective with, of course, different valuations. To its opponents, popular culture encouraged the replacement of self-sufficiency and the work ethic with an ethos of gratification and consumption that was associated with African Americans and immigrants; the rhythmically complex and sometimes dissonant music reinforced this sense of upheaval and rebellion. The attack on jazz thus came from two emerging strands of ideology: the idea that the poor, immigrants, and people of color lack reason and self-control, the capacity for "labor and self-denial," and the notion that mass culture appeals to base, antisocial desires. To its critics, jazz's social dangers and its aesthetic disorderliness were inseparable.[16]

Disorderly Music and Unruly Behavior

In addition to encouraging race mixing and sexual immorality, according to critics of saloons and honky-tonks, the music itself fundamentally threatened the social order. A famous editorial in the 1918 *New Orleans Times-Picayune* railed against the dangers of "jass":

Why is the jass music, and, therefore, the jass band? As well ask why is the dime novel or the grease-dripping doughnut? All are manifestations of a low streak in man's tastes that has not yet come out in civilization's wash . . . In its youth, it was listened to blushingly behind closed doors and drawn curtains, but, like all vice, it grew bolder until it dared decent surroundings. . . .

In the matter of jass, New Orleans is particularly interested, since it has been widely suggested that this particular form of musical vice had its birth in this city—that it came, in fact, from doubtful surroundings in our slums. We do not recognize the honor of parenthood, but with such a story in circulation, it behooves us to be last to accept the atrocity in polite society, and where it has crept in we should make it a point of civic honor to suppress it. Its musical value is nil, and its possibilities of harm are great.[17]

In the eyes of such opponents, jazz was anarchic noise that simulated and stimulated social breakdown.

The critique of "unruly" music and was not new; from Puritan times, some have sought to keep music within strict boundaries, associating the breaking of musical rules with social disorder. One observer complained in 1721 that psalms "are now miserably tortured, and twisted, and qua-vered, in some Churches, into an horrid Medly of confused and disor-derly Noises." Opponents of "lining out," in which a deacon sang a line of a psalm upon which the congregation improvised "flourishes, grace notes, and turns," sought to bring back "regular singing," using writ-ten sources. Later criticism centered on the "fuguing tunes" of William Billings (1746–1800), which featured dissonant, raucous polyphony, with (according to Billings) "each part striving for mastery and victory, [t]he audience entertained and delighted, their minds surprisingly ag-itated and extremely fluctuated, sometimes declaring for one part and sometimes for another." Billings described it as a kind of participatory liberation, but his critics saw it as dangerous and disorderly.[18]

Opponents of early jazz similarly connected the defiance of musical conventions with the breakdown of social order. To its critics, music at "ratty" clubs mirrored and encouraged the unrestrained behavior of its listeners. A 1902 newspaper article portrayed musicians emitting loud, wild, uncontrollable sounds at a sarcastically described "grand ball" at a Storyville club: "The orchestra consisted of a clarionet, a guitar and a bass fiddle. The guitar was picked by a bullet-headed negro with a far-away look in his eyes, and a molasses-colored musician that blew the clarionet had to brace his feet against the railing of the players' stand to prevent himself from being hurled backward by the strength of his breath, which at each blast into the instrument had the effect of making the player 'kick' back like a shotgun." While the shotgun imagery suggests both violence and sexuality, another club in the District was described as simply having "an indecent ring about it that was disgusting."[19]

To its critics, the danger of the music stemmed from its rejection of some (but by no means all) European conventions, particularly the priority of composition over performance, the primacy of harmony over melody, and the diatonic scale. "A site of unruliness," jazz resisted (as many pointed out) precise notation because of its blue notes of indefinable pitch and subtle rhythmic manipulations, producing what Nathaniel Mackey calls "fugitive sounds." Such sounds recalled "callithumpians," nineteenth-century masked folk processions where marchers beat drums, blew whistles, and banged on pots and pans: "'Music' is a metaphor for the official social code; 'noise' is implicit violence, a challenge to law's authority, as Carnival is a challenge to Lent, as callithumpians were demons of disorder." Early jazz's very unintelligibility revealed its rootedness in emergent structures of feeling underneath the surface of a culture of racial purity.[20]

"Do Not Shake the Hips"

Critics also lambasted the dances performed to jazz. According to the 1918 *Times-Picayune* editorial, "On certain natures sound loud and meaningless has an exciting, almost an intoxicating effect, like crude colors and strong perfumes, the sight of flesh or the sadic pleasure in blood. . . . A dance to the unstable bray of the sackbut gives a sensual delight more intense and quite different from the languor of a Viennese waltz or the refined sentiment and respectful emotion of an eighteenth century minuet." The "wrong" kind of dancing had been a concern in America as far back as the famous Maypole at Merry Mount in 1628, where renegade Puritans and Indian women danced together, violating both sexual and racial taboos. By the end of that century, Puritans like Increase Mather still decried "profane and promiscuous dancing." Later guardians of purity saw the waltz, introduced in the late eighteenth century, as scandalous because of its "close embrace." One writer declared in 1894, "I do not believe that any woman can or does waltz without being improperly aroused. . . . Any woman with a nature so cold as not to be aroused by a perfect execution of the waltz, is entirely unfit to make any man happy as his wife, and if she be willing to indulge in such pleasures with every ballroom libertine, she is not the woman any man wants for a wife."[21]

Dancing had particularly been an issue in early New Orleans as white Creoles and English-descended Americans fought for their respective national dances, at one point reaching a compromise whereby English country dances alternated with French contredanses or quadrilles. In Congo Square the calinda, considered "lascivious" and "indecent" by missionaries in Martinique, evoked both fascination and outrage, with even some Creoles of Color considering it "common" and undignified. New, more sensual dances, previously discussed, shocked critics as well.[22]

Reformers associated the new dances with sex, arguing that working-class couples did not "dance" but rather engaged in "a series of indecent antics to the accompaniment of music." Similarly, one writer in 1914 complained that at public dance halls in New York City, "vulgar dancing exists everywhere, and the 'spiel,' a form of dancing requiring much twirling and twisting, and one that particularly causes sexual excitement, is popular in all." Rules for dancing were formulated during this period to make dances more "respectable." (Ironically, in light of its earlier reputation, some critics called for the return of the waltz.) The immensely popular Vernon and Irene Castle, who helped spread the ragtime music of James Reese Europe and others, popularized the less provocative one-step and the fox trot and advocated more restraint in body movement: "Do not wiggle the shoulders. Do not shake the hips. Do not twist the body. Do not flounce the elbows. Do not pump the arms. Do not hop—glide instead. Avoid low, fantastic and acrobatic dips." However, dancers like the Castles had to walk a fine line—if they constricted the dances too much, the public would reject them.[23] Like jazz itself, the dances evoked both excitement and fear.

———

Although white criticism of jazz is hardly surprising, some blacks and Creoles distanced themselves from disrespectable venues and the music played there as well. Posters for clubs like Economy Hall used high-toned language to advertise their "respectable" nature, like one from 1909 announcing a "First Grand Disguise, Masquerade & Fancy Dress Soiree Dansante to be given by the garden district social club." Another advertises a similar event at the same venue, assuring prospective patrons that "The Following Committee of Well Known Gentlemen Will Spare No Energy or Finances to Make This Affair Eclipse any of our Former Successes." These posters echoed 1888 newspaper announcements for brass band engagements describing the musicians as "respectable" or "the best and most intelligent colored young men of our town." Advertisements for the newly opened Dixie Park used similar language to reassure potential customers of its safety and respectability, calling it "the most refined Park for colored people in the South. Where order will always be maintained. The park is the best to the colored people for public and private parties or any other respectable amusement." For good measure, it was promised that "the music will be furnished by Prof. Babb Frank and his wonderful Peerless Band in all new Uniforms." A similar reassurance that "the best of order will be maintained" was offered on a poster for a "grand excursion picnic" featuring music by John Robichaux, that icon of Creole respectability.[24] The references to respectability, order, and new uniforms by Creoles and blacks mark the spaces advertised as exclusive, not for the disrespectable, the "ratty." However, as we shall see, New Orleans Creole and black objections to jazz differed, each emerging from distinctive cultures and histories.

"All Bright People": Creole Opposition

Creoles of Color of the older generation harshly criticized the kinds of venues that featured the new music. Of a Sicilian barroom, Danny Barker's mother said, "That smoking, gambling, whiskey—they goin' dead straight down into hell!" Much of the Creoles' opposition to the new music centered on its association with blacks, whom they saw as lower class. As Creole Paul Dominguez put it, "You see, we Downtown people, we try to be intelligent. Everybody learn a trade, like my daddy was a cigarmaker and so was I. . . . We try to bar jail. . . . Uptown, cross Canal yonder, they *used* to jail. . . . There's a vast difference here in this town. Uptown folks are ruffians, cut up in the face and live on the river. All they know is—get out on the levee and truck cotton—be longshoremen, screwmen. And me, I ain't never been on the river *a day in my life*." Although of African ancestry, most Creoles did not see themselves as black; drummer Paul Barbarin said, "I didn't know I was colored until . . . later years." According to some, Creoles were more racist than many whites, and many of them spoke French exclusively.[25] Blacks and Creoles of Color lived fairly separately, the Creoles living "downtown" and the blacks "uptown."

One can surmise that the music's association with recent immigrants also tainted it for Creoles. Because both groups were largely Catholic and bilingual, immigrants and Creoles might have bonded, but they did not, because of the immigrants' lower-class status. For a time at least Creoles and elite whites stuck together; indeed, having elite social connections distanced Creoles from blacks, and they introduced evidence of such connections at trials to prove their whiteness.[26]

Creoles separated themselves from blacks more urgently in response to Jim Crow. Emancipation supported the Creoles by challenging racial hierarchy, but it also called their special position into question because their free status no longer distinguished them from blacks. The absence of slavery to mark a clear line between white and black also led many whites to disassociate themselves from Creoles of Color. Since the days at Saint-Domingue, whites had tried to erect barriers between themselves and Creoles; a 1779 regulation there made it unlawful for free people of color to "affect the dress, hairstyles, style, or bearing of whites." With racial boundaries seemingly more permeable, shades in between black and white represented the possibility of the contamination of the pure white self. The mulatto, in the words of Joel Williamson, represented the white South's worst nightmare, "the absolute damnation of South-ern civilization. . . . He was the walking, talking, breathing indictment of the world the white man had made. He rendered beyond denial the fact that white people had fallen, and white was therefore not totally right. It was apparent in his very person that white and black had inter-penetrated in a graphic and appalling way. Life in the Southern world was not pure, clean, and clear as white people needed to believe." White women in particular resented mixed-race women as a threat to their family in the form of plaçage. Because of the strength of the bonds of plaçage, "the quadroon mistress had the power to destabilize a [white] Creole family and Creole society in general." Grace King called the quadroons "the most insidious and the deadliest foes a community ever possessed."[27]

As a result of this fear of racial impurity, whites increasingly pushed Creoles into the category of black. Some whites took this perspective soon after the end of the Civil War. In an 1867 letter to a newspaper, written in Creole, a Creole of Color complained of being called a "Stink-ing, Stealing, Lazy Nigger" and lamented that while before the war "they said that nigger is a nigger, griffe is a griffe, mulatto is a mulatto; now all of us are people of color, even one who is black as soot, they have to call him a person of color. I don't hear American [i.e., English] much but I know Nigger is not a word to say to a *gentleman* of color."[28] This letter is especially interesting because the writer's fear of becoming black is tied to a potential loss of respectability, of "gentleman" status, which a few decades later would play a part in Creole opposition to jazz.

Most Creoles of Color were ambivalent about their relationship to blacks; even in Saint-Domingue they had simultaneously attacked racism and defended slavery. In New Orleans, though considering themselves separate, Creoles allied with blacks for political purposes; an 1866 edito-rial stated that "our future is indissolubly bound up with that of the ne-gro, and we have resolved . . . to rise or fall with them. We have no rights which we can reckon safe while the same are denied to the fieldhands on the sugar plantations." While some saw such alliances with blacks as a wholehearted embrace of Creoles' own blackness, other Creoles like Rudolphe Desdunes, connected with both the *Plessy* case and brass band musicians, emphasized the need to retain their unique culture. Both using race and calling it into question, by allying with blacks to fight racism Creoles implicitly acknowledged with one hand the biracial black-white taxonomy they rejected on the other, "symbolically stating that race *is* a construct that had been used against them" and then using it "to make the most of Reconstruction's promises."[29]

The end of Reconstruction gave added impetus to the movement to deny special status for Creoles. In 1877 Lafcadio Hearn reported that in "the South there appears to be a widely diffused opinion among the lower classes that the Creoles of New Orleans are 'nothing more'n damned niggers who jabber French.'" The same year a Creole man complained that even "a person having a few drops of African blood in his veins, no matter how white he may be is considered a nigger and has to be cooped in the cockloft of a theatre or stay at home. I think that man has a right to choose for himself weather [sic] he will be a white man or a nigger. So it is, the moral suffering of a man having a little negro blood in his veins is something terrible—for he is always in hot water."[30]

During Reconstruction, Creoles had allowed French-speaking non-Creole blacks to join their organizations. But with the rise of Jim Crow in the late nineteenth century, Creole organizations became more selective, and the community drew into itself, creating a self-contained world of parallel institutions—schools, benevolent societies, social clubs, and musical and literary associations, centered in particular neighborhoods. Even as late as 1915 most Creoles refused to attend black churches. To protect their distinct identity, they started highlighting their French roots by calling themselves "Creoles of Color" rather than "free people of color."[31]

As they closed their borders to keep blacks out, Creoles increasingly cultivated relations with whites and emphasized light skin and the absence of a slave background as criteria of Creole identity. Creoles sought to ally themselves with high culture, typically associated with whiteness; speaking French rather than Creole, having a piano and being able to play it, and practicing skilled labor (rather than domestic work like blacks) gave one higher status in the Creole community. For a time many whites accepted this alliance: as Rose Tio, the daughter of famed clarinetist and teacher Lorenzo Tio Jr., put it, "Regardless of who they were, if they were a mixed people or if they were white, if they were on a certain cultural level, they were intermingled.... Anyone who was not

Figure 8. The John Robichaux Orchestra, 1896, with the leader on violin. The "gentleman" Robichaux's band exemplified Creole respectability. (Photo courtesy of the William Ransom Hogan Archive, Tulane University.)

of the cultural level, who could not speak fluent French . . . whether they were of the same race or not, they were classed among themselves."[32]

Holding on to a European identity, Creoles thus at first resisted African-based music. Older and wealthier Creoles of Color in particular opposed the new music and looked down on younger musicians who embraced the new style. They often spoke of themselves as "decent" and "respected" colored citizens, just as appalled at the dives of Franklin Street as the *Mascot* was, and they refused to let their daughters hear "ratty" music, believing that it (in Johnny St. Cyr's words) "caused the younger set to misbehave on the dance floor." According to Rose Tio, second lines were considered "vulgar," while Barney Bigard's parents let him follow bands only for a few blocks: "They didn't want us to get hung up in those 'second lines' because they were kind of bad."[33] Seeing themselves as purveyors of European "high culture," growing up on a diet of European classical music, even many younger Creoles found the new music foreign.

"Barbaric" African elements of the music particularly distressed the Creole elite. In the words of one historian, speaking of an earlier period, "By repudiating their African heritage and embracing French culture, the free coloreds of antebellum New Orleans signaled the complete triumph of acculturation, for Louisiana whites had always held up France as the essence of civilization and Africa as the epitome of barbarism." This attitude continued to some degree after the war, and remnants of it exist today.[34]

Creoles resisted the new black music by maintaining exclusive clubs for "respectable" entertainment. At these halls the society bands of Armand Piron, John Robichaux, and others, though they often employed jazz musicians, played tame, "sweet" music for the elite. Robichaux was, according to one musician, "light colored" and "dignified," someone who wanted to be seen as a "gentleman" rather than a "low class Negro." Because he was so "straight laced," some musicians did not want to play for him, but Robichaux took pride in his silky hair, a marker of white European heritage and therefore sophistication.[35]

These exclusive clubs served as refuges from a possible association with blacks and their taint of disrespectability, as some Creoles withdrew into themselves, "creating a Creole world over which they alone had a certain degree of control." Creole musician Manuel Manetta on an oral history tape speaks of *respectable* halls, like Perseverance Hall, Cooperators Hall, Artisan (or Artesan) Hall, and Francs Amis, repeating the word *respectable* with great emphasis. Of the Francs Amis (in the Seventh Ward), Manetta says, "That was *respectable*—all bright people was there. . . . You wouldn't see too many of the dark faces. . . . Uptowners wouldn't go there." Here Manetta connects Creoleness, light complexion, and respectability and, by implication, blackness, dark complexion, and "rattiness." At one time the French language would have kept blacks out of such social clubs, but since fewer and fewer Creoles spoke it, clubs required invitations or used peepholes to exclude disrespectable (black) outsiders. These halls were clustered in Creole neighborhoods like Tremé, an area settled by refugees from Saint-Domingue in the early nineteenth century, and the Seventh Ward; both areas were known as residences of Creole craftsmen and tradesmen. Thus were geography, race, class, and respectability intertwined in the emergence of New Orleans jazz.[36]

Although it is tempting to criticize Creoles as elitist or racist, their emphasis on respectability was understandable. It was galling to Creoles that, as one newspaper in 1881 put it, "the most respected colored citizens of our community are deprived of the pleasures and benefits of these [lakefront] resorts by the glaring insults offered them, by bluntly refusing to accommodate them to refreshments in common with others,"

yet "the most despicable, or depraved white man or woman, can enjoy the hospitalities as bountifully as our most respected white citizen."
In their mind, "decent colored people" would not sit in "black" train
cars.[37] Maintaining respectability challenged white stereotypes of people of color by asserting intelligence and sophistication. Yet as we shall
see, a growing number of Creoles rejected older notions of respectability
and instead inserted themselves into the dominant culture through the
sounds of jazz emanating from their instruments.

The Devil's Music: Black Resistance to Jazz

Many blacks also opposed the new music in the name of respectability. Black opposition to jazz, particularly its African features, had roots
in contemporary conflicts over the church's own music. Many religious
leaders and congregants resisted African-influenced church music, and
this resistance reached a peak at the time of jazz's emergence. Like
jazz, emotional, bluesy music, often found in lower-class "Sanctified"
churches, exemplified a primitivism that in their eyes presented an unsophisticated image to whites and held them back in their quest to advance the race.

This battle was an episode in a long struggle within American Protestantism over emotional church music. As early as 1721, Puritan Cotton
Mather had warned against the dangers of singing psalms, contending
that while it could aid memory, its sensuality tempted worshipers away
from God. Though meant to "calm and silence our evil noisy Passions,
to actuate and invigorate pious and devotional Affections," it could also
stir up those very passions.[38]

Some white church leaders labored to convince African Americans to
make their church services more standardized and less emotional. Calling ring dancing and "patting Juba" (striking alternating thighs) "gross
perversions of true religion," Methodist official John F. Watson in 1819
spoke of "a growing evil, in the practice of singing in our places of public
and society worship, merry airs, adapted from old songs, to hymns of
our own composing" mainly by blacks. Watson seemed to have several
objections here, encompassing the composing of hymns by blacks; the
emotional ("merry") quality of the singing; the use of folk tunes, thus
mixing the sacred and the secular; and the movements accompanying
the music. Urging "reverence and stillness on the part of the congregation," Watson recommended that blacks be taught psalms and hymns

so they would cast aside "the extravagant and nonsensical chants, and catches and hallelujah songs of their own composing."[39]

Even black clergy joined the critical chorus. As early as the mid-eighteenth century, one Baptist preacher railed against "noisy Christians," and the African Methodist Episcopal church later passed a resolution "strenuously oppos[ing] . . . the singing of fuge [sic] tunes and hymns of our own composing in our public places and congregations." Yet many black churchgoers resented these restrictions. One former slave, "Old Jenny," complained of a lack of spirituality amidst the decorum of the white church: "Yous so chained up wid' spectability dat yous feared to hab de Sperit work, les' dere some noise wid it."[40]

This debate became particularly acute during the time of jazz's emergence, when blacks sought to fight racism by uplifting the race, which often meant striving for respectability in the eyes of whites. Social class was at the center of debates about African-influenced music in Sanctified churches, with middle- or upper-class blacks seeking to shed what they saw as remnants of primitivism that slowed their upward social path. In the 1880s, a Baptist missionary among the Louisiana freedpeople complained of a "disorderly and disgraceful ceremony" with wild singing and parishioners falling into trances. Around the same time, African Methodist Episcopal Church bishop Daniel Alexander Payne told some ring-shouting churchgoers that their movements constituted "a heathenish way to worship and disgraceful to themselves, the race, and the Christian name." Ordering them to "sit down and sing in a rational manner," he threatened to revoke their church memberships if they disobeyed. Even the renowned James Weldon Johnson, who a few years later edited a collection of spirituals, called shouts "semi-barbaric" leftovers from a "primitive African dance," "not true spirituals nor even truly religious."[41]

The Sanctified Church itself simultaneously embraced and rejected these notions of respectability. While it emphasized strict morality and formal dress ("dress as becometh holiness"), members practiced a kind of ecstatic worship that many Baptists and Methodists considered less than fully respectable.[42] As we shall see, particularly since it allowed instruments while other denominations did not, the Sanctified Church acted as a bridge between the music of the traditional black church and the nightclub, though undoubtedly members would not have looked at it that way.

More often than not, church music "reform" movements had limited success. In response to Payne's admonitions against the ring shout, one worshiper snapped back, "Sinners won't get converted unless there is a ring"; two women at a Baltimore church physically assaulted him for trying to "modify the extravagances in worship." In an 1886 New Orleans church service, missionaries of the American Baptist Home Mission Society trumpeted the success of their efforts to make African American worship more orderly, later demonstrating their seriousness by threatening to expel a group of exclaiming women. However, in his sermon the minister objected to such efforts, proclaiming, "Some folks preaches style and says 'keep still, stop that shoutin',' but I doesn't preach style. Who dares to say to a soul filled with the spirit, 'stop shoutin!'" "Shouting," here referring to both physical movement and verbal cries, was a part of black culture that many churchgoers were reluctant to let go of. As one former slave put it, "I stays independent of what white folks tell me when I shouts. De Spirit moves me every day, dat's how I stays in. White folks don't feel sech as I does."[43]

Persevering in the face of resistance to their attempts to prohibit African features of worship, "respectable" blacks opposed jazz for some of the same reasons, believing it to be "destructive to moral virtue and racial uplift." Responding to urbanization and what they saw as its damaging effects to family and morality, black guardians of respectability valorized the home and the church as havens from the temptations of the street and its immoral dancehalls and nickelodeons. Ironically, given Creole assumptions about African Americans, black Protestant ministers saw the Creole community as a hotbed of sin (gambling, drinking, sensual entertainment), though many Protestants were drawn to Creole music and entertainments in the late nineteenth century.[44]

The language of respectability also reflected gender divisions, with the home and church representing female domains. "Women who strolled the streets or attended dance halls and cheap theaters promiscuously blurred the boundaries of gender." The idea of respectability had class dimensions for blacks as well. The working poor sought respectability to avoid falling into (or being lumped with) the underclass, yet they also differentiated themselves from the hedonism of the upper classes. Jazz's association with the underclass made it particularly harmful in their eyes, and they rejected even the ways of walking or dancing associated with the good time people. Yet the purveyors of respectability were fighting a losing battle, as the church's influence waned amidst urban modernization.[45]

As with their Creole counterparts, it is tempting to view black critics of African-based music as Uncle Toms who abandoned their race in pursuit of assimilation, but such a view would be overly simple. Since, as we have seen, many whites saw blacks as criminals and prostitutes, endemically lazy and immoral, embracing respectability, particularly for women, represented an assertion of dignity and racial self-help and an act of resistance to racism. By clinging to respectability, blacks defined themselves in a way that they thought indicated their moral superiority and would lead to advancement of the race. Those who clung to rural or backward-seeming dress, speech, worship, and music were seen as reinforcing negative stereotypes. Ingrid Monson has reminded us that while academics and white "hipsters" romanticize transgressions against respectability, many musicians and audiences of color emphasize hard work and other "Protestant" values as vehicles for social mobility.[46] The rejection of the new music in the name of respectability, then, had a double edge, simultaneously allying with white opposition to black culture and rejecting it.

Containment

Bolstered by vociferous support, opponents of the new music tried to contain it temporally and spatially. Understanding the threat the music posed to the disciplinary control of time, opponents attempted to regulate the hours it was performed. In 1881, the New Orleans city council passed an ordinance requiring barrooms to close at midnight in order to reduce fighting, and in 1886 the state legislature passed a Sunday closing law.[47] However, such regulations went largely ignored in the Crescent City.

These temporal restrictions were aimed at the carnivalistic ethos of these milieus and the subjectivities they enabled. Interestingly, even some club owners tried to stop the flow of the music and the experience of time it created; they would order musicians to cease playing so that customers would buy drinks.[48] Despite the music's power, the imperatives of commerce and its control of time could not be completely interrupted.

Authorities also responded to the perceived social dangers of jazz by attempting to control public space through segregation and isolation. Undoubtedly "reformers" would have liked to purge the city of "vice" altogether, but since that was impossible, they sought to contain it. The creation of districts for prostitution did not so much indicate an acceptance of vice as an attempt to confine it. This purging of "vice" from business districts or "respectable" neighborhoods was common; by the late nineteenth century, most American cities had red light districts tolerated by law enforcement. These attempts at containment exemplified the racial geography of public amusement; typically, nineteenth-century American theaters reserved the third balcony for prostitutes and their customers, keeping them away from the more "respectable" theatergoers, who voyeuristically gawked at them. African Americans often sat in an even higher balcony, a trend that continued in movie theaters into the 1950s.[49]

Authorities established the prostitution districts in black neighborhoods, suggesting "a rough equality between its population of 'lewd and abandoned women,' both white and black, and the African Americans who lived, went to school, and worshiped in the neighborhood. The Story Ordinances placed people of color on a plane with prostitutes and other sexual sinners, both conceptually and in terms of physical proximity." Many whites believed that blacks, prostitution, and jazz all threatened contagion and needed to be quarantined; one citizen complaint alleged that, in the words of the police report, "a large crowd of negroes living in a small house, with only three rooms[,] would spread disease." Music and dancing compounded the problem; in 1896, one physician at a meeting about controlling smallpox suggested that the city close its "negro dance halls" on Franklin Street to stop the spread of the disease. However, this plan was rejected because many feared that such a closing, according to the *Daily Picayune*, "would only result in the unclean blacks being disseminated among corner groceries and clean drinking dens," but the board voted to limit the movements of blacks in and out of the city for the time being. Thus two months before the *Plessy* decision declared segregation on New Orleans streetcars constitutional, whites tried to seal off music in tenderloin clubs, which they associated with literal disease or the contagion of immorality. Even red light districts themselves were segregated, with each brothel featuring prostitutes of only one race. As always, however, there were loopholes, as when Creole prostitutes passed for white by calling themselves "Spanish."[50]

Not surprisingly, jazz's opponents recruited the police in their fight. As early as 1892, police received citizen complaints over loud late-night partying and ragtime music in "respectable" neighborhoods. Police inspectors fielded such complaints regularly, usually focusing on the loudness of the music and the lateness of the hour, and they granted, withheld, or revoked permits for live music to control vice. In response to a complaint alleging that certain lawn parties "were a nuisance, and . . . the conduct of negroes was intolerable," the police inspector refused to issue further permits; one club was denied a permit for an electric piano, as it would have created a "nuisance to the neighborhood."[51]

Complaints were even made about churches; in St. John Divine, for example, "stamping of feet was so great that same could be heard two squares away, much to the annoyance of the neighborhood," as some were prevented from sleeping. In another case, police revoked a permit to "preach the Gospel on the streets" because a nightly indoor service by the same group had created "a nuisance to the neighborhood." Reinforcing the observation that respectability was not just a white concern, "colored" citizens complained as well; one objected to a Saturday night fish fry that "[kept] him up all hours of the night," while another said the same venue featured "string music and they annoy him very much." Surprisingly, the police seemed to take these protestations by New Orleanians of color seriously: in response to the complaint about the string music, "the men on said beat [were ordered] to give this place their strict attention."[52]

Noise was not the only complaint made about saloons and nightclubs, for police also responded to more general objections to the venues' clientele and their immoral behavior. A permit for a club a few blocks away from, but not in, the District was revoked because, in addition to a string band playing too late, "women who reside in the district which is set aside according to law for prostitutes . . . visit the restaurant and after eating they engage in dancing." Similarly, withdrawing a permit for a lawn party frequented by "the lowest class of negroes" from Black Storyville, police alleged that parents could not leave their children outside because "their dancing is not respectable, and . . . they use very vulgar language, and . . . disturbances are regular." Drug use at clubs also brought police intervention, as in the case of George Foucault, proprietor of the Storyville club "Fewclothes," frequented by important musicians, who was charged with "selling catarrh powder containing cocaine." Other complaints centered on racial mixing at barrooms; Vito La-Rocca's saloon, "strictly for colored people," was alleged to have white patrons (in addition to "noisy" negroes outside).[53]

Even if a permit was not revoked, police harassment could follow a complaint. In response to one citizen's objection to "a negro dive of the lowest type, frequented by Negroes of all classes," the officer assured him that the "usual surveillance will be kept on this place as in places of that character." Police paid particular attention to this club because of its proximity to Union Depot, "directly in the route taken by passengers going to and from the Depot."[54]

Yet the police did not act in a uniformly harsh manner. Sometimes permits would be issued or retained, as in one in July 1907 that allowed a saloon owner "to sing, with cornet and band, also for electrical piano."

Other times authorities dismissed complaints, as in the case of one made about a lawn party on South Rampart by well-known bandleader Babb Frank. The police interviewed twenty-six individuals, white and "colored," and "all claimed that they are not annoyed by the dances and all entertainments which have been conducted there in an orderly manner, excepting an Italian" who complained the music was played too late into the night. The report ends by saying that "this neighborhood is principally inhabited by negroes, and upon investigation made by the Officers find[s] the complaint not well founded," perhaps suggesting that such an event was acceptable in a (disrespectable) "negro" neighborhood even if it might not be elsewhere.[55]

Despite some racially motivated crackdowns by police, at times the authorities turned a blind eye to the "impure" activities surrounding jazz.[56] An article in the 1902 *Daily Picayune* about the dangers of dance halls complained that police stationed there were "oblivious" and actually "enjoy[ed] themselves"; after detailing incidents of drinking minors, swearing, the presence of prostitutes, and "indecent" "raggy ragtime," the article lamented that the police sat at tables or talked to women, either way taking no action to stop the immorality. That some of this indifference resulted from bribes or other forms of corruption is suggested by an editorial some years later complaining that policemen covering "notorious" dance halls were "actually paid by the proprietors of the establishments" and therefore allowed their immoral activities to continue.[57]

Notwithstanding their seeming futility, attempts to regulate jazz and its environment continued. In 1908 and 1909, laws were passed officially segregating brothels and barring musical instruments except where food was served. In 1917, the city council passed an ordinance strictly segregating the downtown and uptown districts, so that, according to its author, "the appearance of a white man in the negro district will cause his arrest" and "a negro woman even stroll[ing] in the white district . . . will be jailed." This created controversy, but the debate became moot when Storyville, uptown and downtown, was abolished later that year.[58]

Fascinating Rhythms

Whites and "respectable" blacks and Creoles might have been repelled by jazz, but many of them found it fascinating as well, and this fascination contributed to the spread of the music. The mayor of New York City on an 1891 visit, in the midst of outrage against vice on Franklin

Street, made a point of stopping at a club there to watch stevedores do an "animal" dance, the "Hog Face."[59] "Respectable" people patronized disrespectable establishments and danced to immoral music, returning to their homes no less respectable for it, while white club owners, often using money-laundering schemes, made huge profits from the immorality they criticized.

Not all Creoles rejected the new music either, as the French-speaking elite represented a small portion of their population. Creoles went to the opera, but they also gambled, put on cockfights and circuses, and ridiculed the dandy mulatto in song. During the period of jazz's formation, working-class Creoles identified themselves as laborers and banded together with whites and blacks; these Creoles frequented "ratty" venues in disrespectable neighborhoods along with working-class blacks and fueled the new music.[60]

Certain white Americans for some time had identified with blacks in order to go beyond the confines of what was socially acceptable and discover new identities. In the early 1800s, one observer in Jamaica complained that white women, drawn to Creole language and culture, spoke "a sort of broken English"; one, in response to the observation that it was cold out said, "Yes, ma-am, *him rail-ly too fra-ish.*" Blackface minstrels of the 1840s and 1850s satirized opera and the wealthy and addressed controversial issues that were difficult to broach in other forums.[61] By the late nineteenth century, African American music for many whites represented values that they saw as disappearing from or forbidden by modern society. In 1901 Caroline Elizabeth Merrick, a New Orleanian who became prominent in the women's rights movement, looked back on her life and feared that the innocence black music represented would disappear:

Will not so-called musical "cultivation" tend to destroy the charmingly distinctive character of the negro's music? Art cannot supply or enhance the quality of his genius. It will be a definite loss if the music of the future shall lack the individualism of his songs, for with them will go the wonderful power of improvisation—the relic of his unfettered imagination, the voices of his native jungles struggling to translate themselves into speech. His happy *insouciance* is already fleeing before the pressure of his growing responsibilities. Very much that constitutes the picturesque and lovable in negro character will disappear with the negro point of view,—for if he survives in this civilization his point of view must merge into the Anglo-Saxon's.[62]

For Merrick, "negro" music conjured up a Rousseauian state of nature, a prefall innocence before the modern imperatives of work, specialization, and self-denial. Listening to such music evoked primitivist fantasies that allowed listeners like Merrick to mentally escape from an increasingly routinized society. Whites saw in African Americans an inversion of Protestant ethic values like hard work and self-denial, values becoming increasingly dominant, evidenced by William Graham Sumner's *What Social Classes Owe to Each Other* (1883) touting "labor and self denial" and Frederick Taylor's time and motion studies aimed at producing an efficient workplace.

The endurance of this view is apparent from a similar statement in 1926 by Paul Whiteman and Mary Margaret McBride: "In America, jazz is at once a revolt and a release. Through it, we get back to a simple, to a savage, if you like, joy in being alive. While we are dancing or singing or even listening to jazz, all the artificial restraints are gone. We are rhythmic, we are emotional, we are natural."[63]

Though based on racist stereotypes of African Americans as childlike, the notion of jazz as free and natural contained a potentially critical perspective on modern capitalist society. Even the harsh criticism of the music can be seen as a kind of repressed wish for the forbidden: in a time of increasing routinization and restraint, whites condemned blacks for emotionality and the pursuit of pleasure at the expense of work precisely because they (whites) were drawn to those qualities. As Richard Ford puts it, qualities racist whites attribute to blacks are the "guilty projections of white society. This white self-regard is at the root of race bigotry in all its forms; it is not a fear of the other, but a fear and loathing of the self. . . . It is the construction of whiteness as the absence of those demons the white subject must project onto the other." Black culture, particularly music, became associated with values that whites both disavowed and desired, as evidenced by the subterranean demimondes, where race mixing took place, in every major Southern city.[64]

Whites in New Orleans from the city's beginnings found themselves drawn to black culture—simultaneously strange, forbidden, and alluring—and its music in particular. In the nineteenth century, observers inevitably described slave music and dance as "savage" and wild, like the missionary who in 1823 summarized the "Saturnalia" and "Congo dances" during slave holidays with the phrase "Every thing is license and revelry."[65]

Whites were sometimes appalled by black church services; their sense of decorum was violated by the bodily movement, wailing, and crying out. As early as the Civil War period, many whites found the music performed in black services foreign and disturbing, probably because of African-influenced features—blue notes, a hoarse tone, improvisation, overlapping rhythms.[66] At the same time, after they stopped laughing or recoiling at its strangeness, the music fascinated and moved them, surreptitiously evoking buried emotions. One New England minister described his response to a black church service in Carrollton, Louisiana, in 1863: "It seemed . . . like a wail, a mournful, dirge-like expression of sorrow. At first, I was inclined to laugh, it was so far from what I had been accustomed to call music; then I felt uncomfortable, as though I could not endure it, and half rose to leave the room; and at last, as the weird chorus rose a little above, and then fell a little below, the key-note, I was overcome by the real sadness and depression of soul which it seemed to symbolize."[67]

Similarly, Mary Boykin Chestnut in 1861 found herself disturbingly swept up into a black service led by "a full-blooded African" who "became wildly excited" when he sang. His "voice rose to the pitch of a shrill shriek, yet was strangely clear and musical, occasionally like a plaintive minor key that went to your heart. Sometimes it rang out like a trumpet. I wept bitterly. It was all sound, however, and emotional pathos. . . . The words had no meaning at all. It was the devotional passion of voice and manner that was so magnetic." As worshipers "sobbed and shouted and swayed backward and forward," Chestnut felt that "it was a little too exciting for me. I would very much have liked to shout, too."[68]

This white fascination with black music, even if ambivalent, helped spread jazz beyond the confines of the tenderloin. In an era in which the concept of "highbrow" culture as something insulated from and better than popular culture was just beginning to emerge, jazz's increasingly popular "modern" sounds challenged such categories and appealed to many whites opposed to elitism. As Karen Sotiropoulos puts it, "On many levels, late nineteenth-century whites understood their own civilized status through distance from blackness, while by the 1910s, whites understood their status as modern through their ability to buy the blackness that the new culture of consumption produced."[69] While for some this attitude substituted for a real reconsideration of their racial views, others experienced subtle but significant shifts.

The Spread of Impurity

When the music expanded beyond rough, forbidden venues, it reached public locales, spaces open to a wide variety of people. In these freer spaces, sometimes as transitory as the street itself, the new music united New Orleanians of various races, sexes, and classes around its infectious pulse, enabling more inclusive subjectivities. Many performance spaces remained segregated, especially "quiet" and exclusive Creole dance halls in Faubourg Marigny and elsewhere, like the Pythian Temple which catered to the Creole elite. However, as Pops Foster puts it, "Way late around New Orleans the dicty people got tired of hearing that violin scratchin' all night and started to hire some bands who'd play some rough music for them." Drawn to the dancing and pleasure-oriented lifestyle associated with the new music, suddenly people wanted to hear "hot" "gutbucket" music played by ear. Even in saloons segregated into white and "colored" sides, Pops Foster remembered, the "colored had so much fun on their side dancing, singing, and guitar playing, that you couldn't get in for the whites." Such impure gatherings took place at Lincoln Park as well, where Bolden projected his cornet's sound for blocks, or even miles, if testimony is to be believed.[70]

Outdoor performances spread the music to diverse audiences because, as Bruce Raeburn puts it, "you can't segregate the streets." A profusion of sounds washed over the streets of New Orleans, including vendors' street cries, tin horns, brass bands, and spasm bands. Outdoor performance—the "street as theater"—was a West African tradition, but it was also integral to white ethnic groups like Sicilians and Jews who were important to the growth of jazz. Canal Street and the French Quarter in particular were designed to be inclusive with public squares, halls, and markets.[71] Not only did a variety of races and classes hear the music, they often listened in close proximity to one another.

Transgressing boundaries, parades encouraged such intermingling from the city's beginning. New Orleans's parades were arenas of impurity, mixing normally segregated elements, like the 1837 procession described in the newspaper as "preceded, followed and hemmed in on every side by a motley collection of all colors, sexes, and conditions." In another march the same year, white revelers dressed as Indians, animals, and circus performers and were later joined by blacks, drawing censorious commentary from the *New Orleans Picayune*: "A lot of masquerades were parading through our streets yesterday and excited considerable speculation as to who they were, what were their motives and what on earth would induce them to turn out in such grotesque and outlandish habiliments."[72]

Such boundary-bursting processions continued into the period of jazz's emergence. "Invented on the streets from a blend of French, African, and Native American folkway," New Orleans's parades by the late nineteenth century were sponsored by Jews, Swiss, Germans, Portuguese, and Italians. Many white musicians first heard black bands

Figure 9. Frank Christian's Band on Quarella's Pier at Milneburg, a popular lakefront resort known for its jazz (1915). (Photo courtesy of the William Ransom Hogan Archive, Tulane University.)

in parades or funeral processions, sometimes marching right by their houses. Sicilian-American cornetist Sharkey Bonano sought out music this way, following parades to hear the great black cornetist Joe Oliver. Parades also connected neighborhoods separated by race and class as the second line continually picked up members along the route.[73]

Milneburg Joys

Other relatively free spaces included waterfront resorts like Milneburg on Lake Pontchartrain. Named for Alexander Milne, who immigrated from Scotland in 1776, the park was designed to be an island of simple gratifications amidst the onslaught of industrialization. Milneburg first drew popular crowds in the 1830s when a railroad ("Smoky Mary") was built to carry passengers from the riverfront in New Orleans; trains made up to sixteen trips a day, with seven extra trips on Sundays and holidays. Featuring ballrooms, bathhouses, restaurants, hotels, and saloons, Milneburg was known as a "poor man's Riviera," because a round trip on Smoky Mary cost a mere fifteen cents, while a nickel bought one a poor boy sandwich or a tall glass of beer. Though some of the hotels and restaurants catered to the elite, all classes partook of Milneburg's pleasures; in 1839 the *New Orleans Picayune* called it "the truly republican stamping ground." All races attended as well, although within the confines of segregation: Creoles of Color used special bathhouses and railroad cars. Although slaves were at first forbidden, it was impossible to prevent them from coming, and bathhouses were built for them as well.[74]

After the Civil War, camps were built on the lake for picnics, fishing, swimming, dancing, and, eventually, jazz. The new music at the lake disturbed some from the older generation who lamented the replacement of the guitar and violin by the trombone and the drum. One disgruntled individual railed against "blatant, raucous noises and revelries," complaining that "swaying, swaggering dances" had crowded out quadrilles and minuets. To his generation, jazz signified a lower-class barbarism associated with people of color, but some younger New Orleanians had less fear of such racial intermingling. On weekends, up to six thousand people gathered at Milneburg, many of them from clubs and fraternal organizations. Nearly every camp had music of one kind or another, providing work for most of the major New Orleans jazz bands. Milneburg also contained dance halls, including some "rough" ones, from which (as one white New Orleanian remembered it) "the hottest jazz came." One writer claims that "no other one location in New Orleans did more to shape jazz into its present and final form" than Milneburg, and the resort was immortalized by the New Orleans standard song "Milneburg Joys."[75] As a haven of pleasure, Milneburg was a more family-friendly version of the District, a fantasy world in which to escape the pressures of an increasingly monotonous and difficult work world.

Both black and white bands played at Milneburg, and members of all races picnicked there. Neither adult listeners nor musicians of different races mixed, but black and white bands, kept separate, heard each other's sounds emanating through the air from adjacent camps. With "five or six bands playing five or six tunes and not over one hundred yards apart," bands would "buck" (compete against) one another. Two white musicians many years later remembered black and white bands at Milneburg "blowin' with each other all day" with "no dissension or trouble," "just blowin,'" allowing musicians of different races to hear and influence one another.[76]

What impact, if any, these interracial musical exchanges had on listeners at Milneburg is unclear, but some found it freeing. "Colored" and white children played together, and as a child, Creole drummer Paul

Figure 10. West End, a lakefront resort featuring jazz. Note the bandstand in the lower right corner of the postcard. (Photo courtesy of the Louisiana State Museum.)

Barbarin walked from camp to camp taking in the music: "Colored, white, out there by the lake you were happy, having a good time and folks were friendly." As with recollections of interracial nightclubs, one must take such descriptions with a grain of salt because many whites were racist and remained so after exposure to such interracial milieus, but some were undoubtedly influenced as a result of the exposure.[77]

Other such lakefront areas that featured jazz, typically with open-air pavilions, included West End, Bucktown, and Spanish Fort. West End was a popular park featuring a Ferris wheel, boathouses, a hotel, several horse sheds, a stable, a soda stand, restaurants, a shooting gallery, a carousel, an ice cream parlor, and a long promenade with electric lights. The *Times Picayune Guidebook* of 1896 called West End "the Coney Island of New Orleans," describing the bandstand as "an immense platform, built on piles over the water of the lake . . . where a fine band discourses music every evening during the summer to all who care to listen. The open air concerts are extremely popular, thousands of people resorting hither nightly to enjoy the music and the cool breezes from the lake." The park featured performances by military bands such as the Mexican Eighth Regiment in the late nineteenth century and later showcased jazz bands at spots like the West End Roof Garden. "The Poor Man's Sin Capital of the South," Bucktown catered to the less well-to-do and contained dance halls and saloons featuring jazz as well as gambling houses. Like Milneburg, it was immortalized in a song ("Bucktown Blues") by Morton.[78]

Other parks, not on the lakefront, featured jazz as well, most notably Lincoln Park and Johnson Park. Established by the Standard Brewing Company in 1902, Lincoln Park was enclosed by a wooden fence and featured a large, one-story dance hall and pavilion. It drew crowds of African Americans for picnics, prizefights, vaudeville shows, movies, balloon ascensions, and fireworks, all accompanied by music, from brass bands to Buddy Bolden. Bolden was more at home in neighboring Johnson Park, which catered to his core lower-class audience; he performed at a hall there for evening dances, and occasionally a holiday or Sunday matinee, beginning in about 1903. Bolden's competition with John Robichaux, the light-skinned Creole who played written "legitimate" music at Lincoln Park, enacted a kind of class rivalry. To take Robichaux's audience away, Bolden would blast a few notes toward Lincoln Park, and "members of the sporting crowd who were at Lincoln Park . . . [would] exit and go to dance to the less disciplined, but more raggy and catchy music of Bolden." After Bolden went insane, Johnson Park declined and eventually was closed.[79]

Particular neighborhoods were also sites for interracial interactions centered on jazz. The Irish Channel was an uptown, mostly white working-class community—"longshoremen and screwmen. . . . [who] made good wages and liked to have a good time, drink and dance"—that spawned many important white jazz musicians like the Brunies brothers, Nick La Rocca, Tony Sbarbaro, Happy Schilling, and Johnny Fisher. According to one musician, the Irish and blacks in the neighborhood lived together harmoniously, with members of either race acting as babysitters for the other; boys played baseball together and fought as a unit against boys from other wards. When jazz musicians talk about the Irish Channel, they inevitably recall the lawn parties there, bands playing on the front porch to the assembled crowd eating and drinking on the grass. For twenty-five or thirty-five cents admission, revelers danced on the ground or on tarps to the light of kerosene lamps or flambeaux (torches); an additional ten cents bought beer or wine. In their hedonistic atmosphere, many such parties featured easy interaction among New Orleanians of differerent races. As clarinetist Emile Barnes put it, "White and black were at the same table. They didn't interfere with it."[80]

Yet parties in the Irish Channel did not always feature such relaxed toleration. The neighborhood was a kind of lawless zone where, according to one musician, "they used to shoot cops in the feet and make them dance." Local whites fought wars with tough kids from Basin Street, so at times it was dangerous for blacks to set foot in the neighborhood.[81] Fights between partiers sometimes forced musicians to "get out of the way," if possible with their instrument, of thrown pop, beer, and whisky bottles; one recalled how a drummer and his entire kit were thrown over a fence. Sometimes the band would be forced to play after the scheduled time for ending (usually 4 a.m.), until all the partygoers collapsed from drinking, exhaustion, or fighting, and to top it off they might not get paid. As Manetta tells it, "When they hired a band it was common enough . . . to take out a big 45 pistol and a big quart bottle of whiskey, say, 'Go ahead, drink now, continue playing.' Till all of 'em fall on the floor, and they fight, and they cuss, then they'd break it up. We hired till one o'clock, when we'd leave out there six o'clock in the morning."[82] Though such violence and exploitation was not overtly racially motivated, it established an atmosphere that allowed intolerance to surface.

―――――

In such parties and lakefront picnics, as in the nightclubs, the music flourished in racially mixed milieus and pockets of leisure set up in opposition to routinization and industrialization. Jazz had begun as a means for lower-class blacks to create freer spaces for themselves within an increasingly racist city, spaces built on an alternative ethos. Now, however, the music and its values spilled into the public square, much to the displeasure of the guardians of purity. As whites were drawn to the music, listeners confirmed the fears of early critics by crossing racial boundaries in places where the grip of established social hierarchies was loosened: parades, parties, and lakefront parks.

Clearly, there were limits to jazz's ability to erase boundaries. Playing before white audiences could be dangerous for Creole and black musicians, like the time a white woman in the audience flirtatiously winked at Creole drummer Paul Barbarin, whereupon her date threatened him until the cornetist, Chris Kelly, pulled a gun on the man.[83] Segregation was increasingly enforced by lynchings and other kinds of violence, and reformers attempted to contain "vice" by aiming at some of jazz's main constituents—working-class or underclass blacks and immigrant whites.

Yet jazz musicians were able to preserve the culture and values of such groups because their members demanded cutting-edge, African-based music. Even further, musicians took that culture into the mainstream, blurring the line between African-based and European music, the ratty and the respectable.

THREE

Musicians

The language of critique is effective . . . to the extent to which it overcomes the given grounds of opposition and opens up a space of translation: a place of hybridity, figuratively speaking, where the construction of a political object that is new, *neither the one nor the other*, properly alienates our political expectations, and changes, as it must, the very forms of our recognition of the moment of politics. HOMI BHABHA

The spread of African-based "ratty" music beyond seedy nightclubs represented a kind of racial mixing, in effect bringing black culture to Creoles and whites. The music's popularity catapulted it beyond the few whites and Creole musicians who would venture into disrespectable neighborhoods to hear it. Yet audience enthusiasm only partly explains the creation and dissemination of the impure music called jazz. To get a fuller picture, we have to look at the lives of New Orleans musicians themselves. Early New Orleans jazz musicians, in pursuit of economic success, learned to negotiate a variety of racially marked milieus, and this learning process broadened their identities and blurred the boundary between African-based and European music.

Musicians, particularly in difficult economic times, wanted to maximize their employment possibilities. Except on special occasions like Mardi Gras, most musical jobs did not pay particularly well, less than skilled labor like that performed by longshoremen, and jobs were usually short term, so that musicians constantly hustled to string together a series of gigs. Fortunately, despite the general economic downturn, there was a shortage of musicians in New Orleans, and this gave musicians opportunities to work in a huge variety of settings. (This shortage also contributed to the development of jazz in that groups became smaller and more conducive to improvisation.) The need to play for as many kinds of audiences as they could—black, white, or Creole, working class or upper class—demanded a kind of versatility that Ingrid Monson calls "polymusicality." Rather than settling on a fixed musical identity catering to a particular group, musicians crossed racial boundaries both physically, by playing for audiences of another race, and musically, playing the sometimes unfamiliar music demanded by those audiences.[1]

In the early years of jazz in New Orleans, the repertory and style that bands employed varied with the race and class of the audience. Bands performed pop numbers, but not the blues, for whites and traditional dances like mazurkas, quadrilles, polkas, and schottisches for Creoles; a waltz might be played "straight" for whites but shifted into 4/4 for black audiences. According to Danny Barker, even though Bolden played primarily for blacks, he altered his style according to the audience's social class. For "upper crust" blacks (doctors, lawyers, dentists), Bolden cleaned up his performance, avoiding risqué songs and playing in a "sweeter" style, but about nine in the evening, when the "low-life characters came out of the District, the notorious pimps, gamblers, hustlers . . . would listen awhile to Bolden's sweet music" and complain, demanding the bluesier, "nastier" music. The master, of course, readily complied, lest they go away unhappy.[2]

At a time, then, when politically, legally, and socially, increasingly rigid racial categories made little room for mixture, economic conditions impelled musicians to listen to, play with, and perform for people of all races, and these experiences entailed a broadening of their racial identities. Thus did economic factors in general, and the working conditions of musicians in particular, come into conflict with the legal framework of segregation. Musicians learned to use race strategically, enacting what Gayle Wald calls "the *dialectics* of identity, through which subjects appropriate 'race'—a discourse they do not control—for their own needs, wishes, and interests." These racial boundary crossings in a sense depended upon the very lines they sought to cross, and yet if one rejects a polarized choice between upholding and transgressing racial lines and instead focuses on the ways they are continually negotiated, challenged, and upheld, the actions of these musicians become comprehensible.[3]

Musicians sometimes had to cross class lines as well. Lower-class musicians had to learn the music and comportment appropriate for more affluent audiences, while their middle- or upper-class counterparts strove to master the lower-class "ratty" music that was not a natural part of their milieu. Crossing these class lines to play music in a variety of settings and negotiating changing racial boundaries also affected musicians' identities and, ultimately, the identities of audiences.

The identities of musicians were not completely fluid, of course. Musicians of color confronted obstacles that whites did not, routinely encountering abuse from customers and proprietors. Guitarist and banjoist Danny Barker recounted a helpful proverb: "Keep your eyes and ears open around them white folks, 'cause you never know when they'll change on you. They'll laugh with you one minute and getcha killed the next." Young black and Creole musicians had to take care not to lose their temper; their elders advised them to take the white customers' money and let them say what they wanted. But for many, it was a frustrating experience. Black clarinetist Johnny Dodds hated playing clubs in the District because when they passed the hat white customers would insult him and he could not respond.[4] In addition, though lumped together by racist whites, Creoles and blacks brought distinct identities to the color line and thus experienced that line differently. Crossing racial and class boundaries challenged black, Creole, and white musicians in differing ways, and the experience of each group will be examined here in turn.

Black Musicians

New Orleans during the time of jazz's birth could be a hostile and dangerous place for blacks. This was, after all, the height of the Jim Crow era, and in addition to discrimination, blacks were beset by poverty and unemployment. Yet since the time of slavery, New Orleans blacks had used music to unite and affirm their community.

Black musicians in turn-of-the-century New Orleans were inheritors of a long-standing African-based culture in which music permeated everyday existence. Community life in black New Orleans revolved around music. It is tempting to see black musicians as conduits for a "pure" black music that was entirely theirs, but such a view would be mistaken. The "black community" in New Orleans consisted of a number of groups in tension with one another, and those groups had different relationships to the emerging "ratty" music. Drummer Warren "Baby" Dodds even claimed that wealthy blacks could not play jazz, though the "next lower" class could.[5] Urban and rural, middle class, working class, and underclass, religious and secular blacks—all had relatively dark skin and spoke English rather than French, but they hardly constituted a monolithic culture, musical or otherwise. Musicians from these different groups took different paths to become musicians, and playing music had different effects on their identity.

In addition, African American music was intertwined with other kinds of music from the beginning, and musicians continued to mix genres and styles. They took the music they knew and transformed it and used new musical knowledge to adapt their playing to a given context. In doing so, they became adept at playing with their racial and class identity, altering it as the situation required.

———

The importance of music for the New Orleans black community goes back to its beginnings. Music for the slaves was a source of solidarity, an expression of the longing for freedom, and (as we shall see) a way of satirizing the master. Through music, the slaves preserved a part of African culture.

In New Orleans, Congo Square stood at the center of African-based music making, constituting "a distinct subculture of New Orleans slave life." Although lower-class Creoles looked on, the musicians themselves were black: Benjamin Latrobe in his well-known account of the square said, "All those who were engaged in the business seemed to be *blacks*. I did not observe a dozen yellow faces" (emphasis in original). Latrobe tells of songs sung in an African language, accompanied by African instruments. His characterization of the music as "brutally savage" indicates African musical devices foreign to him: call and response, melisma ("a detestable burthen on one single note"), and blue notes. Some accounts mention ring dancing at Congo Square and elsewhere, with different rings representing different tribes or nationalities. Though Congo Square is the most famous site of African American music making, apparently there were other gathering points throughout the city. One observer in 1799 wrote of a "vast number of negro slaves, men, women, and children assembled together on the levee, drumming, fifing and dancing in large rings." Authorities prohibited such gatherings sometime in the late 1830s or early 1840s, probably as a result of increased abolitionist activity and the Nat Turner rebellion.[6]

Music making at Congo Square and elsewhere transmitted the African heritage from one generation to the next. According to Daniel Walker, during dances in Congo Square, "physical spaces came alive and the spirits and the ancestors walked about. In this respect the performances . . . aided in the reconstitution and reformation of a particularly African worldview in the Americas. This worldview was one of the mechanisms that gave the African-descended population the power to transcend the extremely dehumanizing experience of slavery and to continue to define themselves and their environment in terms that were conducive to survival and positive self-definition."[7]

Congo Square and other such gathering places were long gone by the time jazz arose and had no direct effect on African American musicians in New Orleans, yet blacks preserved and developed African-based music in other settings. Among these were the seedy dives described in chapter 1. A *New Orleans Mascot* cover drawing in 1887 shows a band in such a club, featuring a tuba, cornet, and possibly a banjo, while another cover portrays a number of brass musicians playing from a balcony, and the music's description suggests an African-based performance.[8] Most commonly, however, budding black jazz musicians in the late nineteenth century heard African-based music at the waterfront and elsewhere on the streets, sometimes performed by folksingers or "songsters," and in church.

Songsters, Roustabouts, and Brass Bands

Many New Orleans blacks heard African-based music simply by taking in the sounds around them as they went about daily life. A variety of itinerant workers and musicians filled the air with song. After emancipation, wandering "songsters" played "country dance tunes, songs from the minstrel stage," spirituals, blues, and narrative ballads, while "musicianers" or "musical physicianers" played instrumentals. In New Orleans, songsters like "Lemon" Nash (who worked on the railroad in a pinch) and Richard "Rabbit" Brown played guitar or ukulele and sang ballads, either traditional folksongs or their own creations, sometimes memorializing local events like the killing of Police Chief Hennessey ("The Downfall of the Lion") or the Tuxedo Dance Hall murder of 1913 ("Gyp the Blood"). Brown had grown up in the tough "battlefield" neighborhood from which Armstrong hailed, and he sang on the streets of the District and at Mama Lou's at Lake Pontchartrain.[9]

The waterfront was especially known for the sound of melodies filling the air. Famed riverboat bandleader (and onetime employer of Armstrong) Fate Marable claimed that "jazz was the outgrowth of Negro life in New Orleans. It developed from the chants of roustabouts loading cotton boats, singing with perfect rhythm as they lifted the bales." Waterfront workers sang and danced as they loaded and unloaded freight and serenaded passengers on ships as they traveled from one destination

Figure 11. Kid Ory's Woodland Band (1905), La Place, Louisiana. An early rural ensemble. (Photo courtesy of the William Ransom Hogan Archive, Tulane University.)

to the next. Like songsters, roustabouts were travelers, collecting and spreading black folk music, singing lurid, sometimes profane tales of "lamentable love-affairs" and "murder trials and mourners," among other subjects. Some musicians were themselves dockworkers at various points.[10]

Someone growing up in New Orleans would hear other black workers singing as well. Willie Foster claimed that the blues came from railroad workers, who would play guitar and sing songs like "Stack O'Lee."[11] Street vendors inevitably sang to advertise their products, from charcoal to strawberries.

Budding rural musicians also absorbed African-based music in their daily lives. A significant number of early black jazz musicians had roots in the plantations or country parishes upriver from New Orleans in towns like Donaldsonville, Oakville, Plaquemine, Raceland, and Bertrandville. (Louis Armstrong's mother and King Oliver's family both emigrated to New Orleans from rural areas.) The "lower plantation belt," a twenty-five-mile strip beginning right below "English turn" contained about nineteen plantations on both sides of the river. According to Karl Koenig, "these plantations, beginning in the last decade of the 19th Century . . . furnished the world some of the first and second generation of jazz musicians."[12]

Rural areas had active music scenes. Like their urban counterparts, rural would-be musicians heard songsters and other folksingers. Trombonist Jim Robinson remembered guitar players at Deer Range Plantation playing harmonica and singing blues, hymns, and folksongs like "Steamboat Bill" and "Casey Jones." Sonny Henry, growing up on Magnolia Plantation, heard workers sing "any kind of a church hymn, anything you want," while cutting cane, and cornetist Punch Miller sang blues to himself as he plowed the sugarcane fields. Out in the country surrounding New Orleans, guitarists walked up and down the levee at the bayou Lafourche singing for change.[13]

The Black Church

In addition to the sounds of the street, one of the first places many black musicians heard African-based music was in church. As we shall see (chapter 4), the music of the church, though usually omitting instruments, had striking similarities to the ratty music that influenced jazz, despite many black churchgoers' opposition to such secular sounds. In the words of Johnny St. Cyr, "The churches always had music—singing—and the congregation would really swing, tapping their feet, swaying as they sang their hymns." Bolden attended St. John Baptist Church on First Street, a house of worship known for its musicality; according to Kid Ory, "Bolden got most of his tunes from the 'Holy Roller Church,'" attending strictly for the music, not the religion.[14]

The connection between early jazz and the church was so strong that the famous Funky Butt Hall, known for its music (sometimes by Bolden) and dangerous atmosphere, would become a church for a while, then re-open as a dance hall. As Ory put it, some "jack-leg preacher" would come in and hold forth, "and then someone would come back and open it for a dance hall." In a single week it might serve both functions: "dance all night Saturday night till Sunday morning, twenty minutes afterward it would be a church." Ory's reference to a "jack-leg preacher"—an uneducated preacher usually associated with the Sanctified movement, holding forth in a storefront or even on the streets—and its temporary abandoned business location suggest that the church at Funky Butt Hall was a Sanctified church.[15]

The Sanctified (Holiness) churches, which reached their peak in the 1890s, had a particularly strong influence on budding jazz musicians. According to Armstrong, New Orleans music "all came from the Old 'Sanctified' Churches." He claimed to have to have "acquired" his "singing tactics" in church and Sunday school, recalling childhood memories of the preacher's hymn and the congregation's "wailing" response. Armstrong may have adopted his signature white handkerchief, a key prop in his stage persona, in response to the handkerchief a preacher would wipe his face with, "signal[ing] . . . the congregation that he's going to say something of importance and they'd better pay close attention."[16]

The Sanctified churches reacted against increasing respectability and decorum in Baptist and Methodist churches, largely in response to pressures by their overseeing organizations, by emphasizing emotional expression. Worshipers sought direct sanctification through possession by the Holy Spirit, evidenced by speaking in tongues. Zora Neale Hurston called the Sanctified Church a "protest against the high-brow tendency in Negro Protestant congregations as the Negroes gain more education and wealth," a "rebirth of song-making," and a "revitalizing element in Negro music and religion" that returned African elements to the service.[17]

The Sanctified Church was a haven for the lower classes, the same lower classes that went to dives to hear ratty music. (How many of the same lower-class individuals went to both venues is unclear.) The Holiness churches typically took "disused garages, vacant shops, gaming and pool halls, even abandoned theaters" and used them for services.[18] The fact that the Sanctified Church tolerated instruments indicated that it may have been more sympathetic to secular music than other Protestant churches were.

Baptist and Methodist churches generally considered jazz and its antecedents disrespectable, the devil's music, even if it shared many features with the sacred music performed in church. The postbellum era saw a growing gulf between sacred and secular music, the latter associated with sin, dives, and brothels, and secular musicians risked the scorn of their elders. When W. C. Handy brought a guitar home in the 1880s, his father told him it was "one of the devil's playthings" and ordered him to get rid of it. The wife of Willie Cornish, a trombonist who played with Bolden, was religious and "never did care for" the dances at which her husband performed.[19] Black jazz musicians drew upon the music of the church yet faced the institution's condemnation and ultimately had to rebel against it.

Some black churches in New Orleans, particularly the larger ones, even rejected religious music sung or played in an African-based style. Johnny and Baby Dodds's Baptist church, where their father was a deacon, demanded the decorum usually found in white houses of worship, prohibiting musical instruments as well as the syncopated clapping, hoarse cries, and call and response heard in lower-class churches: "You could hear a pin drop. We didn't dare chew gum or even look up.

If we weren't gentlemen on the street, we were gentlemen in church. And church was different from what it is now; there was not hollering or whooping. And they didn't have music in the church, there was only singing."[20]

Johnny and Baby Dodds, then, had to find other ways to imbibe the bluesy, African-based music heard at some churches. The Doddses lived near Bolden's church and three other Baptist churches, so they may have heard music there. The family also sang hymns in harmony at home, accompanied by a pump organ played by one of Johnny's sisters, but it seems unlikely that they would have sung in an emotional, bluesy, African-based style.[21] Most likely the Doddses had to learn to cross the border between sacred and secular music, seeking out sounds their parents considered dangerous and becoming religious and class rebels. While Armstrong imbibed the music of the black church in his daily life, his future bandmates the Doddses had to actively search for it, defying their upbringing.

In sum, the church's legacy for the young jazz musician was mixed. Many heard African-based music in church yet had to rebel against the sacred world in order to be a jazz musician. Some, like Bolden, were never believers and attended church only to hear music, but others risked their soul to embrace jazz. Still others, like the Doddses, did not hear such music in their church at all and had to find other ways to assimilate the black music tradition.

Learning to Play

Just hearing music, or course, does not make one a musician. Young New Orleans blacks, whose parents were often unable to afford instruments, had to use creativity to begin making music. Often children started out singing in vocal groups, eliminating the need for instruments altogether; Armstrong and childhood buddies formed a barbershop quartet and went around singing for change. Some children constructed homemade instruments and started "spasm bands." Pops Foster's brother made a string bass for him out of a flour barrel; others used cigar boxes and various household items. Alternatively, children picked up ten-cent kazoos or fifes. Ernest "Punch" Miller finally got a real cornet when some older musicians acquired new instruments and gave him the castoffs.[22]

Budding black musicians often learned through informal apprenticeship. Alfred Williams did not have a teacher but followed Kid Ory's band from job to job; on occasion their drummer would let Williams "fool with his drums," and through such explorations he eventually learned his instrument. Others studied formally with teachers. Willie Hightower was practicing his instrument one day when Dave Perkins passed his house, knocked on the door and asked him if he wanted a music lesson. Hightower said no, "all I want to do is play like Freddie Keppard and Joe Oliver." Perkins admonished him, arguing that while "Joe Oliver is alright, [and] Freddie Keppard is alright...you want to learn [to read] music." Hightower rejected the offer but later, apparently realizing the opportunities music reading would open up for him, did study with Perkins.[23]

Many musicians like Bolden combined experimentation, apprenticeship, and formal study. Bolden studied cornet and music reading from Manuel Hall, strictly a note reader from an older generation. Yet Bolden's prodigious ear helped him learn pieces and licks; according to one musician who was a contemporary of the great cornetist, Bolden "could go hear a band playing in the theater, and he come on out and practice in between dances, and that morning, before the ball was over with, he play that piece and play it well."[24]

Sometimes black musicians found ways to learn from more formally trained Creoles. At times lessons were casual, growing out of friendship between Creole "professors" and black musicians. After bringing King Oliver to his house for late-night dinners, "Professor" Manuel Manetta taught Joe Oliver "division"—the ability to read and negotiate the time values of written notes, from sixteenths to whole notes. Oliver offered to pay Manetta, but the teacher declined to accept any remuneration. Others learned music reading and "legitimate" technique in formal lessons with Creole or mulatto teachers like Dave Perkins and Lorenzo Tio Jr. Some of Perkins's black students, like Baby Dodds, went on to great fame.[25]

Sometimes black musicians took the deliberate step of, in effect, crossing Canal Street by listening to or playing with Creole musicians. Roy Palmer was born uptown but made a point of listening to downtown bands and eventually sought out a Creole teacher.[26] Black musicians also listened to and learned from white bands, although they were prohibited from playing with them.

One particular teacher facilitated the cross-fertilization between blacks and Creoles, in the context of the brass band: "Professor" James Brown (J. B.) Humphrey. Humphrey, a well-off Creole and a member of a classical Creole orchestra, had been hired by former governor Henry C. Warmoth to create a brass band at Magnolia Plantation. Once a week in the 1890s he traveled from New Orleans to organize and teach bands at Magnolia and other plantations along the river. Many of his students who had been field hands went on to become well-known jazz musicians, earning their reputation when Humphrey took his plantation ensemble into New Orleans for big events when there were not enough bands in the city.[27]

Many Creoles of Humphrey's generation refused to have anything to do with the emerging jazz music, preferring traditional written arrangements, and would not teach or work with black musicians. Humphrey, however, saw the new music as a vehicle to help country blacks advance in the world and expand their possibilities. In the first fifteen years or so of the twentieth century, musicians from the country who had been trained by Humphrey and others moved to New Orleans, and some of them found work, integrating the brass bands, including the famous Excelsior Band.[28]

Although Humphrey taught a variety of styles, some of his students, like Chris Kelly, stuck to blues-based music when they moved to New Orleans, even knowing that they would be unemployable in more "respectable" places. This meant that record companies did not record Kelly, he was never hired by "the sophisticated white or Creole bands," and he was unable to play respectable Creole enclaves like Jeunes Amis or Pythian Temple Roof Gardens. However, according to one musician, "the common people kept Chris Kelly so busy that he didn't often get time to play the 'strictly' classy places."[29]

Others took advantage of the mixture of styles taught by Humphrey, finding that the musical versatility they learned made them more employable in New Orleans. Though Humphrey's country bands played the traditional march repertory, they started incorporating Bolden's ideas as well. These musicians were already familiar with the church music at the root of Bolden's style; sometimes Baptist hymns were played in 4/4, and this may have been an entry point into Bolden's music. In fact, one night Humphrey's country band, the Eclipse Brass Band, marched through Storyville playing Bolden's tunes, and the prostitutes all ran out to the streets, thinking it was Bolden. Like Bolden, blacks in Humphrey's bands, under the tutelage of their Creole leader, transformed march music through the incorporation of black musical conventions. Humphrey in a sense integrated blacks and Creoles, Protestants and Catholics (all the field hands were Protestants), city and country.[30]

Along with musical flexibility, blacks sometimes acquired racially fluid identities. Light-skinned blacks like Lee Collins passed for white; Collins once played in an all-white band, claiming to be Spanish. The lighter one's skin, the more likely this impersonation would succeed, but even blacks who could not literally pass used New Orleans's ambiguous racial classification scheme to their advantage. Black musicians and bands with few or no Creoles identified themselves as Creole as a defense against racism or to create a more respectable image, as in Oliver's "Creole Jazz Band" or Amos White's "New Orleans Creole Jazz Band." According to guitarist Clarence "Little Dad" Vincent, at one club (the Old Absinthe) some patrons demanded to know, "What kind of band is this? You ain't white, you ain't Mexican, you ain't Indian," to which he responded, "This is just [a] high-yellow, Creole Negro band," quieting their protests. When audience members at an engagement in San Francisco taunted members of the King Oliver band with racial epithets, the musicians quickly began speaking Creole. According to Bruce Raeburn, Oliver "adopted Creole speech and mannerisms despite his Baptist upbringing because he found them conducive to promoting an image of refinement and sophistication in his musical endeavors."[31] Since the enactment of respectability broadened one's economic opportunities, making a living as a jazz musician required a racial and class fluidity that collided with the spread of the one-drop rule.

Negotiating Racism

Racial impersonations worked only up to a point, particularly for those with a dark complexion. According to Armstrong, "They had lots of players in the District that could play lots better than Jelly [Roll Morton], but their dark Color kept them from getting the job." Interestingly, Armstrong also lamented the fact that he did not get to know any white musicians in New Orleans because the city was "so Disgustingly Segregated and Prejudiced." King Oliver and others left the city for precisely this reason. Armstrong left only when King Oliver offered him a job in Chicago, but for many years afterward he, like Johnny Dodds and others, avoided New Orleans because of the prejudice he had experienced there.[32]

Even in ordinary jobs, black musicians had to negotiate the customs of segregation. Sometimes musicians would learn the hard way. Willie Hightower's first job took him to Audubon Park, a posh white neighborhood, and he made the mistake of coming to his employer's front door, where he was greeted by a shocked servant who told him, "Oh my God, go to the back, don't come in the front, go around the back." According to Hightower, the woman of the house didn't like "colored people to come to the front door, say[ing] you should know better than that," but he explained that he was unaware of the custom.[33]

To adapt in such an environment, musicians learned to present themselves in a manner that was acceptable to whites. In the incident described above, one of the band members who had gone to the front door with Hightower had no coat on, so the woman of the house gave him her husband's coat to wear. Looking back, Hightower marveled at the fact that they ultimately completed the job successfully: "Now, they give us credit for that job. I don't know how we got away with it, or nothin' like that, but we just commenced to playin' music." Part of Bolden's success was the fact that, according to Manetta, he was a "neat fellow" who "dressed in rich white man's clothes" and "always had a coat and tie on." Interestingly, his band members dressed sloppily and were rather ill mannered, entering people's houses with their "high roller" hats and neglecting to take them off.[34] But in general, blacks had to learn to act the part demanded by whites.

————

The experience of racism was shared by all black musicians, yet the commonality of such experiences did not erase the many differences among them. Black musicians, far from being pure conduits for black vernacular music, had to cross various class and racial lines in order to pursue their craft. Those crossings differed depending upon where the musician started; Armstrong's journey out of the underclass and Johnny Dodds's path from his more "respectable" upbringing presented different challenges for their professional aspirations. Regardless of the particular path, however, such traversals altered the identity of the musician and brought different styles of music in contact, helping to create something that came to be called jazz.

Creole Musicians

Creole musicians, among them major figures like Morton and Sidney Bechet, faced somewhat different challenges from those confronted by their black counterparts. Though sometimes they are seen as part of the "black music" tradition, others argue that Creoles were "not black" since they typically did not identify with their African roots until forced to do so by the rise of Jim Crow.[35] However, either of these two options— seeing Creoles as representatives of "black music" or calling them "not black"—misses the more complex role of Creole musicians in the birth of jazz, for they are more fruitfully viewed as hybrid.

The hybridity of Creoles uniquely equipped them to cross the color line, embodying racial mixing in their very persons, and Jim Crow increasingly pressured them to do so. These pressures, along with jazz's growing popularity, led to their interacting with blacks in unprecedented ways. Both the fact that they were increasingly seen as black and the growing popularity of black music led Creoles of Color to collaborate with black musicians, and these collaborations produced jazz, a music rooted in African, Caribbean, European, and American culture. Thus jazz was made possible both by the hybridity of New Orleans, which allowed the Creoles' blend of African and European culture to develop and flourish, and by the pressures to eliminate hybridity that brought Creoles and blacks together. Not all Creole musicians embraced black music, but those who did played a key role in developing and spreading jazz.

Creoles at the time were in a state of transition. Despite Jim Crow, Creoles' special "third race" status endured in weakened form well into the late nineteenth century and even into the twentieth as they resisted the move to a black-white dichotomy. Creoles did eventually become "black," but the transformation in their legal and social status was much more gradual, the ambiguity much more prolonged, than most jazz histories have indicated. This was particularly true in Creole sections of the city, where segregating statutes were very leniently enforced and Creoles dominated many skilled professions and held large tracts of property.[36]

Plessy v. Ferguson illustrates the ambiguity of the Creoles' postemancipation status. Though we remember Plessy for his argument in 1896 that segregated train cars violated the Thirteenth and Fourteenth amendments, his brief made another claim as well: that he in fact was not black. Jim Crow laws, argued Plessy before the Supreme Court, not only violated the Equal Protection Clause but also took away without due process valuable "property"—the "reputation of being white."[37] Plessy, then, was in the peculiar position of simultaneously challenging racial divisions and seeking to uphold them. In a sense, Creoles like Plessy would have liked to have upheld special status for those of mixed race, and thus they were civil rights activists only reluctantly.

The fact that Plessy thought his assertion of whiteness was worth making in court shows that Creoles' claim to special status was still viable at this point, particularly in New Orleans. One of Plessy's attorneys, Louis Martinet, said in 1891 that "people of tolerably fair complexion, even if unmistakably colored, enjoy here a large degree of immunity from the accursed prejudice. In this respect, New Orleans differs greatly from the interior towns."[38]

Legal and cultural differences between blacks and Creoles were slowly eroding, but racial purity was not fully embodied in law until at least 1910. According to one Louisiana Supreme Court decision, "until.... *Lee v. New Orleans Great Northern Railroad Co* [1910] . . . no one in this state—not the Governor, nor any judge . . . —could have undertaken to say with any degree of authoritativeness what proportion of blood a person had to have in his veins in order to be classed as a person of color."[39]

Yet in another case that very year, the court drew a clear line between blacks ("Negroes") and Creoles ("colored"). Here the issue was whether cohabitation between a white man and an octoroon woman violated a statute making concubinage between a white and a "person of the negro or black race" illegal; the court ruled that the term *negro* included only "pure" blacks. At another point the court said that *negro* could not refer to "persons who, though apparently white, yet had in their veins a perceptible admixture of negro blood"; rather, it meant "negro, plain negro, or persons black as negroes and having the characteristics of the negro."[40]

Despite drawing this sharp line between blacks and Creoles, the court acknowledged that in everyday life the boundaries were blurry, and it even suggested that race could be a manner of culture or manners: "A notice that all negroes were to be driven out of New Orleans would no doubt set everybody inquiring at what point the color line was to be drawn. Few in all likelihood would understand that the many people who have the appearance, education, and culture of whites were intended to be included in such an order." Such a statement, essentially a legal recognition of passing, suggests that one could be of African heritage and still be white in one's appearance and manner and that such a person would be white legally and socially. It also suggests that class is, even at this relatively late date, intertwined with race, that "status is frequently more of a determining factor on group membership than genealogical ancestry."[41]

As we have seen, the fact that one's race in New Orleans sometimes depended on one's class—"middle-class" comportment was likely to be seen as Creole or even white rather than black—reveals something about the opposition to jazz. "Respectable" older-generation Creoles (and perhaps blacks) allied with most middle- and upper-class whites against a music associated with the lower classes, particularly the black lower classes. For Creoles, respectability was a means to avoid falling into the disrespectable categories "black" and "lower class"; shunning jazz was part of such a quest.

Yet the example given by the court, ostensibly a random one for purposes of illustration, reflects the growing push for racial purity, envisioning as it does an expulsion of "negroes" from New Orleans. Increasingly all persons of African ancestry, including Creoles of Color, were being seen as black, as the court acknowledged: "Socially persons of mixed colored blood are known to be classed with negroes. A notice posted at the entrance of a ballroom that negroes are not admitted would certainly mean that colored persons—i.e., persons of mixed negro blood as well as negroes proper—were not admitted."[42] It is telling that the court uses a dance venue in its example. As time went on, the term *colored* was used to designate both Creoles and blacks as second-class citizens in a variety of settings.[43]

In the period during which jazz arose, then, the situation of Creoles was ambiguous. As the court decisions just cited show, the law still distinguished blacks and Creoles. Thus Jerah Johnson, to whom we are in debt for correcting the myth that Creoles were suddenly classified as black in 1894, errs when he claims that "they had no special legal status or privileges in law at the time."[44] However, the special status of Creoles was disappearing, the dividing line between them and blacks becoming less distinct. Socially, one was increasingly either black or white but not something in between.

Some Creoles opted to pass as white. One observer reported that church records of births and deaths looked like "player piano rolls," filled with scratched-out sections. Presumably what was scratched out was the designation "h.c.l" or "f.m.c," indicating *homme de couleur libres* or free man of color. This erasure was ironic, since that classification was once treasured as evidence of aristocratic lineage. Others tried to preserve a sense of racial fluidity, altering their identity depending on the context. In a sense, this simply enacted what has always been true in New Orleans: "What many of us normally assume to be likely *connotations* of membership in a particular group are, in the case of southern Louisiana, often, if not always, the crucial variables that individual New Orleanians manipulate in making themselves members of a group, or in identifying others as members of a group."[45] Creoles used race strategically, sometimes allying with blacks, sometimes with whites, and other times insisting on special "third race" status.

Paradoxically, then, the hardening of racial categories created a whole class of cultural impersonators, Creoles taking on the identity of black and, occasionally, white. The very hybridity that Jim Crow laws were attempting to destroy made it possible for some Creoles to evade those laws. Originally defined by nationality, allied with the white French against Americans, they were now defined racially, as separate from whites, no matter what nationality. Americanization destroyed the basis of Creole identity, as race rather than place now defined them: to become Americans, Creoles had to become black.[46]

Yet remnants of the old culture- and place-based identity remained in exclusive Creole clubs and neighborhoods. Creoles existed on a kind of tightrope, balanced between two modes of defining their identity. As they moved out of exclusive clubs and neighborhoods, their complex struggles with identity affected the course of the music.

The Creole Struggle to Embrace Jazz

As jazz spread from the ratty clubs where it began, some Creoles, like other New Orleanians, wanted to play the new music. Formal musical training was more readily available to Creole children than to blacks, and they were more likely to have instruments, though a few created home-made ones like paper-covered combs or "a cheese-box covered with the skin from a round of beef": famed clarinetist and soprano saxophonist Sidney Bechet began by blowing through the tubing of his mother's douche![47] Teachers like Louis Tio taught a strict regimen of scales, instrumental technique, and theory, although not all Creoles took advantage of such training—apparently Bechet limited himself to a couple of lessons from Tio.

Learning one's instrument was one thing, playing jazz was another. Although blacks had played music for whites since the founding of the country, they had kept the most African music to themselves, often in religious ceremonies. Slaves sang work songs and field hollers, but when performing for whites they played jigs and other European dance music. As we have seen, this insulation from whites continued into the late nineteenth century when the most African-based music was confined to lower-class black clubs.

Like whites, Creoles did not hear much African-influenced music. Creoles and blacks tended to reside on opposite sides of Canal Street— "downtown" and "uptown" respectively. Johnny St. Cyr has said of early days of jazz, "I didn't know too much about what went on uptown—all I knew were the Creole musicians." According to Baby Dodds, "People from the different sections didn't mix. The musicians mixed only if you were good enough."[48]

The gulf between the two groups went beyond geography; Leonard Bechet considered those living uptown "naturally always rough, ignorant," lacking "a background like the . . . Creole people." According to Bechet, Creole musicians "always did hold up a nice prestige . . . and demand great respect," and that meant that they "never played jazz—played nice music." Thus "all such people as that, they . . . kind of hesitate . . . to join in on the other side." Creole parents tried to stop their children from second lining, although "the pull of the music was too strong."[49]

Creoles were unlikely to hear the music at most of their local nightclubs, for upper-crust, "respectable" Creole music halls generally excluded black musicians and customers. At such venues, Armstrong said, "most of the musicians were Creoles. Most of them could pass for white easily. . . . They went a lot of places with ease, because of their light skin. Places we Dark Skinned Cats wouldn't Dare to peep in." Even dark Creole musicians encountered discrimination. George Lewis, a dark-skinned Creole, complained that some Creole bands "wouldn't hire a man whose hair wasn't silky." If clubs did allow dark-skinned musicians, they made things difficult for them: at one club where Lewis was reluctantly accepted as a replacement for the light-skinned Alphonse Picou, he was told by the management to keep his beer glass because no one else would ever use it after he had tainted it. As Pops Foster put it, "The worst Jim Crow around New Orleans was what the colored did to themselves. The uptown clubs and societies were the strictest. You had to be doctor or a lawyer or some kind of big shot to get in. The lighter you were the better they thought you were. The Francs Amis Hall was like that. The place was so dicty that they wouldn't let us come off the bandstand because we were too dark. They would let the lightest guy in the band go downstairs and get drinks for all of us." Conversely, since, as one musician put it with great emphasis, "the majority—I want to be straight—of the black skinned musicians stayed together," Creoles were sometimes cut out of black jobs as well.[50]

To hear ratty music, Creoles had to venture into forbidden, often dangerous black clubs. Manuel Manetta describes a childhood visit to a "saloon" (most likely a controversial "concert saloon") with a big dance hall in the back. Women and men danced the slow drag, and "ratty women," women who "hustle[d]," shook their bodies in time with the music. It must have been a dangerous or forbidden place, because he trembled from both excitement and fear, clinging to the hand of his older brother. A tourist in a foreign land, Manetta was stunned by the strange habits and dress that he observed, including one pianist wearing a "big high roller hat on his head" and another sporting a "big old pompadour." Yet Manetta was drawn to the sound of one piano player after another (he remembers a total of eight) playing the blues while sitting on beer cases. He absorbed as much as he could and went home to practice what he had heard, assimilating black music and learning to be a jazz musician.[51] By entering into the scary, foreign world of the ratty black hall, Manetta not only learned to play jazz but transformed his identity.

In addition to the music's inaccessibility, aspiring Creole jazz musicians faced tremendous disapproval from many in their community. When Sidney Bechet played some bluesy licks for "Papa" Louis Tio, the renowned teacher cried out, "No! No! No! We do not bark like a dog or meow like a cat!" Disparaging jazz musicians as "routiners" who didn't have the discipline to use written music or set arrangements, Tio called jazz "a disgrace to music in anyone's house." ("In anyone's house" implies that if it belonged anywhere, jazz belonged in the streets or honky-tonks, not in the sanctity of a decent home.) Similarly, according to St. Cyr, the Golden Rule Band was "so hot that they were barred from some of the more dignified homes." Creoles saw the home as a bastion of musical and moral purity, and exclusive Creole clubs represented an extension of the home, a safe haven. As we have seen, many were hostile to the music because of its associations with blacks, the lower classes, and disrespectability. When Morton's father first heard him playing ragtime, he beat him with his belt and said, "Son, if you ever play that dirty stuff again, I'll throw you out of here on your ear!" His future common-law wife at first refused to become involved with him because, working in a brothel, he "wasn't decent."[52]

When Creoles like Sidney Bechet learned to play the blues, they rebelled against the Creole upper crust, identifying with a more oppressed culture and refusing to assimilate as the elite had wished. Many of them became near-outcasts in their communities, certainly among the older generation, for playing the new music in ratty venues. They were part of a new, rebellious generation of musicians who did not aspire to playing with their elders and ridiculed them behind their backs. Thus were their identities transformed from, for example, "violinists" to "fiddlers."[53]

If Creole musicians wanted to play the new music, they had to learn to improvise, and this skill was often unfamiliar. The famous Creole clarinetist Alphonse Picou once showed up a gig and asked for the music. When the leader told him he didn't need any, he said, "How am I going to play?" "Playing without music," he later recalled, "was a very new style to me. I think it was impossible to me! It seemed a sort of style of playing without notes." (The leader's instruction to "come in on the choruses" was not much help.)[54]

Jumping Fences: Creoles Learn Black Music

Despite obstacles to the acceptance of black music among Creole audiences and musicians, its popularity slowly grew, and adventurous Creoles began to master the new style. Economics partly explains the music's

Figure 12. The Superior Orchestra (1910), a Creole dance band, with Bunk Johnson on cornet. (Photo courtesy of the William Ransom Hogan Archive, Tulane University.)

inroads in the Creole community. Previously, though Creoles put a great emphasis on music and musical training, few were professional musicians, as the occupation was considered ungentlemanly. But as whites took over skilled trades, Creoles had fewer employment options, and working as a full-time musician gained acceptance. Ironically, such a path was becoming more difficult, as the popularity of white bands, some traveling from other areas, gave Creoles fewer opportunities to play for white audiences.[55]

Creoles had to find ways to work more steadily, and sometimes their ambiguous racial identity came in handy. Occupying a disappearing no-man's-land in the looming black-white divide, Creoles became cultural impersonators adept at "jumping the fence," passing as a member of another race, stylistically or, in some cases, literally. Creoles increasingly played with black musicians and adopted a traditional black, African-influenced style, challenging the racial identities of those they came in contact with and forcing black musicians to adjust their musical personas as well.

Sometimes Creole musicians could genuinely pass for white or, as they say in New Orleans, *passé blanc*. As musician Mike De Lay put it, speaking of a somewhat later period, "I don't know any people that didn't. . . . That was damn near the style in New Orleans. . . . Looks like every Tom, Dick, and Harry jumped over the fence." Two members of the "white" Reliance Brass Band, Achille Baquet and Dave Perkins, were actually of mixed race. Although crossing the color line exacted a psychological cost, Creole musicians made more money playing with white bands than they could have otherwise. Whether a Creole musician could pass for another race did not depend entirely on skin color. Consider the case of two brothers, Eugene and George Moret. Eugene was dark skinned with black hair but played only in white bands, whereas the lighter-skinned "briquette" (red-haired) George performed with blacks. Frequently musicians changed their name to avoid sounding foreign; a new name could give them more options for how to present their identity.[56]

Many people seemed to know who was passing or not. George "Happy" Schilling had three mixed-race musicians in his "white" band, and he later recalled that when it passed by in a parade, those in the know would say, "There goes Happy Schilling and his black and white band." According to one musician, "Nine out of ten, if you was a guy that minded your business, it didn't matter what color you were."[57]

Some musicians could impersonate a number of different ethnicities. "Chink" Martin, of Mexican and Filipino background, gained his racist nickname because on a streetcar white bandleader Jack Laine told the conductor, perhaps to avoid looking as if he was violating segregation codes, that Martin was a "Chinaman." Drummer Abby "Chinee" Foster was a racial chameleon. As he recounted, "When I was a little boy I used to play with white and colored bands. . . . Half of them thought I was Mexican, half of them thought I was Puerto Rican. . . . I got to playing a lot around the French Market with different bands, white and colored. . . . So they didn't know whether I were white or whether I were colored. Some of them used to suspect that I were Indian, just like Lorenzo Tio. . . . One time I went on a show and done a Chinese act, so from then on, white and colored started calling me 'Chinee.'"[58]

Some who passed embraced racial fluidity, playing with whites and blacks, not fixating on one particular identity. Others, like the Creole clarinetist Achille Baquet, rejected blackness altogether, passing completely over to the white side of the color line. When in 1918 a Chicago newspaper described him as "a colored musician," he fired off an indignant letter emphasizing his "wish to impress on the minds of the public that A. J. Baquet is a white man, born and raised in New Orleans, and that he has a Spanish Indian mother and a French father. All of New Orleans will verify this. He is not only the first and original white jazz clarinet player, but is a professional musician and reads music."[59] Even Creoles who did not pass and were seen by many as black were reluctant to view themselves as such.

Creoles who were unable or unwilling to pass for white played with black musicians and for black audiences. Some were simply too dark to be seen as white, while others were light skinned enough to pass but chose not to do so. In some cases, musicians refused to pass because they valued artistic growth over bigger paychecks. Creole Joe Darensbourg performed with Creoles or blacks because he thought they played better, "hotter": "I had guys saying I was crazy to be fooling around with these colored guys, that I could be making more money working with white bands, which was true. But I enjoyed what I was doing. I'd much rather play with these fellows 'cause the colored guys just had it." Similarly, Creole banjoist George Guesnon saw black music as something to embrace. In his view, though the "majority of downtown musicians were well trained, excellent sight readers, with perfect tonation, . . . they played with no soul, heart, drive or beat in their playing," unlike their uptown counterparts. Though Creoles and blacks learned from each other, the Creole musician, in Guesnon's estimation, got the better deal, because "from his uptown brother he had something to steal—beautiful passages and ideas that came from the soul, something that wasn't on the cold sheet he was used to looking at, something that kept him mystified as to how such things could be done without any musical training."[60] Although such a view is overly dichotomized, based on a romantic picture of black primitivism, Guesnon's wholehearted embrace of black music is notable for its clarity and enthusiasm.

Most Creoles had to play for black audiences in order to survive, and this forced changes in their music. This transformation is readily apparent in an exchange between Creoles Albert Glenny and "Papa" Louis Tio, recalled by Glenny many years later. In response to Glenny's request to play a job with him, Tio asked, "Who ya playin' for?"

Glenny replied, rather cagily, "The people that God made. Playing for them Lions."

Tio persisted, addressing his concern more directly: "Who you playing for; you playing for white or for colored?" When Glenny responded that they were playing for blacks ("Lions"), Tio replied, "Lord have mercy," lamenting that such audiences "want ya to make cat on your clarinet. . . . They want ya ta make all that noise ya know, all that monkey shines."

The "musicianer" (music reader) Tio wanted to "play the straight music," but Glenny, like many other Creoles, particularly younger ones, was willing to adapt and play the blacker sounds that the older generation considered "noise." Even when Creoles overcame their resistance to playing for black audiences, it was difficult because they could be very demanding; as Leonard Bechet put it, "You have to play real hard when you play for Negroes. You got to go some . . . to avoid any criticism. You got to come up to the mark."[61]

As Creole musicians learned jazz, they were particularly influenced by Bolden, melding his innovations with their more European-based music. Bolden played on excursion boats from New Orleans to Baton Rouge, and Creole musicians like Kid Ory, who lived outside the city in La Place, would hear him play that way. For a time Creoles sided with John Robichaux ("those Frenchmen from downtown," as Bolden called them) in his rivalry with Bolden, but the charismatic cornetist converted many Creoles with the power of his playing and his ability to electrify crowds. Clarinetist George Baquet was bowled over when he saw Bolden play "Make Me a Pallet on the Floor" at a rough place, and someone cried out, "Oh, Mr. Bolden, play it for us, Buddy, play it!" According to Baquet, "I'd never heard anything like that before, I'd played 'legitimate' stuff. But this—it was something that pulled me! They got me up on the stand that night, and I was playin' with 'em. After that, I didn't play legitimate so much." Blacks also began playing with Robichaux as the differences between the two became less stark.[62]

Bolden's popularity increased the attraction of the blues, and the marketplace demanded that Creoles learn the style. According to Johnny St. Cyr, the blues bands were originally all uptown, but "when in later years they began hiring downtown bands uptown, they started playing blues because that's what they *had* to play." Creole musicians sought out blues musicians to teach them that style. Joe Robichaux (John's nephew) listened to Irish Channel blues pianists, while Alphonse Picou played old classical French songs like "Huguenots" until he learned the blues from a black woman with whom he performed. It was clear that Picou's motivation was commercial; the woman told Picou that she had "a very wonderful blues" learned from her husband, a railroad worker, and if they mastered it, "it's going to be very good for the band."[63]

In contrast to their formal training in European music, Creoles learned African American techniques through listening and apprenticeship, as befits the oral tradition. Picou says that when he went to the woman's house to learn the blues, "I caught on to the melody and I wrote it down, from her, from her voice and . . . with my instrument. . . . And that night . . . we played it." (In a sense, Picou's method was hybrid, learning the tune orally and then writing it down.) Often this apprenticeship entailed following a favorite musician, carrying his instrument, and learning through imitation. Some Creoles were exposed to black music through the church; though the vast majority of Creoles were Catholic, they sometimes attended Protestant churches to hear the music. Other Creoles were exposed to the blues by rural musicians who moved to New Orleans, some of them black family bands playing a blues-based folk music. More rarely, an experienced black musician would give lessons to a younger Creole, as Chris Kelly did to George "Kid Sheik" Cola and Avery "Kid" Howard.[64]

Creoles also increasingly were exposed to the blues in brass bands. The popularity of Bolden, along with a shortage of full-time Creole musicians, led to the integration of blacks into the brass bands, which had been almost exclusively Creole. Black musicians like "Black Benny," Joe Oliver, and others played with influential bands like the Onward Brass Band, and they exposed Creole musicians to "rattier" sounds, which they incorporated in their own playing.[65]

As they played with blacks and performed before audiences accustomed to "ratty" music, Creole musicians altered their style, incorporating more African-based elements. To please black audiences, they had to play black-influenced music, transforming their identities as well as the music itself. The effect of Creoles' having to play for black audiences was the intermingling of European-influenced music with blues-based black music, and such interpenetration was a key step in the creation of jazz.[66]

The "White-Skinned Negro": White Musicians

White Musicians as Impure

White New Orleans jazz musicians are often seen as an inessential part of the music's development, due in part to the white Original Dixieland Jazz Band's (ODJB) exaggerated claim to have invented jazz and its distinction of being the first jazz band to record. At best whites are seen as competent players who contributed little to the music's development.[67]

Such a position ignores the testimony of black and Creole musicians who have acknowledged the influence of white musicians. In particular, the ODJB's influence on New Orleans musicians of all races "can be extensively documented." Armstrong himself stated his admiration for ODJB clarinetist Larry Shields, and Dink Johnson, a black drummer, took up the clarinet after hearing the Original Dixieland Jazz Band's Larry Shields.[68]

Figure 13. Jack Laine's Reliance Brass Band (1910), one of the city's premier white bands. (Photo courtesy of the William Ransom Hogan Archive, Tulane University.)

Since whites did not teach blacks and Creoles or play for their functions, it was not easy for New Orleanians of color to learn from white players or even to listen to them up close. Yet some black and Creole musicians in interviews have mentioned hearing white bands play in their neighborhoods, in bucking contests, on the streets in parades, and at lakefront resorts like Milneburg; Jack Laine's Reliance Band often attracted an enthusiastic African American second line. Blacks and Creoles would also, like white musicians, listen to the music outside segregated venues; according to one musician, "when white bands played a dance, the Negroes listened outside and danced in the street."[69]

Whites, then, contributed to the racial circulation of the music, creating hybrid identities themselves. From the inception of slavery, white musicians were intrigued by African devices and incorporated them into their music making, adopting black melodies and performance practices. White fiddlers played black jigs, and society ladies and gentlemen learned and danced African American dances.[70]

Whites who played jazz altered their racial identity, becoming less white in the eyes of "respectable" Caucasians. Of course, many working-class whites had close contact with blacks to begin with; although segregation was the custom in upscale "society" restaurants, theaters, and clubs, working-class blacks and whites often lived on the same block, "frequently under the same roof in double-occupancy rectangular wooden cottages."[71]

A large number of white musicians came from families of relatively recent immigrants, often lower-class Jews or Sicilians, and for that reason were seen as less white, or even nonwhite, to begin with. Italians in particular were outcasts, more despised, according to some, than blacks. The word *guinea* had referred to African slaves and descendants, but beginning in about the late 1890s, it was applied to Sicilians and southern Italians. In the 1898 Louisiana state constitutional convention, one speaker exclaimed that "according to the spirit of our meaning when we speak of 'white man's government,' [the Italians] are as black as the blackest negro in existence." An Italian government official investigated Sicilian sharecroppers in Louisiana in 1906 and found that "a majority of plantation owners cannot comprehend that . . . Italians are white" but saw the Sicilian immigrant as "a white-skinned negro," "black dagoes." At the same time, Italians were not subject to Jim Crow laws and were able to become citizens, marry whites, and join white unions, among other privileges.[72]

Sicilians, who made up the vast majority of Italian immigrants (and Italian jazz musicians) during this period, were particularly despised. Southern Italians were looked down on in much of Italy itself; Italian positivist anthropologists tried to scientifically prove that southern Italians were a different, more African race than northerners. According to one, "One of the two Italies, the northern one, shows a civilization greatly diffused, more fresh, and more modern. The Italy of the South [however] shows a moral and social structure reminiscent of primitive and even quasibarbarian times, a civilization quite inferior." One still hears the saying "Europe ends at Naples. Calabria, Sicily, and all the rest belong to Africa." This prejudice against southern Italians made its way to America, adapting itself to homegrown racism. In 1891, the mayor of New Orleans, Joseph A. Shakespeare, called southern Italian and Sicilian immigrants "the most idle, vicious, and worthless people among us. . . . They are without courage, honor, pride, religion or any quality that goes to make the good citizen." Even the progressive-minded Lafcadio Hearn spoke of "something viperine in this sultry Sicilian blood."[73]

This hatred was due partly to New Orleans Sicilians' willingness to associate with blacks as equals. Italians' whiteness was what motivated Southern Americans to bring them to the United States—Southern planters wanted to have white laborers instead of blacks—yet they did not behave like whites, at least toward African Americans. During the period of jazz's emergence, "Sicilian immigrants and African Americans developed a relationship that allowed some interaction and cooperation which modified, to some extent, the rigid boundaries of segregation and the blatant injustices of the Jim Crow system." Italians had been encouraged to immigrate because it was thought they would accept menial jobs, but many of them refused and were forced into the French Quarter, often living in poverty. According to one critic at the time, "The worst part of this quarter is inhabited by the lower class Sicilians, the Mafia, and Negroes, an area of gin, wine, and dope."[74]

Italians inhabited plantations as well. In 1900 at Deer Range Plantations, from which several great black jazz musicians came, two Italian workers lived in a double house with blacks, and a newspaper in 1904 reported that an Italian attended a "Negro Ball" at Crescent Plantation near Houma.[75] Italians predominated as fruit sellers in the French Market, and as a result they interacted with a huge variety of New Orleanians of different races and nationalities.

In the eyes of racist whites, both Italians and jazz music threatened racial purity, and the same social groups inveighed against both. In 1890 a vigilantelike committee led by Edgar Farrar, appointed by the mayor as part of a campaign against Italians ("criminals or paupers from Europe"), was also summoned in a *Mascot* newspaper editorial decrying a proto-jazz band of "'coons' armed with pieces of brass . . . inflict[ing] torture upon this suffering community." Infamously, eleven Italians were lynched after police chief Henessey was killed, reportedly by a Sicilian connected with organized crime. The police would sometimes harass or arrest Italian fruit vendors because of protests that they took jobs away from "Americans," and in one instance police dismissed a complaint about loud jazz music in a neighborhood because the only one objecting was, in the police report's words, "an Italian named Jake Tamberello," whose testimony was apparently not worth taking seriously.[76]

But the connection between Italians and New Orleans jazz went beyond their similarity in the eyes of racists. The Sicilian underworld helped revive the jazz entertainment industry in the city, employing Buddy Bolden and others, and important clubs in the District, Black Storyville, and elsewhere like Mantraga's, Joe Segretta's, Tonti's Social Club, and Lala's Big 25 were owned by Italians. More fundamentally, because of their concentration in mixed downtown neighborhoods, Italians like Luke Schiro, who grew up in Tremé and lived around the corner from Economy Hall and a few blocks from Perseverance Hall in the Seventh Ward, heard a lot of jazz or proto-jazz simply by going about their daily lives. In addition, Sicilians were attracted to jazz because New Orleans's nightclubs, wandering musicians, brass bands, and parades recalled similar institutions in their ancestral land.[77]

Another sizable group of white jazz musicians in New Orleans was Jewish. Although the Louisiana Code Noir of 1724 ordered the expulsion of Jews, by the late nineteenth century they were quite assimilated, often in mercantile professions. Similar to other groups, they had their own social aid societies, like the Hebrew Benevolent Society, founded in 1828, which paid medical and burial costs. Sometimes seen as less than fully white, Jews, like Italians, had musical connections to blacks; as opposed to Irish and northern European sounds, Italian, black, and Jewish music featured minor keys and syncopation. Armstrong has talked about the influence of a Jewish family he worked for, and one white musician, George Brunis, compared the blues to a "Jewish hymn, like Eli, Eli."[78]

John Wigginton Hyman, who changed his name to Johnny Wiggs, was such a Jewish jazz musician. Born in a well-to-do neighborhood, he grew up hearing his mother play piano by ear, accompanying herself and his father as they sang. His childhood recollections included some of the ambient sounds that influenced jazz, from a black washerwoman singing with a kind of beautiful roughness to the bottlemen who roamed the town playing three-feet-long tin horns, with a brass reed and a wooden mouthpiece. Wiggs remembered hearing them blocks away, and when they approached he ran to get bottles to trade them for children's miniature dolls or candy. The bottlemen were gifted at playing what he called the "blues," and when he later heard black cornet players like King Oliver, he was reminded of their "bending of notes" as well as the street cries of the blackberry woman. At a subscription dance at Tulane, he and his friends listened in awe of Oliver, oblivious to the girls they were supposed to be courting. (A subscription dance took place when boys with an entrepreneurial spirit rented the Tulane gym and hired a band, charging a dollar admission.) Wiggs also took lessons from an Italian woman, whom he thought of as very severe.[79]

Thus were Italians, Jews, and jazz tied together as threats to racial purity. Even Christian, non-Italian white jazz musicians became impure and crossed racial boundaries to practice their art, if only because white audiences demanded black music, whether played by blacks, Creoles, or whites. To work, the white musician had to risk his or her identity and become disrespectable, until jazz itself, partly due to such whites, became not only respectable but integral to American culture.

Learning the Music

Like many Creole and black musicians, some whites began playing music without formal training. These budding musicians played homemade instruments in children's spasm bands like the one Jack Laine organized at age twelve: "We'd commence to marchin' around the neighborhood playin' anything that come into our heads, makin' up little sounds as we went along." Under the circumstances, a good ear was invaluable; like Buddy Bolden, Frank Christian would hear a tune once, even from a balcony, and then be able to play it himself.[80]

However, unlike most black musicians, whites often had formal musical training. Luke Schiro took lessons at the Italian Hall from a professor from the Contessa Entellina Benevolent Society Band, an Arbreshe organization. (The Arbreshe were Sicilians whose ancestors originated in Albania.)[81] Tony Parenti and Arnold Loyacano studied solfeggio, the latter at the Milano Conservatory in the old French Opera House when he was seven years old. This method, based on singing syllables (do, re, mi, and so on) to internalize musical relationships, was ideal for impoverished Italians who could not afford instruments.[82]

A few whites studied with music teachers of color. Mulatto Dave Perkins instructed Jack Laine and Monk Hazel, Creole Kid Rena taught Sharkey Bonano and Louis Prima, and renowned teacher Lorenzo Tio Jr. had white students (and apparently few black ones). Although Creole teachers focused on reading and technique (particularly scales), undoubtedly there was a stylistic influence as well. Future ODJB trombonist Eddie Edwards took lessons from a Mexican musician who had stayed in New Orleans after the famous exposition in 1884.[83]

Like Creoles, whites who played jazz risked being labeled rebels; the father of Italian American (and future Original Dixieland Jazz Band member) Nick La Rocca called him "worse than a bum" because he had decided to become a musician. White musicians did not play for black audiences and thus did not get the encouragement for jazz that they might have. Even if they were willing to become outcasts, white musicians did not typically hear African-based music but were more likely to be familiar with opera.[84] True, whites had an easier time hearing Creole and black musicians than vice versa, since musicians of color routinely played at white functions. However, such functions usually did not include working-class whites—the most likely to want to play jazz—and whites who did attend would not hear the most innovative, blues-based music.

Aspiring white jazz musicians sometimes had to work hard to hear black bands, congregating on the sidewalk when black bands marched by for a funeral or sitting outside black or Creole clubs and "sweating" the band to pick up musical ideas. Tony Parenti sneaked into the Lyric, a "colored theater" in the French quarter, while clarinetist Harry Shields listened all night to Johnny Dodds outside Nolte's Hall, close to where Shields lived but off limits to whites. He also sat on the banks of the Claiborne Canal and listened to black and Creole musicians like Sam Morgan, Kid Rena, and Punch Miller play Monday-night dances at the National Baseball Park, two blocks from his home yet worlds away.[85] As a child, trombonist George Brunis went to the District, wearing long pants and posing as a midget, with wrinkles drawn on his forehead, to hear black musicians; when his mother found out, she "beat the Dickens" out of him. Leon Rappolo, later of the New Orleans Rhythm Kings, had an easier time: he learned jazz clarinet licks from African American musicians playing at a "Negro Saloon" owned by his father.[86]

White musicians also heard blacks playing music outdoors, where notes traveled through the air unimpeded by Jim Crow. Parenti recalled learning some of his favorite tunes by hearing African American Fate Marable play them on the steamer *Sidney*'s calliope, which could be heard all over the city. Somewhat later, Louis Prima used similar tactics: "I used to follow those black cats on the flatbed trucks that went through black neighborhoods advertising the dances. The trucks stopped at the corners and black cats would blow to draw a crowd. If the man who owned the corner grocery store sent out some beer, the cats would blow some more, but when the truck moved on, I'd run behind it to the next stop."[87]

Bassist and tuba player Steve Brown described the great lengths he went to in order to hear black musicians. "We took ideas from out in . . . the country as well as through the darkies that we heard play, around here . . . We took the ideas, the white people did—that's the poor white trash as we called ourselves in those days. And we played what sound good to us." As a child he would go to the "Negro section and they'd have tarpaulins spread over the yard and the back and the Negro bands would play and as kids we'd go listen to 'em. . . . Hear 'em play all types of tunes." Brown sought out black music up and down the city, from the waterfront to churches: "I used to, many a time, when I was a kid, go along the river and these Negro roustabouts would be sitting out on the cotton bales waiting for the boats, and they'd be singing. And they'd harmonize so beautifully . . . oh, you've never heard anything like it in your life; I'd just sit around and listen to them for hours." Some would have banjos or "an ole' battered up trumpet; and they'd play their tune, some, some popular number . . . like they'd think it should be played, ya know—improvising and playing . . . it in their way, their style. And . . . I heard a Negro one time in . . . one of the churches, playing an organ. . . . For harmony, we used to love to pass by these Negro churches and hear 'em sing."[88]

Although white musicians could not openly play with blacks and Creoles, "bucking contests" brought them together. Such contests began when bands advertised upcoming performances or other events by riding around town in the back of a furniture wagon driven by three mules, yelling to onlookers and passing out handbills. The musicians sat in the back on folding chairs, and when the wagon stopped at a corner, the band played, drawing dancing crowds. "Bucking" took place when two such bands met and, someone locking the wagons' wheels together to prevent a premature retreat, dueled until one was declared the winner. Some white musicians have spoken of the joys of "bucking" with a black band, describing it as an elaborate dance—coupling, uncoupling, meeting, separating, all in the service of the forbidden pleasure of playing music together: "Buddy Petit'd be advertising a colored dance, we'd be advertising a dance, we'd meet on the corner, and we'd challenge each other; and they'd pull in one direction, we'd go another direction, and play 'Get over dirty' with the instruments, you know; then maybe an hour or so later, we'd meet on another street, another corner."[89] One could argue that such contests encouraged competition rather than mutual influence, but in jazz the two are indistinguishable, particularly when such rivalry represented one of the few ways to hear bands of another race.

Occasionally a white musician violated racial boundaries by playing with musicians of color. Louis Prima was able to mingle with black musicians in the South because of his dark skin tone, while other white musicians played with musicians of color light enough to pass. In one such encounter, Parenti jammed with Creole Barney Bigard, who had a gig across the street, during intermissions. "This was a 'sneak in' endeavor, because of the Jim Crow laws; but at the early hours of the morning, and in a dimly lit night club, most people didn't know the difference, especially as Barney was light complected."[90]

Whites also violated the color line by hiring light-skinned New Orleanians of color. White bandleader George "Happy" Schilling, mentioned previously, hired Dave Perkins and Achille Baquet, as had his predecessor

Jack Laine, along with Creole Batiste Aucoin. As he recounted it, Schilling had heard good things about Baquet's clarinet playing, and someone reassured him, "He's colored, he's a nigger, you notice, but don't pay attention; he looks like white."[91] Despite using the racist terminology, Schilling, recounting the incident in 1957, seemed quite proud of his integrated band; whether he had felt the same emotions decades earlier when he hired Baquet or had simply been interested in getting a good clarinetist is impossible to determine. Such encounters furthered the education of the whites in the band as well as that of the musician hired, complicating the identity of both, and these musical negotiations influenced the course of the music.

Versatility as Hybridity: Impurity as an Occupational Requirement

Thus in presenting his racial identity in his music and sometimes in his very person, the jazz musician had to be a protean figure, altering himself with his surroundings and speaking a variety of cultural languages in the music itself. Black, white, and Creole musicians utilized and transformed African, European, and American forms of music, creating something new: jazz. Contrary to the claims of melting-pot historians, jazz did not emerge from a harmonic blending of cultures into a seamless whole. Rather, it came out of the struggles of musicians to negotiate changing political conditions, struggles that forced them to contend with different kinds of musicians and musical genres and in the process alter their identity. Out of these encounters, there emerged a new, hybrid music that refused to stay within the confines of a binary, hierarchical racial system.

In the pursuit of jobs, New Orleans musicians of all races exhibited incredible entrepreneurship. Ory began as a child by organizing fish fries, inviting people to listen to his music in an empty house and paying girls fifty cents a night to fry fish. Soon he began to branch out on weekends, playing country dance halls and picnics in the mill towns and society halls between LaPlace and Baton Rouge. In New Orleans itself, Ory played venues as diverse as Economy Hall, Cooperators Hall, Milneburg, the Yacht Club, society parties down St. Charles Street, parades, Lincoln Park, Spanish Fort, and Bucktown. As he put it, "I played in every corner where they liked music." He claims to have rented Economy Hall and Cooperators Hall and "tied them up for a whole year," keeping them empty just to avoid competition. He tried to advertise more than any other band, driving his furniture wagon to announce upcoming gigs.[92]

Other musicians displayed similar entrepreneurial skills. Chris Kelly's wife described him as "something like a manager" who would negotiate contracts and hire sidemen: he would book himself for three or four jobs in one night but play only one of them, sending other musicians to perform the rest under his name. Rural musicians like Pops Foster's father organized bands with just as much entrepreneurship as those in the city, giving dances on their farm and inviting people from neighboring plantations. Charlie Love, born in Plaquemine in 1885, characterized his father's band as a collective: every time they had a meeting, each member would contribute some money, and when they had enough they would buy a set of instruments and pay for a teacher. The understanding was that if someone quit the band he would leave his instruments.[93]

But success in turn-of-the-century Jim Crow New Orleans required more than entrepreneurship. To make a living, musicians had to display musical versatility and the fluid sense of racial and class identity that it required. In a sense, versatility grew naturally out of New Orleans's Afro-Caribbean Creole heritage: "In the Caribbean, the individual musician who specializes in a single form or style to the exclusion of all others is a rarity; just as the instrumentalist who limits himself to a single instrument is an exception."[94] But although Creoles of Color, most of them with Caribbean roots, embodied hybridity most directly, eventually all New Orleans jazz musicians became "Creoles," crossing racial and class lines in order to make a living.

When jazz first emerged, the world of New Orleans musicians was divided into a series of oppositions roughly corresponding to race and class divisions. Creoles and whites tended to be "legitimate" music readers ("musicianers") who opposed the new, improvised music and played strictly written music, typically with a soft, light attack; they "couldn't jazz." Blacks and lower-class musicians were mostly "fakers" or "head" musicians, who could not read but improvised or learned melodies by ear. (Those who could decipher individual written notes but not read music fluently were called "spellers.")[95] The rivalry between Robichaux and Bolden was a kind of shorthand for this opposition, even though Bolden (though not his sidemen) apparently could read music. There were important exceptions to this grouping—for example, virtuoso Creole Sidney Bechet did not read music. But for the most part, early on, two separate worlds existed: uptown (black, faking) musicians playing "ratty" music and (Creole, reading) "legitimate" players from downtown.[96]

As jazz developed, some bands stuck with one audience and one style of music, like the black and Creole bands that exclusively played "society" jobs with white audiences; though they were accused of abandoning their race, the lure of high-paying jobs took precedence. According to leader Oscar Celestin, "The coloreds said we did not want to play for them but this was not so, we just did not have any time left."[97] Undoubtedly the society jobs paid more, so it was not a matter of time so much as money.

Others, like black cornetist Chris Kelly, went the other way, primarily playing ratty music for black, lower-class audiences. Wildly popular at the time, he played "low down music, more of what you would call barrelhouse music. Played the blues and all that rough stuff." As a result, record companies considered him unsophisticated, and he is little known today though at the time his passionate, bluesy style made him Bolden's heir apparent. His son even recalls a story where Kelly came to do a job, was told that the gig was canceled for lack of an audience, and then, Bolden style, stuck the horn out of the man's window and blew, drawing a crowd.[98] Yet unlike Bolden, he had no interest in broadening his audience.

Because of his near exclusive "blues" repertory, many considered Kelly a limited player; most Creole bandleaders would not hire him.[99] In reality, despite his reputation, he could play more mainstream fare like "Maryland, My Maryland" and all of Joplin's ragtime compositions from the "Red Book," and he occasionally played white dances. However, unlike most New Orleans musicians, he was so popular among blacks that he simply did not have to branch out—he could make a living playing the "rough" blues. As Avery "Kid" Howard put it, "In other words, money, money, money. First come, first served."[100]

Kelly's self-limited audience gave him a freedom that musicians who worked for more varied audiences did not have. Because of his draw among the "ratty" crowd, Kelly could dress in a haphazard fashion; musicians laughed when they saw him walking down the street with clothes that were frayed at the elbows and knees. According to Barker, "Chris would come on the job with a tuxedo, a red-striped shirt, a black tie, a brown derby, and a tan shoe and a black shoe. Whatever he picked up in the house when he left, that's what he wore." George Lewis called him "my rag man" (note the double meaning—wears rags, plays rags) and said he was "the most liked among all colored people in New Orleans." Even his son admitted that Kelly "wasn't no fancy dresser, no indeed."[101]

Kelly's ability to ignore middle- and upper-class audiences—both their taste in music and the style of dress they wanted to see on a performer— was unusual. By necessity, most musicians played for, as Leonard Bechet put it, "all varieties of people."[102] In the words of Johnny St. Cyr, "There were musicians who specialized in brass band work and would not play dance music, but the better musicians played both. . . . We played for white and colored, all over New Orleans—one night out on St. Charles Avenue for a private party at a fine home for wealthy white people, next night we might play in the District."[103] Playing for diverse audiences entailed the ability to cross racial and class lines in musical style and in deportment.

The most successful musicians became musical chameleons, playing ratty or legitimate, improvised or composed music, with uptown or downtown musicians, in "rough" or society halls, simply to maximize their employment opportunities. Willie Cornish, who played with Bolden, was, according to his wife, "well-known amongst white people. . . . play-[ing] for big weddings and everything . . . [because] he knowed how to play. . . . If he didn't know, they wouldn't have hired him." But he and most other musicians had to be willing and able to play ratty, in rough venues, as well. When one musician was asked whether cornetist Oscar Celestin played ratty, he said, "It kind of depend who he was playing for. Celestin had a band there when they was playing for rough people, in them rough place there . . . they knew how to play. And when he go to them great big to-do . . . like the country club," they knew how to play for "rich white people." In short, "he had a good band there; he had a good band to go both ways."[104] (This was presumably before he began exclusively playing society jobs.)

The need for versatility was heightened by the fact that some jobs, particularly in the District, paid mainly through tips. At clubs like the Tuxedo, musicians were paid $1.25 a night, which was "carfare," but tips made up for the low pay. Tips required playing a particular song for a customer; after someone requested a particular song, the hat would be passed. Once a woman named Willie from Mobile came in with around a thousand dollars and wanted to repeatedly hear the song "Walk the Dog," giving the musicians a $5 or $10 tip every time they played it.[105]

Such musical versatility involved a varied repertoire. As Pops Foster put it, "It was a rule in New Orleans if you didn't play any blues you didn't get any colored jobs," and if you didn't play quadrilles and other traditional dances, Creoles would not hire you. But versatility also encompassed playing the same tunes differently for different audiences. Musicians like Morton played "high" and "low" versions of the same tune, depending on the audience, the low version featuring raunchier lyrics and bluesier music. Most students of jazz think taking a 4/4 tune and playing it in 3/4 is a modern technique, but Big Bill Thompson performed "Chinatown My Chinatown" as a waltz for the more sedate (white) crowd but "jazzed it up" to its standard 4/4 for the hipper audiences. Similarly, King Oliver played bluesy and rough at the Big 25 in the District but sweetened his style for subscription dances at Tulane: "At 'Big 25' it was hard-hitting, rough and ready, full of fire and drive. He subdued this to please the different patrons at the gym dances."[106]

The chameleonlike nature of New Orleans musicians included the ability to play more than one instrument. Manuel Manetta was a virtual one-man band, playing piano, violin, guitar, cornet, and trombone, sometimes in combination with one another. Frank Christian, a white cornetist, remembers being asked to play clarinet or other instruments in Laine's band. It did not matter that Christian was not an expert on those instruments; Laine needed someone to fill in, and the assumption was that a competent musician could branch out.[107] This ability to play a number of instruments was a rejection by New Orleans musicians of all races of the European virtuosic tradition in favor of an African-based craft aesthetic.

Versatility also required the ability to project the right image for a particular situation; musicians had to be adept at performing various social class identities. Both Robichaux and Bolden, supposed opposites, one the refined Creole and other the ratty playing black, could project an image of middle-class professionalism when necessary, so much so they wore identical suits from the same stylish tailor, Godchaux, featuring cuffed pants with big pleats and sporting black silk handkerchiefs around their necks. Willie Cornish, who had played rough jobs with Bolden, later insisted that his sidemen wear coats and ties for certain gigs. The Tuxedo Band wore tuxedos in order to get "respectable" jobs but elsewhere dressed more casually.[108]

In a sense, then, jazz musicians had to be class chameleons as well as racial impersonators, playing and acting "ratty" or respectable as the situation required. The ability to make such shifts required "middle-class" versatility and general professionalism. In addition to skillfully playing their instruments, musicians had to manage an ever-changing schedule of gigs, dress in appropriate attire, and play a repertory that a particular audience demanded in its favorite style. As Scott DeVeaux has written of a later period, "[Musicians'] work entailed the routine and anonymity of playing in any orchestra, demanding the same unglamorous traits of dependability, versatility, and unobtrusive competence. These work requirements, as much as anything, fostered values that could only be called middle-class where one would least expect to find them—at the heart of the jazz world." The Eclipse Brass Band, originally James Humphrey's plantation band, was a perfect example of this versatility. The band transcended the usual lines—uptown and downtown, black and Creole, honky-tonk and society, readers and fakers—by being able to read music and improvise in whatever style was needed, and thus flourished professionally.[109]

———

As musicians circulated through different venues and different audiences, the boundary lines between the various kinds of music became less clear, and "respectable" audiences were drawn to ratty music. The dissolving of the boundary between uptown and downtown, black and Creole, reader and faker, changed the music itself. The popularity of this "jazz" or "barrel house music" made older musicians, much to their chagrin, look old fashioned. Thus, according to Pops Foster, the Carey band, "a real whatchacall honky tonk band" that did not read music, "would get up side any band, a reading band, and make a fool out of them."[110]

The new impure music, a mixing of European conventions and black folk music, was opposed by guardians of purity, whether Creoles like Lorenzo Tio Sr., religious blacks who thought it the "devil's music," or racist whites who believed that the mixing of cultures would create a degenerate America. For the jazz musician, however, impurity was an occupational requirement. As we have seen, some Creoles were able to play with both white and black bands, thus violating the laws of purity in the most fundamental ways. Other musicians, though playing only with members of their own race, became musically impure by altering their style for different audiences, musically changing their identity as the occasion demanded.

Not all employers or audiences allowed their horizons to be broadened. Sometimes employers would insist on a particular kind of playing or even specific tunes. Once a white man who had hired Punch Miller's band told him, "We don't want that old stuff here; we want music," referring to written music, so the band eschewed improvisation for the engagement. Sometimes whites actually gave a band written music to play, even when the band had its own; the musicians might acquiesce or rebel by playing their own arrangements. One musician recalled working for wealthy whites at the Cotton Exchange who would pay them $25, an enormous sum for a job at that time (Manetta would get $1.25 a night to play at the Tuxedo), and insist that they play "The Star Spangled Banner" numerous times.[111] In other words, some whites did not want to have their identity stretched by exposure to the new music.

However, others were drawn to the new sounds, despite their strangeness. The change was not sudden. Bolden's popularity made it imperative that musicians play in the newer style, yet one could not present it in pure form to white audiences. But as the music circulated among black, white, and Creole audiences, in ratty and society venues, it picked up scraps and incorporated them. Musicians learned new styles and audiences altered their taste, in small ways stretching their racial identities. In an increasingly modern America, audiences hungered for novelty; in the words of St. Cyr, club owners "would hire the band that had the new stuff." Such was the competition to play the latest offerings that bands would cut off the titles of new sheet music, or even destroy the cornet and violin parts after memorizing them, to make sure other bands could not play the tune.[112]

Because of economic pressures on musicians as well as white fascination with black culture and discomfort with the new routinized world that was emerging, the racial purity demanded by Southern ideology and increasingly codified into law did not extend to musical performances and venues. Indeed, the push for purity in the Jim Crow era helped create in music and its venues a more open space to preserve and enhance the countertradition, especially prevalent in New Orleans, of racial interaction and intermixture. As we shall see, the racial circulation of musicians through various venues and the creation of relatively free musical spaces profoundly altered the music itself, creating an impure mixture of the African and the European. Like Bakhtin's "overpopulated" words, still echoing with the voices of previous speakers, the music bore traces of its travels, traces that refused to melt and become generically American.[113]

FOUR

Music

How differently in the two [kinds of songs], the African has smitten his image into every line: in the one sort, the white, uprolled eyes and low wail of the savage captive, who dares not lift the cry of mourning high enough for the jealous ear of the master; in the other, the antic form, the grimacing face, the brazen laugh, and self-abasing confessions of the buffoon, almost within the whisk of the public jailer's lash. GEORGE WASHINGTON CABLE, 1886

Music and Domination

When Africans were kidnapped and taken to North America, they were thrust into a world of monologue. As Frederick Douglass put it, telling about a slave who had been falsely accused: "To all these complaints, no matter how unjust, the slave must never answer a word. Colonel Lloyd could not brook any contradiction from a slave. When he spoke, a slave must stand, listen, and tremble."[1] To teach a slave to read or write was illegal in many states.

Yet these Africans, and then African Americans, expressed themselves through music. Indeed, they were ordered to sing and dance, beginning on the perilous "middle passage" to America. In the master's eyes, such singing and dancing maintained his property, exercising his captives and boosting morale.[2] Singing slaves were also useful for propaganda purposes, evidence of their "happy" lives; abolitionists at first denied that the slaves sang and danced, attributing such reports to Southern lies. From the master's point of view, then, slave music increased his power, and he expected, one supposes, that such songs would praise him.

Slaves, however, took a potential tool of the masters and used it against them, condemning their oppressors and imagining liberation. They also "signified" upon European music, transforming it with African musical devices and creating an impure form called jazz.

"Dey Gib Us de Crust": Music as Critique

Slaves used music to protest their condition from the very beginning. Even on slave ships, when ordered to sing, Africans intoned mournful dirges lamenting the loss of their homes, families, and friends. In 1795, one observer in Louisiana heard slaves singing "Jacobin songs," threatening the lives of local officials, promising to guillotine the "swine governor," and expressing a longing for freedom. Slaves sang of "the proud defiance of the runaway, the courage of the black rebels, the stupidity of the patrollers, the heartlessness of the slave traders, and the kindness and cruelty of masters." One report said that slave complaints about matters like having to work on Sunday were "sung with peculiar vivacity, when the Negroes come under [the master's] window, or near his house."[3]

In addition to airing complaints against individuals, songs opposed slavery in general:

The big bee flies high,
the little bee makes the honey.
The black folks make the cotton,
and the white folks gets the money.
We raise the wheat
Dey gib us de corn
We bake de bread
Dey gib us de crust.

The spirituals in particular, though a bit less overtly, became instruments of protest. These sacred songs began with white encouragement: in 1784, an Anglican bishop wrote to Barbados from London suggesting that the slaves compose hymns using their own melodies, which they could sing not only in church but during laboring. Surely the bishop did not envision that the spirituals would become vehicles to express black aspirations for freedom, affirm a better future, and negate the present. When slaves sang these ostensibly Christian, European songs, they performed a kind of racial cross-dressing in which the Israelites became black, their struggles for freedom against the Egyptians standing in for those of African Americans. Slaves even altered spirituals to comment on contemporary events, as when the Emancipation Proclamation prompted runway slaves to sing, "Go down, Abraham / Away down in Dixie land / Tell Jeff Davis / To let my people go."[4]

Periodically authorities tried to prohibit such songs. If the protesting message was too obvious, slaves could be punished, like those jailed in South Carolina for singing "We'll Soon Be Free," featuring the stanzas "We'll soon be free / When de Lord will call us home," and "We'll fight for liberty / When de Lord will call us home." Masters accused slaves of plotting rebellions during Sunday festivities, and eventually slave singing and dancing were heavily regulated or banned because they were thought to be impious. One law mandated "death or imprisonment at hard labor for life" to whoever should be guilty of "writing, printing, publishing, or distributing anything having a tendency to create discontent among the free colored population." A 1849 edict in St. John's Parish, Louisiana, prohibited slaves "from beating the drum or dancing after sundown."[5]

For the most part, however, public officials looked the other way when critical songs were sung.[6] Music's status as "entertainment" insulated it, especially in New Orleans, from the punishment that would have been forthcoming had the same sentiments been expressed in nonmusical form. The "low" status of popular entertainment, used to denigrate black musical accomplishments as unintellectual, also allowed African Americans the freedom to express otherwise forbidden viewpoints.

"Killed His Sweet Little Sister": Black Ballads

By the last decade of the nineteenth century, slavery had ended but so had Reconstruction, and African Americans faced an increasingly hostile white society that sought to solidify the boundaries between the races. A generation of blacks came of age that had never known slavery and wanted full inclusion in America, but whites fought harder than ever to exclude them. In response, some blacks rejected America.

This rejection was expressed in black ballads, which celebrated outlaws, rebellious slaves, and folk heroes. Such songs immortalized "bad niggers," violent men legendary in the oppositional culture of lower-class black New Orleans:

I's Wild Nigger Bill
From Redpepper Hill

I never did work, an' I never will.
I's done kill the boss,
I's knocked down the hoss,
I eats up raw goose without apple sauce.

These "bad men" were loners who stood apart from the legal and moral order and rejected all rules:

I'm so bad, I don't ever want to be good, uh, huh;
I'm going to de devil and I wouldn't go to heaven, uh, huh;
No I wouldn't go to heaven if I could.

Many of these songs celebrated those who endured great trials, like the "heroic goose, who, after being shot, picked, cooked, carved, and run through the sawmill, was last seen with a large, derisively honking flock of goslings, flying over the ocean," or John DeConqueror, "a trickster folk hero famous for outwitting his white owners during slavery."[7]

Such ballads permeated the culture of black New Orleans during the period jazz arose. Jelly Roll Morton sang a blues recounting the murderous exploits of Aaron Harris, born in New Orleans between 1875 and 1880, who killed eleven people yet never was convicted of a crime, supposedly because a "hoodoo woman" protected him with her magic. Harris, sings Morton, was "the baddest man / That was in this land . . . killed his sweet little sister and his brother-in-law / About a cup of coffee."[8]

Women, too, were celebrated in such ballads, though some of them gained notoriety through their sexuality rather than violence. Such "bad women" included "Lillian Smith, who shot down the most fabulous of the New Orleans pimps, Thomas Wade, alias Clark, like a dog; . . . Louise Blackstein, the beautiful octoroon prostitute from Gasouet Street, whose ravishing beauty drove men mad; Corrine Mantley, who had her name in lights over her Iberville Street bordello, something the great Lulu White didn't have; the bad prostitute, Louise Benjamin, killer of five men; [and] Mary Porter, the big-time landlady of Bienville Street, with many houses of ill-fame and girls of every description and color and race." Morton's rendition of "The Murder Ballad" recounts the tale of a woman who suspects another of sleeping with her man and, after warning her rival, "I'll cut your throat and drink your fuckin' blood like wine," "pulled out a pistol and shot her right in her eyes."[9]

Some musicians, like famed bass drummer Black Benny, who could drive a band with each powerful stroke of his mallet, were themselves such "bad men." Though a violent man, Black Benny invariably escaped the law. In a story recounted by Armstrong, after refusing to comply with a police order to appear for questioning, Benny is chased by an officer, who slips, leaving his face "so spattered with mud that he looked like a black face comedian. 'I told you I wasn't going to jail today,' Benny shouted at him, and went on about his business."[10] In Armstrong's telling, Black Benny's humiliation of the officer is a kind of signifying reversal: the police officer ends up in blackface, but blackface that humiliates the white man who (unintentionally) puts it on. The bad man takes the blackface symbol and reverses it, using it against whites.

Yet songs did not always glorify such men and women. Morton described Harris as "terrible," "the toughest," "the most heartless man I've ever heard of or ever seen," someone who could "chew pig iron and spit it out razor blades." In "Aaron Harris Blues" Morton gives voice to his mortal fear of the man, whom he unknowingly hustled in pool. Morton gives a double-edged performance, expressing his fear but also showing how he was able to hustle Harris and get away with it. Morton mastered the violence of a man like Harris, whose vocabulary was reputed to be under one hundred words—he "spoke" by means of his gun—by telling his story in song.[11]

Such songs reflected African American ambivalence about these bad men. On the one hand, they were admired for standing up to the law, typically killing a police officer or sheriff, the very embodiment of white oppression. At the same time, such men often provoked retribution by whites, and these ballads inevitably ended with the death of the "hero," as if to reestablish order. At the end of "The Murder Ballad," the tough killer of her rival regrets that she "jeopardized [her] . . . life for that no-good man" and prays "that the Lord will show me another day," in the end urging the listener to "try to be a good girl."[12]

Because of their power, such critical songs became increasingly dangerous in the Jim Crow era. Morton tells Lomax that although he knew a song about Robert Charles, the "bad man" who killed several police officers, he "found it was best . . . to forget it . . . in order to go along with the world on the peaceful side." Yet musicians of color found other ways to criticize the established order.

Signifying

The rejection of white society present in some black ballads did not appeal to most African Americans. Most wished, as DuBois put it, "to be both a Negro and an American." One option was to try to live up to American ideals, to become respectable, proving whites wrong about blacks. Advocates of such respectability, as we have seen, opposed jazz because it was associated with pariahs and oppositional values. Another possibility, however, was to use satire, which Douglass called "scorching irony," to criticize racism.[13]

These contrasting approaches can be seen in two photographs of the pioneering jazz band of Joe "King" Oliver. In the first, the large Oliver, dressed in a tuxedo, sits near the center of the frame. His right hand rests stiffly on one knee, while his left props his cornet firmly upon the other. The cornetist stares downward and to the distance with a serious, reflective expression, as if contemplating a profound and difficult question. The effect, as befitting his "title," is regal.[14] The six other members of the band, including a young Louis Armstrong, stand behind him. The musicians to Oliver's left all have their left arm at their side, creating an image of great symmetry, reinforced by the vertical folds in the black curtains behind them. Each band member sports a tuxedo, with the exception of the only woman in the group, pianist Lil Hardin, who wears a light-colored evening gown with a single strand of pearls around her neck and flowers in her hair. The band's instruments are displayed in front of them, carefully arranged in an abstract pattern: a banjo, drumsticks, another cornet, and a mute, all vertical, reinforce the series of uprights that characterize the photo and give it its dignity. On the horizontal axis sit two clarinets, crossed in an X; a trombone; another cornet-type instrument; and a bass violin on its side. The effect is of great formality, seriousness, and dignity. Oliver and his men exude respectability.

The second photograph consists of the group (with slightly altered personnel) in a wildly different pose.[15] The musicians are dressed as field hands, with large cuffed overalls, neck kerchiefs, and various types of headgear: a flat, floppy worker's cap, a straw hat, and, on the leader, a bowler (derby). Hardin appears in the guise of a farmer's daughter, wearing a checked, short-sleeved, calf-length gingham dress with square neck. The musicians stand in a row on a sidewalk directly in front of a brick wall in various humorous poses. Some kneel, instruments pointing skyward; Oliver aims the bell of his cornet at Hardin, who covers her ear in mock pain. The violinist looks skyward, protecting himself from a falling object or perhaps asking heaven for guidance. The bass player faces the camera and holds his bow in front of him, saberlike.

Two photographs, two stances: respectability and satire. In a time of racism and segregation in the South, both of these stances undermined the expectations of white Americans, who regarded black musicians as idiot savants, nothing more than talented mimics. The "serious" photograph asserts dignity, combating the racist stereotype of laziness, and the formal attire enacts the kind of respectability usually associated with the higher-status Creoles. Under Jim Crow, dressing up could be seen as an impudent violation of social boundaries, and by striving for respectability, black musicians asserted their rightful place within American society.[16]

The "humorous" photograph takes a different approach. It could be seen as a kind of racial self-hatred, a "tomming" enactment of white fantasies of happy slaves on the plantation, a sacrifice of the very dignity embodied in the other photograph in order to entertain whites and reassure them of their superiority. However, one can also read the image as parody. That is, the musicians self-consciously enact stereotypes in an exaggerated way in order to show their ridiculousness, "consciously us[ing] racist stereotype in their performances, in part, to distance themselves from these images since it was abundantly clear (at least to themselves and their black audiences) that they were *performing* these roles not embracing them as representative behavior." Such parody exemplifies a broader African American device called *signifying*, "repetition with a signal difference," that difference sometimes constituting a "reversal."[17]

This repetition with an overturning effect can be seen in another story recounted in Armstrong's autobiography, in which, remembering his boyhood experience with New Orleans's segregated train cars, he mockingly refers to the blackface minstrel symbolizing racial separatism as "James Crow."[18] Armstrong, himself sometimes accused of minstrelsy, by formalizing Crow's name signifies on it, simultaneously evoking and reversing it. In fact, Armstrong's move is a reversal of a reversal; he formalizes the name, implying respect, but the formalization exposes the ridiculousness of "Mr. Crow" and ultimately shows disrespect for a practice built on disdain for African Americans. Armstrong, by signifying on Crow's name, enacts the verbal equivalent of Plessy's assault on the color line. As we shall see, such signifying was central to the creation of jazz.

"Cruel Satires": The African (American) Tradition of Parody

Satirical songs and dances play a central role in West African society, because no punishment is more feared than ridicule. In the region's history, songs criticized both local authority figures and colonists, and those mocked were expected to endure the insult in a good-natured manner lest they be seen as hypersensitive. "In such songs, cleverly veiled but pointed references to the sources of social injustice were broadcast throughout the marketplace to the widespread enjoyment and satisfaction of the public." Despite operating by clever allusion, satirical songs and dances were so potent that in what is now Zambia, colonial authorities enacted a statute specifying that "no person may organize or take part in any dance which is calculated to hold up to ridicule or to bring into contempt any person, religion, or duly constituted authority."[19]

Sung satire permeated black life in the Americas as well. "The topical song, relying for its effect on such devices as double entendre, irony, and veiled allusions, is a Caribbean specialty that cuts across many musical genres." In Martinique in 1887, Hearn observed "cruel" and "coarse" "Carnival songs . . . of which the local meaning is unintelligible to those unacquainted with the incident inspiring the improvisation," whose barbs would eventually resound through "all the burghs of the island." Such songs often ridiculed by mimicking the victim.[20]

This tradition continued in the United States, as visitors to plantations often found themselves on the receiving end of satirical slave songs. In 1774, Edward Long heard slave work songs full of "derision, and not unfrequently at the expense of the overseer, if he happens to be near, and listening; this only serves to add a poignancy to their satire, and heightens the fun." Similarly, two white women in 1832 criticized a slave singer only to immediately find themselves the object of satirical choruses. The same women saw the slave Clotilda satirize her fellow slaves in song and then ridicule the dancing ability of the master himself in verse, performing a "laughable imitation" of an unsuccessful attempt to dance the Juba. Slaves mimicked their masters using both gesture and music, and the owner would sometimes be flattered, especially because such satire might be preceded by a song ridiculing the singer himself or herself or praising the master. In the end, satirical songs allowed slaves to make criticisms that would not be acceptable in other forms and sometimes resulted in actual improvements, because the master might respond to the "complaint" by making small changes in the life of the slaves.[21]

While some such satire was tolerated as harmless entertainment, it was not without dangers, and for this reason singers sometimes concealed their barbs. For much of U.S. history, to be African American required the ability to say one thing while meaning another. Speaking forthrightly to a white person brought risk of harm or even death; one had to, in the words of poet Paul Laurence Dunbar, "wear the mask." But masks reveal as well as conceal, and singing, dancing, and music making by African Americans were always rich with multiple meanings.

African Americans thus became adept at insinuation. Slaves were expert dissimulators, pretending to be ignorant or unobservant when they were anything but. According to Douglass, the slaves sang songs praising the master when he was in earshot, but along with such flattery they inserted "other words of their own improvising—jargon to others, but full of meaning to themselves." Thus slave singing had multiple layers, simulating contentment while criticizing bondage. Some slave songs signified upon the persona of the master in order to enact a carnivalistic reversal:

O massa take that bran' new coat
and hang it on the wall.
The darky take the same ole coat
and wear it to the ball.

Slaves on occasion actually did dress up like the master and mistress, imitating their manners and dancing, to the amusement of observers.[22]

Slaves used dance for satirical purposes as well. As one former slave put it, "Us slaves watched white folks' parties, where the guests danced a minuet and then paraded in a grand march, with the ladies and gentlemen going different ways and then meeting again, arm in arm, and marching down the center together. Then we'd do it, too, *but we used to mock 'em*, every step. Sometimes the white folks noticed it, but they seemed to like it; I guess they thought we couldn't dance any better." The ultimate example of this was the cakewalk, in which African Americans dressed formally and high-stepped in imitation of high-society whites, who thought they were being emulated without realizing they were being satirized.[23]

New Orleans's Culture of Satire

New Orleans in particular is a city rich with satire, and much of its music had parodic overtones. Congo Square was itself a kind of a parody of the Place d'Armes, at the opposite end of Orleans Street. According to a contemporary observer, George Washington Cable, while the Place d'Armes represented "all that was best"—high society, fine goods, "the ruling class"—Congo Square embodied the "worst," the workman, the quadroon, the slave, the prostitute. "One was on the highest ground; the other on the lowest." Even its name represented debasement, for the "negro was the most despised of human creatures and the Congo

the plebeian among the negroes." The famous calinda dance performed in the square was always "a grossly personal satirical ballad." In the
brothels of Storyville, pianists and prostitutes sang "dirty" parodies of
popular songs, while other tunes had titles like "The Shit" or "Go to
Hell." Buddy Bolden had a song making fun of a certain judge, the performance of which could lead to arrest.[24]

New Orleanians of color used satire in their own community as well,
as a kind of comment on class and color divisions. Songs deplored
in mocking language the fate of free mulatto (or quadroon) women,
black men, and the free male quadroon, who could attend the famous
"quadroon" balls only with the "menial" occupation of a fiddler.[25] By
the 1920s, blacks who resented the increasingly "respectable" church
services recorded mock sermons and spirituals, turning "I Heard a Voice
from Heaven Say" into "I Heard the Voice of a Pork Chop" or replacing "God" in prayers with "Silver Dollar" ("Without you, Silver Dollar, I
wouldn't have nowhere to go").[26] It is likely that such songs circulated
in the underground culture of earlier New Orleans as well.

In New Orleans, a city known for the funeral and the carnival (Mardi
Gras), simultaneously opposites and twins, every dignified ritual had its
satirical counterpart. At times events were what Bakhtin calls "double
voiced," with the satire built into the very ritual it parodied. The dignity of a parade was ridiculed by the second line, a group of "children,
prostitutes, gamblers, and novice musicians" and other spectators, who
followed the musicians along the side of the road, marching, clapping,
"capering before the band and parodying the dignified but lively posture
of the grand marshal," sometimes even disrupting the proceedings.[27]
During Mardi Gras, blacks offered their parody of King Rex, King Zulu,
who instead of handing out coins and trinkets threw coconuts into the
crowd. Even dignity could be exaggerated to the point of satire, like
the evocation of Chopin's funeral march that begins Jelly Roll Morton's
"Dead Man's Blues."[28]

The jazz funeral itself contains a kind of built-in satire, the march to
the cemetery dignified and somber, the march back joyous and upbeat.
At the church and on the way to the cemetery, the band plays hymns
like "Just a Closer Walk with Thee" and "Amazing Grace," with little, if
any, improvisation. The snare drummer muffles his instrument with a
handkerchief until the minister's words "Ashes to ashes, dust to dust"
signal its removal, and after a drum roll the band accelerates the tempo
with "Didn't He Ramble," celebrating the wildness of the deceased, or
"When the Saints Go Marching In," a joyous procession turning the
gloom inside out, transforming mourning into mirth.[29]

"The Blacks Danced Out Their Mocking Reply"

The "double voiced" nature of New Orleans rituals reveals satire's kinship with homage. What Creoles called "signifying songs" could take the form of "loving insults" like "I'll be glad when you're dead, you rascal you."[30] Signifying thus builds upon the very thing it criticizes, for whatever the tension between them, the marching band and the second line together make up the parade. Ralph Ellison illustrates how signifying criticizes and builds upon its object by imagining a group of slaves dancing:

> Looking through the windows of a plantation manor house from the yard, [they] imitated the steps so gravely performed by the masters within and then added to them their own special flair, burlesquing the white folks and then going on to force the steps into a choreography uniquely their own. The whites, looking out at the activity in the yard, thought they were being flattered by imitation, and were amused by the incongruity of flattered blacks dancing courtly steps, while missing completely the fact that before their eyes a European cultural form was becoming Americanized, undergoing a metamorphosis through the mocking activity of a people partially sprung from Africa. So, blissfully unaware, the whites laughed while the blacks danced out their mocking reply.[31]

Signifying is thus akin to Hegel's *Aufhebung*, simultaneously nullifying, preserving, and transforming, although perhaps a more appropriate reference is to W. E. B. DuBois's evocation of a self that wishes to affirm its blackness without abolishing its Americanness. It is no coincidence that DuBois came up with the concept of double consciousness during this period of heightened awareness of African Americans' relationship to the larger American culture. As opposed to separatism, double consciousness suggests the possibility of African Americans' inserting themselves into America through culture, one of the few accepted avenues of expression, by signifying on it. This insertion is not a joining of preexisting entities but a transformation of the whole, bridging the "immeasurable distance" between black and white. Not a melting pot but polyphony, in which each new voice changes the whole.[32]

The coexistence of homage and satire reflects the double consciousness of African Americans: part of the dominant culture and aspiring to advance in it, but also apart, commenting on it and satirizing it. Signifying seen in this light can forge connections across disparate communities. Gary Tomlinson calls signifying "a trope of mediation between or among texts or languages," "a figure representing the strategies by which a text or voice finds its place between (among) differing discourses," and "the linguistic process by which we traverse the space between self and other, or, better, by which we locate meaning in that space," coming to terms with the otherness inside us.[33]

Signifying allows African Americans to both insert themselves into and transform the dominant culture, simultaneously showing respect for received texts and criticizing or parodying them. According to Zora Neale Hurston, this "modification of ideas" is the essence of originality: "So if we look at it squarely, the Negro is a very original being. While he lives and moves in the midst of a white civilization, everything he touches is re-interpreted for his own use."[34]

A simultaneous drawing upon and criticizing mainstream culture was apparent in black bands' performances in the city's ubiquitous parades, which combined patriotism and parody. Such a combination is apparent in a march by the (black) Excelsior Band, described in a contemporary newspaper account as having "new and beautiful uniforms, planned after the style of the Prussian military costume, with dark blue helmet hats, ribbed with burnished brass, corded in white, with long white horse hair plumes, long military coats, three rows of brass buttons, corded in white, with epaulets, pants of dark navy blue cloth with white stripes." On the one hand, the musicians clearly took pride in the uniforms and the parade, yet the exaggerated nature of the uniforms and the march constituted both a "caricature of white folks' pomposity" and "subtler self-parody."[35]

Musical Signifying

Music has served as one of the key vehicles for African American signifying because, in the words of Paul Gilroy, the "special power" of black musical forms "derives from a doubleness, their unsteady location simultaneously inside and outside the conventions, assumptions, and aesthetic rules which distinguish and periodise modernity."[36] Musicians of color signified upon American culture, inserting themselves into it and transforming it. After being ripped from their African homeland, they might have rejected American music and created a pan–West African music separate from white culture, but the slaves did not have the autonomy to do so and instead Africanized European and American forms. In New Orleans slaves continued to play African music, most notably in Congo Square, but they soon took up Western instruments like violins and played jigs and reels, filtered through an African musical sensibility.

Thus, a usually astute observer of early black music errs when he argues that "African-American musicians often 'crossed over' to perform and compose European-style music, but they also built their own separate musical culture on an African foundation."[37] Rather, the two types of music were intertwined from the beginning, with blacks signifying on white music and whites, fascinated with the emotional resonance of black music (and seeing opportunities for moneymaking), borrowing from it in turn.

The subversive yet integrative potential of signifying can be seen in the transformation of American patriotic songs by Americans of color, using African-based devices. "Old Corn Meal," or "Signor Cornmeali," a popular black singer who had started as a street peddler and then became the first black to appear on the stage in American New Orleans, sang variations on "The Star Spangled Banner." Danny Barker describes one "General Zachariah," a fat, dark-skinned man, who wore a military uniform mixing Union and Confederate garments and led a "three-piece military group—a fife or flute or clarinet, a huge bass drum beater and a snare drummer similar to the Uncle Sam posters"—that played only "the first dozen bars" of "Dixie" and part of "The Battle Hymn of the Republic." (As Barker puts it, "His uniform showed him to be neutral about the Civil War.") Similarly, in response to requests for "Dixie," pianist Manuel Manetta played "Dixie" with one hand and "Yankee Doodle Dandy" with the other, putting Northern and Southern anthems in dialogue, each signifying on the other, calling into question the supremacy of either one.[38] Although white Northern pianists also played these songs simultaneously, African American performers more directly felt the contrast between Northern and Southern social orders and thus more fully rendered it in music.

Ingrid Monson argues that signifying's process of repetition and variation is central to mainstream jazz, which often takes popular songs and transforms them into very different works, like John Coltrane's modal explorations on Rodgers and Hammerstein's "My Favorite Things." Musicians also create variations on melodies by past performers or respond to instrumentalists sharing the bandstand, but in a sense audiences signify as well. Since "standard" tunes are performed by many artists over a period of many years, listeners often hear echoes of an older version in a newer performance, as when Coltrane's 1960 "Body and Soul" evokes Coleman Hawkins's 1939 version. Signifying thus connects present and past, creating a community of sound stretching across time. Unlike Romantic artists' attempts to escape the "anxiety of influence" by establishing their independence from predecessors, jazz musicians revel in the "joy of influence," drawing on previous improvisers even as they assert their individuality by signifying on them.[39]

Yet what has been little noticed is that signifying spurred jazz's very creation, giving birth to a dialogic, racially impure American music in the midst of Jim Crow New Orleans. Crescent City musicians used African devices to signify upon European and American music, inserting themselves into and transforming the dominant culture.

African and European, Caribbean and Mexican

That jazz draws on African music is a commonplace, yet the relationship between the two goes beyond devices like syncopation. One can posit a West African cultural aesthetic, an approach to expression that, even when we acknowledge the variety among African and African American cultures, represents a kind of lingua franca. In this aesthetic, art is inseparable from the community interactions (religious ceremonies, rites of passage, celebrations) of which it is a part. From this perspective, New Orleans musicians were not "artists" operating apart from everyday life and commerce; their "art" was inseparable from work and from the community events it accompanied. Offering "music for all *occasions*," musicians' business cards emphasized the primacy of the event in the act of making music.[40]

Given the central role of the community, West African–derived art forms also blur the distinction between artist and audience, making listeners as much a part of the performance as the musicians themselves. While audience members at European classical performances sit in quiet contemplation, Africans and African Americans dance, shake, tap their feet, clap their hands rhythmically, and cry out in response to music. Musicians in turn react to listeners, playing louder or softer, with more or less rhythmic intensity, or even changing the beat, in order to keep the audience moving. Many jazz musicians from Armstrong to Charlie Parker and beyond have talked about the audience's part in their music making.

African American art is thus inherently dialogic, and "call and response" is just one example of a larger structural principle. From this perspective, the second line street parades crucial to the development of jazz in New Orleans have roots in African practice. "The African-American parade typically featured a raucous improvised style of music and a back-and-forth interaction between spectators and parade performers; these features were not typical of white parades and processions of the era but they were prevalent in black rites in both West Africa and the nearby Caribbean."[41]

Admittedly, neither "African culture" nor "European culture" was pure to begin with, sharing as they did a long history of mutual influence. The earliest blacks to come to North America were skilled traders, sometimes of mixed race, from the African coast. Many of them fluent in multiple languages, they drew upon a variety of European cultures in their travels; one African merchant and politician from the Gold Coast, Abee Coffu Jantie Seniees, was known as Jan Snees, Jacque Senece, Johan Sinesen, and Jantee Snees, in different European accounts. These "Atlantic Creoles" had a "genius for intercultural negotiation" or "cultural brokerage," and this cosmopolitanism helped create the black Atlantic; Senegambia, from which two-thirds of New Orleans slaves came, was a particularly syncretic culture. Though some have described the music in Congo Square as purely African, others remembered hearing European musical forms like "jigs, fandangos, and Virginia breakdowns."[42]

In the other direction, European culture very early on was influenced by Africa. For example, Spanish music (which later had an influence on jazz) was shaped hundreds of years ago by African music.[43] Despite this intermingling, important features of West African music were underdeveloped in European music, and these devices played a key role in the development of jazz.

Transforming Music: African (American) Devices

Without denying the diversity in African music, one finds "fundamental affinities—and easy compatibility—of African musical traditions south of the Sahara." According to musicologist Olly Wilson, "The empirical evidence overwhelmingly supports the notion that there is indeed a distinct set of musical qualities which are an expression of the collective cultural values of peoples of African descent . . . [and] which, taken together, comprise the essence of the black musical tradition." Four such musical features of the music were central to the creation of jazz: syncopation, polyphony, a manipulation of pitch I call "bluing," and improvisation. From the beginnings of slavery, these devices constituted a key part of the African American musical vocabulary, and each of them played a crucial role in transforming European forms.[44]

Cross Rhythms and Syncopation

A fundamental principle of African music that differentiates it from European forms is its emphasis on rhythm. Africans "understand" a piece of music if they know the dance that accompanies it: "black music is not a purely aesthetic phenomenon, but brings its faithful into communion, more intimately, to the rhythm of the community which dances, of the World which dances."[45] In African music a melody is inseparable from its rhythm, the dance that accompanies it, and ultimately the occasion and community of which it is a part.

Beyond the importance of rhythm itself, African music is noted for its rhythmic complexity. In contrast to Western music's unifying meter— for example, a measure consisting of four beats with emphasis on the first beat—African performances feature *"always at least two rhythms,"* each competing for our attention. Where such polymeters exist, no natural central thread holds the music together, because the "interweaving of diverse and multiple rhythms is coherent only when one actively participates by finding and maintaining a point of reference," and this point of reference differs depending on the listener.[46] Rhythm has an openness and flexibility largely absent from Western music, presenting a kaleidoscope of possibilities for the listener or musician to attend to.

Early jazz did not approach the rhythmic complexity of African music, but it did have a weaker version of it: syncopation, an emphasis on the "offbeats," either the upbeat or beats 2 and 4. Syncopation is literally decentering, a deviation from the expected. In that sense, syncopation signifies on the ground beat, avoiding it yet referring to it in that avoidance. Through ragtime and then jazz, syncopation radically transformed American melodies.[47]

Polyphony

In addition to its numerous rhythmic layers, African-based music uses multiple melodic lines, whether through "call and response" (antiphony) or simultaneously through polyphony. Call and response is just as it sounds, one melody answered by another in a kind of conversation. Polyphony, with two or more melodies sounding simultaneously, takes call and response one step further, each melody signifying on the other. In polyphonic improvisation each instrumentalist simultaneously listens and responds to the other; such improvisation is a form of signifying because each melody must be related to the next but cannot merely repeat what has been said, because then it would not be polyphony.[48] Thus, polyphony is repetition with a signal difference. Heterophony, simultaneous singing or playing of variations of the same melody, represents a similar process.

Polyphony, heterophony, and call and response inject dialogue into a culture bent on the monologism of racial purity. As Bakhtin suggests, any utterance contains or implies a response; while some kinds of music omit or suppress the response, polyphony foregrounds it, substituting dialogue for monologue, multiplicity for singularity. Even more than call and response, which separates the statement and its answer, polyphony suggests that a musical utterance and its response are intertwined. The dialogic nature of polyphony in jazz is heightened by the African-based emphasis on the timbral contrast between different instruments. As opposed to, for example, a string quartet, African-based music highlights the different tonal qualities of each instrument in the ensemble, creating a "mosaic of varying tone colors" rather than a smooth blend.[49]

Polyphony even creates dialogic listening. Monophonic music demands that the music be heard in a preordained way, with the main melody holding listeners' hands and guiding them down a path, pulling them back to attention when their feet wander off the main road. Polyphony, on the other hand, with its simultaneous melodic lines gives the listener a choice of melodies on which to focus, forcing the listener to, in effect, make his or her own composition. Paul Gilroy sees in the dialogue built into African and African American music an "ethics of antiphony," "a democratic moment enshrined in the practice of antiphony which anticipates new, non-dominating social relationships," blurring the line between self and other and giving rise to "special forms of pleasure."[50]

Bluing

The flexibility of rhythm and melody that syncopation and polyphony create in African music are joined by an equally malleable sense of pitch. The bending of notes slightly flat or (less often) sharp, which in the absence of an available verb I will call, after a composition by Miles Davis, "bluing," is perhaps the most distinctive feature of African music. (After all, Beethoven used syncopation and Bach improvised.) As one early observer of the relationship between jazz and African music put it: "No note is attacked straight; the voice or instrument always approaches it from above or below, plays around the implied pitch without ever remaining on it for any length of time, and departs from it without ever having committed itself to a single meaning. The timbre is veiled and paraphrased by constantly changing vibrato, tremolo and overtone effects."[51] Bluing signifies upon Western tonality by playing with and distorting it. Although seen by some as noise or "out of tune" playing, bluing was not mere undermining but in fact something new—not just the distortion of American music but the creation of African American music.

The essence of bluing is the manipulation of the timbre of an instrument or voice, making it "dirty" or impure, using devices like growling, melisma, and falsetto. In addition to such "distortion," a single performance might feature a variety of timbres, as when slave songs "move[d] from speechlike sounds . . . through ranges of musical compass to screaming and yelling, all within the confines of a single performance." This emphasis on varied and expressive tone production violates "correct" European American instrumental and vocal technique. Bluing also distorts the diatonic scale, slightly lowering various scale degrees to produce "blue notes," which in effect sit in between the piano keys. Blue notes are not only (as is sometimes asserted) playing a flatted third (or fifth) over a major harmony, but bending a note in between the minor and major third, creating sounds that cannot readily be transcribed with standard notation. King Oliver was a master of bluing, "the best gut bucket man," creating "freak" wa-wa effects through manipulation of a variety of mutes, including cups, buckets, Coca-Cola bottles, and derby hats; his oft-imitated solo on "Dippermouth Blues" illustrates such effects perfectly.[52]

Bluing predates the emergence of the twelve-measure blues form in the early twentieth century. As early as the 1830s and 1840s, observers described field hollers and work songs as "extra-ordinarily wild and unaccountable" or "plaintive," matching later descriptions of the blues. Although no one knows for sure how the blues began, some trace its origins to folk music played on cotton plantations in the South which spread to lumber workers, stevedores on the docks of Southern seaports, railroad laborers, and roustabouts on riverboats.[53] According to Sunnyland Slim (Albert Luandrew), who grew up in Mississippi in the early 1900s, "They were singing the blues in Mississippi and Louisiana ever since there were colored peoples living there to my way of knowing . . . in cotton fields and in the prison camps and the levee camps." Religious and upper-class African Americans shunned it, the former because it was "the devil's music" and the latter because it was too primitive, not projecting the respectable, middle-class, and educated image necessary for blacks to advance in America.[54]

Observers reported hearing the blues in New Orleans around the turn of the century or before, and "nowhere in the country (except possibly in St. Louis) was there a stronger African-American blues piano tradition during this period," encompassing "slow drags" and (faster) "stomps."[55] Without bluing, jazz never would have developed; we would have been left with a sophisticated form of ragtime represented by James Reese Europe and other Northern bands. Thanks to uptown blacks as well as agricultural workers in the areas surrounding New Orleans, some of whom were trained by "professors" like James Humphrey, the Crescent City's blues sensibility combined with ragtime and other kinds of popular music to create jazz.

Improvisation

The African feature people most associate with jazz is improvisation. Improvisation provides the musician with a sense of freedom unavailable in the classical tradition, and for that reason alone it has political implications for African Americans. At the same time, improvisation is never entirely free, for the musician is only part of a larger whole encompassing a particular tradition, the other performers, and the audience. One can see improvisation's freedom within boundaries in the practices of African drumming. Drummers alter their playing in response to the movements of dancers, but when they do so they must meld their variations into the rhythms of the other drummers, because any individual changes alter the effect of the ensemble as a whole. Improvisation is also bounded by its context: "in an African musical event, everyone present plays a part, and from a musician's standpoint, making music is never simply a matter of creating fresh improvisations but a matter of expressing the sense of an occasion, the appropriateness at that moment of the part the music is contributing to the rest."[56] Performed at parties, parades, and funerals, New Orleans jazz was similarly functional, and musicians improvised in response to the constantly shifting imperatives of the moment.

Improvising New Orleans musicians generally did not create extended new melodies as later jazz musicians would but instead embellished the songs they played, like Bolden, who if he had "four, five, six notes or eight notes to one bar... put sixteen to it." However, contrary to those who have suggested that New Orleans musicians did not improvise, at times elaborate embellishments became virtually new melodies.[57] As Johnny St. Cyr put it, "You had to keep within the boundaries of the melody, but our old heads had great ability to beautify the number....

When we'd buy the regular stock arrangements, we would familiarize ourselves with the melody and then add what *we* wanted till we sounded like we had special orchestrations." In St. Cyr's view, the slow move away from the written melody began with clarinet embellishments and was taken up and expanded by cornetists like Freddie Keppard.[58] More important, New Orleans improvisation-as-embellishment more fully fit the African model of collective art than did later, more individualistic jazz soloing. In embellishing melodies, New Orleans musicians signified upon them: repetition with a signal difference.

Other musicians recall Bolden's on occasion improvising entirely new melodies that they called "head music" or "a make-up piece." According to Paul Domínguez, Bolden would transform a melody not by adding extra notes but by keeping the rhythm constant (or very similar) and changing the melody notes themselves; instead of the William Tell Over-ture's "Dum, duh duh dum, duh duh dum, dum dum dum," Bolden would play "Ya dah dah, da-da-da, dah dah dah, dee dee!" According to Albert Glenny, Bolden picked up his cornet until he "just play[ed] something," sometimes telling the musicians on the bandstand, "Watch me, I'm going to come up with something new," and expecting them to join in. Similarly, according to Morton, Freddie Keppard in 1907 "could play one chorus eight or ten different ways."[59]

"The Spanish Tinge": Caribbean and Mexican Influences

Through these African American devices—syncopation, polyphony, bluing, and improvisation—turn-of-the-century musicians in New Orleans signified on a variety of kinds of music and ultimately produced jazz. However, this process was actually set in motion earlier in the Caribbean, particularly Cuba and Saint-Domingue, and Mexico, and carried to New Orleans by black and Creole refugees.

According to Roger Abrahams, one should view the Crescent City "not as the bottom of the United States, but as the crown of the Caribbean," the hub of "Greater Afro-America," the two regions sharing carnival, work songs, voodoo, "songs of derision and praise," and the French Creole language. Even the quintessential New Orleans jazz funeral, featuring slow, sad music before the burial and joyous tunes afterward, has roots in the West Indies: in 1809 in Jamaica, one observer noted that during a funeral burial there was a "melancholy dirge," but that after the interment "the drums resound with a livelier beat, the song grows animated and cheerful; dancing and apparent merriment commences, and the remainder of the night is spent in feasting." Similarly, the mutual aid societies' marching bands that were so important in New Orleans can be traced back to their equivalents in early eighteenth-century Cuba, called *cabildos*.[60]

The most obvious sources of Caribbean culture in New Orleans were the Creoles and blacks from Saint-Domingue who fled to the Crescent City during the revolution there. In Saint-Domingue, French culture combined with Kongo-Angolan forms, central to black ways of being in the Americas. "Congolese patterns of movement and worship, drumming and dancing provide the lingua franca for all the Transatlantic Black World—a way of organizing and calling down the spirit." A number of dances in the city had "Congo" in the title, as did, of course, Congo Square. The "Kongo pose" (left hand on hip, right in the air) defines Mardi Gras parades, as do baton twirling and waving umbrellas, which have also been seen in West Africa.[61]

But the story is more complicated, because blacks and Creoles from Saint-Domingue did not come directly to New Orleans but first went to Cuba, the Caribbean country in which the West African musical influence remained the strongest. The strength of West African music in Cuba was bolstered by the popularity of black and mulatto musicians among whites: one writer in 1832 exclaimed with dismay, "The arts are in the hands of people of color!" In Cuba, African and European musical forms combined, Yoruba and other melodies interacting with Spanish folk music.

When French-speaking Creole and black refugees from Saint-Domingue arrived in Cuba, the mix became more complex, resulting in a blend of African, Spanish, and French music. In Cuba, "sailors' chanteys, church hymns, military marches, and, especially, social dances like the quadrille and contredanse" intertwined and became Africanized. Set (suite) dances like the French contredanse merged with local music to create the *contradanza habanera* (contradance from Havana; later simply the *habanera*), incorporating syncopation and the Latin Clavé rhythm (*one*-and-two-and-*three*-and-*four*). In the process the movements themselves were transformed into couple dances and given new titles like "Tu madre es conga" (Your Mother Is Congolese). As would happen later in the Crescent City, in the Caribbean the cutting-edge, racially mixed music began with the lower classes and only later, after much denunciation by elites, spread to the larger society. The intermixing continued as the nineteenth century progressed; by 1880, Cubans had incorporated saxophones and cornets, sometimes using improvisation, in the *danzón*.[62]

Cuban music, with its French, Spanish, and African influences, came to New Orleans with Creole and black refugees, but there were other Cuban connections to the Crescent City as well: the Onward Brass Band performed in Cuba in the 1880s; influential cornetist Manuel Perez had strong family connections to Cuba; bandleader Jack Laine's wife, Blanche Nunez, was of Cuban ancestry; and one of Laine's cornetists, Manuel Mello, visited Cuba often for his work in the sugar business. New Orleans musicians also worked with circuses traveling to Cuba, and black American soldiers, some of them musicians, stationed in Cuba in the Spanish American War later brought Cuban culture to the city as well. Some have traced the development of ragtime and jazz in New Orleans to the influence of the Cuban contradanza, habanera, and danzón.[63]

Cuban music also came to New Orleans by way of Mexico, which added its own ingredients. Habanera rhythms, renamed *danzas*, became popular in Mexico in the 1870s, and in 1884, a Havana band played in Mexico City, setting off a fashion in Mexico for Cuban dance music.[64] Mexicans also used Cuban style, itself influenced by African, Spanish, and French rhythms, to signify upon European waltzes and schottisches, Latinizing them.

This Cuban-Mexican compound then influenced American music, the "significant and largely unwritten history of Mexican and African-American interaction" centering in New Orleans. Mexico created a huge sensation when it sent its Eighth Regiment Cavalry Band, featuring more than sixty musicians, to New Orleans as part of the Cotton Centennial Exposition of 1884–85. A local publisher put out sheet music versions of the Eighth Regiment Band's most popular songs, and they sold thousands of copies, eventually influencing the music that would become jazz. At the turn of the century, one musician recalled a good number of Mexicans in the French Quarter, and important New Orleans Creole musicians had Mexican roots, including the Tios, "Yellow" Nunez, and "Chink" Martin. Latinos had an influence on black bands as well; Perlops Nunez allegedly led one of the first black bands in the city, and Jimmy "Spriggs" Palau played with Bolden.[65]

New Orleans's connections with the Caribbean and Mexico strongly influenced jazz and the dances accompanying it. Congo Square dances like the calinda and bamboula, sometimes seen as purely African, were in reality Caribbean blends of the African and the European; one observer noticed similarities between dances he had seen in Saint-Domingue before the revolution and performances in Congo Square ten years later, while George Washington Cable referred to the calinda as "a sort of vehement cotillion." According to Roger Abrahams, the habanera beat is at the center of the second line rhythm.[66]

Although the dances accompanying jazz had Caribbean roots, they were transformed in New Orleans. In general, dance forms tended to be treated with flexibility by people of color in America; according to Shane White and Graham White, "Even if the steps black dancers were using were familiar to whites, those steps were being performed at different speeds, combined in different ways, and executed with different movements of the torso and limbs." Lafcadio Hearn in 1876 saw Cincinnati roustabouts at a riverfront dive gradually transform a quadrille into a Virginia reel and then into a "juba dance," featuring call and response by the band.[67] In the Crescent City, Creoles set in motion a further Africanization of European set dances like the contradance, cotillion, mazurka, schottische, and waltz.

However, the most important Caribbean-European set dance in New Orleans jazz culture was the quadrille, danced in lower-class black clubs. According to Pops Foster, "The quadrille people were the rough gang, most of those guys were uptown." Though originally a formal, elite dance, the quadrille in the seediest clubs became the property of the working and underclasses, who further Africanized the form. Morton says that at "low class dance halls," the quadrille "was very low when they danced it," though it was not intrinsically so.[68]

The structures of such dances influenced the music accompanying them. African Americans used quadrilles to construct musical "patchworks," "joining together otherwise incongruous materials, or . . . using music in unorthodox ways." According to one scholar, "Quadrilles consumed melodies at a fearful rate, and it was common to make the music up out of bits of popular songs or snatches from opera arias." Some remember Bolden's turning quadrilles into ragtime, and Morton demonstrated on record how "an old quadrille" was transformed into the New Orleans standard "Tiger Rag."[69]

———

Whether derived directly from Africa or through the Caribbean and Mexico, African-based music gave New Orleans musicians the tools to transform European forms into African American music. Early anthropologists spoke of African "survivals" in the New World, but such a vocabulary is too passive. American slaves from the beginning actively chose to hold on to African culture as a way of affirming and shaping their identity within a dehumanizing environment, and their attempts were periodically refueled, as it were, by new slaves arriving from Africa.[70] In New Orleans, musicians, partly in response to audience demand, used African devices, filtered through the Caribbean and Mexico, to signify on European forms, transforming them into jazz. This process began in the black church, to which we now turn.

Shouting: The Black Church and the African American Aesthetic

In the black church, as in African religious ceremonies, "music tends to undergird everything else that is done."[71] The church played a key role in the development of jazz, preserving and transmitting an African-based musical aesthetic that incorporated and transformed European conventions. Black churchgoers used polyphony, syncopation, and bluing to transform sacred music through individual and collective improvisation.

The most obvious African feature of black church music is its polyphony, rooted in the practice of "lining out." Begun by whites to teach hymns to illiterate church members, in this ritual the preacher intoned a line of a hymn, which was then sung by the congregation. Black congregations, however, in the African tradition did not literally repeat the line but instead changed the melody or rhythm slightly, creating an overlapping texture of melodic lines sung at different tempos or meters.[72] In 1867 one observer described such a process at a black church:

There is no singing in parts, as we understand it, and yet no two appear to be singing the same thing—the leading singer starts the words of each verse, often improvising, and the others, who "base" him, as it is called, strike in with the refrain, or even join in the solo, when the words are familiar. When the "base" begins, the leader often stops, leaving his words to be guessed at, or it may be they are taken up by one of the other singers. And the "basers" themselves seem to follow their own whims, beginning when they please and leaving off when they please.

Alternatively, preacher and congregation or even members of the congregation engaged in call and response. Individuals later incorporated such call and response into their solo singing—once a white man was walking home and thought he heard a group of black workers singing, but it was in fact (in his words) "one man, who was digging a ditch, and at the same time giving out lines and singing them at the top of his voice."[73]

Bluing was central to black church music as well, as singers used their voices in ways that startled whites. In 1866 one observer of a New Orleans black church service saw "the most singular and impressive sights imaginable, consisting of weird songs, incoherent, irreverent shouts, mingled with violent contortions, wails and moans, quaint prayers and responses." Even sympathetic whites found that such "contortions" could not be precisely notated because of their flexible use of pitch; in spirituals, "tones are frequently employed which we have no musical characters to represent . . . these tones are variable in pitch, ranging through an entire interval on different occasions." "Like birds," blacks were known "to strike sounds that cannot be precisely represented by the gamut," featuring "slides from one note to another, and turns and cadences not in articulated notes," creating "odd turns made in the throat."[74]

Singers "distorted" notes in two ways. First, they utilized blue notes, typically pitched below the standard notes of the diatonic scale. Though observers heard them as wrong or strange, these tones represented the introduction to whites of a blues aesthetic that remains central to popular music today. Second, singers evoked the blues by bending notes, employing melisma ("vocal contortions to which the simplest words seemed" to be subject), the singing of a number of notes on a single syllable.[75]

Observers also noticed unusual rhythms, "apparent irregularities in the time, which it is no less difficult to express accurately."[76] Such "irregularities" could refer to a variable tempo, as when a congregation slowed down or accelerated a particular melody with the emotional flow of the service, or to syncopations that obscured the downbeat, making the time seem less distinct by creating polymeters or polyrhythms.

Using polyphony, syncopation, and bluing, black churchgoers spun limitless variations on sacred songs. Each rendition was unique, the "song" a collectively created performance that might never be sung the same way twice because it was dependent on the makeup of the congregation, their mood, and their interaction with one another. One ex-slave described the creation of spirituals as a process of collective improvisation: "We'd all be at the 'prayer house' de Lord's day, and de white preacher he'd splain de word and read whar Ezekial done say— Dry bones gwine to lib ergin. And, honey, de Lord would come a'shinin' thoo dem pages and revive dis ole nigger's heart, and I'd jump up dar and den and holler and shout and sing and pat, and dey would all cotch de words and I'd sing it to some ole shout song I'd heard 'em sing from

Africa, and dey'd all take it up, and keep a'addin' to it, and den it would be a spiritual." This process continued into the early twentieth century, as one can see from a report of a church service from that period: "Up from the depths of some 'sinner's' remorse and imploring came a pitiful plea . . . sobbed in musical cadence. From somewhere in the bowed gathering another voice improvised a response . . . then other voices joined the answer, shaping it into a musical phrase; and so, before our ears, as one might say, from this molten metal of music a new song was smithed out, composed then and there by no one in particular and by everyone in general."[77]

The songs resulting from such transformation were often characterized as "patchworks." One observer described spirituals as "fragments, caught here and there, and pieced into mosaic, hap-hazard as they come," "patchwork[s], made up from the most striking part[s] of popular Methodist hymns." Rather than seamless artifices in the style of Isaac Watts, such songs were makeshift constructions built from standard hymns and lines of prayer or the Bible, lengthened with often spontaneous choruses referring to everyday life. A hymnal written by African Methodist Episcopal minister Richard Allen in 1801 codified this practice using "wandering refrains," "refrain verses or short choruses attached at random to orthodox hymn stanzas." The materials for such patchworks went beyond hymns; one observer in Alabama in 1894 saw congregants incorporating plantation songs into the mix.[78]

These songs' hodgepodge construction, which a former slave described as a "mixtery," illustrates a larger African American aesthetic principle: the juxtaposition of apparently diverse elements. West African music combines a range of timbres in a manner that Europeans considered discordant, just as they were startled by the way West African textiles or slaves' summer clothing combined apparently incompatible colors, fabrics, and textures.[79] Such juxtaposition changes each element by putting it into a foreign context where it "sounds" against another, producing resonances and dissonances that put both sources in a new light.

The improvised, patchwork quality of black church music called into question the idea of aesthetic purity and wholeness. One black singer, when asked by a WPA interviewer how many stanzas there were in his song, replied, "Until you get tired." As White and White put it, "For large numbers of slaves, a song was never a stable text and an unvarying tune; it was a frame to be filled as the moment dictated."[80]

The Africanization of European sacred music questioned the idea of ethnic or racial purity as well. Spirituals were often denigrated as white hymns with distorted words or melodies, a judgment that ignores the fact that when black "sorrow songs" borrowed from European sources, they radically transformed them. Melville Herskovits described a recording from Trinidad in which a hymn is played straight and then Africanized through rhythmic changes. In a 1939 recording of Trinidad Shouters singing "Jesus, Lover of My Soul," one can see the Africanization of a hymn. The performance begins in a droning, straight-ahead manner, but slowly rhythms and counterrhythms, falsetto cry, and call and response are added, creating a new, ecstatic performance.[81]

Another spiritual performance, "What a Friend We Have in Jesus," recorded by Herskovits the same month, reveals a similar signifying process. The Trinidadian musicians, led by Henry Williams, are Spiritual Baptists (Shouters), who combine Protestantism with syncretic, Yorisha-derived Orisha worship. The performance begins with two men and two women singing the hymn in unison, yet soon the two men start scatting using an ever-changing vocabulary of syllables. With an emphasis on beats one and three, phrases like "rum-ba, ruma-ba," constitute a percussive accompaniment that competes for our attention with the hymn sung by the women. Soon the syllables are replaced by a rhythmic groaning called "trumping" or "hocketing," a "typically African feature" that sounds like a drum with flexible pitch, "induc[ing] . . . light-headedness and then spirit possession" while subtly shifting the emphasis to beats two and four, creating syncopation. One can still hear the hymn, but the African accompaniments threaten to overtake it, the syncopated, percussive scat syllables signifying on the stolid renditions of the words.[82] Though not recorded in New Orleans, "What a Friend We Have in Jesus" illustrates the African American "communal re-creation" of sacred songs, in which the new (European) is incorporated and the old (African) continually reaffirmed.[83]

Jazzin' God

Late-nineteenth- and early-twentieth-century musicians in New Orleans took these African devices from the church and applied them to other European music, setting in motion the creation of jazz. According to Kid Ory's wife, everyone went to hear church music because "that's where it really started." The music of the Sanctified Church was particularly important for jazz because unlike other denominations its services featured musical instruments, taking their cue from the 150th psalm: "Praise him with the sound of the trumpet; praise him with the psaltery and harp;

praise him with the timbrel and dance; praise him with stringed instruments and organs." As Pops Foster explains, "The Holiness church was the only one that didn't consider music to be sinful. Their music was something. They'd clap their hands and bang a tambourine and sing. Sometimes they had a piano player, and he'd really play a whole lot of jazz." Mahalia Jackson described what she heard at the Sanctified Church near her home in the late 1910s and early 1920s: "These people had no choir and no organ. They used the drum, the cymbal, the tambourine, and the steel triangle. Everybody in there sang and they clapped and stomped their feet and sang with their whole bodies. They had a beat, a powerful beat, a rhythm we held on to from slavery days, and their music was so strong and expressive it used to bring tears to my eyes."[84]

The sacred music that influenced jazz was not confined to the church. Plantation workers sang spirituals, and urban slaves utilized psalms or hymns as work songs. One observer in Richmond, Virginia, told of workers' singing psalms in a tobacco factory that, akin to the Funky Butt, used to be a church: "Here also fine psalmody may be heard, as of yore, and the organ loft is still occupied by a choir, but one whose music *ceases* on Sabbaths and Holy days."[85]

Regardless of where they first heard it, early jazz musicians drew on African American religious music. Bolden played a key role in incorporating the sounds of the church to preserve and disseminate African-based music; according to Bud Scott, "each Sunday, Bolden went to church and that's where he got his idea of jazz music." Ory and others recalled Bolden in 1904 or 1905 leaving church "swinging": "on those old, slow, low down blues, he had a moan in his cornet that went all through you, just like you were in church or something."[86] Bolden's music was inevitably described as new and exciting by listeners, and this exhilaration came from his mixture of the sacred and the secular.

Jazz musicians like Bolden used religious songs as part of their repertory, playing spirituals like "Ride On, King," "I'm Going When Jesus Calls Me," "Nearer My God to Thee," "What a Friend We Have in Jesus," and "When the Saints Go Marching In." Oliver, whose father was a Baptist minister, took hymns and made songs out of them, or played them in tandem with "some real low down dirty blues," much to the dismay of his religious wife. Chris Kelly, the famous bluesy cornetist, always ended his performances with the hymn "When the Saints Go Marching In," played, contrary to modern practice, as a "sacred song"—slowly.[87]

More important, jazz's style was influenced by the church. Many black musicians, including Bolden, Kelly, Dave Perkins, Sam Morgan, and Jim Robinson, developed their bluesy styles, with bent notes and growls, in

151

part by exposure to the music of the Baptist or Sanctified church.[88] As one musician put it, "They sang the blues in church; the words were religious, but it was the blues," and it was this blueslike quality, with its intense kinetic effects, that was new in the music of Bolden and others. Even when playing secular material, Oliver drew on the church's African aesthetic; according to cornetist Mutt Carey, with various mutes Oliver could "make his horn sound like a holy-roller meeting"; "jazzin' God" was how one musician characterized such influence. Kelly was also known for using a wailing "wa-wa" sound on his famous bluesy rendition of "Careless Love."[89]

The church also contributed to jazz's rhythms. According to George Lewis, Kelly, "the best blues player I ever heard," took his ability to count off a tune in a swinging fashion from the church: "He kept the tempo with his heel and toe. He got that in church, that's where he got that beat. Just like what we used to call 'coonjaille.'" Musicians gravitated to church music because, in the words of Johnny St. Cyr, "those Baptist rhythms were similar to the jazz rhythms, and the singing was very much on the blues side. You could dance as well as shout to those rhythms." "Swinging like crazy," Baptist churches featured bluesy "jubilee singing," consisting of spirituals sung in rhythmic fashion with hand clapping, often with drums, piano, or even cornet or trombone. Another musician, Paul Barnes, has highlighted syncopation, with the congregation clapping on the offbeat, as the feature that jazz took from the Baptist Church. As he put it, "The pure races hit on the beat, but the mixed races, the New Orleans people, hit on the after beat."[90]

Jazz musicians drew upon the physicality and passion of church music to excite audiences. Cornetist Kelly, growing up on Deer Range Plantation, got no encouragement for his interest in music from his parents, who were religious Christians, yet he "played everything in the sacred style." According to his brother Ben, when he played his signature blues "Careless Love," "all the women say, 'Oh, preach, preacher, preach, preacher, play that *Careless Love*.' . . . I'm telling you . . . them women— they open their house and say, 'Oh come on, preach, preacher!'"[91] On the one hand, this is his religious parents' nightmare—seducing women with his "preaching" cornet. Yet from another perspective, like the singers in the Sanctified Church, Kelly drew on the power of African-based music to excite and stir the soul.

Ironically, then, though Baptists railed against secular music and its associated gambling, dancing, and promiscuity, the music played in the black church and the "devil's music" heard in dens of iniquity shared many musical features: polyphony (including antiphony and

heterophony), syncopation, melisma, blue notes, improvisation, gut-
tural tone, and a connection with bodily movement. As Hurston put it
in her study of the Sanctified Church, "the tunes from the street and
church change places often."[92]

Bolden took the African-influenced music of the Baptist "Holy Roller"
church he attended, transformed it by incorporating secular influences,
and brought it into the public square. In Ory's words, "He'd hear these
songs and he would change them a little," "put[ting] his own feeling" in
the religious music he played; as we have seen, this practice is very much
in keeping with spirituals and black church music in general, which continually transformed hymns and other materials. Danny Barker described
(or imagined) Bolden mixing blues and hymns, as if in a battle between
God and the devil. Bolden signified on church music to help create something both European and African, and his immense popularity spread
the music, even if he rarely, if ever, played for whites.[93]

"Voodoo Rhythms": Creoles and Religious Music

The black church influenced Creole musicians as well, through Bolden
and their observation of black church services.[94] But Creole religious
music may have also contributed to jazz through the music accompanying voodoo ceremonies. Admittedly, the evidence for this is sketchy.
Early opponents of jazz tied it to voodoo as a way of discrediting it, as
in a 1921 *Ladies' Home Journal* article titled "Does Jazz Put the Sin in
Syncopation?" "Jazz originally was the accompaniment of the voodoo
dancer, stimulating the half-crazed barbarian to the vilest deeds. The
weird chant, accompanied by the syncopated rhythm of the voodoo in-
vokers, has also been employed by other barbaric people to stimulate
brutality and sensuality."

One is tempted to dismiss any link between voodoo and jazz as merely
an attempt to disparage the music as barbaric, but recent writers have
hinted at connections between the two not based in racism. Voodoo
came to New Orleans, its "birthplace . . . in North America," from Haiti,
where it is part of everyday life and "even the songs of revolution were
keyed across the island by voodoo rhythms," uniting opponents of colonial rule. Voodoo is a syncretic religion, developed in Haiti from a variety
of African religions and Catholicism—"Africa *reblended*"; in New Orleans,
Catholic songs and elements like altars, incense, candles, and holy water were similarly combined with African customs. According to Jason
Berry, "local voodoo pockets" kept the slaves' African heritage alive after

the end of Congo Square celebrations, continuing the dances in ceremonies "in woods, on bayous and at Lake Pontchartrain, with torch-lit
gatherings."[95]

Important Creole musicians also had ties to voodoo, a woman-cen-
tered religion, often through female practitioners. Mamie Desdunes, Jelly
Roll Morton's piano teacher, was a "voodoo priestess," while his godmother, Eulalie Echo, practiced the religion, and Morton himself, according to a contemporary, had "tendencies toward voodoo." Influential
bassist Alcide "Slow Drag" Pavageau was reportedly the nephew of famed
voodoo practitioner Marie Laveau.[96]

Various features of African American music and dance have been connected to voodoo as well. Folklorists John and Alan Lomax found fundamental similarities between "shouts" in Louisiana and Haitian voodoo
rituals, including a ring moving counterclockwise, call and response,
and a gradual increase in intensity culminating in trancelike states. Blues
songs passed on voodoo beliefs, making frequent reference to voodoo
and conjure.[97]

One should not overstate the case for voodoo's connection to jazz,
because only a small number of people actively practiced it, yet for Creoles it performed functions similar to those of the black church. As in
the black church, in voodoo ceremonies women played an important
role in African-based music making. The use of African musical devices
and ecstatic movements brought on by spirit possession connect Creole
voodoo ceremonies with the black Sanctified Church as well: both represent arenas where African music was preserved and synthesized with
European culture, and both were environments where New Orleanians
of color could promote solidarity through music.

The two were, of course, quite different. The black church incorporated European culture through hymns, while voodoo did the same
through Catholic ritual. (There were some reports that Baptist and
Methodist hymns were used in voodoo, but the descriptions show
singing mostly in French or Creole.)[98] But even though black Protestants
would be appalled at being compared to voodoo practitioners, whom
they would consider disciples of the devil, they had more in common
than they might like to admit.

Ragtime

Though crucial for the development of African American music, Creole and black religious music was confined at first to their respective

segments of the population. However, in the 1890s African devices, nurtured in the church, reached a wide and diverse audience through ragtime. Ragtime arose when musicians and composers like Scott Joplin used African devices to signify on a variety of musical styles and forms including vaudeville, minstrelsy, and, most important, the march. As a young man Joplin had wandered the South, hearing a variety of folk songs; he later played cornet and led a brass band, playing overtures, marches, and waltzes, and syncopating classical melodies for audiences. Taking its multipart form from marches (and perhaps European classical dances), ragtime was a hybrid form of music, with ragtime bands in the 1890s playing "overtures, potpourris of traditional dance tunes," "standard marches," cakewalks and "coon songs."[99] In this sense it represented a continuation of the "patchwork" aesthetic found in the black church.

Ragtime's most notable feature was syncopation, its distinctive feeling the result of superimposing syncopated rhythms on top of the march's duple pulse, creating tension between the ground rhythm and offbeats. For most people, ragging meant syncopation; indeed, the name of the music is perhaps derived from this use, i.e., "ragged time." In fact, music publishers routinely issued songs in regular and ragged form, the latter syncopating the melody. Teachers and instruction manuals taught students to rag any kind of tune by "incorporat[ing] . . . a standard ragtime boom-chick bass and . . . insert[ing] . . . regular right-hand syncopations."[100]

Recognizing syncopation's subversion of the downbeat, opponents attacked it. According to critics, while in moderation ragtime's syncopation was acceptable, in excess it "overstimulates" and is addictive and unhealthy. "Ragtime," wrote one, "is syncopation gone mad, and its victims, in my opinion, can only be treated successfully, like the dog with rabies, with a dose of lead." Its "unnatural rhythms" were said to disrupt body and mind, destabilizing the steady pulse and heart rhythms necessary for health.[101]

Opponents of the music also associated it with African Americans and attacked it with racist stereotypes. To its critics ragtime utterly lacked intellect and was founded instead on a "primeval conception of music, whose basis was a rhythm that appealed to the physical rather than to the mental senses." One writer called ragtime "symbolic of the primitive morality and perceptible moral limitations of the negro type," warning that through its influence, "America is falling prey to the collective soul of the negro."[102]

Critics associated ragging with race mixing, and they were right to do so. Through ragtime, syncopation disrupted the traditional course of American melodies, Africanizing them. However, although early ragtime was a means for African Americans to influence white culture, its communicatory and emancipatory potential was limited, particularly in its solo piano form. First, while it relied on syncopation, some of its practitioners accepted Eurocentric models of music and art; Joplin strove to have ragtime accepted as "high" culture and wrote larger forms like operas to make him "legitimate." Ragtime thus did not connect with the blues and other African American genres as centrally as jazz would. Second, ragtime eschews improvisation, which is central to jazz as a vehicle for self-expression and freedom. Finally, much early ragtime was centered on the home and the nuclear family. Before the phonograph, it was disseminated through the sale of sheet music meant to be played in people's homes and thus did not have the public impact that, say, a marching band could. These features limited ragtime's potential to express the more blues and folk based music that was being played by Bolden and thus hindered its appeal to the black masses.[103]

But if ragtime itself had limited emancipatory potential, later musicians took its distinctive syncopation, its "ragging," and used it to signify on American themes and melodies, transforming them into jazz. In New Orleans, as Creole musician Lawrence Duhé put it, "they ragged all the pieces"—cakewalks, marches, popular songs, hymns, and classical compositions. Pioneering white bandleader Jack Laine even recalled ragging songs like "The Stars and Stripes Forever": "We'd tear it up . . . We'd rag it up. . . . I mean as far as we could go."[104]

Ragging Ragtime

Black church music and ragtime provided musicians with a set of African-based signifying devices—improvisation, bluing, syncopation, and polyphony—that they then heightened and applied to ragtime itself and to brass band music. From Buddy Bolden to King Oliver, musicians played classic rags and popular ragtime songs but further Africanized them, transforming them into jazz.[105]

A comparison of three versions of Joplin's "Maple Leaf Rag" illustrates this metamorphosis of ragtime into jazz. The first, by the United States Marine Band in 1906, foregrounds the piece's most European features, omitting improvisation entirely.[106] The band reproduces the written melody's syncopation, and there is a bit of call and response, but the ensemble overwhelmingly emphasizes beats 1 and 3 and plays mostly in unison. Time is insistent and stiff, with little fluidity, creating a martial feeling ideal for propelling soldiers to march in lockstep.

The second version, recorded in 1925 by Albert "Abbie" Brunies, a white cornetist, presents a marked contrast with the Marine Band's rendition. A New Orleanian, Brunies brings out the more African features of the piece, particularly its syncopation, with the drum emphasizing beats 2 and 4 and Brunies accenting the upbeats. The piece is also rife with polyphony, cornet and clarinet in dialogue with one another, and the musicians take improvised breaks and (perhaps reflecting the later time period) short solos. Although the performance's feeling is light and fluid, the tempo is much faster than that of the other two versions, perhaps in response to the Original Dixieland Jazz Band's frenetic records; this tempo does not allow for the relaxed manipulation of the time that would have provided a multitude of rhythmic levels.

In the third version, Jelly Roll Morton in 1938 brings to fruition the African American potential of "Maple Leaf Rag," particularly its syncopation. Using a relaxed tempo, Morton continuously plays with the time, beginning phrases at unpredictable points in the measure, creating the antithesis of the Marine Band's insistent, military downbeats. His manipulation of the beat produces a sense of continual surprise as phrases vie with one another for attention, generating a collage that never settles into a fixed picture and a feeling of openness absent from the other versions. Despite the piano's fixed pitches, Morton evokes the blues by accenting flatted thirds and by sliding up to melody notes using glissandi, the pianist's equivalent of a blues player's bent notes. Profusely signifying, Morton emphasizes the features of the piece that most decenter American music—syncopation, polyphony, and bluing—evoking unexpected modes of feeling in the listener.

Ragging Europe

Jazz's destabilization of European and American culture can also be seen in Morton's ragging of the "Miserere" from Verdi's *Il Trovatore*, a staple of brass bands in the late nineteenth and early twentieth centuries.[107] He first plays the composition "straight," in waltz time, putting the accent on the first of each of the three beats of the measure. Played rubato (without a steady beat, in a ruminating fashion) in the Romantic manner, the performance is melancholy, befitting the title, yet delicate and refined. One imagines the Romantic poet in his drawing room, contemplating the vale of tears called life.

In a second, "jazz" performance, Morton radically transforms the piece while retaining significant portions of the melody. One first notices the livelier tempo and shift from waltz time into 4/4, but Morton Africanizes the piece as well. After a brief introduction, the pianist vamps for four measures on a syncopated, Latin-tinged riff before launching into a stride style, single notes alternating with chords accented on 2 and 4 (oom-pah). Later he introduces the stop-time "breaks" so characteristic of New Orleans jazz, in which the left-hand rhythm stops and allows the right to insert a comment before continuing.

In short, Morton transforms melancholy into affirmation and rubato ruminations into rousing stomp (indeed, Morton stomps his foot as he plays). Through the "break" he also introduces African American call and response, creating an internal dialogue in addition to his conversation with European high culture. The beauty of Verdi's melody is still present, yet it has been hijacked into another musical tradition, as if to say, "The 'classical' tradition belongs to us as well, and we can use it to create African-American music." Thus does Morton illustrate the manifold ways jazz signified upon European culture, musically inserting people of color into its center.

"Sousa Played in Ragtime"

Such musical signifying culminated in New Orleans's brass bands. A Paul Laurence Dunbar poem, "The Colored Band," speaks of "Sousa played in ragtime," but it was not only marches that were ragged, for brass band musicians also Africanized hymns, spirituals, ragtime, popular songs, and nineteenth-century ballroom dances (waltzes, mazurkas, polkas, schottisches, and quadrilles).[108] New Orleanians of color gravitated to marching bands because, consistent with the African tradition, the ensembles set music to movement and displayed a blues aesthetic through "timbral contrast between various sections." Through the brass band, spirituals and ragtime left the church and the parlor, respectively, and strode into the public square, accompanying "circuses, carnivals, minstrel and medicine shows, political rallies, churches, picnics, dances, athletic contests, holiday gatherings." Rural towns had brass bands as well, some consisting of (as one newspaper described them) "respectable colored men of our town." According to cornetist Punch Miller, brass bands in the country played the same marches and hymns as did New Orleans ensembles, and just as well as the city bands, the only difference being that they played on dirt roads instead of pavement.[109]

Dating back to the Revolution, the American brass band was actually a small marching ensemble featuring brass, woodwinds, and percussion, ultimately derived from seventeenth-century European military bands. By the late 1860s, African Americans and Creoles began forming their own marching bands, typically featuring about ten instruments: two or three cornets, a snare drum, a bass drum, and trombones, clarinets, baritone horns, alto horns, and (less often) saxophones.[110] The brass band was poised for polyphony: over the drums' percussive base, cornets blared the melody while other horns wove rhythmically accented counterpoint.

The marching band transformed its European American sources, but this process took time. Early Creole brass band musicians tended to be classically trained; some of their fathers or brothers had light enough skin to play in white brass bands, and until about 1900 Creole bands probably sounded little different from countless other American brass bands. When asked whether the Excelsior Band read music, Albert Glenny and Leonard Bechet answered, "Yes sir, oh, yes, sure! Yeah," with great emphasis, as if to stress the respectable, "legitimate" nature of the venerable band in contrast to the later ratty ones. However, as the Creole brass bands began to accept black (Baptist or Methodist) musicians, albeit reluctantly at first, their sound became more ratty and African. Brass bands were thus a key site for the coming together of Creole and black musicians; as cornetist Wooden Joe Nicholas put it, "Brass bands were mixed bands. Creole and uptown in a brass band—they were solid. They were one, Joe Oliver and Manuel Perez, see?"[111]

The mixture of Creoles and blacks in the brass bands changed the music as the earthier, more "gutbucket" style and improvisation of the black dance bands became intertwined with European music. In a superficial sense, black marching bands carried on the European tradition, allowing blacks to integrate themselves into American culture, but they simultaneously commented upon it and altered it. Rather than simply reproducing the vast European and American sources they drew on, brass bands transformed them, signifying upon them through rhythmic and tonal alterations. Early brass bands experimented with syncopation, shifting the accent from beats 1 and 3 to 2 and 4, and these innovations were "absorbed and altered" by ragtime piano players, finally reentering the marching band in standardized form. Pianists like Morton then moved jazz forward by playing syncopated brass band rhythms in the left hand, as one can see in his two renditions of "Maple Leaf Rag."[112]

The brass band's sound changed as well, for musicians incorporated "dirty" blues sounds—bent notes, growls, and smears—and a "hoarse and crying" tone came to characterize New Orleans jazz; the use of such sounds was encouraged when brass bands played hymns in Protestant churches.[113] Creoles also had to play the blues in the brass band, altering these musicians' sounds.

Improvisation transformed brass band music as well. Early bands played exclusively from written scores; one musician tried improvising in his father's brass band and was told "he did not have music like that in his band and if he did it again he would be sent home." But sometime in the early twentieth century, a number of groups started featuring improvisation, called "head music" or "ratty" music, with the first cornetist playing the melody straight and the second, the "hot man," polyphonically adding embellishments or harmony parts. In addition, new kinds of brass bands arose—"ratty" or "barrelhouse" bands—that played entirely by ear, performing hymns and popular songs rather than the complicated "heavy marches" of the traditional brass bands. Bolden himself formed a nonreading brass band, helping to bring the black music style he pioneered into the European-oriented ensembles, though he seemed not to put a high priority on the group.[114]

The brass bands' transformation of the European "legitimate" tradition through African devices can be seen in a Baby Dodds recording, featuring legendary trumpeter Bunk Johnson, of "Maryland, My Maryland." Although recorded in 1944, it features New Orleans musicians from jazz's formative period and illustrates the sometimes tense juxtaposition of the European and African American traditions. On the one hand, the band heavily accents the downbeats, giving the piece an insistent, heavy feeling little different from that of traditional marches. Yet Johnson plays the melody with slight upbeat accents, syncopating it, and lags behind the beat, while George Lewis's clarinet and Jim Robinson's trombone weave countermelodies, creating a polyphonic texture. Though the heavy European marching beat clashes with the decentering syncopation and polyphony, later musicians would more fully bring the two traditions together.

High Society: Signifying Performances

Many styles of music played in turn-of-the-century New Orleans brass bands and other ensembles had their counterparts elsewhere in the country. As early as 1850, according to one report, a trumpeter in a New York City nightclub played in a hot, perhaps bluesy style, accompanied by an African-influenced drummer: "You cannot *see* the red-hot knitting-needles spirted [sic] out by that red-faced trumpeter...which needles aforesaid penetrating the tympanum, pierce through and through your brain without remorse. Nor can you perceive the frightful mechanical contortions of the bass-drummer as he sweats and deals his blows on every side, in all violation of the laws of rhythm."

Long before Morton, musicians in other regions signified on pieces like the "Miserere" from *Il Trovatore*. Indeed, many practices attributed to New Orleans musicians were widespread in the eighteen thousand or so brass bands that existed in early-twentieth-century America: bands associated with fraternal lodges that played at members' funerals, playing slow dirges to the cemetery and lighter music on the way back, calling bandmasters "professors," battling bands, and improvisation (or at least embellishment).[115]

What was relatively unique to New Orleans was the melding of the blues and ragtime in the small ensemble. In most of the country at the time jazz developed, groups were getting larger, growing from an average of sixteen to eighteen members in 1890 to twenty in 1910. But in New Orleans, the trend moved in the opposite direction, partly because there were so many jobs for too few musicians that they split into smaller groups.[116]

When New Orleans musicians played brass band pieces in small ensembles, reinterpreting them through the black blues tradition, the result was jazz. Bolden is again a key figure, for he took the blues-influenced ragtime of the brass band and played it in a small group. Weaving its way into the fabric of everyday life, this new music graced parades, picnics, dances, and funerals.

The small group transformation of ragtime through the blues tradition, hauling it onto the streets where it marched, can be seen in a performance of "High Society Rag" by King Oliver's Creole Jazz Band, featuring a young Louis Armstrong. This tune defined New Orleans jazz, for as Lee Collins put it, "at that time when you heard a clarinet play 'High Society' you didn't ask him where he was from. You knew he was from New Orleans. As a kid I found bands playing the tune, and it was the first standard I learnt. Creoles wouldn't come to a dance then unless you could perform 'High Society.'"[117] First performed as a slow, "grand" march by brass bands like the Excelsior and Onward, it was transformed into jazz by younger musicians. One of the sections features a standard clarinet solo thought for many years to be originated by the Creole clarinetist Alphonse Picou. The piece's transformation through the use of

Figure 14. King Oliver's Creole Jazz Band, with Armstrong kneeling in front. The other members are Honoré Dutrey on trombone, Baby Dodds on drums, Lillian Hardin on piano, Bill Johnson on banjo, and Johnny Dodds on clarinet. (Photo courtesy of the William Ransom Hogan Archive, Tulane University.)

African devices—most prominently its "patchwork" aesthetic, mixing disparate styles—can be seen in Oliver's rendition.

The performance begins with a military-style fanfare in unison, heralding the origins of jazz in the street parade. The band then breaks into eight measures of polyphony, the clarinet playing the melody and cornets interjecting syncopated figures while the trombone plays walking bass lines. Four measures of a minor-key marchlike melody follows, with somewhat fewer comments by the cornets. The band then repeats the previous sixteen measures, though of course not exactly given the improvisatory nature of the music. Thirty-two bars of highly polyphonic music follows, with the cornets taking the melody and clarinet paraphrasing the solo that is to follow.

A brief (four-measure) fanfare signals a shift in the performance. What follows is a melody with a kind of national anthem feel to it, performed in unison. Elements of jazz enter in by means of a clarinet break after sixteen measures; the melody begins to repeat, but after eight measures, Armstrong's cornet improvisations take over, supplanting the theme. What follows is eight measures of a severe-sounding march-type melody, played in unison. The exaggerated nature of the playing, with trills for filigree, suggests a kind of parody of "serious" music. Finally, the clarinet plays the famous Picou solo with polyphony and smearing trombone breaks.[118]

In this remarkable performance, African elements burst through the European march form. Throughout, the rendition incorporates elements of the blues, most notably in Oliver's raspy, "dirty" cornet sound and his bent notes and smears. His throaty tone exemplifies a key element of blues-influenced music: its invocation of the human voice, even through musical instruments. Musicians like Oliver used instruments designed for the orchestral and marching band traditions to Africanize American culture: "Trumpets and trombones . . . sang, grunted, and growled in the hands of New Orleans jazz players. Smears, slides, and quavers were all indicators of a musical attack that differed significantly from the formal European approach."[119]

Oliver and his band conjure up the European American military march tradition, with its joyous fanfares and serious, downbeat-oriented melodies, only to make that tradition their own by recasting the piece as a polyphonic jazz performance. The interaction between blues-oriented black music and the Creoles' more European sounds is embodied in the group itself, including as it does both blacks and Creoles. Yet despite the varieties of cultures with which the performance engages, it holds together as a unified work of jazz.

"High Society," then, is a classic example of signifying: Oliver integrates himself into, comments upon, and alters mainstream culture, amplifying ragtime's syncopation and polyphony and transforming it by means of the blues and improvisation. But the musicians also signify through their juxtaposition of sometimes disparate elements into a musical patchwork or collage. Many standard New Orleans jazz tunes were similarly patched together from a variety of sources and genres. Like spirituals, tunes at this time "were subject to various modifications, including disassembly, reassembly in different order, and insertion into other pieces as beginnings, middles, or endings. They sometimes crossed subcultures, where they were adapted to different words and stories and played in markedly different styles."[120]

Such collages reject monologic unity because each part signifies on the others. In this respect, Oliver's rendition of "High Society" evokes what Bakhtin calls "carnivalized literature," particularly the "multi-styled and hetero-voiced" "serio-comical" form: "Characteristic of these genres are a multi-toned narration [note the possible musical image of 'tone'], the mixing of high and low, serious and comic; they make wide use of inserted genres—letters, found manuscripts, retold dialogues, parodies on the high genres, parodically reinterpreted citations; in some of them we observe a mixing of prosaic and poetic speech." By exaggerating the serious-sounding march motif in the middle of "High Society," Oliver changes its meaning, presenting it as a parody in relation to the rest of the performance but simultaneously claiming it for the New Orleans tradition.[121] Oliver's signifying through collage challenges racial purity by calling into question the monologic European or American realm of culture from which people of color are excluded.

Interestingly, "High Society" was written by a white man, Porter Steele, an undergraduate member of the Yale mandolin club, and was subsequently taken up by a duo of vaudeville banjoists (Ruby Brooks and E. J. Denton), who commissioned an arrangement of it for a large ensemble. Jazz cornetist King Oliver reveals the tune's roots in popular song, vaudeville, and marches and simultaneously signifies upon those traditions, making it into something new: jazz. This is not a "synthesis" but a dialogue and a transformation: not the liberal melting pot but an African American appropriation of an art object from the dominant culture that simultaneously stakes a claim on that culture, bursting into "high society."

Signifying, then, illustrates once again New Orleans jazz's "impurity," its ability to draw on and transform a variety of kinds of music from different ethnic groups. By not melting them down but allowing them to coexist, New Orleans jazz called into question the idea of racial purity itself. Signifying blurred racial boundaries, "travers[ing] the space between self and other," and at the same time represented an assertion by African Americans, a means of challenging and transforming a resistant culture.

FIVE

Dissemination: Morton, La Rocca, and Armstrong

From its beginnings, jazz leaped beyond the boundaries of the Crescent City. Train excursions, sometimes sponsored by organizations like longshoremen's clubs, spread the sounds to surrounding areas like LaPlace, Houma, Pointe a la Hache, Thibodaux, Baton Rouge, and Shreveport. In a typical route, passengers boarded a train on Esplanade Avenue which crossed the river on barges, hooked up to engines, and pulled into Gretna, whence it embarked upon its westward journey. For a dollar, usually on a Sunday, a passenger from New Orleans could travel with the band and listen to the musicians hold forth from the baggage car. At each stop, the band entertained locals at a pavilion near the train station or at nightclubs in the black section of town. Riverboats also spread the music. When Baby Dodds worked on the riverboats, the bands mostly played for whites, but once a week "colored excursions" "gave us an altogether different sensation because we were free to talk to people and the people could talk to us, and that's a great deal in playing music. We were less tense because it was our own people."[1]

These early forays out of New Orleans had relatively limited impact. Though some excursions went as far as Chicago, preparing the way for the later concentration of musicians there, most were confined to Louisiana. Contrary to the myth that the 1917 closing of Storyville caused the exodus of musicians from the city, New Orleans jazz musicians had started taking the new music on the road several years earlier, perhaps as early as 1902. Between 1914 and 1916, three important groups—the Creole Band, Brown's Band, and the Original Dixieland Band—began to disseminate the music to Chicago, New York, California, and countless small towns throughout the country. The closing of Storyville in 1917 had a limited effect anyway, because, according to some musicians, one could find as much work in the District after the end of legalized prostitution as before. Rather, like many people of color during the Great Northern Migration, jazz musicians moved to Chicago to better their chances in life.[2]

Some musicians left New Orleans because of the city's increasingly violent racism, illustrated by the Robert Charles riots. Trombonist Preston Jackson moved to Chicago in 1917 to get away from the violence against blacks and authorities' acceptance of it: "There was no defense against them. See, whenever a black got shot, he was just shot. All the police had to say was, 'This nigger, he threatened me,' and the law would take his word."[3] Unfortunately, Jackson felt the effects of this personally when an unarmed friend of his was shot. But despite hopes that moving North would mean the end of such troubles, some musicians—especially Creoles like Morton who were used to somewhat higher status—found worse racism when they left New Orleans.

The spread of the music—its nationalization, as it were, abetted by the rise of records and radio—dramatically altered its character from a local, functional amusement to part of a burgeoning American entertainment industry.[4] How would this transformation affect the political meaning and impact of the music? What changes in the music and its presentation were necessitated when musicians traveled in parts of the country that, without a history of Creole culture, were less tolerant of racial ambiguity, though not necessarily more racist? Would jazz continue to challenge racial purity, or was this subversive ability unique to the Crescent City?

To address these questions, I look at three influential figures who spread the music: Jelly Roll Morton, Nick La Rocca (of the Original Dixieland Jazz Band), and Louis Armstrong. Creole, white, and black respectively, each teaches us something about the music's meaning and impact as it spread throughout the country. In particular, each man's story illustrates the complex relationship between physiognomy, racial identity, musical style, and commercial success. Each musician made a series of choices that shaped his music and its audience, limiting or expanding its popular appeal. First, how should he present his own ethnic identity? Should he emphasize his race or not? Was Morton black or Creole? Was La Rocca white, Italian, or New Orleanian first of all? To some extent these decisions were made for them; Armstrong could hardly present himself as white. Yet matters of meaning and emphasis—what did it mean to be black? would Armstrong downplay his blackness?—were under individual control. A second set of decisions, not always conscious, involved the music itself. What racially marked devices (like blues techniques) would be used? Did the musician acknowledge the influence of the music of other races? Finally, there was the question of how to present oneself as an entertainer. What persona would most appeal to audiences? Should one embrace or hold at arm's length the growing entertainment industry? Each of the choices these and other musicians made influenced the music and its dissemination throughout the United States.

Though the musicians are considered separately in this chapter, each account follows a similar thematic trajectory. I begin with New Orleans, examining how each man learned the music and the city's carnivalistic values. I then ask how they experienced their racial identity. How did they react to racism? How did they negotiate the complex racial politics of New Orleans, and then elsewhere in the country, in their day-to-day lives as working musicians? I then turn to racial influences in the music itself. To what extent did each man incorporate various ethnic influences into his music, and to what degree did he acknowledge such mixing, as opposed to seeing his music as "pure"? Finally, I look at each musician's experience in the marketplace. Why did each individual succeed or fail? To what extent did they use New Orleans values to transform American music?

Morton

Learning New Orleans Music, Living Its Values

Raised in a Creole neighborhood, Jelly Roll Morton was steeped in European music and inspired by the sounds he heard at the French Opera House. Like most Creoles, he grew up in a house filled with musical instruments, allowing him to experiment with guitar, piano, trombone, and drums, among others. But his influences did not end with arias and overtures, for the young Morton found himself drawn to the music he heard in the street, like the parades where "the drums would start off, the trumpets and trombones rolling into something like *Stars and Stripes* or *The National Anthem*." He also heard the blues when he was, in his words, "knee-high to a duck" from various players and the ragmen with their ten-cent horns.[5]

Like Armstrong, Ory, and others, Morton began his musical training in a childhood vocal group, in his case a quartet that "specialized in spirituals," helping him learn harmony and internalize African American musical devices. Starting out on homemade instruments like "two chair rounds and a tin pan," he soon graduated to harmonica and Jew's harp, ultimately studying guitar "with a Spanish gentleman in the neighborhood." Before long he was playing in a string band (bass, mandolin, and guitar), serenading New Orleanians late at night with popular songs like "Hot Time in the Old Town Tonight" as well as blues and ragtime. Taken by the piano he saw played at the French Opera House, he longed to take up that instrument but did not do so until he met his match on guitar in the person of Bud Scott; he later studied the keyboard formally at St. Joseph's University and with a Professor Nickerson. As a teenager, he put on his father's long pants and stole down to the District to listen to the piano players, and by eighteen he was frequenting "ratty" honky-tonks like Kaiser's.[6]

Though he was one of early jazz's greatest artists, Morton was an atypical New Orleans musician. Working mainly in the District, he did not play lawn parties, parades, and funerals as Armstrong and others did. He also left the Crescent City relatively early (1902), later making recordings with New Orleans musicians but not in New Orleans. Despite his atypicality, his importance as a musician and his Creole background teach us much about the dissemination of the music. His very lack of success in the broader entertainment industry, in contrast to the immense fame of La Rocca and Armstrong, sheds light on the role that race played in the spread of jazz throughout the country.

Night People: Celebrating Masculinity and "Impure" Sexuality

Though a Creole, Morton plied his trade in the heart of New Orleans's carnivalesque underworld. Initially mortified to play in a brothel in Storyville, he soon became enamored of the red light district and mastered its bawdy folklore and songs. Singing tunes like "New Orleans Blues," "Winin' Boy Blues," "Make Me a Pallet on the Floor," "The Dirty Dozen," and "If You Don't Shake, Don't Get No Cake," Morton celebrated uninhibited, "impure" sexuality. In a society increasingly demanding monogamy and sexual purity, Morton communicated the opposite message:

I never believe in havin' no one woman at a time
Never believe in havin' one woman at a time
I always have six, seven, eight or nine. ("New Orleans Blues")

Similarly, "The Murder Ballad" evokes polymorphous sexuality, as a woman who has been sent to prison and can no longer be with her man looks forward to masturbation and lesbian sex:

Time is comin' that a woman don't need no man . . .
Time is comin' a woman won't need no man,
You can get it all with your beautiful hand. . . .
I can't have a man, so a woman is my next bet,
I can't have a man in here, a woman is my next bet,
She said to a good-lookin' mama, "Baby, I'll get you yet."

The sexual images in these songs sometime have a Rabelaisian flavor, like the woman in "The Murder Ballad" who brags, "Years and years I could take a prick just like a mule." In "Make Me a Pallet on the Floor," Morton even blasphemously mixes religion and sex, telling his woman to "throw up your legs like a church steeple, / so I can think I'm fuckin' all the people." Such imagery, coupled with Morton's blustery persona, evoked the black tradition of Stagolee and playing the dozens.[7]

Consonant with the patriarchal culture of the District, these songs primarily celebrate male sexuality, treating women as objects of male lust, as when Morton in "Winin' Boy Blues" boasts, "I screwed her till her pussy stunk." "The Murder Ballad" is an exception to this, with a woman learning that she doesn't need a man for sexual satisfaction. But though generally reinforcing traditional sex roles, the songs opposed monogamy in favor of freer, more "impure" practices.

A master at playing Scott Joplin, Morton also spread impurity by "ragging" European melodies. He was particularly fond of signifying on operatic melodies like the "Sextet" from *Lucia*, "transform[ing]" them, as he put it, "into jazz time. . . . There's different little variations and ideas in it that no doubt would have a tendency to detract or to masquerade the tunes."[8] Morton used ragtime to insert people of color into European culture and to develop a new style that would come to be called "jazz."

When Morton left New Orleans, he took his carnivalesque repertoire and his ragging skills with him, seeking out demimondes in other cities. His first stop was Biloxi, Mississippi, the home of his godmother, where he easily found work in a "sporting house," a pattern that would continue elsewhere in his travels. In the words of Danny Barker, "Jelly was night people—red-light district—good times. . . . Early in this century, about every large city in America had its tenderloin or red-light district, and Jelly, at an early age, started entertaining and took on the life-style of the notorious night people of the underworld." As Morton himself put it, "At that particular time, the sporting houses were all over the country and you could go in any town, if you was a good piano player, just as soon as you hit town, you had ten jobs waiting for you. So we all made a lot of money." Like many pianists, Morton kept moving in search of jobs or money, and in each new town he sought out the tenderloin, found a crowded bar, and sat down at the piano.⁹

In Biloxi, in addition to playing in brothels, Morton learned how to hustle pool from "the gambling fraternity, eager to bet on a challenge or contest," and he used piano playing as a cover: "Playing piano fooled them on pool." At times Morton's music was a mere sideline to his gambling and pimping. These illicit activities bolstered his sense of masculinity—"sporting women went for notorious men as it gave them prestige and the spot light"—and he "returned to New Orleans feeling quite a man." As a child he had believed the piano was for "sissies"; he had taken up the instrument only after he saw a ragtime pianist with short hair at a party. In contrast to his idol Tony Jackson, who was gay, Morton dispelled the association of piano playing with femininity by adopting a "tough guy" persona. (His embrace of sporting-life culture did not extend to drinking: although he believed "you can be a real man only if you take half a pint of whiskey, throw it up to your mouth and drink the whole thing straight down," doing precisely this resulted in his spending three days nearly unconscious under his bed, an experience that inoculated him against alcoholism.)¹⁰ As we shall see, however, the values of the New Orleans underclass that served Morton so well in the red light districts of the South hindered him when he tried to make it in the growing national entertainment industry.

Morton, Race, and Racism

Morton's travels brought him face to face with a kind of racism he had not experienced before. In New Orleans, the still ambiguous status of Creoles had insulated him from some of the slights that a black like Armstrong received. Armstrong, explaining resentfully how he was cut out of many jobs because of his dark skin, explicitly contrasted his fate to Morton's: "Jelly Roll with lighter skin than the average piano players, got the job because they did not want a Black piano player for the job. He claimed—he was from an Indian or Spanish race. No Cullud at all."¹¹ Yet outside the Crescent City, Morton encountered a different world, one in which he was effectively just as black as "Satchmo." But as a Creole, he responded differently to racism from Armstrong, and their divergent responses influenced their vastly differing career trajectories.

In one of his earliest trips to Biloxi, Morton came face to face with the virulence of turn-of-the-century Southern racism. At the time he worked at a white brothel run by one Mattie Bailey, who trusted Morton enough to let him lock up at night. The establishment was "a dangerous place," however, and Bailey's reliance on Morton was taken as a sign that they were "intimate," conjuring up the racist Southerner's greatest nightmare and evoking the standard response: "One night some of the bums and low riff-raff decided to lynch me, but Mattie heard about it and got me out the back door in time." After this taste of Mississippi mores, Morton decided "it was a good time to leave for New Orleans." However, either finding the Crescent City only marginally better or willing to take risks to pursue travel, he did not stay there long. It was not until several years later in Chicago that he found a more hospitable environment: "Both colored and white went to the theater and there was no ill feelings. . . . You could go anywhere you wanted regardless of creed or color."[12]

Morton's response to racism ran the gamut from defiance to acquiescence. Once in Gulfport (just west of Biloxi), he chuckled when he chanced upon some white men beating a mule, unsuccessfully trying to get the animal to move. Despite one of the men's threat that "whoever laughs, I'll give him the same I gave the mules," Morton continued to laugh and was beaten up. He also once withdrew from an engagement when he found out a white band was getting paid more for the same gig.[13]

At other times, Morton dismissed or defended racist actions. In Biloxi he "came in view of a lynching" of a black man accused of attacking a white girl. Despite having narrowly escaped the same fate there himself, Morton expressed indifference because "a lot of those cases is lies and plenty of them is truth," and in this instance "most of the people in Biloxi, white and black, were satisfied. They seemed to think he really had attacked the girl." Around the same time in Greenwood he witnessed the lynching of "a colored boy" who shot a white man who had been trying to horsewhip him. Despite describing a frightening atmosphere— there was "nobody on the streets," and someone had to tell him "where to go and how to get there"—he denied being afraid and appraised the lynching as "an even break. He killed a man who wanted to whip him and they killed him." The whipping of the boy, in Morton's telling, disappears from the narrative, leaving a cold mathematical equation, an equal exchange of lives.[14]

Morton made other, even more blatantly racist statements. According to his wife, Mabel, Morton "didn't like Negroes. He always said they would mess up your business." "Don't pay any attention to any of those niggers," he wrote to her, "I know all niggers do is try to find out anyone's business and stop gossiping." Morton particularly disparaged dark-skinned blacks: "If one of the coal black, blue-gummed Negroes bites you, they'll poison you. They hate everybody in the world but they self. I don't like to be around them."[15] At the peak of his popularity, according to Mabel, Morton "never had to play a colored engagement" because "he was so well liked by the white people" and "the colored places couldn't afford him." Morton also played blackface, although apparently he was not very good at it. Consistent with these actions, Morton denied his African roots, describing himself as "all French."[16]

Yet other evidence calls into question Morton's apparent racism. According to his sister, "At one time, some of the Creole people in downtown New Orleans believed in class and caste, but my brother wasn't prejudiced against dark people. He was crazy about King Oliver, and King Oliver was a great big black man." In the middle of an Oliver performance, Morton once called out, "Hey, Blondie!" but more in the spirit of fun than in rancor, and the two men played together beautifully on two sides in 1924. Furthermore, in San Francisco he and Anita endured considerable police harassment for operating (in his words) a "black and tan—for colored and white alike."[17]

Other accounts of Morton's attitudes on race are ambiguous. According to one musician, Morton was "interested in the race problem. If you wanted an argument you'd get it out of Jelly on the race problem, but he was fair to all races, to everybody. He was a Creole, but he also had darker colored members in his band, too."[18] Here it is unclear what position of his generated so much argument, but its apparent unpopularity among blacks is revealed by the caveat "*but* he was fair to all races." Perhaps he spoke in a racist manner at times but treated people fairly.

The most likely explanation is that his racism was directed mainly at lower-class blacks, particularly those who did not hail from the Crescent City. Non–New Orleans musicians in Chicago generally complained of discrimination by the Southern arrivals; as trombonist Preston Jackson (from New Orleans) put it, "there was strained relations between the Chicago musicians and the Louisiana musicians." Morton happily employed blacks like Johnny and Baby Dodds on his classic Red Hot Peppers sessions, but he believed non–New Orleanians could not play his compositions correctly. Tellingly, in 1917 he spoke of leaving Chicago because "a different class of people were invading the city at the time"—presumably lower-class blacks.[19] He viewed himself as a modern composer and felt that lower-class, unsophisticated blacks could not appreciate his music.

Whatever his general attitude about racism, when it threatened his livelihood, he vigorously fought against it. Arguing that "those white people, they know if they hold me down they hold the rest of us down," he engaged in a spirited campaign to procure the royalties owed to him and other musicians of color. When ASCAP, which secured royalties from performances of compositions, rejected his application because of his race, he wrote letters and published articles criticizing them; more than two hundred letters to his friend Roy Carew detail Morton's battles over copyrights, royalties, record companies, and booking agencies. Even after ASCAP admitted him, he brought a lawsuit against it because it relegated him to the lowest-earning category. In his battle for royalties he also took on unscrupulous publishers, particularly Melrose Music, but failed and ended up in near poverty while Benny Goodman made millions playing "King Porter Stomp" and other Morton compositions. For a time, he descended into ranting about "Jews and Communists" who supposedly controlled the "union, radio stations, publishers [and] booking agents" and expressed satisfaction that the FBI was investigating "5th colum[n] activities" in unions. These desperate comments aside, his tenacity and his insistence that he could take on the powers that be show an admirable refusal to acquiesce in inequality, if only when his own interests were at stake.[20]

Morton in the Marketplace

Despite his vast abilities, Morton, except for a brief period, failed in the popular entertainment industry. One ambitious comeback scheme after another fizzled, and he died unable to afford needed medical treatment. Part of this was due to exploitation and racism in the industry. In addition to unpaid songwriting royalties, African Americans initially faced a hostile recording industry; no black jazz band recorded until five years after the 1917 debut by the white Original Dixieland Jazz Band. When they did record, blacks were shunted into "race records," and their repertory was restricted to "Negro" material—typically the blues—rather than a larger variety of sounds and more modern tunes. The rise of radio hurt African American performers, because they were excluded from the most popular shows, as did the ascendance of large, national booking agencies, which slighted black musicians.[21] Prominent hotels and commercial radio stations refused to employ black bands for fear of offending Southern listeners and sponsors.[22]

One could also blame Morton's lack of success on his style, increasingly seen as old fashioned as the thirty-two-measure pop song replaced ragtime and marches. New Yorkers wanted faster, more precise music and, according to Danny Barker, "could not even dance to the rhythm we had in New Orleans, or in Chicago, or in the South."[23] But Morton was hardly stuck in the past: in the early 1940s he created advanced works that commentators have compared to those of Mingus and other moderns. Many of his riffs fueled the big bands of the swing era, yet Morton never had the financing to regularly work with a large ensemble.

Morton's personal qualities also contributed to his failures. First and foremost, as one of his employers in Chicago put it, "Jelly just couldn't handle money. He would collect the fees from the promoters, but instead of using the money for salaries and transportation, he spent it somewhere else." One could also blame his woes on his abrasive manner, infused with self-praise and disparagement of other musicians. Yet his "arrogance" was a manifestation of Creole pride, his belief that he deserved recognition and monetary reward for his creative endeavors, evident in his insistence on playing his own compositions. One promoter created a popular variety show for him featuring dancers and other entertainers, yet within days, unbeknownst to the promoter, Morton had fired the other performers and made the show a revue of his own works.[24] Even when he signified, it was often upon his own compositions. (One can compare his two recorded versions of "King Porter Stomp" to see his revisions of his own works: the later one features dissonant sounding chords, an orchestrally filled-out background, and increased rhythmic complexity, with offbeat accents in unexpected places.) In contrast, as we shall see, Armstrong would engage more fully with American popular songs, giving his music a broader appeal.

In the end, it was Morton's independence, his refusal (in one musician's words) "to bend," that hurt him in a racist marketplace.[25] While Armstrong turned all his booking and financial dealings over to manager Joe Glaser and made millions, Morton insisted on handling his own business arrangements. While such refusal to trust others was understandable given the extensive discrimination he had experienced in the music industry, it left him virtually penniless. "Jelly Roll Morton" was as creative and compelling a persona as "Satchmo," but while his style worked well in the red light district of New Orleans, most listeners,

Figure 15. The Original Dixieland Jazz Band with Nick La Rocca on cornet, Henry Ragas on piano, Larry Shields on clarinet, Eddie Edwards on trombone, and Tony Sbarbaro on drums. (Photo courtesy of the William Ransom Hogan Archive, Tulane University.)

record companies, and radio stations did not love an independent, fast-talking Creole musician, no matter how gifted.

Nick La Rocca

Like Morton, Dominic "Nick" La Rocca grew up playing music in New Orleans and left to travel the country, but the two had, to put it mildly, different degrees of success in the broader American marketplace. Whereas Morton died (in Armstrong's phraseology) "broker than the ten commandments," La Rocca and his fellow Original Dixieland Jazz Band (ODJB) members earned twelve hundred dollars a week within a month of their famous engagement at New York City's Reisenweber's Restaurant in 1917.[26] (Recall that New Orleans musicians around the same time might be paid $2.50 for an eight-hour gig.) That same year they made the first jazz record, which sold more than a million copies. The irony (and injustice) of a white band's being the first to record jazz has often been remarked upon, but that is only the beginning of the racial politics bound up with the career of Nick La Rocca and the ODJB. The way his and the ODJB's success was built on the simultaneous utilization of black musical devices and denial of such influences is part of the story as well.

"Some of My Musical Education"

La Rocca's early life resembled that of many white New Orleans musicians. His parents hailed from Salaparuta, Sicily, and had settled in the Irish Channel neighborhood in 1876. Nick's father, Girolamo, was a shoemaker by trade who played cornet from written music with other Italian musicians, just as he had in his town band in Sicily. Like many Crescent City musicians, Nick first heard music in the streets and at public functions: in addition to his father's playing at West End and Spanish Fort, he imbibed music at Italian and German birthday parties, at parks, or along the river, "which was the poor people's promenade." Describing his childhood, La Rocca evoked accordions and piccolos on Portuguese boats, Italian clarinets, and German brass bands: "All these men would go around... the front part of the city playing the street corners accepting gratuities from the people with a hat. That was some of my musical education."[27]

Like many Crescent City Sicilians, most of the La Rocca family played music: his sister Antonia held forth on mandolin and guitar, his sister Maria on the zither, and his brother Rosario on the violin.[28] Nick began with a homemade instrument, "an empty spaghetti box with baling wire for strings, and a bow which made use of horsehairs obtained from a nearby livery stable."[29] He graduated to the bugle, and during the Spanish American War he and other children dressed up as soldiers, armed with washboilers, tin pans, old kitchen utensils, an American flag, and a sign that said "Down with Spain," and marched to Nick's accompaniment. He soon advanced to popular songs like "Bill Bailey."

In spite of his family's copious musicianship, La Rocca's father, like Morton's, discouraged his son from becoming a professional musician, for he considered them "tramps." Nick stole his father's horn and secretly practiced it anyway, but when the elder La Rocca found out, he destroyed it with an ax.[30] Despite his father's disapproval, Nick persevered, putting together an ensemble consisting of guitar, violin, bass, and cornet in 1903 and playing in string bands.

Though not singing risqué ballads like Morton, La Rocca to some degree shared in the Crescent City's carnivalistic aesthetic, claiming a scatological origin for a section of the ODJB's "Tiger Rag." He was in the habit of practicing cornet on the toilet, and his mother once gave him a laxative called Hunyardi, contained in a box featuring a red devil with a pitchfork. According to La Rocca, "In blowing on this horn, some of these sounds emanated from elsewhere"; he later incorporated the sounds into the tune.[31] One can hear what he refers to in the rapid descending smears played by Edwards's trombone, ostensibly imitating the roar of a tiger, during the stop-time sections of the tune. Whether the story is true is beside the point, although La Rocca's embarrassment and reluctance to tell it speak to at least its psychological veracity. Regardless, it shows how La Rocca connected excretion, transgression, and musical creativity—a connection he shared with Armstrong, as we shall see.

*"As White as They Can Possibly Be": La Rocca, Race,
and Signifying*

In the New Orleans tradition, La Rocca developed his style by signifying on other kinds of music—in his own recollection, hymns, popular songs, Sousa marches, German and Italian brass band melodies, and opera arias. Like Armstrong and other black musicians, La Rocca was influenced by the church, but in his case the white Catholic Church. While black musicians sang spirituals in the Sanctified Church, La Rocca improvised vocal countermelodies on hymns like "Hosanna" and "The Holy City." He claimed, bizarrely, that he discovered the blues through these improvisations, though he feared he was disgracing the Bible.[32]

In addition to hymns, La Rocca professed to have learned from Italian operas (as did Armstrong and Morton), having worked the lights at the Old French Opera House for two seasons. From the "background contramelody and different melodies against one another," he learned to create a "conversation of instruments," like the polyphony of "Livery Stable Blues." He also claimed to have taken harmonies from operas and put different melodies to them.[33]

La Rocca and his friends also learned licks and improvisational skills by playing along with phonograph records; when he was rehearsing with his violinist friend Henry Young, at times Young's mother would yell "Breakdown," a signal for them to discard the written music and "play whatever melodies you could fit in there." (In New Orleans, "breakdown" designated the last chorus of a tune, featuring raucous polyphony and improvisation.) He particularly recalled using Sousa's marches as a springboard for his own melodies: "from the noodles in there I built my own tunes."[34]

La Rocca's stint with Jack Laine's Reliance Band from 1910 to 1916 reinforced these practices, teaching him to signify on familiar melodies through embellishment and syncopation. Echoing Morton's dictum "Any kind of a tune may be transformed to jazz," La Rocca explained that "any tune becomes a jazz tune when you put the idioms to it. . . . It's nothing but march time, syncopated. . . . It's working up different embellishments on a chord construction, that's all it is."[35]

What La Rocca leaves out, of course, is any mention of the blues and black church music. Though growing up in New Orleans's kaleidoscopic musical environment during the music's formative period, La Rocca claimed that he developed his style without any influence from musicians of color, and he insisted that jazz was "the white man's music and not colored." In the band's semiofficial biography, H. O. Brunn's *The Story of the Dixieland Jazz Band*, based largely on interviews with La Rocca, no mention is made of Buddy Bolden, Kid Ory, Freddie Keppard, Joe Oliver, or any of the countless other New Orleanians of color who played regularly during his youth. Throughout his life, he argued that "the negro did not play any kind of music equal to white men at any time. Even the poorest band of white men played better than the negroes in my days." In an interview at the Hogan Jazz Archive, he had the questioner play records by Oliver, Armstrong, and Ory and then explained how "these Negroes copies us."[36]

At the same time that he distanced himself from blacks, La Rocca tried to assume the mantle of "naturalness" usually attributed to African Americans. Never able to decipher written notes, he was proud of his "primitivism," famously remarking, "I don't know how many pianists we tried until we found one who couldn't read music."[37] It was as if he had to reject upper-class respectable white culture along with black music.

Of course, one could not live in New Orleans without hearing black and Creole bands at public events, and La Rocca himself acknowledged hearing Creole bandleader Armand Piron at white society dances and "colored" bands at the DeSoto Hotel.[38] He also recalled his sisters' playing songs like "La Paloma" and "Over the Waves" on zither, providing some exposure to Latin music. (Morton also played "La Paloma.")[39] Interestingly, La Rocca clung to the black-Creole distinction, arguing that Creoles like Piron, Robichaux and Perez, unlike blacks, did make good music; he also made an exception for Armstrong, who is quoted in Brunn's book praising the ODJB.[40] Despite these small concessions, in keeping with the ODJB's advertisements as "The Creators of Jazz," La

Rocca saw himself as the font of the music, even pointing out that in the early days the word *jazz* was sometimes spelled "jas," the abbreviation of his middle name, James.

Consistent with its whitewashed narrative, the band and its supporters actively tried to maintain a racially pure image. The ODJB worked to shed the associations between its music and African Americans, although undoubtedly that association intrigued as many as it repelled. On the occasion of the band's 1919 visit to England, the London *Daily News* disputed that jazz—the word or the music—was of black origin and reassured its readers about the band's racial composition: "In view of the unkind and disrespectful things which have been said about Red Indians and Negroids and West African savages, it should be stated that the players are all white—as white as they can possibly be." In 1923 the band cut some records for Okeh, but, in the words of biographer Brunn, the "series came to an abrupt halt when La Rocca discovered that they were being advertised by the company as 'race' records"; the group wanted "no part in this kind of masquerade."[41]

La Rocca's claim to have invented jazz not only earned him the scorn of many critics but also landed him in legal trouble. The ODJB's first issued record, "Dixieland Jass Band One-Step," took one of its sections from African American composer Joe Jordan's "That Teasin' Rag," and the band was forced to reissue it under the title "Introducing 'That Teasin' Rag.'" Other arguments, not reaching litigious proportions, centered on the band's authorship of specific tunes, most famously "Tiger Rag." According to Johnny St. Cyr, "'Tiger Rag' wasn't nobody's particular melody. It was a combination of several different melodies they picked up and just put 'em together." Ed Garland claimed the tune is a traditional New Orleans melody called "Jack Carey": "Folks think that Nick La Rocca wrote it, but we were playin' the tune in New Orleans when he was still wearin' short pants."[42]

La Rocca did acknowledge that "Tiger Rag" took some sections from various (white) tunes—"National Emblem March," "London Bridge Is Falling Down," a Sousa march, "Over the Waves," and the "get over dirty" lick—but he called Morton's claim to have developed it from a quadrille "lies concocted by a bunch of Communists who received money from Russia and the NAACP."[43] Thus La Rocca acknowledged the "patchwork" songwriting tradition but divested it of its African American content.

In addition to its patchwork quality, the group's performance of "Tiger Rag" shows its roots in both African and European sources in other ways. The smears and slides by the trombone and clarinet evoke the blues tradition but also the circus and vaudeville. (Many New Orleans musicians remember playing in the circus.) The use of clarinet breaks, alternating with the full band, creates call and response. "Tiger Rag" is also a truly polyphonic performance, with cornet, trombone, and clarinet constantly vying for our attention; despite a verbal braggadocio equal to Morton's, La Rocca was not a musical prima donna. Indeed, in contrast to the cornet-centered music of Oliver and most New Orleans ensembles, in the performances of the ODJB La Rocca can barely be heard amidst the other instrumentalists, and he rarely took "breaks." La Rocca was proud of such interplay and used a sewing metaphor to picture how the sum of each man's contribution creates a coherent whole: "It's like a dress—I cut up the material, [clarinetist Larry] Shields puts on the lace, and [trombonist Eddie] Edwards sews it up." (His use of a feminine image is surprising here—it is hard to imagine a similar pronouncement from Morton or Armstrong.) The band's collective nature extended to financial matters: the members split royalties five ways, even distributing songwriting credits among them.[44]

Critics for many years disparaged the ODJB as white musicians playing poor imitations of blacks, but increasingly scholars are recognizing the contributions of the band and its influence on black musicians. Yet despite the band's successful incorporation of African and European musical devices, the band did not fully master African-based music. In "Tiger Rag," the rhythm, in spite of its drive, has a certain sloppiness to it; compared to Morton's precision and constantly shifting accents, the ODJB's "Tiger Rag" features predictable patterns and sometimes wavering time. Flaws in the performance can also be seen when one compares it to Bunk Johnson's rendition (on a Baby Dodds record), where he accents the offbeats and lags behind the beat, creating a lightness missing from the ODJB's account. In addition, though his rhythmic drive anchored the band, La Rocca rarely, if ever, improvised, apparently reserving the melodic inventiveness he learned as a child for composing. This absence of improvisation is especially apparent in contrast to clarinetist Larry Shields's numerous keening "breaks."

Even with its flaws, the ODJB's music clearly draws on black and Creole music of the Crescent City, incorporating African-based techniques like glissandi, growls, call and response, and polyphony. Despite La Rocca's denials, like other New Orleans ensembles the ODJB signified on European sources with African musical devices, even if its use of such devices was less than fully realized.

ODJB and the Marketplace

Like much early jazz, the ODJB's music engendered considerable resistance at first. Interestingly, critics disparaged it in terms usually reserved for African American bands, berating the "immoral" frenzy its music aroused in audiences, particularly females. Respectable citizens were hardly thrilled to hear of a Chicago audience's response to the ODJB's music that was reminiscent of Armstrong's description of black New Orleans dives. As recounted by La Rocca, "Women stood up on the dance floor, doing wild dances.... The more they would carry on, the better we could play.... I can still see these women who would try and put on a show dance, raise their dresses above their knees and carry on, men shrieking and everybody having a good time. I would let go a horse whinny on my cornet and the house would go wild." Critics portrayed the music as incomprehensible noise generated by an out-of-control machine: according to the *New York Sun* of 1917, the trombone "chokes and gargles," "the piano vibrates like a torpedo boat destroyer at high speed," and "the drum, labored by a drummer who is surrounded by all the most up-to-date accessories and instruments of torture, becomes the heavy artillery of the piece and makes the performance a devastating barrage." The band itself sometimes encouraged such imagery, as the very moralistic criticism that was meant to silence the band enticed many more to want to hear them. In La Rocca's words, "jazz is the assassination, the murdering, the slaying of syncopation. In fact it is a revolution in this kind of music.... I even go so far as to confess we are musical anarchists."[45]

Despite, or perhaps because of, this early criticism, the ODJB's engagement at Reisenweber's catapulted them to success, taking them to England, where they gave a command performance for the king and royal family, and to Europe. Domestically, they became the first jazz band to gain national recognition, and their first released record, "Livery Stable Blues," set a record for Victor, outpacing Caruso and Sousa, both of whom had recorded for the company.[46]

As with Armstrong, the key to the ODJB's success, learned in countless gigs in New Orleans, was its responsiveness to listeners. La Rocca had an ability to gauge what the audience was ready for and deliver it, yet at the same time he sought to educate listeners by slowly introducing less familiar material, using more embellishment as the engagement progressed. In his words,

What I added to the music pleased the people; and they like it. And whenever I played for an audience, I didn't play to the musicians, I played to the audience because they were the paying customers. That's psychology. And I prided myself on trying to be a good business man in that way. If the tune was too ratty, had too much to it, I'd tone it down, give 'em a little more melody, so they could understand it. But after we'd get there three or four weeks, and they heard me play the same tune, I'd cut it up and they'd like it. . . . But you could not just play to a green audience these harsh numbers that . . . had no melody. . . . They wouldn't understand that music. A musician would. They didn't.[47]

La Rocca particularly paid attention to what would make audiences move their bodies. Boasting that he was "one of the best dancers they ever had in New Orleans," he described the band's music as "wine," "inject[ing] life" into the audience. At Reisenweber's, people were used to soft music with strings and did not know what to make of "Tiger Rag," but once the management urged people to dance, everything changed. Like Bolden, after urging people to stomp their feet La Rocca stopped the instruments one by one until only the sound of the audience pounding the floor remained. The band's experience doing vaudeville in Chicago in 1917 also contributed to its success, and novelty effects like simulated animal sounds, the trombonist's moving the slide with his foot, and tin can "mutes" on the clarinet were influenced by minstrel shows.[48]

The band's style reflected changing dance fashions, which themselves had social significance. The shift from the refinement of ballroom steps to faster, rhythmic, and more expressive moves helped make the band a huge success. These fast tempos created a kind of "jazz age" frenzy that some saw as wild and immoral but most believed more decent because they avoided the erotic overtones of the toddle and the shimmy, let alone the New Orleans "slow drag." When dance hall owners asked the Juvenile Protective Association, formed to protect youth from immoral entertainment, "What can we do to make our dance halls more respectable?" the answer was "Speed up your music."[49]

The ODJB's success did not last, however. Unlike Armstrong, La Rocca and company could not make the transition from late ragtime to Tin Pan Alley. The record companies forced them to record more trendy material and fewer originals, but the results, like "Margie" or "Broadway Rose," had an insipid feeling to them, often featuring a melody played by saxophone and trumpet in a kind of out-of-tune unison. The sloppy time and intonation that had minimally affected the band's earlier breakneck performances became more noticeable at a slower tempo. ("Margie" was a big hit but an anomaly in this regard.) In addition, even a white band like the ODJB got caught up in the attack on jazz as injurious to morals, as dancers, finally catching up to the "good time people" in New Orleans dives, began to stand in one spot and grind together.[50]

La Rocca ultimately retired after a nervous breakdown and descended into racism and paranoia. While Morton had occasionally blamed Jews and Communists for his troubles, La Rocca was obsessed with what he saw as these twin perils to civilization. Like Morton, but with less (if any) justification, he engaged in a letter-writing campaign to repair his besmirched reputation, imploring the racist Senator James Eastland of Mississippi to look into the "propaganda" regarding New Orleans jazz history "compiled by the northern carpetbaggers" like the "Jew" Marshall Stearns (who in actuality was not Jewish). "These people control the press because of their position in the social world. . . . This jazz movement is nothing but to bring on integration between the poor white man and the colored race, as these parasites are already segregated from their own poor white people." Like Morton, he claimed that the big bands of the swing era became rich by emulating his riffs, another example of blacks' receiving unmerited credit for jazz. His final interview for the Hogan Jazz Archive, at the end of 261 pages of transcript, shows his fully developed racism: After describing Africans as uncultured and "lazy," he says, "I'm a segregationist, and a die-hard one because I don't think the colored man has earned his place, so far. Maybe [in] the years to come, yes, but not now. Any other questions?" Hogan: "Turn it off."[51]

Though exacerbated by psychological problems, La Rocca's racism had larger social causes and effects. Unlike Armstrong, and to some degree Morton, La Rocca would not acknowledge the mixed-race roots of his music but created an unconvincing myth of pure white origin, consistent with the nation's quest for racial purity. Hiding the signifying nature of his songwriting and playing, he retreated into a solipsistic world without the Other, a world that ultimately drove him mad.

Armstrong: The Coffee Poisoner

The true revolutionary is one that's not apparent. I mean the revolutionary that's waving a gun out in the streets is never effective; the police just arrest him. But the police don't ever know about the guy that smiles and drops a little poison in their coffee. Well, Louis, in that sense, was that sort of revolutionary, a true revolutionary. LESTER BOWIE

The New Orleans musician who did the most to circulate the new music throughout the United States and ultimately the world was Louis

Figure 16. Louis Armstrong. (Photo courtesy of the William Ransom Hogan Archive, Tulane University.)

Armstrong. A look at his life and music suggests that through him the music spread some of its social influence beyond the city of its origin.

Admittedly, anyone making the argument that Armstrong furthered the cause of racial equality, bringing mixture and impurity to American culture, must overcome his minstrel-like Uncle Tom image. One pictures "Satchmo" running around the stage, back hunched, mugging and grinning, bulging his eyes like a blackface minstrel, while singing sentimental songs about the South. An account of a 1933 concert captures Armstrong's stage presence: "He announces 'When You're Smiling.'. . . He backs off, downstage left, leans half-way over like a quartermiler, begins to count (swaying as he does) 'one, two, three.'. . . He has already started racing toward the rear where the orchestra is ranged, and he hits four, executes a slide and a pirouette; winds up facing the audience and blowing the first note as the orchestra swings into the tune." At the same time, Armstrong's genius produced brilliantly sculpted solos and revolutionized not only jazz but all of popular music, instrumental and vocal. As Miles Davis put it, "You can't play anything on a horn that Louis hasn't played—I mean even modern."[52]

Contemporary jazz scholars have taken a variety of approaches to Armstrong's apparent contradictions. Some interpret what looks like minstrelsy as "subversive comic art," the work of an "Elizabethan fool," "disrupting from the sidelines." From this perspective he is a trickster, "winking at his audience" while performing. Others view his work as postmodern, arguing that his scat singing "points at something outside the sayable," while his use of swing and quotation reveals a "bricolage" aesthetic rooted in contingency and provisionality.[53]

While drawing on these analyses to a degree, my emphasis is different. Rather than seeing him as evading or going beyond the racial and political strictures of his time, I see him as engaging with them, playing with them—signifying on them. I also emphasize Armstrong's own views of music, which he saw as both entertaining and politically transformative, bringing people of different races together.

Though many argue that Armstrong as a powerful soloist represented the end of New Orleans jazz, I see him as a New Orleanian first of all and contend that Armstrong's music blurred racial boundaries in a manner consistent with the musical practices of his hometown. In his music and in the way he lived his life, Armstrong held on to the carnivalesque philosophy of the disrespectable dives of the city of his birth. When he left that city, his view of music's role broadened, and he came to believe that music could be a force for interracial harmony; his music reflected that belief as he signified upon American popular songs with African-based musical devices. As an entertainer, Armstrong was able to achieve phenomenal success for decades in a way that eluded Morton and La Rocca, using elements of minstrelsy to penetrate into the consciousness of millions of Americans and transform American popular music. Like other New Orleans musicians, but to a far greater degree, he Africanized American music and brought the music to "impure," interracial audiences.

"We Were Colored, and We Knew What That Meant"

Armstrong grew up in an impoverished, dangerous neighborhood in the heart of Black Storyville, near the seediest of the honky-tonks, where he heard bluesy piano from levee workers, and the district's carnivalesque values can be seen in his life and his music.[54] In his neighborhood, he said, "there were honky-tonks at every corner," including Funky Butt Hall, "and in each one of them musical instruments of all kinds were played." He second lined to parades as well, following brass bands and listening intently, noting "the things they played and how they played them." Unlike Morton and La Rocca, Armstrong could not afford music lessons, and there were no phonographs or musical instruments in the family. Instead, Armstrong learned to play through a stroke of ill fortune—his detention in the Colored Waifs Home, where he received formal training in the brass band and performed tunes like "At the Animals' Ball," which Morton played as well. In the African American tradition, he continued to learn through informal apprenticeship, following King Oliver all day long in street parades, running errands for his wife, and ultimately going to the older man's house for a free lesson.[55]

Armstrong grew up steeped in black New Orleans's underclass culture. It is telling that this key event in his life—the stay at the Waifs Home— was precipitated by his taking part in the quintessentially African American ritual of firing a gun into the air during festivities. As we have seen, Armstrong claimed to have taken his musical style from the black church, and I have suggested his use of a handkerchief in performances is taken from there as well. Even his use of herbal laxatives, which I will analyze later, is part of African culture, traceable back to the West Indies, where women used herbs to cure a variety of ailments and bewitchments.[56]

Growing up in New Orleans, Armstrong learned about racism early. Entering a streetcar for the first time at the age of five, he sat down in the "white" (front) section, unable to read the signs in the back saying "for colored passengers only." Upon witnessing this action, a black woman ran up from the rear, grabbed him, and dragged him to the "colored" section. When he asked what the signs said, the woman responded, "Don't ask so many questions! Shut your mouth, you little fool." Other incidents taught him quickly that openly opposing racism would only get him in trouble. When a white man lured his cousin Flora to his house and got her pregnant, some urged her father to have him arrested. From Armstrong's perspective, "That did not make sense. He was a white man. If we had tried to have him arrested, the judge would have had us all thrown out in the street."[57]

Armstrong's fear of racist violence is palpable in his writings. In New Orleans, he recounts, the police would "whip our heads first and ask questions later." Once while working as a musician on a riverboat, Armstrong saw a white woman slip on the deck, at which point a black passenger cried out, "Thank God!" Armstrong immediately felt a wave of terror. As he reminisced later, "My, my the lord was with us colored people that night, because nothing happened. I'm still wondering why. I have seen trouble start down there from less than that." One night, arriving late at the house of some white people for whom his wife worked, he was stopped by the night watchman and questioned suspiciously. The next morning he awakened his family before dawn and told them they had to move out at once.[58]

On the surface, Armstrong accepted segregation. Describing his work on the riverboat, he said, "We were colored, and we knew what that meant. We were not allowed to mingle with the white guests under any circumstances. We were there to play good music for them, and that was all." Being from the South, "we understood, so we never had any hard feelings. I have always loved my white folks, and they have always proved that they loved me and my music."[59]

Subservience, in certain respects, toward whites was a necessity for survival. As he put it later in life, "If you didn't have a white captain to back you in the old days—to put his hand on your shoulder—you was just a damn sad nigger. . . . If a Negro had the proper white man to reach the law and say, 'What the hell you mean locking up MY nigger?' then— quite naturally—the law would walk him free. Get in that jail *without* your white boss, and yonder comes the chain gang!" Even after leaving the South, he deferred to whites on some occasions. His manager Johnny Collins once called him a "nigger," and Armstrong was enraged. But recounting it later, he says, "I could bash his fucking brains out. . . . But, it's a different story. It's a white man. So I don't fuck with Johnny."[60]

To have been openly confrontational would have endangered his life. There were other avenues besides open rebellion, however. Right after recounting the incident with the New Orleans streetcar, Armstrong says that on Sunday evenings African Americans "took the whole car over, sitting as far up front as we wanted to. It felt good to sit up there once in a while. . . . Maybe it was because we weren't supposed to be there." The fact that he follows his account of being dragged to the back of a streetcar with this story, even though the two are chronologically unrelated, suggests that in his mind, black solidarity mitigated the effects of racism. That is, in response to racism African Americans in New Orleans bonded together for support and protection. Armstrong often notes the sense of fraternity within the New Orleans black community. As he puts it when describing a night of bar hopping with his mother, "We were both having a fine time meeting the people who loved us and spoke our language. We knew we were among our people. That was all that mattered. We did not care about the outside world."[61] To the extent possible, the New Orleans black community governed itself; people would settle their own violent fights rather than call the police. Yet Armstrong soon would conquer the "outside world," becoming known and loved by the white public in a way no African American had before.

Armstrong's Carnivalesque Life Philosophy

Armstrong took the values of New Orleans with him when he left, communicating them to the public through his autobiographies, magazine articles, and public statements. Though he embodied and described the classic rags-to-riches American success story, he rewrote the tale, inverting some of its values and maxims to spread the carnivalesque philosophy of New Orleans. The protagonist of the American Dream rises through hard work, thrift, and asceticism—a life of renunciation and sacrifice results in prosperity and happiness. Armstrong's autobiographies show a man who values and practices hard work but who also learns and teaches a carnivalesque philosophy that inverts other "Protestant" values. Like the dancers in the dives of the District and his childhood neighborhood in Black Storyville, Armstrong celebrated pleasure and the "lower" body in the midst of a culture ambivalent, at best, about sensuality.

It is useful to compare Armstrong's philosophy to that of another famous autobiographer, Ben Franklin. Franklin's central idea is that, as he puts it, "nothing brings more pain than too much pleasure; nothing more bondage than too much liberty."[62] Elaborating on this, he lists several values to be embraced by the successful person. In his autobiographical writings, Armstrong rejects each of these values.

FRANKLIN

TEMPERANCE: Eat not to dullness; drink not to elevation.

FRUGALITY: Make no expense but to do good to others or yourself; *i.e.,* waste nothing.[63]

ARMSTRONG

David Jones [a fellow musician on a riverboat] . . . starved himself the whole summer. . . . He saved every nickel and sent all his money to a farm down South where employees and relatives were raising cotton for him. . . . Every day he would eat an apple instead of a good hot meal. What was the result? The boll weevils ate all of his cotton before the season was over.

This incident taught me never to deprive my stomach. . . . I'll probably never be rich, but I will be a fat man.[64]

FRANKLIN

CHASTITY: Rarely use venery but for health or offspring, never to dullness, weakness, or the injury of your own or another's peace or reputation.[65]

ARMSTRONG

[Black Benny] said to me: . . . "Always remember, no matter how many times you get married; always have another woman for a sweetheart on the outside."

[Lucille, my wife, must] [k]eep our Citadel (I call's it) with that wall to wall Bed Fresh "n" Ready to go at all times.[66]

Armstrong celebrated the body and its appetites. His delight in sexuality was apparent in his frequent recounting of lewd jokes and stories; he also wrote pornography and invited his wife and others to read it aloud.[67] For him all appetites were part of one life force, as when he compares sex to "something to eat" in "I'll Be Glad When You're Dead, You Rascal, You." In a letter to a well-known jazz critic, Armstrong utilized a similar trope to explain how he avoided indigestion by shying away from late-night snacks: "So you can quote me as saying I ain't ever gonna' eat at nights before I go to bed. Now wait a minute. No wisecracks—ha-ha."[68]

Armstrong's celebration of bodily functions was not limited to the appetites but extended to the other end of the digestive process—excretion. In psychoanalytic terms, Armstrong rejected the dominance of genitality, polymorphously reveling in the oral and anal as well. In a trivial sense, the origin of Armstrong's fascination with excretion is clear; his mother told him that good bowel movements were the key to health, and throughout his childhood she gave him herbal "physics." Focusing on this origin, however, would be misleading, because it would suggest that

Armstrong's engrossment with his lower bodily functions was anxious or fearfully obsessive. On the contrary, he reveled in his bowel movements; to him, they were a source of great joy. In fact, the counterpart of his wall-to-wall bed was a bathroom covered with mirrors, since he and Lucille were (in his words) "disciples to laxatives."[69] Whereas mirrored rooms are usually reserved for sex, Armstrong chose to watch himself performing another bodily function. Armstrong's sensualism extended to all rooms of the house: bedroom, kitchen, and bathroom.

In Bakhtin's description of the spirit of carnival, excretion represents fertility, partly because of its proximity to the genitals, as well as laughter. "The images of feces . . . debase, destroy, regenerate, and renew simultaneously." Like La Rocca, Armstrong associated bowel movements with creativity, comparing the sounds of defecating with music. One night after taking his favorite laxative, he is awakened by rumblings in his stomach, and when he gets to the toilet ("the Throne"), "All of a Sudden, music came—Riffs—Arpeggios—Biff notes—etc. Sounded just like ('Applause') Sousa's Band playing 'Stars and Stripes Forever,' returning to the Channel of the Song—Three Times. Wonderful."[70]

One could interpret Armstrong's evocation of "Stars and Stripes Forever" in the context of bowel sounds as ironic, ridiculing patriotism and America itself, but this does not fit in with Armstrong's known love of patriotic songs. Rather, in his view his music emanates from the same life force that animates his bodily functions and pleasures; for him, art, sexuality, and excretion are all expressions of his creativity. In fact, he routinely used the same word—"wailin'"—to refer to playing music, copulating, and defecating. When explaining to a trumpet mouthpiece designer what shape he desired, Armstrong pointed at the inside of a toilet bowl and said, "I want a curve just like that!"[71] This celebration of the body, and particularly its "lower" functions, represents a repudiation of the Enlightenment valuation of the mind over the body and its sense of shame.

Consonant with this rejection of bodily shame, Armstrong publicly celebrated what is usually considered a "private" function as he routinely handed out packages of his favorite herbal laxative, Swiss Kriss, to friends and visitors and signed his letters "Swiss Krissly Yours." One year he sent out a Christmas card with a photograph of him on the toilet, pants down, with a background simulating the view through a keyhole and the caption "SATCHMO-SLOGAN (Leave it all behind you)." A friend took a full-length photograph of him in his dressing room, naked, facing away from the camera, and Armstrong's reply was "Print up thousands of 'em"—a piece of advice that was ignored.[72]

Armstrong's manager, among others, made sure that most of his fans were unaware of his bodily obsessions, yet Armstrong never tried to hide this aspect of his personality. Even had it been more widely known, Armstrong's delight in bodily functions could reinforce stereotypes of blacks as hypersexual, or more generally tied to the body. However, in his case whites may have been less likely to make such an association because of his status as a beloved and "wholesome" entertainer.

Armstrong's philosophy of life is carnivalesque in another sense. During Carnival, rank and hierarchy were suspended; there was a kind of celebration of what was normally considered "low." Armstrong came from, and remained psychologically tied to, "disrespectable" blacks and lower-class whites and Creoles and their values. Pimps, whores, and petty criminals were "his people," and he never in his writings criticized them or rejected them in favor of "polite society." His hipster slang and frequent marijuana use predated the counterculture by decades; he accomplished the difficult feat of helping to spawn an underground culture while simultaneously achieving mass popularity. At the same time, he treated authority figures with a kind of irreverence that punctured their sacredness. For example, Pope Pius XII liked Armstrong's music and wanted to meet him; Louis and Lucille Armstrong were thus granted an audience with the Holy See. All went fine until the pope asked the couple if they had any children, to which Louis allegedly replied, "No, but we're having a hell of a lot of fun trying!" Similarly, at one concert he "broke all rules of theatrical protocol" (according to an Associated Press report) by acknowledging the presence of Princess Margaret, announcing, "We've got one of our special fans in the house, and we're going to lay this one on for the Princess."[73]

In another sense, Armstrong upset traditional hierarchies by intermixing high and low genres. Armstrong was an instrumental genius, playing popular songs on records sold to millions and played on countless radios. Even within a single song, he would follow a bit of risqué vaudeville with a brilliant trumpet solo. Gary Giddins puts it quite well, speaking of a recording called "Tight like That," which featured pianist Earl Hines saying things in falsetto like "Tight like that, Louis?" "The entertainer and the artist are inseparable. . . . What manner of artist spices his performance with rude jokes about the pleasures of the flesh? What sort of entertainer can so forthrightly convey the acute sadness of the human comedy? Setting up the final payoff, Armstrong interpolates an adolescent jingle ('Oh, the girls in France . . . ') and then makes that very phrase the stuff of great passion."[74] Like jazz itself, Armstrong brought values, genres, and styles associated with the lower classes and African Americans into mainstream America.

Music and Racial Harmony

Although sometimes seen as an Uncle Tom, Armstrong celebrated and championed black culture. He made collages of newspaper photos of prominent African Americans and owned a copy of the two-volume *World's Great Men of Color*, from which he crossed off completed chapters. In the years after his departure from New Orleans, Armstrong stood up for his race, beginning with his refusal to straighten his hair as early as 1930, decades before the celebration of naturalness. Years later, Armstrong wrote a letter to President Dwight Eisenhower condemning his failure to act in response to Governor Orval Faubus's blocking of desegregation in Little Rock. He simultaneously canceled a tour of Russia, writing to the president, "The way they are treating my people in the South, the government can go to hell," and "It's getting almost so bad, a colored man hasn't got any country." His road manager publicly apologized for Armstrong's statements, and he promptly fired him, saying, "Do you dig me when I still say I have a right to blow my top over injustice?" On tour, he insisted that he be allowed to stay at luxury hotels from which blacks had been excluded: "I had it put in my contracts that I wouldn't *play* no place I couldn't *stay*."[75]

This assertive attitude went hand in hand with his vision of his music's role, for very early in his career, Armstrong began to believe that music could be a vehicle to challenge the boundaries between the races. When the riverboats he played music on stopped up North, the audience was often hostile, never having seen black dance musicians. However, the band just ignored this, and as he tells it, "Before the evening was over they loved us. We couldn't turn for them singing our praises and begging us to hurry back."[76] Though band members on the riverboat could not "mingle" with the guests, they communicated with them through music, creating a bond between black performer and white audience.

In Armstrong's view, the emotional power of music and its transcendence of language and nationality can be a force for harmony among human beings. He proudly recounted a concert he gave in the Congo, then in the midst of a civil war after Patrice Lumumba's assassination. According to Armstrong, when the concert was imminent, both sides called a truce; "both armies came to the concert and sat side by side, and had a ball. As soon as we left they were fighting again." His philosophy is summed up by the answer he gave in Lebanon to a question as to why he was going to play in Israel: "You see that horn? That horn ain't prejudiced. A note's a note in any language."[77]

Armstrong's choice of, and even alteration of, lyrics also opened up a space in American popular culture for criticism of racism. Although he performed racist songs like "When It's Sleepy Time Down South," he recorded others that criticized racism. One, "Little Joe," is a father's ode to his son that features antiracist lines like "Though your color isn't white, you're more than like a mighty rose to me," and the narrator professes his love to his son "even though the white folks may think nothing of you." On the other hand, a line like "Your eyes are black as coal, but your little soul is white as snow to me" represents a double-edged sword, reinforcing the superiority of white over black (snow over coal) at the same time it is criticizing that system of evaluation.

Another such song is Fats Waller and Andy Razaf's "(What Did I Do to Be So) Black and Blue." Originally a song about color prejudice within the black community, Armstrong turns it into a lament about racism, featuring the lyrics "They laugh at you, and scorn you too. / What did I do, to be so black and blue?" (and "my only sin is in my skin"). However, as in "Little Joe," the line "I'm white inside, but that don't help my case, / 'Cause I can't hide what is in my face" reinforces the idea that white is good and black is bad.

Elsewhere, Armstrong creates an antiracist message in a different way—by altering lyrics. In a 1931 recording of "Just a Gigolo," he changes the ending of the line "When the end comes I know, they'll say just another gigolo" to "just another jig I know." Obviously, this parodic signifying changes the song's theme dramatically from lack of romance to the evils of racism. Many black listeners delighted in such wordplay, although some objected to the epithet "jig."[78] However, Armstrong's undermining of racial purity can be seen more strongly in his alteration of the music itself.

From Polyphony to Virtuosity

Armstrong transformed American popular culture by using his instrumental virtuosity to signify on American and European sources, "blackening" popular music. However, he did not do so right away; his early recorded works reflect the more group-oriented New Orleans polyphonic tradition. Although cornetists like Buddy Bolden, Joe Oliver, and Freddie Keppard were given the title "King," the emphasis was on an ensemble sound, with texture created by the simultaneous melodies of the instruments, rather than the individual performer. "You're Next," recorded in 1926, begins with a somber rubato piano introduction in the classical style that ends with a cascade of descending arpeggios associated with nineteenth-century romanticism. After a short vamp with a march feeling to it, a minor blues chorus follows, continuing the somber tone, with Armstrong's trumpet added to the piano. Just near the end of the chorus, Armstrong surges into the major key, followed by the rest of the band playing classic New Orleans polyphony. From his new home in Chicago, Armstrong evokes the world of his youth and particularly its funeral processions—somber music played on the walk to the grave, cheerful polyphony leaving it. A piano solo follows in filigreed ragtime style, reminiscent of some of Morton's work or even Scott Joplin's. After a rather stiff clarinet solo (accompanied by piano) featuring New Orleans–style breaks, the band comes in again with some stop-time trombone, Armstrong playing the melody.

Consonant with the New Orleans polyphonic tradition, "You're Next" showcases the group rather than the individual musicians; Armstrong allows everyone to have his or her say, never dominating the proceedings as he later would. The tune is centered on the fundamental ceremony in New Orleans and an important site for musicians: the funeral with its bifurcated sadness and joy. The title "You're Next" suggests mortality, a reminder that those watching the funeral will have their own one day. The performance also evokes the ragtime tradition with its foursquare rhythms reminiscent of a parlor or brothel rather than a parade. This is the Armstrong who insisted that King Oliver, the master of classic New Orleans jazz for whom he had worked, was his idol.

Armstrong recorded other performances early in his career, however, more indicative of the future—the age of the virtuoso soloist who would transform American popular music. "Cornet Chop Suey" is one of these. The piece begins and ends with unaccompanied trumpet demonstrating Armstrong's formidable technique and inventiveness. The heart of the piece, though, is a series of breaks that Armstrong negotiates with such subtlety and assuredness that he makes everybody else in the band look like amateurs. His ability to manipulate the beat—holding back, riding on top, or edging ahead—combined with his melodic genius, points to his recordings to follow, which would increasingly emphasize Armstrong the soloist rather than Armstrong the Joe Oliver–style bandleader. The breaks would grow and, so to speak, take over the polyphony surrounding them. The next step in this process can be seen in "Potato Head Blues," recorded a year later. The performance is similar in structure to "Cornet Chop Suey," except that the sections devoted to Armstrong's solo and breaks are longer, overshadowing the polyphonic material (and clarinet solo) surrounding it. He also is more willing to "show off," punching out stratospheric riffs and proudly displaying his virtuoso technique.

Armstrong's inventiveness extended to his singing, as he increasingly featured popular "Tin Pan Alley" songs rather than the tunes of his youth. He did not simply fit himself into this preexisting genre but rather profoundly signified upon American songs, transforming popular singing. Armstrong's 1929 recording of "When You're Smiling," an inane song featuring lyrics like "When you're smiling / the whole world smiles with you," illustrates this process of signifying: while adhering to the basic structure of the tune (harmony, number of measures), he changes the song in every other way. To begin with, he alters the rhythm of the words—holding back, rushing, sustaining one note longer than it is written, punching out notes in short accents as a trumpet would. Even more radically, he completely changes the melody itself. The written melody begins with the phrase "when you're smiling," consisting of three notes, ascending in pitch; a second "when you're smiling" repeats the melody with a slightly different ending. In Armstrong's version, the band plays an insipid rendition of the written melody, at which point Armstrong enters singing "Oh when you're" as three accented notes of the same pitch and then *descends* to the "smiling." In his enunciation of the word *smiling*, he changes the rhythm; the two syllables are sung short-long instead of long-long. The second phrase repeats the change, descending from an even higher pitch, creating an exact inversion of the melody. When he gets to the phrase "the whole world," he begins on a lower note than is written and then creates a different melody.

Two other alterations should be noted. The first is that he says "when you smiling," evoking black dialect, instead of "when you're smiling." The second is the use of different vocal timbres—he growls and smears some notes like a trumpet and sweetly croons others. This emphasis on different timbres rather than a single ideal sound or a perfect blend of instruments is central to West African music and the American blues tradition that grew out of it.[79] Thus does Armstrong "blacken" American popular music, illustrating signifying's "repetition with a signal difference," bridging the gap between languages, cultures, and selves.

These changes in rhythm, melody, and timbre would not be surprising in an instrumental solo, but the application of such techniques, particularly the dramatic alteration of the melody, was seldom, if ever, seen before in popular singing. In fact, in Armstrong's performance the usual relationship between instrumental and vocal is reversed. Usually the singer sings the melody relatively straight and then the instrumentalist plays variations on it (or on the chords). Here he alters the melody in the vocal and follows it with a relatively straight reading by his trumpet.

"After You've Gone," recorded two months later, is even more dramatic. The melody is completely obliterated as words are first stretched and then spat out percussively, at times sliding imperceptibly into scat (nonsense syllables). In this back and forth between words and scat even in the same line of the song, one is sometimes hard pressed to distinguish the two. In a kind of West Africanization of American popular music, Armstrong reduces words to percussive sounds and ultimately to rhythms, turning his voice into a drum.

What follows is an approximation of Armstrong's alchemy; words that are percussively clipped are underscored, and stretched words are indicated by repeated vowels:

You feeeel blue
Oh you feel sad
[break: instruments drop out]
Miss that baby bop she bop no do may bo aaan
[instruments resume]
They'll come a tiiiime
Yoooooul regret it
Theyyyl coooome aaa time [floating across the beat]
I'll bet it

Thus, in the course of the song, Armstrong takes four approaches to the melody: clipped, on-the-beat accents; drawn out, stretched words; normally sung words; and scat. The interplay between these various approaches to the words creates a new composition that is entirely Armstrong's. The singer takes precedence over the song, which is almost a tabula rasa for his invention. Armstrong thus transforms the popular song into a vehicle both for the West African/blues tradition and for his individual radical invention.

In short, Armstrong transformed American popular music through his use of humor, his virtuosic trumpet playing, and his alteration of the melody and lyrics of songs. While Morton and the ODJB influenced the swing music of the 1930s, Armstrong's innovative phrasing virtually created the genre through his effect on Fletcher Henderson's orchestra. Armstrong's transformations represent a public assertion of individuality, and such assertions by African Americans were not welcomed, to say the least, by most whites. Many African Americans have described how segregation forced one to be as unassuming and self-effacing as possible; anything less would draw retaliation by whites who saw it as a threat. As Richard Wright put it, "The safety of my life in the South depended upon how well I concealed from all whites what I felt."[80] Armstrong's playful, even eccentric distortion of popular songs, then, represented the antithesis of the stereotypical "darky" that he sang about in some of his songs, shuffling along, eyes to the ground, stepping aside for any white who crossed his path. Yet this was not just an assertion of individuality but an insertion of African American elements into American culture. Thus Armstrong hastened the hybridity of American culture by signifying on it, incorporating West African and blues elements into popular song, a practice that would ultimately produce rock and roll.

Did Armstrong actually improve whites' perception of blacks? Despite his popularity, there is the possibility of a kind of racial compartmentalization, whereby whites loved "Satchmo" but shuddered at the thought of an African American living next door. In addition, Armstrong's admission that fighting resumed as soon as he left the Congo suggests that the harmonizing effect of his music was temporary. One white civil rights activist, however, bears witness to the possibility that Armstrong's music could create more permanent change. Charles L. Black, a Southerner who ultimately worked for the legal team that won *Brown v. Board of Education*, said that he became involved in civil rights after hearing Armstrong play at a 1931 dance. In Black's words, "It is impossible to overstate the significance of a sixteen-year-old Southern boy's seeing genius for the first time in a black. We literally never saw a black then in any but a servant's capacity. It had simply never entered my mind—that I would see this for the first time in a black man. But Louis opened my eyes wide, and put me to a choice. Blacks, the saying went, were 'all right in their place.' What was the 'place' of such a man, and of the people from which he sprung?"[81]

King of the Zulus: Armstrong, the Marketplace, and Minstrelsy

Unlike Morton and La Rocca, Armstrong was an enduring star in the marketplace, becoming one of the first modern pop stars, commanding huge audiences, and appearing in films. His first hit song was in 1926; one of his last was "Hello, Dolly!" in 1967, which reached the number-one spot on the popular music charts—the last jazz record to achieve that position—displacing the Beatles.[82] This fame allowed him to break some racial barriers, in effect leaving behind the safety of the group solidarity that characterized segregated New Orleans.

In addition to his path-breaking music, a key to Armstrong's success was undoubtedly his ability to entertain. Throughout his career, even as an international star playing large concert halls, Armstrong maintained a remarkable capacity to emotionally connect with the audience. Walking onstage, Armstrong "gave the impression of approaching the room as one approaches a person, as if he did credit to a host and wanted to share as quickly as possible the extraordinary force that animated him. Contact was immediately established, one was irresistibly captured by the incredible dynamism that was released by his entire being."[83]

His success as an entertainer brought him scorn as well as praise. Early in his career, Armstrong was a role model for many African Americans; Harlemites imitated his sartorial elegance, and the black press described him as someone who won the respect of whites without self-abasement. However, he later came to be seen by many African Americans as an Uncle Tom and an embarrassment. In particular, he lost a large portion of his black audience when he dressed up in whiteface as the Mardi Gras "King of the Zulus." Many African Americans saw the image of him in whiteface as absurd and clownlike, detracting from their struggle for respect. Even now, some writers argue that Armstrong's minstrelsy was a kind of self-abasement designed to get the approval of whites; *Africana: The Encyclopedia of the African and African American Experience* speaks of "the troubling legacy of Armstrong's persona" and contends that "Armstrong's happy-go-lucky disposition and good humor provided a convenient reinforcement for the racial prejudices of many white listeners."[84]

There is little doubt that Armstrong identified with blackface comedians. Telling of how he sold coal as an adolescent, he says he looked like "Al Jolson when he used to get down on his knees and sing *Mammy*." Minstrel-like routines appeared in his performances, like one recording called, interestingly in light of the event described above, "King of the Zulus." In this and other songs, either spoken banter or the lyrics themselves are based on traditional minstrel themes like food (fried chicken, chitlins) and sex (marital infidelity). Typical is "I'll Be Glad When You're Dead, You Rascal You," which tells the story of a man who is invited into the singer's house and sleeps with his wife: "I brought you into my home / You wouldn't leave my wife alone / You dog!" Among the guest's other sins were eating his fried chicken, which Armstrong, in a spoken aside, equates with adultery, both involving "something to eat." This was later acted out in a short film of the song ("soundies" were precursors to MTV), with portly vocalist Velma Middleton cuddling up to the band's guitarist and sending provocative glances in his direction; Armstrong responds by walking up to the guitarist and singing the song, thus accusing him of being a "rascal." In another song, "You're Driving Me Crazy," Armstrong interrupts the musical introduction in an exaggerated, slurred voice, "Hey, hey, what's the matter with you cats? Don't y'all know that y'all are *driving* me *crazy*!" to which another musician answers, stammering, "Pops, we just muggin' lightly." Armstrong responds in a stammering voice himself but then abruptly stops and announces, "Y'all got me talking that chop suey . . . " I suppose one could argue that Armstrong rejects the stereotype by criticizing himself for adopting the stammer, but nevertheless an old stereotypical routine is reenacted.

Even worse, Armstrong adopted as his theme song, recording it nearly one hundred times, "When It's Sleepy Time Down South." Written specifically for Armstrong by two New Orleans Creoles, the song nostalgically evokes the "dear old Southland . . . where I belong," with a "mammy . . . on her knees," "folks . . . liv[ing] a life of ease," and fields with "the darkies crooning songs soft and low." Armstrong was even asked in a film appearance to change the word *darkies* to "folks," and he refused.[85]

A 1942 film short of "When It's Sleepy Time Down South" features Armstrong and others dressed as slaves or farm workers, a mammy figure with a bow in her hair (Velma Middleton) grooming small children, and a shiftless man in a ragged suit sleeping on a bale of cotton.[86] The "mammy" enticingly waves a drumstick at the lazy man as Armstrong, an intense look in his eye, begins a forceful solo. Taking the drumstick from Middleton and chewing on it, the man in the ragged suit does a lazy dance, drops to his knees, and then goes back to sleep on the cotton bale. Armstrong finishes his powerful solo to end the film.

What saves these performances from self-inflicted racism is Armstrong's signifying on the material. For example, following the initial chorus of "I'll Be Glad When You're Dead, You Rascal You," Armstrong repeats the lyrics but radically alters the rhythm, punching out the words like a trumpet in the first line (*"I'll be glad . . . "*) and then gliding over the beat in the second line ("I will be glad . . . "). After other instruments hold forth, with vocal interjections by Armstrong ("Boy, what makes you so no good?"), he plays a bravura trumpet solo, paraphrasing the melody with long notes and clipped, offbeat accents. It is as if his trumpet were saying, "Enough of this hokum; now I'll show you what I can do." The change is even more dramatic in the film versions of this song and "Sleepy Time," where Armstrong, following the corny and racist acting, stares straight ahead, eyes in steely concentration, and plays beautiful solos. Both the look in his eyes and the virtuosity and passion of his playing give the lie to the stereotypical images of lazy "darkies" that have preceded it. In addition, in the "Rascal" film, the entire band is wearing immaculate, fashionable suits, suggesting dignity.

What many took to be Armstrong's minstrel mask was ultimately a window into African American vernacular culture and his joy at his self-assertion and success in a racist environment. Dizzy Gillespie, who had once chastised Armstrong for his "plantation image," came to look at him differently: "I began to recognize what I had considered Pops' grinning in the face of racism as his refusal to let anything, even anger about racism, steal the joy from his life." Perhaps this is what Billie Holiday meant when she said that Armstrong "Tommed from the heart." At the same time, intimations of subservience in his stage routines allowed whites to absorb Armstrong's self-assertion, both in the sense of his stardom and in his brilliant musicianship, without being overly threatened.[87]

Why, then, did Armstrong participate in minstrelsy? On a superficial level, he did it because it entertained. Armstrong thought of himself as an entertainer rather than, or certainly more than, an artist; as he once put it, "The real test is entertainment. Does it interest your audience?" Yet there were limits to his support for stereotypes. Armstrong admired Bill "Bojangles" Robinson because he used humor without degrading himself: "He did not wear old Raggedy Top Hat and Tails with the Pants cut off—Black Cork with thick white lips, etc. But the Audiences loved him very much. He was funny from the first time he opened his mouth til he finished. So to me that's what counted."[88]

Armstrong could also use the minstrel persona as a weapon. In one instance, the subservient Stepin Fetchit mask allowed him to outwit racist authorities. As he recounts it, "two old cracker sheriffs" at a concert approach Armstrong and say "kinda roughly," "Are you Louis Armstrong?" "I said: 'Yassuh.' Then one of them asked me: 'Is that your band?' I hurriedly said: 'No, suh. I only play in the band—(tee hee)[']." Then the sheriffs tell him that they will confiscate his trumpet after the concert. Armstrong describes the denouement:

And sho 'nuff, when we finish the dance and finish playing "The Star Spangled Banner" here they come right into me reaching for my trumpet. But I tricked them so pretty. When they asked me—"where's your trumpet?"—I pointed to the trumpet case and said: "There it is." The promoter was kind of hip'd to the jive and asked me: "Are you sure that is your trumpet?" I said: "Yassuh, boss. That's the one I blow every night." But it wasn't. I gave them Joe Jardan's . . . and that was that—Tee hee? Cute? You see, Joe and I made the switch during our intermission, right under their noses. So they weren't so smart after all.[89]

Armstrong uses subservient language like "yassuh," "no, suh," and "boss" to outfox the sheriffs, while fully enjoying the game (the interjected "tee hee"). In retelling the incident, Armstrong skewers the sheriffs once again, exposing his triumph over them for all to see, and by pointing out that they moved to confiscate his instrument right after the playing of the national anthem, he hints at the disconnect between America's ideals and the reality of African American life in the South.

In the tradition of black satirical songs, Armstrong even used minstrel humor to criticize racist authorities and emerge unscathed. In one of many encounters with racism on the road, Armstrong and his entire band were arrested and jailed in Memphis in 1931. While they were in jail, a policeman told them, "You ain't gonna come down to Memphis and try to run the city. We'll kill all you niggers." But someone contacted the manager of the theater at which they were scheduled to perform, and he bailed them out. When the band finally made a radio broadcast at the theater, police nervously paced the room. At one point Armstrong announced, "Ladies and gentlemen, I'm now going to dedicate this song to the Memphis Police Force," and then began to sing "I'll Be Glad When You're Dead, You Rascal, You."

After the song was over, band members literally feared for their lives as several police officers hurried toward the stage. Instead, the officers were thrilled, one of them blurting out, "You're the first band that ever dedicated a tune to the Memphis Police Force."[90] This incident suggests an alternative to the opposition between Armstrong the minstrel and Armstrong the civil rights advocate: he was able to use the minstrel persona to attack racism, "poisoning the coffee" of white Americans as he smiled.

Ultimately, Armstrong's music challenged the racial divide that many Americans so tenaciously sought to uphold. Morton and La Rocca had also brought African American elements into popular music, despite the latter's belief that jazz was purely white. But Armstrong, through his immense popularity, carried race mixing and a carnivalesque perspective into the public realm in a way the other two men could not. This is ironic since Armstrong came from the least privileged, most "ratty" background, yet he did not have to give up all of black New Orleans's subversive values to become a success. La Rocca had the advantage of whiteness and the desire and ability to please audiences but could not move forward stylistically. Morton, though more innovative, failed in the face of racism in the music industry, a racism he had not fully experienced in New Orleans, compounded by an inability to manage his finances and an understandable refusal to let anyone else do so.

Armstrong succeeded where the other men failed, through a combination of bold musical assertiveness, an ability to charm (and disarm) audiences, and the relinquishment of business affairs to his "white captain," Joe Glaser. His innovative, virtuosic soloing simultaneously catapulted him beyond the musical conventions of New Orleans and allowed him to carry the Crescent City's spirit to the rest of the nation. He carried with him a respect for and rapport with the audience, and a generosity of spirit that kept him from being mired in bitterness despite the pervasive racism, particularly in the recording industry, that would have given him good reason to do so. His minstrel mask reassured whites that he would not challenge their fundamental assumptions at the same time he did exactly that, through his music, his lifestyle, and sometimes the minstrel persona itself. Those impervious to change saw only the mask. But through the power of his music many others absorbed, in subtle ways, Armstrong's revision of American culture and its values. Poisoned coffee never tasted so good.

Conclusion

The emergence of jazz in New Orleans was unique, a function of the city's complex race relations and profusion of musical forms. At the same time, the story of jazz's birth reflects America's intricate racial negotiations, negotiations that continue to this day. In this conclusion I use the story of early New Orleans jazz to explore larger issues concerning the relationship between music, racial classifications, and racial identities. I argue that we still implicitly embrace racial purity but that early New Orleans jazz offers a new way of thinking about race relations. I then return to the music itself, presenting an alternative approach to thinking about jazz and race and suggesting how this approach might alter the ways we write jazz history.

Racial Purity Redux

As we have seen, from its beginnings, jazz has been tied by both admirers and opponents to the question of America's racial identity. I have argued that early jazz in various ways subverted the push for racial purity in New Orleans. But the quest for racial purity in the realm of culture is still with us. In *Who Are We? The Challenges to America's National Identity*, Samuel Huntington argues that America's "Anglo-Protestant" culture is threatened by multiculturalism and immigration from Latin America and Asia. According to Huntington, America can be united only when those of all races and backgrounds adopt such a culture. Similarly, in the 1990s, writer Richard Brookhiser claimed that "the

WASP character is the American character," while conservative author Laurence Auster argued that "the U.S. has always been an Anglo-Saxon civilization."[1] As we have seen, Wynton Marsalis, Stanley Crouch, and others have put forward a kind of Afrocentric equivalent, albeit not nearly as extreme, arguing that jazz is black music that must be kept free from outside (white) influences.

Even though a majority of Americans would reject calls for racial purity, most still cling to the idea that distinct races exist in nature. Indeed, racial mixture has only recently been officially recognized by the U.S. government. But while the 2000 census for the first time allowed respondents to identify themselves as multiracial, fewer than one-third of those with racially mixed backgrounds chose to do so.[2]

A continuing attachment to racial purity can also be seen in the unexamined persistence of the "one drop of blood" rule in popular consciousness. American racial classifications mystify many foreigners, who have trouble understanding why a person who is one-quarter black is seen as "passing for white" if she self-identifies as white but not "passing for black" if she, like most Americans, sees herself as black. "The personnel officer, the census taker, the judge, the school admissions staff, the affirmative action officer, and the black political caucus leader all readily classify a predominantly white mulatto as a black person." As Ian Haney-López puts it, "There may be light-skinned Blacks, but there are no dark-skinned Whites." Both the pervasiveness and the absurdity of this way of thinking became apparent during the telecast of the 2001 Academy Awards, when after Halle Berry won an Oscar and became (as it was trumpeted in the press) the "first black Best Actress," the camera cut to a shot of her white mother. As Homer Plessy's lawyer recognized more than one hundred years ago, the one-drop rule is rooted in the racist notion of white purity: "There is but one reason to wit, the domination of the white race."[3]

The "melting-pot" model, apparently a nonracist alternative, is merely a different version of racial purity, because it ultimately celebrates an assimilation to dominant (white, Protestant) culture rather than an appreciation of differences. That is, the melting pot is fine as long as the resulting brew is white. Werner Sollors discusses a 1917 poster to promote Victory Liberty Loans (war bonds) with the big letters "Americans All!" and an "honor roll" of ethnic names—DuBois, Smith, O'Brien, Levy, Kowalski, Gonzales, and others—underneath a wreath held by a woman. However, the woman holding the wreath does not appear ethnically mixed but is pale, fragile, and English looking. Thus, there is a double message—all are Americans, but the ethnics "are asked to assimilate to an Anglo Saxon norm."[4] This vision of unity, an America without dissonance, while claiming to embrace diversity, is the equivalent of the racist quest for purity in that it ultimately asks people to cast off their racial identities.

By way of analogy, colors mix differently as light and as paint. The melting-pot model blends colors like a series of light beams—with enough colors, the result is white. The one-drop rule mixes hues like so many drops of paint: blend enough colors on the palette, and a pool of black is left. The melting pot and the one-drop rule are mirror images, both designed to ward off impurity, the former by absorbing the nonwhite into the white, the latter by casting anything tainted with nonwhiteness into the category "black." Yet the story of early New Orleans jazz suggests a different way of looking at racial mixing.

Jazz and Racial Subjectivity

Early on in jazz's history, commentators articulated alternatives to the melting-pot model. Horace Kallen, in a 1915 article entitled "Democracy versus the Melting-Pot," used a musical analogy to argue that American identity is best celebrated by appreciating differences rather than melting them down: "As in an orchestra, every type of instrument has its specific tonality, founded in its substance and form; as every type has its appropriate theme and melody in the whole symphony, so in society each ethnic group is the natural instrument, its spirit and culture are its theme and melody, and the harmony and dissonances and discords of them all make the symphony of civilization, with this difference: a musical symphony is written before it is played; in the symphony of civilization the playing is the writing."[5] In this early version of multiculturalism, Kallen rejects a reified, racially pure America in favor of an evolving multiracial society. By saying that "the playing is the writing," Kallen imagines different ethnic groups improvising their parts, creating a kind of polyphonic jazz.

Although Kallen's model is an advance over racial purity, he still presents the various races or ethnic groups, represented by the different instruments, as static essences. The story of jazz's evolution in New Orleans provides a fundamentally different model of race relations in which, continuing with Kallen's analogy, the instruments themselves constantly change, generating a kind of shape-shifting orchestra. In the Crescent City, musical ideas from different ethnic groups continually circulated, in turn changing those groups. Though they were legally either "black" or "white," jazz musicians and listeners in small ways gained different, more hybrid racial identities.

This process can best be seen in the versatility of musicians. Though musicians tailored their style to particular audiences, when they moved from one engagement to the next, the music retained traces of its previous encounters. As Bakhtin puts it, in a sentence equally applicable to musical phrases, "Each word 'tastes' of the . . . contexts in which it has lived its socially charged life."[6] Racial interchange of a sort, then, came about through the circulation of the music through various venues, as jazz evolved through a continual process of interpretation and reinterpretation—of signifying. When Buddy Bolden put his cornet to his lips and blew, the echoes of white marching bands, Creole quadrilles, and the black church, among others, sounded in his notes, yet were reshaped. Similarly, the phrases of white jazz musicians contained the accents of black musicians, themselves signifying on European and American forms. In order to speak such a variety of musical languages, musicians had to cross racial boundaries, literally and figuratively, learning music that might be foreign to them, listening to and playing with those of other races. Such boundary crossings were severely circumscribed by segregation in law and custom, yet musicians were able in various ways to evade such segregation. As music circulated through society, picking up traces of different racial groups and then becoming part of the mainstream culture, it created more permeable boundaries between the races, challenging the imperatives for racial purity that were solidifying at this time.

The process of racial interchange brought about through circulation differs fundamentally from the melting-pot model. The process of circulation is never complete, and further, the various influences that circulate have never entirely melted. Whereas the melting-pot image assumes a kind of musical and national purity, an essence of Americanness, early jazz embodied the principle of impurity. Bent notes, bluesy growls, Latin rhythms, traces of mazurkas—these all showed up in the music without ever melting down. Jazz did in fact bridge racial boundaries but not through the homogenizing blending of the melting pot but by means of the labyrinthine circulation of music throughout various New Orleans venues with audiences of different races and classes, like a parade with its second line followers.

Circulation also suggests a new way of looking at racial identity itself. One must speculate a bit here, because we have very few direct accounts of how the music affected ordinary listeners. Yet one can imagine that, given the powerful effect of music on identity, New Orleans jazz laid the groundwork for what I call *racial intersubjectivity*, a kind of inner shift that goes beyond being exposed to another's culture. The notion of intersubjectivity emphasizes the way our identity, even our basic experience of the world and of ourselves, is inseparable from our relationships with others.[7] Psychoanalysts have written about the child's development of subjectivity in relation to that of the parent, or the way in which analyst and analysand inhabit a shared reality—eclipsing the Freudian paradigm in which the analyst discovers the truth of the patient from a safe distance.

Although psychoanalysts and philosophers have emphasized a kind of unmediated dyad, intersubjectivity can be understood politically as well. As individuals encountered music, particularly in intimate settings where the borders of the self are loosened, their racial identity opened to the Other. When Creoles and blacks played side by side or whites and African Americans listened together, they entered a shared reality that phenomenologist Alfred Schutz calls "inner time," a "sharing of the other's flux of experiences . . . living through a vivid present in common, [which] constitutes . . . the mutual tuning-in relationship, the experience of the 'We,' which is at the foundation of all possible communication."[8]

Rhythm in particular connects disparate bodies without touching. As Raymond Williams puts it, rhythm is "a way of transmitting a description of experience, in such a way that the experience is re-created in the person receiving it, not merely as an 'abstraction,' or an 'emotion' but as a physical effect on the organism . . . [a] means of transmitting our experience in so powerful a way that the experience can be literally lived by others." Jazz illustrates, in the words of Scott DeVeaux, "the power of African-derived rhythm to animate people's bodies and draw their minds, even against their conscious will, into a distinctively African-American cultural orbit."[9] When Manuel Manetta, an Afro-Italian Creole of Color, ventured into seedy black clubs and heard the blues, learned the idiom, and played it before a variety of audiences, boundaries between self and Other, racially speaking, were made more porous.

Writing Race in Jazz History

Early New Orleans jazz also points us toward new ways of writing jazz history. First, we should be skeptical of statements that assume a kind of essence of jazz. In New Orleans, "jazz" was a constantly mutating collection of musical forms that combined and recombined depending on the musicians involved and the context, particularly the audience. If one simply looks at the variety of songs King Oliver recorded, it is difficult to make the case that they are all the same kind of music: blues ("Dippermouth Blues"); multipart rags ("Weather Bird Rag"); popular songs ("Sweet Lovin' Man"); indefinable performances like "Sobbin' Blues," which is not a blues but a sentimental tune featuring a "sobbing" slide whistle; and evocations of Chopin's funeral march ("Dead Man Blues"). Moreover, the tunes Oliver recorded were a small fraction of what he played; according to his drummer Baby Dodds, the band could play for five hours without repeating a tune. We have no recordings of the waltzes, mazurkas, schottisches, and national anthems that the band played in countless gigs.[10]

Something called "jazz" did emerge that incorporated elements of various kinds of music characteristic of different races and classes, but that category was a result of the imperative of record companies, concert promoters, and critics. Other forms of music, now called something other than jazz (e.g., brass band music), still exist in New Orleans and elsewhere. Our musical landscape is strewn with cast-off possibilities, rejected as impure by the taxonomists and marketers yet still vital.[11]

The ever-changing musical mélange winding its way through the streets of New Orleans, with musicians taking on multiple racial roles before different audiences, signifying on various kinds of music, is an ongoing process that does not fit essentialist categories of racial art, either "black music" or "the melting pot." Despite being captured and tamed by the word *jazz*, the racial identity of the music was mixed, contextual, and constantly in flux.

To understand jazz politically, it is not sufficient to look at the way racism held back musicians and show how they eventually overcame those barriers. Jazz was not simply the free expression of individuals who happened to be black, Creole, or white. Race shaped the music, but the effect of race goes beyond the race of musicians. A political analysis of the music must take into account the multifaceted interactions among musicians, audience members, and opponents of the music. In particular, the role of the audience and its race has been underappreciated; Lawrence Levine's assertion, made in 1992, that "the audience remains the missing link, the forgotten element, in cultural history," still stands.[12] From the working-class or underclass audiences that early on supported the music's most innovative forms to white audiences to whom musicians of color tailored performances, ordinary listeners in subtle ways were cocreators of the music, shaping its hybrid form.

One must look at the effects of hostility toward jazz as well, for opponents of the music had a "productive" role, not just an inhibiting one. The purveyors of purity tried to translate segregation laws on the books into the lived reality of culture. Yet their actions had unintended consequences, foiling their expectations and desires, for opposition to jazz actively shaped the music. The very segregation laws that tried to squeeze Creoles of Color into a binary racial system helped create cultural race mixing by drawing people of various races into common spaces to experience pleasure, giving impetus to the creation of "impure" music. Racial categories limited musicians, but they also brought black and Creole musicians together and facilitated the fashioning of a music that would profoundly alter American culture. The push for purity merely diverted impurity from the political and social arena into the realm of culture; culture then remained ahead of politics, keeping emancipatory impulses alive, embodied in music where they could be heard and felt.

In addition, not enough attention has been paid to what might be called the geography of race in looking at the development of jazz. The standard narrative is linear—racism existed, and musicians were confronted with certain barriers, and as those barriers were eliminated, the life of musicians became freer, allowing the music to spread in different ways. Yet at any given point, as we have seen in New Orleans in the late nineteenth and early twentieth centuries, some neighborhoods and venues were freer than others. The relationship between those freer spaces and the pervasive legal and social racism lies at the center of the story of jazz's emergence.

Finally, early New Orleans jazz suggests a more complex understanding of the relationship between culture and political reality. Rather than being purely hegemonic or emancipatory, New Orleans jazz both reflected and challenged political reality. Political reality, in the form of Jim Crow, limited what musicians could do—whom they could play with, whom they could play for, and what they could play in certain situations. The dissemination of the music was bounded by power relationships; certain spaces were segregated, and musicians could play with only those of their own race. Yet within that system of racial domination, which was becoming more rigid, jazz exploited and widened boundary crossings. Jazz shows us that while identity is always mediated through culture and therefore structured by power, culture is not simply a Foucaultian disciplining mechanism but can be a vehicle for the stretching of identities, opening individuals to the world of the Other.

Jazz Diaspora

The popularization of jazz by Armstrong and others fundamentally changed its function and meaning. Essentially, the music shifted from being functional local entertainment to become part of the burgeoning American popular culture industry, and in the process it lost some of its racial fluidity. While the music still was and is played differently for audiences of various races and classes, with the spread of radio and phonographs it became more homogenized. The kind of interpenetration of black and white that had existed in New Orleans, embodied in the very persons of Creoles of Color, was soon no longer possible in the Crescent City or elsewhere, as Creoles discovered. The anonymity of radio did preserve some racial fluidity, however, as in the white group who called themselves the "Black Aces" and put out "race records."[13]

Modern jazz has less connection to everyday local urban life than it did in New Orleans. Jazz became a national product, though with different subspecies, sparking debates about authentic versus inauthentic jazz that never could have happened in New Orleans, since there it was just "music" for whatever an occasion demanded. Presently, jazz is seen by many as an elite art music, yet even now in New Orleans, the line between jazz as art and jazz as entertainment, or even between different styles of music, is less distinct than in New York, the current jazz capital, and elsewhere in the United States. At clubs in New Orleans today, jazz musicians may play a straight-ahead jazz tune followed by a vocal rendition of a nostalgic or popular song. On a recent trip there I saw a gifted trumpeter, playing before a mixed audience, who interwove "traditional" New Orleans jazz licks with bebop phrases reminiscent of the 1950s virtuoso Clifford Brown.[14] In the face of our relative musical segregation and attachment to racial purity, the subversive sounds of New Orleans jazz remind us of the inevitable intertwining of black and white, racial self and racial Other, in American culture.

Notes

1. All recordings discussed are listed in the discography. Sources for the maps include Campanella, *Geographies*; Koenig, "Sites of Jazz"; Koenig, *Jazz Map*; Miller, "New Orleans Jazz and R&B Landmarks"; Marquis, *In Search of Buddy Bolden*.
2. When and why he changed his name is not totally clear. Morton was his stepfather's name, itself an anglicization of Mouton. Morton may have taken it earlier in life, before he was a musician, but he probably did find it helped his career. Some other Creoles anglicized their names, like George Lewis, born George Joseph François Louis Zeno.
3. Levine, *Black Culture*, 411; Roberts, *From Trickster to Badman*, 203, 206. Some have reported that those of mixed race are more likely to be "bad men," confirming their fluid, slippery identities, although this is not a prevalent view. Brearly, "Ba-ad Nigger," 585. The nicknames are taken from Lomax, "Unrecorded Interview Material," 178, 196; Pops Foster interview, August 23, 1967–August 1969; Russell, *"Oh, Mister Jelly,"* 107 (George Guesnon).
4. Douglass, *Oxford Frederick Douglass Reader*, 116. It should be noted that Douglass did not ultimately reject America but is making a rhetorical point.
5. Rose, *Storyville*, 105.

1. *Plessy v. Ferguson*. The Court in its description is paraphrasing Plessy's own legal petition, but it does not repudiate this characterization.
2. Panetta, "'For Godsake Stop!'" 19; Evans, *Writing Jazz*, 33.

3. *New Orleans Daily Picayune*, January 22, 1894, 4, quoted in Winston, "News Reporting," 27–28; Evans, *Writing Jazz*, 57, 104.

4. See Bakhtin, *Rabelais*.

5. Tucker, *Swing Shift*; Porter, *What Is This Thing*; DeVeaux, *Birth of Bebop*. For new jazz historical analysis of New Orleans, see Ake, *Jazz Cultures*; Raeburn, "Submerging Ethnicity"; Raeburn, "Stars of David and Sons of Sicily"; Raeburn, "King Oliver, Jelly Roll Morton, and Sidney Bechet"; Taylor, "Early Origins of Jazz," especially 46–50. The book focusing on early jazz as an example of the black vernacular, published late in the revision process of this study, is Brothers, *Louis Armstrong's New Orleans*.

6. Ramsey and Smith, *Jazzmen*, 4, 6; Russell and Smith, "New Orleans Music," 9–10; Smith, "White New Orleans," 57. On *Jazzmen* and the Popular Front, see Erenberg, *Swingin' the Dream*, 120–49.

7. Baraka, *Blues People*, 30; Marsalis interview, 6. Marsalis is talking about white musicians in Chicago like Benny Goodman, but these comments reflect his larger point of view.

8. Jenkins, "Wynton Bites Back," 263; Marsalis and Hancock, "Soul, Craft, and Cultural Hierarchy," 345. In the latter interview, Marsalis sets himself up as an arbiter of authentic blackness, declaring that the sound of the music of Michael Jackson and Prince is "*not* black" (349; emphasis in original).

9. Gioia, *History of Jazz*, 6–7; Ward and Burns, *Jazz*, 117 (Marsalis interview); Giddins, *Visions of Jazz*, 70. Yet another metaphor, with somewhat different implications, is "cross-pollination." "Jazz resulted from a complex and exciting period of cross-pollination between musicians and groups." Taylor, "Early Origins of Jazz," 46.

10. Ellington's story in particular is told as a Horatio Alger tale, as when we are told that his mother taught him that nothing could stop him. "Unpleasant facts and potential barriers were simply to be ignored. In *his* life there were to be 'no boxes'; he 'could do anything anyone else could do.' In part because she believed that, he would believe it, too." When asked about not being able to stay or eat at hotels in which he played, Ellington said, "I took the energy it takes to pout and wrote some blues." Similarly, according to Burns, the great blues singer Bessie Smith, when confronted by a group of Klansmen during a performance, scared them off by running after them with her fist upraised, cursing, and threatening to recruit the audience to defend her. Ward and Burns, *Jazz*, 50, 151, 247.

11. Crouch, *Always in Pursuit*, 45; Murray, *Omni-Americans*; Marsalis and Hancock, "Soul, Craft, and Cultural Hierarchy."

12. Baron and Cara, "Introduction"; Szwed, *Crossovers*, 231–32.

13. Baron, "Amalgams and Mosaics," 94.

14. Haney López, "Mean Streets," 165.

15. Barrett and Roediger, "How White People Became White," 446; Hoffman, "Race Amalgamation," 80.

16. Thompson, "Passing of a People," 9–13; *Lee et al. v. New Orleans Great Northern Co.*, 184; Haney López, *White by Law*, 164.

17. Radano, *Lying Up a Nation*, 26.

18. Williams, *Marxism and Literature*, 132–33, 189; Stokes, "Introduction," 5.

19. G. Ramsey, *Race Music;* Mezzrow, *Really the Blues.* On Johnny Otis, born John Veliotes to Greek parents (a fact absent from his official website), see www.johnnyotisworld.com; on "wiggaz," see www.wiggaz.com or, from the perspective of a contemporary version of the fear of race mixing described in this book, www.nationalist.org/alt/2001/nov/wiggers.html.

20. Stokes, "Introduction," 8–10.

21. Kelley, *Race Rebels*, 9–10.

CHAPTER ONE

1. Shapiro and Hentoff, *Hear Me Talkin'*, 3 (Danny Barker).

2. Blassingame, *Black New Orleans,* 33–36; Ory interview; Carew, "Glimpses of the Past"; Koenig, "Four Country Brass Bands," 13–23; Richard Brunies interview.

3. Marquis, *In Search of Buddy Bolden*, 18; Shapiro and Hentoff, *Hear Me Talkin'*, 65, 27–28; Ory interview; Armstrong, *Satchmo*, 34.

4. Bigard, *With Louis and the Duke*, 10–11. On accordions, see Jones, Willie Foster, and Parker interviews. For the Keppard story, see Eddie Dawson in Martyn, ed., *End of the Beginning*, 53. Peter Bocage says there was no brass allowed in the District on Sundays. Peter Bocage in Martyn, ed., *End of the Beginning*, 53, 59.

5. Examples of such early ragtime are contained on Various Artists, *Ragtime to Jazz 1, 1912–1919.*

6. W. Russell, *"Oh, Mister Jelly,"* 467. Another musician reports that early New Orleans drummers in Chicago "did things the Chicago people had never heard," and "other musicians in New Orleans bands played rhythms the [Chicagoans] hadn't heard," sometimes leading to tensions between New Orleans musicians in Chicago and native Chicagoans: ibid., 384, quoting Glover Compton (1884–1964) from an interview at Tulane Jazz Archive, June 30, 1959. Yet another musician claims that a kind of "swinging syncopation" was "unique with the New Orleans musicians": ibid., 562, quoting Paul Howard.

7. Berry, "African Cultural Memory," 4, 10.

8. Hall, *Africans in Colonial Louisiana*, 3, 129–33, 29, 200, 160–61; see also 238, 155; Lovejoy, "African Diaspora," 6–7.

9. Hirsch, Introduction, 9; Harlan, "Segregation in New Orleans Public Schools," 323; Somers, "Black and White in New Orleans," 31; Scruggs, "Economic and Racial Components of Jim Crow," 64; Dethloff and Jones, "Race Relations in Louisiana," 311.

10. Blassingame, *Black New Orleans*, xvi, 182. Before emancipation, even slaves in New Orleans were able to show more independence than blacks were permitted in other parts of the country (8).

11. Somers, "Black and White in New Orleans," 20–21; Haskins, *Creoles of Color*, 15; R. Harris, *Jazz*, 49.

12. Somers, "Black and White in New Orleans," 24, 28; Harlan, "Segregation in New Orleans Public Schools," 327.

13. Anthony, "Negro Creole Community," 165; Senter, "Creole Poets on the Verge of a Nation," 281, 274.

14. Tregle, "Creoles and Americans," 137–38, 141; Domínguez, *White by Definition*, 23; Ostransky, *Jazz City*, 18; Zeno interviews, November 14 and December 10, 1958. On the Caribbean roots of plaçage, see Hearn, *Two Years in the French West Indies*, 251–54.

15. Fiehrer, "From Quadrille to Stomp," 26.

16. Manuel with Bilby and Largey, *Caribbean Currents*, 144–45; Benfey, *Degas in New Orleans*, 14–15; Alice Moore Dunbar-Nelson, "People of Color in Louisiana"; Fiehrer, "From Quadrille to Stomp," 26; Hunt, *Haiti's Influence*, 81–2.

17. Benfey, *Degas in New Orleans*, 5; Bocage interviews; Gehman, "Visible Means of Support," 217; Fabre, "New Orleans Creole Expatriates in France," 181.

18. Rose Tio interview; Elgar interview; Kinzer, "Tios of New Orleans." The Tios descended from free people of color from the early days of New Orleans, owning much real estate, including a large plantation. James Lincoln Collier claims that the Tios were not Creoles since they were not of French extraction, which is doubly false: they did have Gallic roots, yet such roots were not a requirement to be considered Creole. Collier, *Louis Armstrong*, 38.

19. Elgar interview; Raeburn, "Stars of David,"16; Keppard interview. Though it is not clear that the Tios had any Mexican ancestors, one musician claimed that "when you saw them you knew you were lookin' at a Mexican" (Dominique interview). Natty Dominique in his interview also calls Perez "colored."

20. Domínguez, *White by Definition*, 54–55; Bontemps and Conroy, *Anyplace But Here*, 123.

21. Hall, *Africans in Colonial Louisiana*, 263; Olsen, *Thin Disguise*, 56–57; De Lay interview.

22. Knight, *Caribbean*, 122; Hearn, *Two Years in the French West Indies*, 255; Anthony, "Negro Creole Community," 24, 71, 94–5, 107–8.

23. Darensbourg, *Telling It Like It Is*, 50; Manuel with Bilby and Largey, *Caribbean Currents*, 145; Rose Tio interview; Keppard interview.

24. S. Thompson, "Passing of a People."

25. Gilroy, *Black Atlantic*, 4, 15.

26. For 1898 as a turning point, see Dethloff and Jones, "Race Relations in Louisiana," 301–23; Medley, *We as Freemen*, 212.

27. Somers, "Black and White in New Orleans," 37; see also Tregle, "Creoles and Americans," 183.

28. Litwack, *Trouble in Mind*, 405–10. See Hair, *Carnival of Fury*. On Louis Nelson Deslile's father, see Goffin, "'Big Eye' Louis Nelson," 126–29.

29. Gioia, *History of Jazz*, 30; Blassingame, *Black New Orleans*, 163, 234, 239, 238; Morris, *Wait until Dark*, 85. It is difficult to tell from Blassingame's table whether Creoles of Color are included, and though about one-third of black women worked, there are no unemployment tables in Blassingame for women.

30. Arnesen, *Waterfront Workers of New Orleans*, 119–20; Bains, "New Orleans Race Riot of 1900," 14, 43–44. Official documents did not distinguish between blacks and Creoles of Color.

31. For numerous examples, see Litwack, *Been in the Storm So Long*.

32. Berry, Foose, and Jones, *Up from the Cradle of Jazz*, 3; Armstrong, *Satchmo*, 78.

33. Haskins, *Creoles of Color of New Orleans*, 20, 34–35, 40–52. According to Jacqui Malone, the roots of mutual aid societies can be traced to West Africa. Malone, *Steppin'*, 169–70.

34. Wilkinson, *Jazz on the Road*, 11.

35. Medley, *We as Freemen*, 32–33, 127, 130, 135–36, 156–57; Raeburn, "Submerging Ethnicity," 10; Chilton, *Sidney Bechet*, 2; Sancton, *Song for My Fathers*, 190.

36. Southern, *Music of Black Americans*, 82; Pitts, *Old Ship of Zion*, 27–28; Higgenbotham, *Righteous Discontent*, 7–11 ("nation within a nation" from E. Franklin Frazier); Holt, "Stylin' Outta the Black Pulpit," 332; Hurston, *Sanctified Church*, 91; Jacobs and Kaslow, *Spiritual Churches of New Orleans*, 29.

37. White and White, *Stylin'*, 172–77.

38. Levine, *Black Culture*, 53.

39. Herskovits, *Myth of the Negro Past*, 268; Van der Merwe, *Origins of the Popular Style*, 78; Roberts, *From Trickster to Badman*, 121; Stuckey, *Slave Culture*, 26–30.

40. Sobel, *Trabelin' On*, 142; White and White, *Sounds of Slavery*, 11; Marquis, *In Search of Buddy Bolden*, 31, citing "paraphrased script from tape of Allen and Russell interview with Harrison Barnes, January 29, 1959, Hogan Jazz Archive." By "shout" Barnes clearly is referring to the dance, like a ring shout, not a sound.

41. Stuckey, *Slave Culture*, 10–17, 53–63; Hurston, *Sanctified Church*, 104; White and White, *Sounds of Slavery*, 139. For a good example of a ring shout, complete with rhythmic foot stamping, listen to "Run Old Jeremiah" sung by Joe Washington Brown and Austin Coleman at Jennings, Louisiana, 1934, *Afro-American Spirituals, Work Songs, and Ballads*.

42. Stuckey, *Slave Culture*, 90–91, 93; Berry, *Spirit of Black Hawk*, 102. Levine, *Black Culture*, 21, 37–38, also discusses reports of ring shouts at camp meetings.

43. Stuckey, *Slave Culture*, 56.

44. White and White, *Sounds of Slavery*, 110; Jacobs and Kaslow, *Spiritual Churches of New Orleans*, 27.

45. Van der Merwe, *Origins of the Popular Style*, 76; Herskovits, *Myth of the Negro Past*, 209, 233; Whalum, *Black Hymnody*, 168; Sanders, *Saints in Exile*, 18; Harvey, *Redeeming the South*, 119.

46. Maultsby, "Africanisms," 195; Herskovits, *Myth of the Negro Past*, 214–16; Levine, *Black Culture*, 31; Holt, "Stylin' Outta the Black Pulpit," 337.

47. Barker, *Life in Jazz*, 61. On class in Southern urban communities in the late nineteenth century, see Litwack, *Trouble in Mind*, 377.

48. Although the ordinance creating Storyville passed in 1897, most prostitutes did not set up shop there until around 1900. Hair, *Carnival of Fury*, 79; Panetta, "'For Godsake Stop!'" 19.

49. Shapiro and Hentoff, *Hear Me Talkin'*, 7, 12–13; Hazzard-Gordon, *Jookin'*, 85; Gushee, "Nineteenth-Century Origins of Jazz," 108n, 115–17; Manetta interview, May 13, 1958; Manetta interview, March 12, 1957.

50. Hair, *Carnival of Fury*, 78; Medley, *We as Freemen*, 332–38. On "pig ankle corners," see Winston, *News Reporting*, 31–32.

51. Lomax, "Selections from the 1949 New Orleans Jazz Interviews," 165 (interview with Leonard Bechet); Winston, *News Reporting*, 31–32, quoting *New Orleans Item*, November 10, 1900, 10; Hair, *Carnival of Fury*, 76–78; Charles interview; Ory interview. There is a controversy about how many musicians were employed in the District. Early accounts portrayed the District as the birthplace of jazz, contributing to the music's image as depraved and disrespectable. Perhaps in an attempt to elevate jazz's image, some later writers claimed that very few jazz musicians actually played in the District. The truth seems to be that, in contrast to revisionist accounts, many important musicians did play there at one time or another, but it was not necessarily their main place of employment. As Johnny St. Cyr put it, "At one time or another all the musicians in New Orleans must have worked someplace in the District." St. Cyr, "Jazz as I Remember It: Part 2," 22.

52. Marquis, *In Search of Buddy Bolden*, 53, 67. The Odd Fellows Hall charged only fifteen cents for admission. F. Ramsey, "Vet Tells Story of the Original Creole Orchestra." More respectable halls charged twenty-five to fifty cents admission. Kernfeld, *New Grove Encyclopedia of Jazz*, 886. On working-class patrons, see Koenig, "Sites of Jazz." Armstrong, Johnny Dodds, Sidney Bechet, and Lee Collins played at the Red Onion at various times.

53. Manetta interview, March 12, 1957; Amacker interviews; Lomax, "Unrecorded Interview Material and Research Notes," 186, 199; W. Russell, *"Oh, Mister Jelly,"* 142; Bigard interview; Jones, *Talking Jazz*, 28 (Albert Nicholas interview).

54. Amacker interview, July 1, 1960; Lomax, "Unrecorded Interview Material and Research Notes," 178, 186.

55. Glenny interview. Listening to the tape itself reveals some errors in the transcript.

56. Drummer Henry Zeno was also a pimp. Shapiro and Hentoff, *Hear Me Talkin'*, 12, 44. Armstrong, *Satchmo*, 64; Foster, *Pops Foster*, 61; Mitchell, *All on a Mardi Gras Day*, 160; Raeburn, "Stars of David." Morton's great-grandmother was Jewish. According to his sister, Francis M. Oliver, "My brother and I both got our large Jewish noses from our great grandmother Mimi . . . so, of course, we're Jewish." Quoted in W. Russell, *"Oh, Mister Jelly,"* 87.

57. Shapiro and Hentoff, *Hear Me Talkin'*, 12 (Danny Barker); Hair, *Carnival of Fury*, 78; Kenney, *Jazz on the River*, 29, 51. According to Kenney, minstrel-like stereotypes were applied to roustabouts, so newspaper and magazine reports about them should be taken with a grain of salt.

58. Fremaux, *Leon Fremaux's New Orleans Characters;* Hearn, *Lafcadio Hearn's America*, 48–49.

59. Barker, *Life in Jazz*, 16, 61–62. Shapiro and Hentoff, *Hear Me Talkin'*, 50–52. It should be noted that Kelly apparently did play with Creoles like Manuel Manetta. Manetta interview, November 20, 1968.

60. Barker, *Life in Jazz*, 12–15. Here he is speaking of Animule (or Animal) Hall, which was in the Eighth Ward, but his remarks apply to other clubs as well.

61. W. Russell, *New Orleans Style*, 104 (Pops Foster).

62. Bigard, *With Louis and the Duke*, 8; Oliver interview; Barker, *Buddy Bolden*, 63, 68–69.

63. Foucault, "Of Other Spaces." Even the common practice of buying drinks for fellow patrons can be seen as a reversion to precapitalist, more egalitarian forms of social relationships. Ogren, "Nightlife," 60.

64. Litwack, *Trouble in Mind*, 434.

65. Bakhtin, *Rabelais*; DaMatta, *Carnivals, Rogues, and Heroes*, 41.

66. Hall, "Formation of Afro-Creole Culture," 63; Hall, *Africans in Colonial Louisiana*, 238. For an approach that emphasizes the survival of African culture in other colonies and contests some of Hall's conclusions, see Lovejoy, "African Diaspora."

67. Hall, *Africans in Colonial Louisiana*, 160–61, 131, 14, 115, 118; Abrahams et al., *Blues for New Orleans*, 86.

68. Medley, *We as Freemen*, 91.

69. Marquis, *In Search of Buddy Bolden*, 22; Raeburn, "Submerging Ethnicity," 1–4.

70. Levine, *Black Culture*, 22; Southern, *Readings*, 105, 88, 84; Sobel, *Trabelin' On*, 140.

71. Hazzard-Gordon, *Jookin'*, 57.

72. Kmen, *Music in New Orleans*, 7, 46, 43; Mitchell, *All on a Mardi Gras Day*, 36.

73. Woodward, *Strange Career of Jim Crow*, 15. Woodward quotes Richard C. Wade, *Slavery in the Cities*.

74. Berry, "African Cultural Memory," 6; Johnson, "New Orleans's Congo Square," 141–42. On Congo Square, see also D. Walker, *No More, No More*. For a dissenting view on the importance of Congo Square, see Kmen, "Roots of Jazz and the Dance in Place Congo," 5–16. Kmen argues that any

connection between Congo Square and jazz is quite distant. In addition, early jazz drumming was quite simple, unlike the complex rhythms described in Congo Square. Early jazz musicians used snare drums and bass drums from brass bands, not African drums. Congas and bongos came much later in jazz, with the influx of Latin American bands.

75. Cable, "Dance in Place Congo and Creole Slave Songs," 33; D. Walker, "Cultures of Control / Cultures of Resistance," 162, 187, 396; Johnson, "New Orleans's Congo Square," 139–40; Fischer, "Post–Civil War Segregation Struggle," 291–92. The agitation had begun with a series of articles by Creoles of Color in the *New Orleans Tribune*.

76. Berry, "African Cultural Memory," 5–6; Hearn, *Lafcadio Hearn's America*, 131.

77. Long, *Great Southern Babylon*, 60–62. This cover was a response to an 1887 *Harper's New Monthly Magazine* article on New Orleans stating that "no other city of the United States so abounds in stories pathetic and tragic . . . growing out of the mingling of races . . . especially out of the relations between whites and the fair women who had in their thin veins drops of African blood," but arguing that such racial intermixing was coming to an end. Thus the article was titled "Sights of New Orleans, the Harpers [sic] Did Not See."

78. Hair, *Carnival of Fury*, 76–78; W. Russell, *"Oh, Mister Jelly,"* 133, 135, 139.

79. W. Russell, *"Oh, Mister Jelly,"* 135.

80. Ibid., 133.

81. V. Turner, *Ritual Process*, 95–96, 125–28; Bhabha, *Location of Culture*, 2.

82. The Morton quote is from W. Russell, *"Oh, Mister Jelly,"* 132–33; Long, *Great Southern Babylon*, 197.

83. Paul Barbarin interview, December 23, 1959; Barbarin and Bolin, "All Gone Now," 21–22.

84. Morton and Lomax, "Library of Congress Narrative"; Provenzano, "Jazz Music of the Gay '90s."

85. Bocage interview; Foster, *Pops Foster*, 16; Ory interview.

86. Brown interview.

87. Foucault, "Of Other Spaces"; W. Russell, *New Orleans Style*, 103, 115; Foster, *Pops Foster*, 41–42; Barker, *Buddy Bolden*, 20–21; Souchon interview. On the blues as "trash" see W. Russell, *"Oh, Mister Jelly,"* 17 (recollections of Roy Carew).

88. Szwed with Abrahams, "After the Myth," 104. On serenading, see Hightower interview and Willie Foster interview. Foster describes a police officer who enjoyed being serenaded, but Hightower tells of serenading waltzes like "Over the Waves" and being chased away by an officer on the street named Pat Kennedy.

89. V. Turner, *Ritual Process*, 96; Monson, *Saying Something*, 68.

90. Abrahams, *Singing the Master*, 98; White and White, *Stylin'*, 72–77.

91. According to Pops Foster, Bolden "played nothing but blues and all that stink music." *Pops Foster*, 16.

92. Morton and Lomax, "Library of Congress Narrative."

93. Vincent and Miller interview, December 3, 1959; Morton and Lomax, "Library of Congress Narrative"; Stearns and Stearns, *Jazz Dance*, 21–22; Barker, *Buddy Bolden*, 20. Lawrence Gushee argues, against those who see jazz growing out of older dances like mazurkas and quadrilles, that the music developed in tandem with these newer dances (Gushee, "Nineteenth-Century Origins," 117).

94. According to Manuel Manetta, people would pop paper bags during the breaks in the quadrilles. Manetta interview, March 21, 1957. On the Buzzard Lope, see Stuckey, *Slave Culture*, 64–65. In general, see J. Malone, *Steppin'*.

95. Morath, "Ragtime Then and Now," 38.

96. Lefebvre, *Production of Space*, 206; Hanchard, "Afro-Modernity," 282–85.

97. Raeburn, "Early New Orleans Jazz in Theaters," 47, 51.

98. Ory interview; Armstrong, *Louis Armstrong—A Self-Portrait*, 8; Manetta interview, January 4, 1969. Kid Ross and other musicians "smoked dope" as well—"they were all dope fiends." Manetta interview, June 9, 1969.

99. Manetta interview, March 21, 1957.

100. Lomax, "Selections from the 1949 New Orleans Jazz Interviews," 148 (Albert Glenny and Leonard Bechet).

101. White and White, *Stylin'*, 242.

102. Morton and Lomax, "Library of Congress Narrative"; Long, *Great Southern Babylon*, 66–7. See also Porter, *What Is This Thing*, 29. On Oliver's wearing of red undershirts, see W. Russell, *"Oh, Mister Jelly,"* 503.

103. Barbarin interview, March 27, 1957; Morton and Lomax, "Library of Congress Narrative."

104. Stoddard, *Jazz on the Barbary Coast*, 47; Raeburn, "Louis and Women"; Lomax, *Mister Jelly Roll*, 167; Chamberlain, "Goodson Sisters."

105. Unterbrink, *Jazz Women at the Keyboard*, 10–11; Manetta interview, March 28, 1957; Nicholas interview; Miller interview, April 4, 1960. Camilla Todd sang with the Tuxedo Band.

106. Manetta interview, January 4, 1969; Long, *Great Southern Babylon*, 208; Hetherington, *Badlands of Modernity*, 31, 51.

107. Orsi, "Parades, Holidays, and Public Rituals," 1913, 1920.

108. Hazel interview; Vincent interview, December 3, 1959; Manetta interview, March 21, 1957; Parenti and Sbarbaro interview.

109. Alecia Long has dispelled the myth that the two vice districts, Storyville and Black Storyville, were strictly segregated: "Women and men of all classes, colors, and descriptions worked in, patronized, or went slumming in the two neighborhoods deemed vice districts by Ordinance 13,485 C.S." Long, *Great Southern Babylon*, 194.

110. Barker, *Life in Jazz*, 12–15.

111. Shapiro and Hentoff, *Hear Me Talkin'*, 50–52; Koenig, "Sites of Jazz," 8; Koenig, *Under the Influence*, 57; Foster, *Pops Foster*, 41–42.

112. Garland interview, August 16, 1958; Manetta interview, June 17, 1958. Manetta tells of Dodds's being hit with brass knuckles once: Manetta interview, July 11, 1969.

113. Charles, "Hypolite Charles Interview," 29; George Lewis interview, October 21, 1968; W. Russell, *New Orleans Style*, 175; Rose Tio interview. See Regis, "Second Lines," on the domestication and revitalizing of second line parades, including funerals.

114. Shapiro and Hentoff, *Hear Me Talkin'*, 44; Barker, *Life in Jazz*, 62, 34; Lomax, "Selections from the 1949 New Orleans Jazz Interviews" (Albert Glenny and Leonard Bechet); Morton and Lomax, "Library of Congress Narrative"; George Lewis interview, November 25, 1968.

115. Barbarin interview, March 27, 1957; Loyacano interview; Barker, *Life in Jazz*, 34.

116. Knowles, *Fallen Heroes*, 53–54; Barker, *Life in Jazz*, 50.

CHAPTER TWO

1. Quoted in Berry, *Spirit of Black Hawk*, 87.

2. Latrobe, *Impressions*, 51n. Emphasis in original.

3. C. Harris, "Story of *Plessy*," 184, 194, 208. On cases denying citizenship to immigrants of color, see in Haney López, *White by Law*.

4. Although an article in 1684 represented the first attempt to classify the races, the idea that racial identity was something biological, fixed by nature, did not become prevalent until the mid-nineteenth century. One influential theory, polygenism, proposed that the races had each been created separately. Others claimed that the races formed a distinct hierarchy, with blacks at the bottom. These views were held by prominent scientists, who in the name of science supported racial inequality. Darwin's notion of evolution called into question many of these conclusions, since it posited nature as being constantly in flux, with even the boundary between "species," let alone races, being essentially arbitrary. However, many scientists and intellectuals, as well as the general public, were reluctant to embrace the implications of Darwinism for race relations. Gossett, *Race*, 33, 49; Menand, *Metaphysical Club*, 109–16, 123.

5. Long, *Great Southern Babylon*, 149, 163–68. Josie Arlington was the pseudonym of Mary A. Deubler. Cursing by prostitutes brought a $5 fine, while drunkenness cost the woman $10. W. Russell, *"Oh, Mister Jelly,"* 151.

6. Manetta interview, January 4, 1969; Barker, *Buddy Bolden*, 27.

7. Nasaw, *Going Out*, 1–2; Rorabaugh, "Alcohol and Alcoholism," 2139. In many cities, saloons offered a free lunch and inexpensive beer, also serving as employment agencies and banks. Saloons were an integral part of political machines; patrons often voted as the saloonkeeper directed.

8. Hazzard-Gordon, *Jookin'*, 59; Mitchell, *All on a Mardi Gras Day*, 36; Kmen, *Music in New Orleans*, 33.

9. Minstrel shows did regularly travel to New Orleans; see www.uttyl.edu/ vbetts/new_orleans_picayune_My55-De55.htm for *Picayune* references to minstrel shows in 1855. I know of no account of jazz musicians performing minstrelsy in New Orleans; however, when they traveled elsewhere, they sometimes were required to do so in order to play their music. See Gushee, "How the Creole Band Came to Be." There are also pictures of Morton in blackface in Reich and Gaines, *Jelly's Blues*.

10. Long, Great Southern Babylon, 86.

11. Gossett, *Race*, 281; Kousser, "Before *Plessy*," 230. The opinion was printed in the *New Orleans Daily Picayune*, May 21, 1878, 1.

12. Joyner, "Ragtime Controversy," 242–44; Berlin, *King of Ragtime*, 88.

13. For an example of the kind of report issued and regulations created to control dance halls, see Public Dance Hall Commission, *Public Dance Halls Investigation and Ordinance*.

14. McBee, *Dance Hall Days*, 69–70, 87; Ogren, "Nightlife," 1713; "Dance Hall Feud," *New Orleans Daily Picayune*; "Keep the Dance Halls Closed," *New Orleans Daily Picayune*; R. Edwards, *Popular Amusements*, 76; Long, *Great Southern Babylon*, 86.

15. Hair, *Carnival of Fury*, 152.

16. Starr and Waterman, *American Popular Music*, 35; Ogren, "Debating with Beethoven," 249–50; Romanowski, *Pop Culture Wars*, 62. On segregation and protecting white women, see C. Harris, "Story of *Plessy*," 200. On the poor as lacking in self-control, see Sumner, *What Social Classes Owe to Each Other*. On the attack on mass culture, see Hersch, *Democratic Artworks*, chap. 1.

17. "Jass and Jassism," *New Orleans Times-Picayune*.

18. Runyon, "Popular Music before 1950," 1787–88.

19. "Dance Halls Wide Open," *New Orleans Item*.

20. B. Johnson, "Jazz as Cultural Practice," 96; Mackey, "Other," 517; Cockrell, *Demons of Disorder*, 80. On the "emergent" and "structures of feeling," see Williams, *Marxism and Literature*, 132–33, 189.

21. "Jass and Jassism"; Needham, *I See America*, 98, 117. Along the same lines, Ambrose Bierce in 1877 called the modern waltz "not merely 'suggestive' . . . but an open and shameless gratification of sexual desire and a cooler of burning lust," "a realization of a certain physical ecstasy which should at least be indulged in private, and, as some would go so far as to say, under the matrimonial restrictions." In 1901, writers referred to modern dancing as "hugging set to music," which acted "to fan the flame of passion, to gratify as far as possible an unhallowed lust, to lead the unwary into lascivious nets." Wagner, *Adversaries of Dance*, 202.

22. Needham, *I See America Dancing*, 68; Stearns and Stearns, *Jazz Dance*, 21. Stearns and Stearns quote Alice Zeno characterizing the dances at Congo Square as "common."

23. McBee, *Dance Hall Days*, 63–64; R. Edwards, *Popular Amusements*, 78; Nasaw, *Going Out*, 106, 108, quoting Mr. and Mrs. Vernon Castle. On the

relationship between the Castles and James Reese Europe, see Badger, *Life in Ragtime*.

24. 1909 poster for Economy Hall; 1910 poster for Economy Hall; Koenig, "Four Country Brass Bands," 14; 1910 poster for Dixie Park; 1907 poster for Lincoln Park Picnic.

25. Barker, *Life in Jazz*, 5; Paul Barbarin interview, January 7, 1959; Logsdon and Bell, "Americanization of Black New Orleans," 203.

26. Lomax, *Mister Jelly Roll*, 145, 168.

27. L. DuBois, *Avengers of the New World*, 62; Williamson, *New People*, 95; Guillory, "Under One Roof," 82.

28. Kein, "Use of Louisiana Creole," 127.

29. Domínguez, *White by Definition*, 136; L. DuBois, *Avengers of the New World*, 65; S. Thompson, "Ah Toucoutou," 243–45, and "Passing of a People," 287–88; Bennett, "Catholics, Creoles," 191; Senter, "Creole Poets," 283–84.

30. Hearn, *Inventing New Orleans*, 31; Brasseaux, "Creoles of Color," 83; Somers, "Black and White in New Orleans," 29. Somers refers to the letter writer as "black," but given the writer's point of view (and Somers's lack of distinction between black and Creole) he was probably Creole.

31. Bennett, "Catholics, Creoles," 193–94; J. Johnson, "New Orleans's Congo Square," 139.

32. Anthony, "Negro Creole Community," 46; Rose Tio interview.

33. Lomax, *Mister Jelly Roll*, 78; St. Cyr, "Jazz as I Remember It: Part 2," 23; Martyn, *End of the Beginning*, 129 (Rose Tio); Bigard, *With Louis*, 7. For middle-class Creole or black references to themselves as decent and respectable in the 1880s, see Somers, *Rise of Sports*, 143, 148. St. Cyr is speaking of the Golden Rule Band.

34. Rankin, "Forgotten People," 135, 245, 286. On the complicated relationship between Creoles of Color and blacks, see Bell, *Revolution, Romanticism*.

35. Barker, *Life in Jazz*, 61. On Robichaux's hair, see Ory interview, comments by Mrs. Ory (page 52 of transcript). On the necessity for "silky" hair in certain bands, see George Lewis interview, November 25, 1968. On Robichaux as a "gentleman," see Wiggs and Schilling interview.

36. Manetta interview, May 13, 1958; Anthony, "Negro Creole Community," 44, 110–114; Kernfeld, *New Grove Dictionary of Jazz*, 882–87 ("Nightclubs—New Orleans"); Karl Koenig, "Sites of Jazz"; Miller, "New Orleans Jazz." Perseverance Hall and Economy Hall were in Tremé, while Artisan Hall and Francs Amis were in the Seventh Ward. Jazz musicians living in Tremé included George Lewis, Chris Kelly, Jimmy Noone, and Henry Ragas, while those hailing from the Seventh Ward include Buddy Petit, Lizzie Miles, Lorenzo Tio Jr., Barney Bigard, Omar Simeon, Paul Barbarin, Manuel Perez, and Armand Piron. For information on these two neighborhoods, see the website of the Greater New Orleans Community Data Center: www.gnocdc.org/orleans/4/14/snapshot.html and www.gnoc.org/orleans/4/42/snapshot.html.

37. Somers, *Rise of Sports*, 143, 148.
38. Crawford, "Mainstreams and Backwaters," 4–5.
39. Southern, *Readings*, 62–3; Southern, *Music of Black Americans*, 146.
40. White and White, *Sounds of Slavery* 103–5; Southern, *Music of Black Americans*, 131.
41. Southern, *Readings*, 69; Stuckey, *Slave Culture*, 93–94; J. W. Johnson, *Books of American Negro Spirituals*, 33.
42. Gilkes, "Together and in Harness," 230, 238.
43. Stuckey, *Slave Culture*, 93; Harvey, *Redeeming the South*, 122, 107–8.
44. Higgenbotham, *Righteous Discontent*, 200; Logsdon and Bell, "Americanization of Black New Orleans," 236, 243.
45. White and White, *Stylin'*, 222–23; Higgenbotham, *Righteous Discontent*, 199–209.
46. Higgenbotham, *Righteous Discontent*, 187–96; Long, *Great Southern Babylon*, 139; Monson, "Problem with White Hipness," 420.
47. Jackson, *New Orleans in the Gilded Age*, 254–55.
48. Loyacano interview.
49. Hobson, "Prostitution," 2159–60; Nasaw, *Going Out*, 11. On segregation and movie theater balconies, see Lewis, *Walking with the Wind*, 36.
50. Letter to Boyle, May 16, 1911; Long, *Great Southern Babylon*, 139, 103; Longstreet, *Sportin' House*, 167.
51. Letter to Berman, April 10, 1911; letter to Whitaker from Rawlings, November 9, 1906.
52. Letter to Gaster from Walsh, November 1898; letter to Boyle from police captain, February 9, 1911; letter to O'Connor, January 24, 1910.
53. Letter to Reynolds from O'Mullen, April 1, 1911; letter to Boyle from Azcona, April 9, 1911; letter to Whitaker from two detectives, September 8, 1907. In the case of La-Rocca's saloon, the police found the complaint to be "not well founded." Letter to Boyle from police sergeant, May 4, 1911.
54. Letter to Whitaker from Rawlings, November 9, 1906.
55. Letter to Boyle from Driscoll, July 10, 1907; letter to Reynolds from commanding sergeant, May 31, 1911. Another complaint was lodged against "Two Well Known Gentlemen" putting on a function at Odd Fellows Hall for violating the Gay-Shattuck law, a 1908 state statute banning saloons within three hundred feet of a church or school and mandating segregated bars. The police, however, found "no sign of intoxicating liquor," since only "soft drinks were sold." Letter to Reynolds from Rawlings, March 1, 1911.
56. The police could clearly be racist, as when an officer was told "to break up . . . negroes from playing ball" in a particular neighborhood but "not to interfere with the white boys playing ball" because the "negro boys" used obscene language and hung their coats on the trees, breaking branches. Letter to Reynolds from Gorman, March 26, 1913.
57. "Dance Halls Wide Open"; "Keep the Dance Halls Closed."
58. Long, *Great Southern Babylon*, 181, 145–47, 216.

59. Jackson, *New Orleans in the Gilded Age*, 274–75.
60. Arnesen, *Waterfront Workers*, 16, 158, 181; Borders, "Researching Creole and Cajun Musics," 19; Blassingame, *Black New Orleans*, 13; Berry, "African Cultural Memory," 6; Regis, "Blackness and the Politics of Memory," and "Second Lines, Minstrelsy."
61. Knight, *Caribbean*, 146; Mahar, *Behind the Burnt Cork Mask*, 2–3, 342–45. Mahar notes that such minstrels also criticized immigrants and schemes for reform. Interestingly, though they used the black mask for such identity changes and satire, they also drew on burlesques drawn from English stage comedy (59).
62. Merrick, *Old Times in Dixie Land*, 164–65.
63. Leonard, *Jazz and the White Americans*, 34.
64. Ford, "Urban Space and the Color Line"; C. Harris, "Story of *Plessy*," 186.
65. Epstein, *Sinful Tunes*, 23, 133.
66. Ibid., 133, 206, 232, 295.
67. Ibid., 291.
68. Ibid., 226.
69. Levine, *Unpredictable Past*, 172–88, especially 181; Sotiropoulos, *Staging Race*, 221–22.
70. Foster, *Pops Foster*, 44, 64.
71. Koenig, "Sites of Jazz," 8; Raeburn, "Ethnic Diversity"; Fiehrer, "From Quadrille to Stomp," 23–24; Ryan, *Civic Wars*, 43.
72. Kmen, *Music in New Orleans*, 202, quoting the *New Orleans Times-Picayune*, February 14, 1837; Ryan, *Civic Wars*, 47.
73. Ryan, *Civic Wars*, 47, 227–28; Christian interview; Brunies interview; Brunis interview; Bonano interview; Regis, "Second Lines," 483.
74. Dixon, "Milneburg Joys," 11; U.S. Department of the Interior, National Park Service, "National Register of Historic Places Inventory: Nomination Form"; Kmen, "Joys of Milneburg," 18–19.
75. Koenig, "Sites of Jazz," 9; Kmen, "Joys of Milneburg," 19; Souchon, "Places in Early Jazz," 5–6; W. Russell, *"Oh, Mr. Jelly,"* 12. The camps had cottages and boardwalks. At one point there were apparently 115 such camps. See also Dixon, "Milneburg Joys." The tune "Milneburg Joys" was written by Morton, Paul Mares, and Leon Ropollo.
76. Barbarin interview, December 23, 1959; Sbarbaro and Christian interview.
77. Barbarin and Bolton, "All Gone Now," 20–21; Keppard interview. Dance halls and casinos were open at night at Milneburg, but it is unclear how integrated they were. As in the evening hours elsewhere in the city, things became more raucous. As someone put it, "The beer flowed like water and everything was free!" There was a jail between a dance hall and a saloon; those who did not sober up were booked. On Monday morning the drunks were put on the train and sent back. Dixon, "Milneburg Joys," 20.
78. Cangelosi, "West End"; Swanson, "History of Bucktown." For testimony by musicians on the area's influence, see Edwards interview and La Rocca

interview, May 21, 1958. For additional photos of West End and Spanish Fort in the late 1800s, see www.stphilipneri.org/teacher/pontchartrain/section.php?id=144, as well as Huber, *New Orleans*; Mugnier, *Louisiana Images*; and Mugnier, *New Orleans and Bayou Country*.

79. Marquis, "Lincoln Park"; Clementin interview.

80. St. Cyr, "Jazz as I Remember It: Part 2," 22; Kimball interview; Bailey interview; Nicholas interview; Dawson interview; Emile Barnes interview. For a discussion of the Irish Channel, including debates about its boundaries, see Campanella, *Geographies*, 227–45.

81. Brunis interview; Saxon, Dreyer, and Tallant, *Gumbo Ya-Ya*, 50–58. According to this account, part of a Works Progress Administration Louisiana Writer's Project, one man says, "It was all good clean fighting. We kept the niggers and other people who didn't belong out of the Channel and we made the bastards on the riverfront pay us good money."

82. Barbarin interview, January 7, 1959; Loyacano interview; Christian interview; Manetta interview, March 21, 1957; St. Cyr, "Jazz as I Remember It: Part 2," 22, also says similar things.

83. Barbarin interview, December 23, 1959.

CHAPTER THREE

1. Musicians typically made $2.50 or less (perhaps $1.50 or $2.00, plus tips) for playing 8:00 p.m. to 4:00 a.m., though "society" jobs could pay more, perhaps $4; parades paid $3 or $4. During Mardi Gras, a musician might earn $7 for a parade. These figures were taken from Brunis interview; Manetta interview, March 21, 1957; Nicholas interview; Sbarbaro interviews, February 11, 1959, and June 29, 1959; Souchon interview; St. Cyr interview. By way of comparison, in the 1880s, house carpenters, "among the worst paid skilled laborers," earned $2 a day, and longshoreman and screwmen could make $4–5 a day. Longshoremen were paid similar wages in the 1890s, but work was somewhat irregular. Arnesan, *Waterfront Workers*, 94, 157.

2. See Dodds, *Baby Dodds Story*, 10, 20, 29. Barker, *Buddy Bolden*, 21.

3. Wald, *Crossing the Line*, 10 (emphasis in original), 80; R. Williams, *Marxism and Literature*, 112.

4. Barker, *Life in Jazz*, 37; Dodds interview.

5. Dodds, *Baby Dodds Story*, 62.

6. Donaldson, "Window on Slave Culture," 63–64, 67; Latrobe, *Impressions*, 50–51. Others have described Congo Square dances as the calinda and bamboula, which were Caribbean, giving them a European influence as well as an African one. But observers agree that the words were in African languages. Hearn, *Lafcadio Hearn's America*, 131.

7. Walker, "Cultures of Control," 187.

8. *New Orleans Mascot* cover, January 22, 1887; Panetta, "For Godsake Stop!"

9. Palmer, *Deep Blues*, 24–25, 41; Nash interviews; Fontenot, "Times Ain't Like." Nash mentions "Stack-O-Lee," "St. Louis Blues," "It's a Long Way to Tipperary," "Yes We Have No Bananas," "Steamboat Bill," and "Casey Jones."

10. Kenney, *Jazz on the River*, 50–53; Hearn, *Lafcadio Hearn's America*, 48. See also Southern, *Music of Black Americans*, 148. On the sometimes unclear distinction between roustabouts, who traveled with ships, and longshoremen, who worked at the docks unloading them, see Kenney, *Jazz on the River*, 51. Barker, quoted by Kenney, speaks of roustabouts as traveling. See Bailey interview on hearing dockworkers. Willie Parker and Pops Foster worked on the docks; see Parker interview.

11. Willie Foster interview.

12. Koenig, "Plantation Belt," 24. Musicians from these areas are Pops Foster, Israel Gorman, Charlie Love, Punch Miller, Sam Morgan, and Willie Parker, respectively. Many came from Deer Range, including Jim Robinson and Chris Kelly.

13. Robinson interview; Miller interview, August 20, 1959; Pops Foster interview, April 21, 1957; Henry interview.

14. "Holy Roller" would imply a Sanctified church, but all the evidence says Bolden attended a Baptist church. St. John the Baptist was the patron saint of the ultra-emotional voodoo practitioners, but this may simply be a coincidence. According to St. Cyr, the smaller Baptist churches met in storefronts or homes and had a lot in common with the Sanctified Church (unless he is simply conflating the two). St. Cyr, "Jazz as I Remember It: Part 1," 7. On the complex relationship between black religious and secular music and rituals, see Murray, *Stomping the Blues*, 24–38.

15. Ory interview; Garland interviews; W. Russell, *New Orleans Style*, 176. On "jack-leg" preachers see Oliver, *Songsters and Saints*, 200–201.

16. Armstrong, *In His Own Words*, 170; Armstrong *Satchmo*, 11; Holt, "Stylin' Outta the Black Pulpit," 334.

17. Oliver, *Songsters and Saints*, 170–71; Hurston, *Sanctified Church*, 103.

18. Oliver, *Songsters and Saints*, 175.

19. Levine, *Black Culture*, 177; Cornish interview.

20. Dodds, *Baby Dodds Story*, 3. According to Johnny St. Cyr, in contrast to storefront or home-based churches, "the big churches were more solemn": "Jazz as I Remember It: Part 1," 7.

21. Anderson, "Johnny Dodds," 412.

22. Miller interviews, April 9, 1957, and August 20, 1959.

23. Hightower interview.

24. Jones interview.

25. Manetta interview, May 13, 1958. *Division* is Manetta's term; Knowles, *Fallen Heroes*, 81–82; Soderberg, "All about Baby"; Keppard interview.

26. Palmer interview.

27. Koenig, "Plantation Belt"; Koenig, "Professor James B. Humphrey, Part 2"; and Koenig, "Magnolia Plantation."

28. Berry, Foose, and Jones, *Up from the Cradle*, 11; Knowles, *Fallen Heroes*, 32. According to Albert Nicholas, the brass bands were the first place Creoles and blacks played together. Jones, *Talking Jazz*, 26–27.

29. Koenig, *Under the Influence*, 57 (quoting Kid Howard), 65.

30. Knowles, *Fallen Heroes*, 38, 25, 78, 76; Schafer, *Brass Bands*, 14.

31. Collins, *Oh, Didn't He Ramble*, 67; Vincent interview, December 11, 1959; Dodds, *Baby Dodds Story*, 34. One member of King Oliver's band, Honoré Dutrey, actually was a Creole. Raeburn, "Confessions of a New Orleans Jazz Archivist," 306.

32. Armstrong, *Own Words*, 35, 24. On Dodds, see Anderson, "Johnny Dodds," 428.

33. Hightower interview.

34. Hightower interview; Manetta interview, June 10, 1958.

35. See, for example, Collier, *Jazz*, 189–202.

36. Turner, *Remembering Song*, 21.

37. Woodward, "Case of the Louisiana Traveler," 167.

38. Olsen, *Thin Disguise*, 56–57.

39. Domínguez, *White by Definition*, 32–33; *State v. Treadway*.

40. According to the court, "educated people" in Louisiana know the clear meaning of the terms *mulatto*, *quadroon*, and *octoroon*; those terms have "as definite meaning as the word 'man' or 'child.'" The word *griff*, though less widely known, clearly means the offspring of a negro and a mulatto. The griff is "too black to be a mulatto and too pale in color to be a negro." "The person too dark to be a white, and too bright to be a griff, is a mulatto. Between these different shades, we do not believe there is much, if any, difficulty in distinguishing." *State v. Treadway*, 508–9.

41. Johnson, "Jim Crow Laws," 248–49; Domínguez, *White by Definition*, 263. Cf. *Lee et al. v. New Orleans Great Northern*, 184.

42. The court thus seems confused as to whether race is determined by "blood" (ancestry, mixture) or "appearance, education, and culture." *State v. Treadway*, 509.

43. *Lee et al. v. New Orleans*, 183. One white observer remembering his experiences in New Orleans at this time said that for whites, if a person was darker than an octoroon, he or she was black; whites did not distinguish between blacks and Creoles of Color. Carew, "Reflections," 6. When asked whether he played with Achille Baquet, Creole Manuel Manetta expressed surprise, because he (Manetta) played with a "colored band" and Baquet did not play with them. Manetta interview, May 10, 1968.

44. Johnson, "Jim Crow Laws," 248. His statement is true only if he is referring exclusively to statutory law, excluding judicial opinions.

45. Bontemps and Conroy, *Anyplace But Here*, 131–32; Haskins, *Creoles of Color*, 64; Johnson, "Jim Crow Laws," 243–51; Domínguez, *White by Definition*, 263.

46. Thompson, "Passing of a People."

47. Chilton, *Sidney Bechet*, 3.

48. Dodds, *Baby Dodds Story*, 15. The Creole Kid Ory's band featured black musicians.

49. Lomax, "Selections from the 1949 New Orleans Jazz Interviews," 143–44 (Leonard Bechet); St. Cyr, "Jazz as I Remember It: Part 1," 7.

50. Armstrong, *In His Own Words*, 24, 32; George Lewis interviews, October 21, 1968, November 25, 1968, and December 9, 1968; Foster, *Pops Foster*, 105.

51. Manetta interview, July 1, 1958.

52. Chilton, *Sidney Bechet*, 7; Louis Tio interview; W. Russell, *New Orleans Style*, 140 (Natty Dominque); St. Cyr, "Jazz as I Remember It: Part 1," 7; W. Russell, *"Oh, Mister Jelly,"* 62; Lomax, *Mister Jelly Roll*, 166. Pastras is skeptical of Gonzalez's statement; see Pastras, *Dead Man Blues*, 53.

53. St. Cyr, "Jazz as I Remember It: Part 2," 23. See also Ake, *Jazz Cultures*, 10–41; Lomax, *Mister Jelly Roll*, 83–86.

54. Turner, *Remembering Song*, 23–24.

55. Lewis interview, April 1966; Rose Tio interview.

56. De Lay interview; Keppard interview; Charles interview; Fiehrer, "From Quadrille to Stomp," 32. While Baquet and Perkins were the best-known musicians of color who passed for white, Knowles also lists Eddie Cherie and Arnold Metoyer as "black musicians passing for white" in the Reliance Brass Band. Knowles, *Fallen Heroes*, 81. Musicians who changed their names to sound less "foreign" included George Lewis, Don Albert, George Brunis, Raymond Burke, Lizzy Miles, "Big Eye" Louis Nelson, DeeDee Pierce, and Dolly Adams.

57. Schilling interview; De Lay interview.

58. Martin interview; Abby "Chinee" Foster interview, March 9, 1961. Martin calls himself "Spanish," but Raeburn, "Stars of David," 10, says Martin was Filipino. Note that there is a somewhat different version of the Foster quote in W. Russell, *New Orleans Style*, 48.

59. Barrell, "Baquets," 9.

60. Darensbourg, *Telling It Like It Is*, 52; Martyn, *End of the Beginning*, 98 (George Guesnon).

61. Glenny interview; Lomax, "Selections from the 1949 New Orleans Jazz Interviews," 151 (Leonard Bechet).

62. Ory interview; Ramsey, "Vet Tells Story," 3.

63. St. Cyr, "Jazz as I Remember It: Part 1," 7; Robichaux interview; Picou interview; Miles interview; Lomax, "Selections from the 1949 New Orleans Jazz Interviews," 158 (Alphonse Picou). Picou's story is not totally clear; in the Hogan Jazz Archive interview, he says he learned the blues from a bassist named Jimmy Brown, but he tells Lomax the story of the woman married to a railroad worker.

64. Lomax, "Selections from the 1949 New Orleans Jazz Interviews," 158 (Alphonse Picou); St. Cyr interview; Wilkinson, *Jazz on the Road*, 14–19; Peretti, *Creation of Jazz*, 17–21; Martyn, *End of the Beginning*, 83 (Ben Kelley).

65. Knowles, *Fallen Heroes*, 38.

66. Carter, *Preservation Hall*, 38–9.

67. See Brothers, *Louis Armstrong's New Orleans*, who argues that jazz was simply the development of a "black vernacular," directly disputing Morton's more integrative understanding of the music. According to Brothers, "Armstrong's musical development would not have been one bit different had he never heard an Italian aria or a French folk song" (303).

68. Raeburn, "Jazz and the Italian Connection"; Shapiro and Hentoff, *Hear Me Talkin'*, 61 (Jack Weber). For an interesting argument that the ODJB did in fact create a fundamental shift from ragtime to jazz by changing the meter from 2/4 to 4/4, see Stewart, "Original Dixieland Jazz Band's Place."

69. Keppard interview; Shapiro and Hentoff, *Hear Me Talkin'*, 61 (Jack Weber). Keppard says that as a kid he heard white bands playing across the street.

70. Epstein, *Sinful Tunes*, 114, 120–21.

71. Hair, *Carnival of Fury*, 73. Compare Armstrong's comments that he "did not get to know any of the White Musicians personally, because New Orleans was so Disgustingly Segregated and Prejudiced at the time—it didn't even run across our minds" (*In His Own Words*, 33). Boulard, "Blacks, Italians," 56.

72. Mitchell, *All on a Mardi Gras Day*, 160; Raeburn, "Stars of David"; J. Johnson, "New Orleans's Congo Square," 153n. Some historians argue that one's "race" would be considered "Southern Italian," while one's "color" would be white. As evidence for this position, in 1898 the *New Orleans Daily Picayune* reported that "the influx of the Italians between 1890–1900 made Louisiana a white state." Guglielmo, "No Color Barrier," 32, 38–39, quoting the *Daily Picayune*, March 13, 1898, 3.

73. Gambino, *Vendetta*, 49; Guglielmo, "No Color Barrier," 33, quoting Alfredo Niceforo; Guglielmo, "Introduction," 9; Hearn, *Lafcadio Hearn's America*, 65.

74. Scarpaci, "Walking the Color Line," 61; Morris, *Wait until Dark*, 84–85; Jackson, *New Orleans*, 18. On the antipathy of Creoles of Color toward Sicilians, see Barker's grandmother's comment on p. 64, above. Barker, *Life in Jazz*, 5.

75. Scarpaci, "Walking the Color Line," 66–67.

76. Gambino, *Vendetta*, 18, 20; Panetta, "For Godsake Stop!" 8; letter to Reynolds, May 31, 1911. In response to a complaint that "Italians had the fruit wharves and the Poydras Street commission houses all monopolized and it was impossible for Americans to make a living," police officers were "instructed to arrest them when found violating the law," and it is noted that "several of them have been arrested" in the last month: letter to Boyle, February 1, 1911.

77. Morris, *Wait until Dark*, 92–97; Hair, *Carnival of Fury*, 73; Boulard, "Blacks, Italians," 56; Raeburn, "Sons of David," 8; Schiro interview.

78. Malone, "Rabbi Max Heller," 22; Feibelman, "Social and Economic Study"; Armstrong, *In His Own Words*, 6–7; Brunis interview.

79. Wiggs interview.

80. George, "Jazz Was 'Beat Out'"; Christian interview. Tony Parenti also began by playing in spasm bands: Parenti and Sbarbaro interview.

81. This benevolent society was formed in 1886; according to some it was the first Italian society formed in the city. Contessa Entellina is a small mountain village in Sicily that was primarily a home to the Arbreshe; the society was for those in New Orleans from that village. Schiro interview; Wonk, "Sons of Contessa Entellina."

82. Loyacano interview; Parenti and Sbarbaro interview.

83. Oliver interview; Laine and Laine interview; Hazel interview; Rose Tio interview; Edwards interview.

84. Sbarbaro and Christian interview; Parenti and Sbarbaro interview. Parenti and other budding jazz musicians were familiar with opera; his parents often attended the French Opera, though they sat in the highest balcony because that is all they could afford. Eddie Edwards also cited the French Opera and military bands at West End or Spanish Fort as influences: Edwards interview. This love of opera was shared by Armstrong as well.

85. Bessie Smith once told Parenti she would like to hear his band but could not because of Jim Crow laws. Shields interview; Parenti, "Early Years"; Shapiro and Hentoff, *Hear Me Talkin'*, 61 (Jack Weber).

86. Brunis interview; Shapiro and Hentoff, *Hear Me Talkin'*, 58–59 (Jack Weber). "Happy" Schilling also tells of standing outside a club in the District to hear Oliver play: Schilling interview.

87. Parenti and Sbarbaro interview; Boulard, "Blacks, Italians," 60, citing the *Philadelphia Inquirer*, June 20, 1974. On the importance of Marable in general and the calliope in particular, see Kenney, *Jazz on the River*, 41–42, 56–60.

88. Brown interview. According to Brown, instead of the usual style he would play arpeggios on the basses.

89. Manetta interview, March 12, 1957; Sbarbaro and Christian interview; Brunis interview.

90. Boulard, "Blacks, Italians," 60; Parenti, "Early Years."

91. Schilling interview.

92. Ory interview.

93. Martyn, *End of the Beginning*, 187 (Edna Kelly); Miller interview, August 20, 1959; Love interview. On Kelly's taking multiple jobs in the same night, see George "Kid Sheik" Cola in Martyn, *End of the Beginning*, 190; and Howard interview, May 26, 1961.

94. Knight and Bilby, "Music in Africa and the Caribbean," 272.

95. Vincent and Miller interview, November 17, 1959. George Lewis described "spelling" (which he could do) as opposed to reading music: "I know all the signs of the music, but I can't read. . . . You say you're going to read a book? You pick it up and you go right on. You don't say, 'Uh, I,T,E,M . . . item,' you say 'item' right off. That's a reader. So the guy who rehearses it, comes back and makes it over, he's a speller. And most of the musicians around here are spellers, not readers": Bethell, *George Lewis*, 43.

96. Raeburn, "King Oliver, Jelly Roll Morton, and Sidney Bechet"; Chinee Foster interview, June 29, 1960.

97. Ward, "Hot Tuxedos," 7.
98. Martyn, *End of the Beginning*, 189 (Jack Kelly).
99. Koenig, *Under the Influence*, 65. Joseph "Fan" Bourgeau described him as only a blues player: Bourgeau interview.
100. Howard interview, December 22, 1958. Emile Barnes also remembered playing Joplin with Kelly—"not off the dots but pretty close": Martyn, *End of the Beginning*, 87. The countervailing view is given by Kelly's son Jack, who said that Kelly "played mostly for whites, that's who would engage him. They loved his music. Colored would hire him when they could get him because he was always busy." However, Jack Kelly was born in 1923 and had no first-hand knowledge of his father's earlier career. Martyn, *End of the Beginning*, 83. Howard, his pupil, said though he played for a number of Italian audiences, he played "mostly for colored": Martyn, *End of the Beginning*, 189.
101. Bethell, *George Lewis*, 63. Martyn, *End of the Beginning*, 85 (Jack Kelly).
102. Chilton, *Sidney Bechet*, 17. Leonard Bechet says he played "with all varieties of people," but the next sentence and the rest of the paragraph make clear he is referring to playing for different audiences as well.
103. St. Cyr, "Jazz as I Remember It: Part 1," 7–8.
104. Cornish interview; Phillips interview.
105. Manetta interview, January 4, 1969.
106. Foster, *Pops Foster*, 54; Lomax, *Mister Jelly Roll*, 31; Thompson interview; Souchon, "King Oliver," 344.
107. Christian interview.
108. Manetta interview, May 13, 1958; Cornish interview; W. Russell, *New Orleans Style*, 128 ("Sweet" Emma Barrett). Apparently the band received the tuxedos in exchange for advertising on the balcony of the tailor who made them.
109. DeVeaux, *Birth of Bebop*, 49; Koenig, "Magnolia Plantation," 35, 37.
110. Chinee Foster interview, June 29, 1960. When asked who the best trumpeter was, Foster answered "Joe Oliver," but qualified it by saying, "That's on the regular jazz, barrel house music. Now for real smoothness, musical trumpet player, I think [Creole] Manuel Perez." Similarly, Freddie Keppard "wasn't a real musical player, he was a blues player." Foster interview, March 9, 1961.
111. Vincent interview, December 3, 1959.
112. St. Cyr, "Jazz as I Remember It: Part 2," 10.
113. Bakhtin, *Speech Genres*, 145.

CHAPTER FOUR

1. Douglass, *Oxford Frederick Douglass Reader*, 40.
2. Epstein, *Sinful Tunes*, 8, 79.
3. Blassingame, *Slave Community*, 115; Epstein, *Sinful Tunes*, 186–88. A 1739 slave rebellion in South Carolina saw slaves dancing, singing, and playing drums in order to attract more slaves, as they killed whites and burnt land. Epstein, *Sinful Tunes*, 32, 42, 39–40, 60.

4. Levine, *Black Culture*, 37–38; Morgan and Barlow, *From Cakewalks to Concert Halls*, 7.

5. White and White, *Sounds of Slavery*, 117–18; Epstein, *Sinful Tunes*, 60. White spirituals had some similar themes, but they tended to be more "other-worldly," focusing more on Jesus and less on Old Testament imagery than those of blacks. Levine, *Black Culture*, 23.

6. Cable, "Dance in Place Congo," 51.

7. Levine, *Black Culture*, 408; Barlow, *Looking Up at Down*, 21–23; Southern, *Music of Black Americans*, 14, 18. Morgan and Barlow, *From Cakewalks to Concert Halls*, 8–9, 11.

8. Morton and Lomax, "Library of Congress Narrative."

9. Martyn, *End of the Beginning*, 100 (George Guenson); Morton, "Murder Ballad."

10. Armstrong, *Satchmo*, 132.

11. Morton and Lomax, "Library of Congress Narrative"; Levine, *Black Culture*, 412.

12. Brearley, "Ba-ad Nigger," 581n; Morton, "Murder Ballad."

13. Douglass, *Oxford Frederick Douglass Reader*, 118.

14. In Keepnews and Grauer, *Pictorial History of Jazz*, 15. The use of titles of nobility by African American jazz musicians, as a bid for respect in "democratic" America, deserves further study. In New Orleans, the best trumpeter (or cornetist) was called "King," a title bestowed on Buddy Bolden and Freddie Keppard before Oliver gained the "crown." In the post–New Orleans era, this trend continued less formally. One thinks of "Count" Basie, "Duke" Ellington, "Sir" Charles Thompson, and "Sir" Roland Hanna. The avant-garde bandleader "Sun Ra," harking back to ancient Egyptian Royalty, takes this trend to a seemingly higher level.

15. Ibid., 30.

16. White and White, *Stylin'*, 154.

17. Sotiropoulos, *Staging Race*, 9; Gates, *Signifying Monkey*, 51, 63.

18. Armstrong, *In His Own Words*, 59.

19. R. Thompson, "Aesthetic of the Cool," 81–2; Piersen, "Resistance Too Civilized," 348–52.

20. Knight and Bilby, "Music in Africa and the Caribbean," 271; Hearn, *Two Years in the French West Indies*, 159; Piersen, "Resistance Too Civilized," 354–55.

21. Epstein, *Sinful Tunes*, 72, 74; Southern, *Readings*, 73–6, 78–80; Piersen, "Resistance Too Civilized," 357–65. See also Southern, *Music of Black Americans*, 49, 183–85.

22. Douglass, *My Bondage and My Freedom*, 81, 98; Epstein, *Sinful Tunes*, 82–3. Blassingame describes such a situation: "At one of the balls . . . the domestic servants came dressed in their masters' cast-off clothing and brought some of their owners' silverware, table cloths, wine, and food for the guests who were dancing to the tunes played by a slave fiddler." Blassingame, *Slave Community*, 108.

23. Stearns and Stearns, *Jazz Dance*, 22; Blesh and Janis, *They All Played Ragtime*, 96.

24. Cable, "Dance in Place Congo"; Rose, *Storyville*, 103, 105; Manetta interview, June 20, 1958; Amacker interview, July 1, 1960; Ward and Burns, *Jazz*, 21. Morton sang a verse criticizing a Judge Fogarty—it is likely this originated around Bolden's time, because the judge had sentenced some band members to jail at times. Barlow, *Looking Up at Down*, 190.

25. Cable, "Dance in Place Congo," 48. See also Thompson, "Ah Toucoutou."

26. Oliver, *Songsters and Saints*, 135, 138.

27. Peretti, *Creation of Jazz*, 33; Schafer, *Brass Bands*, 53. According to musician Hypolite Charles, "We only played a few blocks outside of the graveyard because things usually got real bad with all the people by then. It was a disgrace the way some of them acted. The police would always have to be there to try and keep trouble down." Charles, "Hypolite Charles Interview," 29.

28. Schafer, *Brass Bands*, 95; Morton, "Dead Man Blues." On King Zulu as a parody of King Rex, see also Mitchell, *All on a Mardi Gras Day*, 151. Mitchell argues that Mardi Gras temporarily "broke down the city's system of racial control," which may have been part of its appeal for both races (36).

29. Marsalis's introduction to Touchet, Bagneris, and Marsalis, *Rejoice When You Die*, 2; Armstrong, *In His Own Words*, 171. Some funerals had as many as three or four bands (Stearns, *Story of Jazz*, 58). According to New Orleans jazz great Sidney Bechet, the procession marched past places the deceased used to frequent. The music was "seeing the world for him [the deceased] again," one final time (Bechet, *Treat It Gentle*, 217).

30. On double voicedness, see Bakhtin, *Problems of Dostoevsky's Poetics*, 40, 73–74; Stearns, *Story of Jazz*, 11–12.

31. Ellison, *Living with Music*, quoted in O'Meally, "Checking Our Balances," 282.

32. The "immeasurable distance" between black and white is what Douglass sees in "What to the Slave Is the Fourth of July?" Douglass, *Oxford Frederick Douglass Reader*, 116.

33. Tomlinson, "Cultural Dialogics and Jazz," 66.

34. Mackey, "Other: From Noun to Verb," 515.

35. Marquis, *In Search of Buddy Bolden*, 16; Schafer, *Brass Bands*, 94.

36. Walser, "Out of Notes," 168; Floyd, "Ring Shout," 271; Hurston, *Sanctified Church*, 49–68; Gilroy, *Black Atlantic*, 73.

37. Barlow, *Looking Up at Down*, 15.

38. Kmen, *Music in New Orleans*, 239–41; Barker, *Buddy Bolden*, 113–14; Collins, *New Orleans Jazz*, 29.

39. Monson, *Saying Something*, 116–17, 98; Floyd, "Ring Shout," 271; Murphy, "Jazz Improvisation."

40. On an African cultural aesthetic, see Caponi, "Introduction," especially 7–17.

41. Piersen, "African-American Festive Style," 418.

42. I. Berlin, "From Creole to African," 19–21, 26, 37, 48; Hall, *Africans in Colonial Louisiana*, 200. Compare Kmen, *Music in New Orleans*, 229 (reports on European forms), with J. Johnson, "New Orleans's Congo Square," 141 (describing Congo Square dances as purely African).

43. Waterman, "African Influence," 85.

44. Knight and Bilby, "Music in Africa and the Caribbean," 262; Wilson, "Black Music as an Art Form," 2. Other features that are often identified as differentiating African from European music, some of which are discussed later, include the dominance of percussion and rhythm, polymeters, a vocalized timbre, the "heterogeneous sound ideal" (a preference for individualized, nonstandard timbre), an inseparable connection with bodily movement, and the priority of performance over composition. In particular, some have argued that in African music "the timing and accentuation, finally, are not *stated*, but *implied* or suggested." Constantly shifting accents also undermine the sense of regularity and straightforwardness.

    It should be noted that many of these features were missing from early New Orleans jazz. Most notably, extensive polyrhythms and rhythmic complexity in general were absent, and jazz musicians used bass and snare drums, not the African drums heard in Congo Square. However, many important features endured, and these features made music a powerful force in New Orleans. Waterman, "African Influence"; Borneman, "Roots of Jazz"; Maultsby, "Africanisms"; Wilson, "Significance"; Wilson, "Heterogeneous Sound Ideal"; Gilroy, *Black Atlantic*, 105; Floyd, "African Roots of Jazz." Wilson argues convincingly that polymeter and syncopation are part of a continuum based on duration rather than two separate phenomena; that is, if syncopation goes on long enough, it establishes an alternate meter alongside the main one (Wilson, "Significance," 9). For an early analysis of the relationship between African and African American music, concluding that African and European music are "constructed on entirely different principles" and cannot be brought together, see von Hornbostel, "African Negro Music." See also Kmen, "Roots of Jazz," 14–16.

45. Chernoff, *African Rhythm*, 23. The quotation is from Léopold Sédar Senghor. According to Chernoff, "If you play a recording of American jazz for an African friend, even though all the formal characteristics of African music are there, he may say, as he sits fidgeting in his chair, 'What are we supposed to do with this?'" (23).

46. Chernoff, *African Rhythm*, 42 (emphasis in the original), 117.

47. See also chapter 1 for more on syncopation.

48. The same melody played simultaneously though rhythmically displaced, like a fugue, would be imitative homophony.

49. Wilson, "Heterogenous Sound Ideal," 162, 168.

50. Gilroy, *Black Atlantic*, 200; Gilroy, *Small Acts*, 138.

51. Miles Davis, "Bluing"; Borneman, "Roots of Jazz," 17. Interestingly, the ODJB also recorded a tune by Henry Ragas called "Bluin' the Blues" in 1920.

52. Southern, *Music of Black Americans*, 201; D. Evans, *Big Road Blues*, 23, 31; Barlow, *Looking Up at Down*, 3–4; R. Russell, *Jazz Styles in Kansas City*, 32; Hodes and Hansen, *Selections from the Gutter*, 70 (quoting Mutt Carey); Miller interview, April 4, 1960. It should be noted that other kinds of American folk music produced similar kinds of vocal and instrumental distortions. Peter van der Merwe has argued that the blues was in fact related to traditional British folk music and its American derivatives. Van der Merwe, *Origins of the Popular Style*.

53. Baraka, *Blues People*, 79; Pratt, *Rhythm and Resistance*, 78; Barlow, *Looking Up at Down*, xii, 3. The blues was a folk music in a number of senses. First, multiple versions of the same songs existed throughout the South. Second, the blues represented an oral tradition. It "borrowed freely from traditional song formats and from the stock of folk sayings, proverbs, and poetic images in the African American oral tradition." Finally, the blues was part of the texture of life, part of "cathartic" communal rituals involving body movement and an emphasis on emotional expression (Barlow, *Looking Up at Down*, 5, 9).

54. Barlow, *Looking Up at Down*, 27; Evans, *Big Road Blues*, 2; Bastin, *Red River Blues*, 5.

55. Titon, *Early Downhome Blues*, 28; Barlow, *Looking Up at Down*, 186.

56. Chernoff, *African Rhythms*, 59–60, 67, 110, 117, 121.

57. Lomax, "Selections from the 1949 New Orleans Jazz Interviews," 145 (Paul Domínguez). James Lincoln Collier is one of the scholars who claims that "when it first became known to the American public, [jazz] . . . was not essentially improvised": Collier, *Jazz*, 27.

58. Lomax, *Mister Jelly Roll*, 94; St. Cyr, "Jazz As I Remember It: Part 1," 8. According to St. Cyr, Keppard "was the first of the 'get off' cornet men—getting away from the melody, more like the clarinet" (8).

59. Lomax, "Selections from the 1949 New Orleans Jazz Interviews," 145–46, 160 (Alphonse Picou and Albert Glenny); Lomax, "Unrecorded Interview Material," 212.

60. Abrahams et al., *Blues for New Orleans*, 1, 8; Epstein, *Sinful Tunes*, 65, 75; Manuel, *Caribbean Currents*, 22, 32.

61. Abrahams et al., *Blues for New Orleans*, 16, 19, 43–49; Lovejoy, "African Diaspora," 14; Epstein, *Sinful Tunes*, 65, 75 (on funerals).

62. Manuel, *Caribbean Currents*, 13, 37, 157, 38, 16; J. S. Roberts, *Latin Tinge*, 5, 29; Leymarie, *Cuban Fire*, 22–34, 78–82.

63. Stewart, "Cuban Influences," 18–19; Narvaez, "Influences of Hispanic Music Cultures," 216; Szwed and Marks, "Afro-American Transformation," 31.

64. J. S. Roberts, *Latin Tinge*, 8, 17, 19; Narvaez, "Influences of Hispanic Music Cultures," 216.

65. J. S. Roberts, *Latin Tinge*, 35–37; Narvaez, "Influences of Hispanic Music Cultures," 213, 216. According to Narvaez, Leadbelly played with Mexican musicians and learned some of their techniques.

66. J. S. Roberts, *Black Music of Two Worlds*, 157; Abrahams et al., *Blues for New Orleans*, 31. The calinda (or kalinda) was a stick-fighting dance in Trinidad and has also been observed in other parts of the Caribbean. Knight and Bilby, "Music in Africa and the Caribbean," 264; Hunt, *Haiti's Influence*, 78. Jerah Johnson describes Congo Square dances as purely African: Johnson, "New Orleans's Congo Square."

67. White and White, *Stylin'*, 79; Hearn, *Lafcadio Hearn's America*, 48–49.

68. W. Russell, *New Orleans Style*, 103; Lomax, "Unrecorded Interview Material," 212.

69. Szwed and Marks, "Afro-American Transformation," 32, 34. The quote that begins "Quadrilles consumed" is from Thornton Hagert.

70. Lovejoy, "African Diaspora," 4–5, 6, 14–15.

71. Sanders, *Saints in Exile*, 54.

72. Southern, *Music of Black Americans*, 30–31, 446; Harvey, *Redeeming the South*, 130–33; White and White, *Sounds of Slavery*, 63. If they were singing the same melody but in an overlapping manner, this would technically be heterophony rather than polyphony. But since there was always some transforming of the original melody, one can accurately describe it as polyphony.

73. Southern, *Readings*, 151–52; White and White, "Listening to Southern Slavery," 251.

74. Southern, *Music of Black Americans*, 447, 146; Blassingame, *Black New Orleans*, 15; Epstein, "White Origin," 54; Southern, *Readings*, 152. (The first quote is from 1874, the second from 1867.)

75. White and White, *Sounds of Slavery*, 27.

76. Southern, *Readings*, 152.

77. White and White, *Sounds of Slavery*, 58; Lincoln and Mamiya, *Black Church*, 349.

78. White and White, *Sounds of Slavery*, 33–34, Epstein, "White Origin," 58; Southern, *Music of Black Americans*, 75–79, 85–86; Harvey, *Redeeming the South*, 130.

79. White and White, *Sounds of Slavery*, 51–54.

80. Levine, *Black Culture*, 159; White and White, *Sounds of Slavery*, 59–60.

81. Wilgus, "Negro-White Spiritual," 80; Herskovits, *Myth of the Negro Past*, 223. The phrase "sorrow songs" to refer to spirituals comes from DuBois, *Souls of Black Folk*.

82. The quotation is from Hill et al., booklet. On Spiritual Baptists, see Manuel, *Caribbean Currents*, 218.

83. Levine, *Black Culture*, 29, 189.

84. Ory interview; Oliver, *Songsters and Saints*, 176; Foster, *Pops Foster*, 21; Levine, *Black Culture*, 183. Today Holiness Church services feature improvisation on a variety of instruments including piano, Hammond organ, drums, bass guitar, saxophones, and tambourines. Reed, *Holy Profane*, 8, 23; Synan, *Holiness-Pentecostal Tradition*, 110.

85. White and White, *Sounds of Slavery*, 180.

86. Marquis, *In Search of Buddy Bolden*, 32, 100; Ory interview; W. Russell, *New Orleans Style*, 90 (Bud Scott).

87. Marquis, *In Search of Buddy Bolden*, 30–31, 43, 108; Cornish interview; Oliver interview; W. Russell, *New Orleans Style*, 163 (Johnny Wiggs); Koenig, "Magnolia Plantation," 37; W. Russell, *New Orleans Style*, 23 (Baby Dodds).

88. Marquis, *In Search of Buddy Bolden*, 30. See also Garland interview, August 16, 1958; Lewis interview, April 1966; Clarence "Little Dad" Vincent in Vincent and Miller interview, November 17, 1959. On the role of the church in this period in New Orleans, see Bennett, *Religion and the Rise of Jim Crow*. Bennett argues that New Orleans churches, Protestant and Catholic, were often interracial "well into the 1910s" and that Protestant denominations, particularly the Methodist Episcopal and Congregational ones, "engaged in a variety of explicit and frequently provocative interracial work, from social interaction during denominational meetings and biracial educational institutions, to advocating political, social, and racial reform" (2–3).

89. Levine, *Black Culture*, 181; Shapiro and Hentoff, *Hear Me Talkin'*, 42 (Mutt Carey); Martyn, *End of the Beginning*, 189 (Kid Howard; see also 91).

90. W. Russell, *New Orleans Style*, 63 (St. Cyr); Bethell, *George Lewis*, 66; Paul Barnes interview. The "coonjaille" (or coonjai) was described by Cable in his account of Congo Square; according to Southern, it was characterized in 1867 as a dance with a leader improvising verses and the rest of the group giving call-and-response shouts. Southern, *Music of Black Americans*, 181–82; see Southern, *Readings*, 174, for the original source. According to Abbott and Seroff, it has been connected to the later "coonjine," a supposed roustabout dance, but they are skeptical. Abbott and Seroff, *Out of Sight*, 308–12. One observer described the coonjine as "the combination song and dance that [was] associated with handling freight" by roustabouts. Kenney, *Jazz on the River*, 52; Marquis, *In Search of Buddy Bolden*, 32; St. Cyr interview; W. Russell, *New Orleans Style*, 60, 63.

91. Hodes and Hansen, *Selections from the Gutter*, 121 (George Lewis); Martyn, *End of the Beginning*, 187 (Ben Kelly).

92. Hurston, *Sanctified Church*, 107; Cone, *Spirituals and the Blues*, 62. Others have argued that the blues and spirituals share similar themes and similarly affirm African American identity: "the blues and the spirituals flow from the same bedrock of experience, and neither is an adequate interpretation of black life without the commentary of the other." According to John Michael Spencer, the blues "is a music that is theological and . . . talks about evil in folk theological language . . . and posits 'theodicies' reconciling the seeming incongruence of evil existing in a world believed to be created and ruled by a good God." The great blues singer Alberta Hunter said that the blues are "like spirituals, almost sacred," an interpretation affirmed by the interjection "oh Lord" in many blues performances. Urban blues singers often replace God's name with "baby" to secularize religious songs. During the 1920s and 1930s, blues singers like Charley Patton and Blind Lemon Jefferson recorded

both blues and religious songs, some out of sincere belief and some only to sell records. Jefferson recorded "I Want to Be Like Jesus in my Heart" under the pseudonym "Deacon L. J. Bates." Spencer, *Blues and Evil*, xxvi, 45–46; Oliver, *Songsters and Saints*, 203–4; Levine, *Black Culture*, 179; Reed, *Holy Profane*, 10.

93. W. Russell, *New Orleans Style*, 90, 118, 174–75; Barker, *Buddy Bolden*, 38. Bud Scott also says Bolden got his ideas from the church: Shapiro and Hentoff, *Hear Me Talkin'*, 37. On Bolden's playing primarily for blacks, see a quote from bassist John Joseph in Carter, *Preservation Hall*, 58.

94. See chapter 3 for a discussion of Creole musicians' attendance at black churches. Catholic churches sometimes had jazz functions; Manetta used to play weekly Sunday night dances in the large yard of the Holy Ghost Church, and Dave Perkins and Clarence "Little Dad" Vincent were members. Manetta interview, June 17, 1958; Vincent interview, December 3, 1959.

95. Ake, *Jazz Cultures*, 117; Koster, *Louisiana Music*, 253; Hunt, *Haiti's Influence*, 16; Berry, "African Cultural Memory," 4–6 ("Africa reblended" is a phrase by Robert Farris Thompson quoted by Berry); Mulira, "Case of Voodoo," 35, 37–57; Baer, *Black Spiritual Movement*, 111; Berry, *Spirit of Black Hawk*, 94.

96. Peretti, *Creation of Jazz*, 36; Rose, *I Remember Jazz*, 7. On Echo see Lomax, *Mister Jelly Roll*; Jasen and Jones, *Black Bottom Stomp*, 131; and W. Russell, *"Oh, Mister Jelly,"* 372 (Hayes Alvis). See also Pastras, *Dead Man Blues*, 55–61, on Morton and voodoo.

97. Stuckey, *Slave Culture*, 95, 362n37; Chireau, *Black Magic*, 145. On music and voodoo ceremonies in Haiti, see Manuel, *Caribbean Currents*, 147.

98. Baer, *Black Spiritual Movement*, 111.

99. Blesh and Janis, *They All Played Ragtime*, 17; E. Berlin, *Ragtime*, 21–23; Schafer and Riedl, *Art of Ragtime*, 6, 15; Curtis, *Dancing to a Black Man's Tune*, 19, 24, 44, 59; Schafer, *Brass Bands*, 17. On the relationship between ragtime and jazz, see Newberger, "Transition from Ragtime," and an article in response, E. Berlin, "Ragtime and Improvised Piano." According to Schafer and Riedl, minstrelsy itself was influenced by black folk music (*Art of Ragtime*, 6).

100. Stearns, *Story of Jazz*, 4–6; Schafer and Riedl, *Art of Ragtime*, 177.

101. E. Berlin, *Ragtime*, 44.

102. Ibid., 43–44.

103. Blesh and Janis, *They All Played Ragtime*, 66. Admittedly, the line between instrumental ragtime and early jazz was not a clear one, and what we now call jazz was at first called ragtime. For an argument that much ragtime piano was actually improvised, see E. Berlin, "Ragtime and Improvised Piano," 6–9.

104. Duhé interview; Laine interview, April 25, 1964.

105. See Newberger, "Transition from Ragtime," on Morton's transformation of "Maple Leaf Rag."

106. New Orleans musicians would be familiar with such renditions, given the tradition of military music in New Orleans beginning with the long occupation by Union troops during the Civil War.

107. On the use of the "Miserere" by brass bands, see Hazen and Hazen, *Music Men*, 118; and Schafer, *Brass Bands*, 39, 8, 42–45.

108. The relation between brass bands and jazz bands was reciprocal. See Schafer, *Brass Bands*, 42–50, 91–95. Schafer claims brass bands were the biggest influence on jazz (38). See also Hazen and Hazen, *Music Men*, 54. Ragtime's origins in the march also tie it to dance, because the march became a popular dance form called the two-step. Indeed, some of Sousa's marches were made directly into two-steps, and ragtime composer Louis Chauvin would warm up by playing Sousa marches. E. Berlin, *King of Ragtime*, 46, 151, 292. Spirituals became part of the brass band repertory and ultimately part of jazz through the funeral processions. Schafer, *Brass Bands*, 39, 8, 42–45.

109. Wilson, "Heterogeneous Sound Ideal," 167; Koenig, "Four Country Brass Bands," 14; Miller interview, April 4, 1960.

110. Schafer, *Brass Bands*, 2; Buerkle and Barker, *Bourbon Street Black*, 9. Baby Dodds once gave the number of instruments in a brass band as nine. Baby Dodds, "Talking: Brass Bands" (see discography).

111. Knowles, *Fallen Heroes*, 31, 7, 20; Lomax, "Selections from the 1949 New Orleans Jazz Interviews," 162 (Albert Glenny and Leonard Bechet); Chilton, *Sidney Bechet*, 18.

112. Schafer, *Brass Bands*, 94; Stearns, *Story of Jazz*, 45.

113. Lomax, *Mister Jelly Roll*, 90; Schafer, *Brass Bands*, 40; Charles interview.

114. Knowles, *Fallen Heroes*, 7, 22–23, 25, 86, 88; Schafer, *Brass Bands*, 21, 87.

115. Southern, *Readings*, 139; Hazen and Hazen, *Music Men*, 27, 52, 66, 120–21, 127. The "Miserere" was a favorite among jazz musicians; Manuel Perez and George Baquet played it as well. Dominique interview.

116. Hazen and Hazen, *Music Men*, 107; see Knowles, *Fallen Heroes*, 20–21. For some reason, around 1910 in New Orleans, unlike in the rest of the country, there were not as many white brass bands in proportion to black. Black culture and brass bands were associated in ways that did not hold true elsewhere in the country.

117. Jones, *Talking Jazz*, 101.

118. Contrary to what had previously been thought, the arranger Robert Recker actually composed the famous clarinet solo, which he wrote as a piccolo solo. Picou or some other Creole clarinetist then transposed the piccolo part to clarinet, and it became part of the New Orleans brass band repertory and was finally played at a faster tempo as a jazz tune. Schafer, "Breaking into 'High Society.'" See also Jasen and Jones, *Spreadin' Rhythm Around*, 299–300.

119. Nanry, *Jazz Text*, 97.

120. Stewart, "Strangest Bedfellows," 26. According to Leroy Ostransky, "High Society" and "Stars and Stripes" have similar last strains. Ostransky, *Anatomy of Jazz*, 150–51. Sudhalter makes a similar point in *Lost Chords*, 761n.

121. Bakhtin, *Problems of Dostoevsky's Poetics*, 108 and (for commentary) 106–7n. Jorge Daniel Veneciano argues that such a collage aesthetic informed Armstrong after he left Oliver as well, in both his music (e.g., inserted opera

quotations) and the visual collages he made on his reel-to-reel tape collection. According to Veneciano, such collages take scraps from other sources and make something new, creating the effect of defamiliarization; collages undermine the separation of art from life (by introducing elements from everyday life) and high from low culture in favor of an "aesthetic of contingency and provisionality," reminiscent of Bakhtin's concept of "unfinalizability," central to dialogic art. According to one commentary, the collage-like "serio-comic" forms in Bakhtin's view "are based on man's inability to know and contain his fate," which "to any vision of a completed set of truth . . . suggests some element outside the system." Veneciano, "Louis Armstrong, Bricolage." On unfinalizability, see Morson and Emerson, *Mikhail Bakhtin*, 36–49.

CHAPTER FIVE

1. Kid Ory saw Bolden play excursions to LaPlace; sometimes trains went as far as Chicago. Pops Foster remembers Sunday railroad excursions in 1910 to local towns like Houma and Thibodaux, Louisiana. Manetta interview, March 21, 1957; Ory interview; Morgan interview; Pops Foster interview, April 21, 1957; Bailey interview. "Big Eye" Louis Nelson described playing at a dive in the black section of town as part of an excursion in Hodes and Hansen, *Selections from the Gutter*, 127. On riverboats, see Dodds, *Baby Dodds Story*, 22.
2. Violinist Charles Elgar claims to have left New Orleans in 1902; Tony Jackson and other solo performers were working in Chicago as early as 1911. Wang, "Researching the New Orleans–Chicago Jazz Connection," 101, 105–6; Gushee, "How the Creole Band Came to Be," 83. According to Morton, "All the greatest hot musicians were in two places, New Orleans and Chicago. The reason of that was that the excursions from New Orleans to Chicago made that possible": quoted in W. Russell, *"Oh, Mister Jelly,"* 59.
3. Jones, *Talking Jazz*, 129.
4. Early critics focused on the supposed commercialization and standardization of a "folk" music. See, for example, Dodge, "Consider the Critics." Today such critiques seem to rest on an overdichotomization of art and commerce as well as other questionable assumptions. Though he writes of a different period, see DeVeaux, *Birth of Bebop*, for an argument that in jazz art and commercial motives are inevitably intertwined.
5. Lomax, *Mister Jelly Roll*, 10; Morton, "Jelly Roll Says He Was the First to Play Jazz."
6. Lomax, *Mister Jelly Roll*, 4–12; W. Russell, *"Oh, Mister Jelly,"* 133. For more on Professor Nickerson, see W. Russell, *"Oh, Mister Jelly,"* 122–23.
7. Pastras, *Dead Man Blues*, 3.
8. Morton claims he knew all of Joplin's tunes "by heart." Lomax, *Mister Jelly Roll*, 139; Morton and Lomax, "Library of Congress Narrative."

9. Morton and Lomax, "Library of Congress Narrative"; W. Russell, *"Oh, Mister Jelly,"* 97 (Danny Barker).

10. Lomax, "Unrecorded Interview Material," 182. According to Marge Creath Singleton, when Morton was in East St. Louis, he "took himself more seriously as a gambler than musician—as a gambler and a hustler." W. Russell, *"Oh, Mister Jelly,"* 495.

11. Armstrong, *In His Own Words*, 35.

12. Lomax, "Unrecorded Interview Material," 180, 200.

13. Lomax, *Mister Jelly Roll*, 162; W. Russell, *"Oh, Mister Jelly,"* 48, 118.

14. Lomax, "Unrecorded Interview Material," 195.

15. Ibid., 201. Some say Morton was kidding when he made remarks about those with dark skin, but others recall his talking seriously in that vein. For some conflicting testimony, see W. Russell, *"Oh, Mister Jelly,"* 367, 496.

16. Lomax, *Mister Jelly Roll*, 196–97, 238–39, 135, 10. The Creole Band, one of the first New Orleans jazz groups to go on the road outside the New Orleans area, also performed minstrel routines.

17. W. Russell, *"Oh, Mister Jelly,"* 91; Stoddard, *Jazz on the Barbary Coast*, 52–53.

18. W. Russell, *"Oh, Mister Jelly,"* 552 (John Spikes).

19. Ibid., 384 (Preston Jackson); Lomax, *Mister Jelly Roll*, 149.

20. W. Russell, *"Oh, Mister Jelly"* (letter to Carew, June 8, 1940, and June 20, 1940); Jones, *Talking Jazz*, 6 (Barney Bigard); Reich and Gaines, *Jelly's Blues*, 131–217. The complete Morton-Carew correspondence is in W. Russell, *"Oh, Mister Jelly,"* 159–305.

21. Kenney, *Chicago Jazz*, 47, 121, 127, 156–57.

22. Erenberg, *Swingin' the Dream*, 170–71.

23. W. Russell, *"Oh, Mister Jelly,"* 98–99 (Danny Barker). According to one musician, "The Oliver band played a lot of slow blues and medium tempo tunes, and when they went to New York they were amazed because New York musicians played so fast." Quoted in ibid., 514.

24. Kramer, "Jelly Roll in Chicago, 1927," 20–21.

25. Lawrence Lucie talks about Morton's refusal "to bend." W. Russell, *"Oh, Mister Jelly,"* 527.

26. Armstrong, *Satchmo*, 106.

27. La Rocca interview, May 21, 1958.

28. Lo Cascio, "Nick La Rocca Story."

29. Brunn, *Story of the Original Dixieland Jazz Band*, 2.

30. La Rocca interview, October 26, 1959.

31. La Rocca interview, May 26, 1958.

32. La Rocca interview, May 21, 1958.

33. Ibid.

34. La Rocca interview, June 2, 1958; Brunn, *Story of the Original Dixieland Jazz Band*, 6.

35. W. Russell, *"Oh, Mister Jelly,"* 484 (quoting Morton's August 1938 letter to *Down Beat* magazine); La Rocca interview, October 26, 1959.

36. La Rocca interviews, October 26, 1959, June 9, 1958, and May 21, 1958.

37. Smith, "White New Orleans," 51.

38. La Rocca interview, June 2, 1958.

39. La Rocca interview October 26, 1959.

40. La Rocca interview, June 9, 1958; Brunn, *Story of the Original Dixieland Jazz Band,* 73.

41. Brunn, *Story of the Original Dixieland Jazz Band,* 125, 178.

42. Lomax, "Selections from the 1949 New Orleans Jazz Interviews," 153 (Johnny St. Cyr); Levin, *Classic Jazz,* 50.

43. La Rocca interviews, May 21, 1958, May 26, 1958, and June 2, 1958; Brunn, *Story of the Original Dixieland Jazz Band,* 94–95.

44. Brunn, *Story of the Original Dixieland Jazz Band,* 23, 89.

45. Ibid., 38, 55 (quoting the *New York Sun* of November 4, 1917), 135.

46. Lo Cascio, "Nick La Rocca Story"; Brunn, *Story of the Original Dixieland Jazz Band,* 70.

47. La Rocca interview, May 26, 1958.

48. Ibid.; Brunn, *Story of the Original Dixieland Jazz Band,* 42–43; M. Williams, *Jazz Masters of New Orleans,* 30.

49. Kenney, *Chicago Jazz,* 45, 71; Kenney, *Jazz on the River,* 35, 48. See also Erenberg, *Swingin' the Dream,* 47–53.

50. La Rocca interview, June 2, 1958. Schuller claims that "the ODJB was not able to absorb into its style the new popular songs coming out of Tin Pan Alley *en masse* in the early twenties" (*Early Jazz,* 182). Sudhalter disputes this (*Lost Chords,* 22).

51. La Rocca interview, October 26, 1959.

52. Giddins, *Satchmo,* 116; Davis quoted in DeMicheal, jacket notes.

53. O'Meally, "Checking Our Balances"; Gabbard, "Actor and Musician," 232; B. Edwards, "Louis Armstrong and the Syntax of Scat," 647; Veneciano, "Louis Armstrong, Bricolage, and the Aesthetics of Swing."

54. When he was four or five, Armstrong's family moved to a house near Liberty and Perdido, although he was born on James (or Jane) Alley, some eighteen blocks away. Armstrong, *Satchmo,* 28, 64; Jones and Chilton, *Louis,* 46.

55. Armstrong, *Satchmo,* 22, 24, 39, 41; Hodes and Chadwick, *Selections from the Gutter,* 78 (interview of Armstrong by Fred Robbins).

56. Piersen, "African American Festive Style," 419. See Hearn, *Two Years in the French West Indies,* 156.

57. Armstrong, *Satchmo,* 14–15, 81.

58. Ibid., 146–47, 222.

59. Ibid., 194–95.

60. Armstrong, *In His Own Words,* 214; Berrett, *Louis Armstrong Companion,* 85.

61. Armstrong, *Satchmo,* 15, 78, 201.

62. Franklin, *Benjamin Franklin Reader,* 285 ("Maxims from Poor Richard").

63. Ibid., 119–20 (*Autobiography*).

64. Armstrong, *Satchmo*, 208–9.

65. Franklin, *Benjamin Franklin Reader,* 120 (*Autobiography*).

66. Berrett, *Louis Armstrong Companion*, 137; Armstrong, *In His Own Words*, 143.

67. Bergreen, *Louis Armstrong*, 463–64. On Armstrong's sexuality see Gabbard, "Actor and Musician."

68. Berrett, *Louis Armstrong Companion,* 114.

69. Ibid., 99.

70. Bakhtin, *Rabelais*, 151; see also 148, 175; Armstrong, *In His Own Words*, 42; cf. 169.

71. See, for example, Armstrong, *In His Own Words*, 170 (music), 180 (excretion); Giddins, *Satchmo*, 181 (sex). The incident with the toilet bowl is recounted in Cogswell, *Louis Armstrong*, 132.

72. Giddins, *Satchmo*, 184. The card is reproduced in Giddins, *Satchmo*, 189. Armstrong and his wife even devised a "diet" program centered on Swiss Kriss (Berrett, *Louis Armstrong Companion*, 99–102). Further evidence for Armstrong's linking of excretion and music is seen in an incident he recounts from childhood: he went to an outhouse only to find a turd on the seat "that looked like a trombone" (Jones and Chilton, *Louis*, 233).

73. Bakhtin, *Rabelais*, 10; Barrett, *Louis Armstrong Companion*, 167, 182. On Armstrong's origination and use of slang, see Berrett, *Louis Armstrong Companion*, 20–23.

74. Giddins, *Satchmo*, 99.

75. Cogswell, *Louis Armstrong*, 89; M. Miller, "Louis Armstrong," 58; R. Long, "Louis Armstrong and African-American Culture," 83; Bergreen, *Louis Armstrong*, 323; Berrett, *Louis Armstrong Companion*, 107; Giddins, *Satchmo*, 163, 165.

76. Armstrong, *Satchmo*, 189.

77. Berrett, *Louis Armstrong Companion*, 168, 174.

78. Jones and Chilton, *Louis*, 132. Whites tended to ignore the change in the lyrics.

79. Wilson, "Significance of the Relationship." Wilson calls this the "heterogeneous . . . sound ideal." According to Barry Kernfeld, Armstrong's voice is "raspy, perfectly suited to the African-American conception of sound upon which jazz timbre is founded. . . . His manipulation of timbre, with details of the grittiness continually changing, is as subtle as the rhythmic play." Kernfeld, *What to Listen For in Jazz*, 167.

80. Hadlock, *Jazz Masters of the Twenties*, 22–23; Wright, *Black Boy*, 255.

81. Berrett, *Louis Armstrong Companion,* 188.

82. Giddins, *Satchmo*, 32.

83. Berrett, *Louis Armstrong Companion*, 65, quoting Hughes Panassié.

84. Early, *Tuxedo Junction*, 296; Bergreen, *Louis Armstrong*, 317, 439; Sellman, "Louis Armstrong." For an example of a writer who sees Armstrong's use of minstrelsy—in this case the singing of "coon songs"—as a

way of ingratiating himself with whites, see Collier, *Louis Armstrong*, 245.

85. Armstrong, *Louis Armstrong and His Orchestra*; Bergreen, *Louis Armstrong*, 287. Armstrong actually walked off the set before the new lyrics could be recorded. When he returned the next day, he said, "What do you want me to call those black sons-of-bitches this morning?" Bigard, *With Louis and the Duke*, 123–24. Dan Morgenstern points out that Paul Robeson also recorded this song, along with "That's Why Darkies Were Born," "Ma Curly Headed Baby," "Piccaninny Shoes," and "Mammy's Little Kinky-Headed Boy." Morganstern, booklet, 25.

86. Armstrong, *Louis Armstrong and His Orchestra*.

87. Gillespie, *To Be or Not to Bop*, 295. Ralph Ellison called Armstrong a "make believe clown" whose trumpet playing makes "even the squarest of squares" aware that he is playacting. Ellison, *Shadow and Act*, 227. Cf. the narrator of Ellison's *Invisible Man*: "Perhaps I like Louis Armstrong because he's made poetry out of being invisible. I think it must be because he's unaware that he *is* invisible." Ellison, *Invisible Man*, 8.

88. Berrett, *Louis Armstrong Companion*, 47; Armstrong, *In His Own Words*, 28; see also 183–86.

89. Berrett, *Louis Armstrong Companion*, 125.

90. Bergreen, *Louis Armstrong*, 347–48.

CONCLUSION

1. Huntington, *Who Are We?* xvi–xvii. Thanks to Jeneen Hobby for this reference. Brookhiser and Auster are quoted in Fishkin, "Interrogating 'Whiteness,'" 454.

2. www.census.gov/population/www/socdemo/race/racefactcb.html; Ferrante and Brown, "Classifying People by Race," 118–19; Roediger, *Colored White*, 9.

3. Davis, *Who Is Black?* 13–15; Haney-López, "Mean Streets," 173; Olsen, *Thin Disguise*, 84–85.

4. Sollors, "National Identity," 94.

5. Menand, *Metaphysical Club*, 393.

6. Bakhtin, *Dialogic Imagination*, 293.

7. "The intrinsic embeddedness of self-experience in intersubjective fields means that our self-esteem, our sense of personal identity, even our experience of ourselves as having distinct and enduring existence are contingent on specific sustaining relations to the human surround." Stolorow and Atwood, *Contexts of Being*, 10.

8. Cook, "Making Music Together," 6.

9. Ibid., 9n; DeVeaux, *Birth of Bebop*, 47.

10. Dodds, *Baby Dodds Story*, 37. These tunes are available on Oliver's album *King Oliver 1923–1930*.

11. On the role of critics in creating "jazz" characterized by a "transcendent principle of continuity," see DeVeaux, "Constructing the Jazz Tradition." On the arbitrariness of the label *jazz*, see Ake, *Jazz Cultures*, especially his discussions of Louis Jordan and Bill Frisell.
12. Levine, "Folklore of Industrial Society," 1379.
13. Kennedy, *Jelly Roll, Bix, and Hoagy*, 52.
14. The trumpeter was Leroy Jones.

Bibliography

Archival Materials

HNOC   Historic New Orleans Collection, New Orleans
NOPL   New Orleans Public Library
WRHA   William Ransom Hogan Archive of New Orleans Jazz,
          Tulane University

Interviews

Written transcripts or summaries unless otherwise noted.

Amacker, Frank. July 1, 1960. WRHA.
_____. September 30, 1960. WRHA.
_____. June 21, 1965. WRHA.
Bailey, Andrew. September 26, 1959. WRHA.
Barbarin, Paul. March 27, 1957. WRHA.
_____. January 7, 1959. WRHA.
_____. December 23, 1959. WRHA
Barnes, Emile. July 29, 1960. WRHA.
Barnes, Paul. June 16, 1969. WRHA.
Bigard, Barney. April 27, 1972. WRHA.
Bocage, Peter. January 29, 1959, and February 6, 1969. WRHA.
Bonano, Sharkey. September 11, 1966. WRHA.
Bourgeau, Joseph "Fan." September 13, 1972. WRHA.
Brown, Steve. April 22, 1958. WRHA.
Brunies, Richard. April 27, 1959. WRHA.
Brunis, George. June 3, 1958. WRHA.
Charles, Hypolite. April 13, 1963, WRHA.
Christian, Frank. September 6, 1965. WRHA.
Clementin, Ferrand. August 2, 1973. WRHA.
Cornish, Bella. January 13, 1959. WRHA.

Dawson, Eddie. August 11, 1959. WRHA.

De Lay, Mike. November 14, 1970. WRHA (transcript and audiotape).

Dodds, Johnny. c. 1938–40. HNOC (William Russell's handwritten notes for *Jazzmen*, MSS 515, folder 15).

Dominique, Natty. May 31, 1958. WRHA.

Duhé, Lawrence. 1960. WRHA.

Edwards, Eddie B. July 1, 1959. WRHA.

Elgar, Charles. May 27, 1958. WRHA.

Foster, Abby "Chinee." June 29, 1960. HNOC.

———. March 9, 1961. HNOC.

Foster, George "Pops." April 21, 1957. WRHA.

———. August 23, 1967–August 1969. WRHA.

Foster, Willie. January 21, 1959. WRHA.

Garland, Ed "Montudie." August 16, 1958. HNOC (handwritten transcript).

———. April 20, 1971. WRHA.

Glenny, Albert. March 27, 1957. WRHA (transcript and audiotape, reel I).

Hazel, Arthur "Monk." July 16, 1959. WRHA.

Henry, Sonny. January 8, 1959. WRHA.

Hightower, Willie. June 3, 1958. WRHA.

Howard, Avery "Kid." December 22, 1958. WRHA.

———. May 26, 1961. WRHA.

Jones, Louis. January 19, 1959. WRHA.

Keppard, Louis. January 19, 1961. WRHA.

Kimball, Narvin H. November 25, 1961. WRHA.

La Rocca, Dominic James "Nick." May 21, 1958. WRHA.

———. May 26, 1958. WRHA.

———. June 2, 1958. WRHA.

———. June 9, 1958. WRHA.

———. October 26, 1959. WRHA.

Laine, Jack. April 25, 1964. WRHA.

Laine, Jack, and Blanche Nunez Laine. February 27, 1959. WRHA.

Lewis, George. April 1966. WRHA.

———. October 21, 1968. WRHA.

———. November 25, 1968. WRHA.

———. December 9, 1968. WRHA.

Love, Charlie. June 19, 1958. WRHA.

Loyacano, Arnold. September 29, 1956. WRHA.

Manetta, Manuel. March 12, 1957. HNOC.

———. March 21, 1957. WRHA.

———. March 28, 1957. HNOC (audiocassette 133A).

———. May 13, 1958. HNOC (audiocassettes 41B, 42A).

———. June 10, 1958. HNOC (audiocassette 49A).

———. June 17, 1958. HNOC (summary of cassette 51B in catalog).

———. June 20, 1958. HNOC (summary of cassette 53A in catalog).

_____. July 1, 1958. HNOC (audiocassette 59A).

_____. May 10, 1968. HNOC (audiocassette 161A).

_____. November 20, 1968. HNOC.

_____. January 4, 1969. HNOC (handwritten transcript, MSS 516, folder 695).

_____. June 9, 1969. HNOC.

_____. July 11, 1969. HNOC.

Marsalis, Wynton. Interview by Ken Burns. June 12, 1999.
    www.pbs.org/jazz/about/pdfs/MarsalisW.pdf.

Martin, Chink. October 19, 1966. WRHA.

Miles, Lizzie. January 18, 1951. WRHA.

Miller, Ernest "Punch." April 9, 1957. WRHA.

_____. August 20, 1959. WRHA.

_____. April 4, 1960. WRHA.

Morgan, Andrew. July 4, 1961. WRHA.

Nash, "Lemon." October 3, 1959. WRHA.

_____. September 28, 1960. WRHA.

Nicholas, "Wooden Joe." November 12, 1956. WRHA.

Oliver, Stella. April 22, 1959. WRHA.

Ory, Edward "Kid." April 20, 1957. HNOC.

Palmer, Roy. September 22, 1955. WRHA.

Parenti, Tony, and Tony Sbarbaro. June 29, 1959. WRHA.

Parker, Willie. November 7, 1958. WRHA.

Phillips, Babe. March 25, 1957. WRHA.

Picou, Alphonse. April 4, 1958. WRHA.

Robichaux, Joe. March 19, 1959. WRHA.

Robinson, Jim. December 10, 1958. WRHA.

Sbarbaro, Tony. June 29, 1959. WRHA.

Sbarbaro, Tony, and Emile Christian. February 11, 1959. WRHA.

Schilling, George "Happy." September 8, 1957. HNOC (audiocassette 249A).

Schiro, Luke. December 5, 1967. WRHA.

Shields, Harry. May 28, 1961. WRHA.

Souchon, Edmond "Doc." February 17, 1962. WRHA.

St. Cyr, Johnny. August 27, 1958. WRHA.

Thompson, "Big Bill." March 1961. WRHA.

Tio, Louis. October 26, 1960. WRHA.

Tio, Rose. Interview by Barry Martyn and Jack Stewart, November 29, 1999.
    WRHA (video).

Vincent, Clarence "Little Dad." December 3, 1959. WRHA.

_____. December 11, 1959. WRHA.

Vincent, Clarence "Little Dad," and Punch Miller. November 17, 1959. WRHA.

_____. December 3, 1959, WRHA.

Wiggs, Johnny. August 26, 1962. WRHA.

Wiggs, Johnny, and George "Happy" Schilling. September 8, 1957. WRHA.

Zeno, Alice. November 14 and December 10, 1958. WRHA.

Letters

All in Louisiana Division, NOPL; listed by recipient.

Berman, Mayor Martin, from sr. captain acting inspector of police (signature illegible). April 10, 1911.

Boyle, John, police captain, from Tim Driscoll. July 10, 1907.

———, acting inspector of police, from police captain (signature illegible). February 1, 1911.

———, from police captain (signature illegible). February 9, 1911.

———, from Sergeant W. F. Azcona. April 9, 1911.

———, from police sergeant (signature illegible). May 4, 1911.

———, signature illegible. May 16, 1911.

Gaster, D. S., superintendent of police, from Captain Richard J. Walsh. November 6, 1898.

O'Connor, William J., inspector of police (signature illegible). January 24, 1910.

Reynolds, James W., inspector of police, from L. W. Rawlings. March 1, 1911.

———, from Captain Garry O' Mullen. April 1, 1911.

———, from commanding sergeant (signature illegible). May 31, 1911.

———, from Captain Paul Gorman. March 26, 1913.

Whitaker, Edward S., inspector of police, from Officer Rawlings. November 9, 1906.

———, from two detectives (signatures illegible). September 8, 1907.

Other

1909 poster for Economy Hall. HNOC (MSS 520, folder 647).

1910 poster for Dixie Park. HNOC (MSS 520, folder 1010).

1910 poster for Economy Hall. HNOC (MSS 520, folder 1005).

New Orleans Mascot cover, January 22, 1887, Louisiana State Museum.

Souchon, Edmond. "The Places in Early Jazz (in and around New Orleans)." Typewritten manuscript in the files of WRHA.

U.S. Department of the Interior, National Park Service. "National Register of Historic Places Inventory: Nomination Form," in Vertical File–Bucktown, WRHA.

Court Cases

Lee et al. v. New Orleans Great Northern Co. 51 So. 184. Supreme Court of Louisiana (1910).

Plessy v. Ferguson, 16 U.S. 537 (1896).

State v. Treadway. 52 So. 510. Supreme Court of Louisiana (1910).

Books and Articles

Abbott, Lynn, and Doug Seroff. *Out of Sight: The Rise of African American Popular Music, 1889–1895*. Jackson: University Press of Mississippi, 2002.

Abrahams, Roger D. *Singing the Master: The Emergence of African American Culture in the Plantation South.* New York: Pantheon, 1992.

Abrahams, Roger D., Nick Spitzer, John F. Szwed, and Robert Farris Thompson. *Blues for New Orleans: Mardi Gras and America's Creole Soul.* Philadelphia: University of Pennsylvania Press, 2006.

Ake, David. *Jazz Cultures.* Berkeley: University of California Press, 2002.

Anderson, Gene. "Johnny Dodds in New Orleans." *American Music* 8, no. 4 (Winter 1990): 405–40.

Anthony, Arthé Agnes. "The Negro Creole Community in New Orleans, 1880–1920: An Oral History." PhD diss., University of California at Irvine, 1978.

Armstrong, Louis. *In His Own Words.* Edited by Thomas Brothers. New York: Oxford University Press, 1999.

_____. *Louis Armstrong—A Self-Portrait: The Interview by Richard Meryman.* New York: Eakins Press, 1971.

_____. *Satchmo: My Life in New Orleans.* New York: Da Capo, 1954.

Arnesen, Eric. *Waterfront Workers of New Orleans: Race, Class, and Politics, 1863–1923.* New York: Oxford University Press, 1991.

Badger, Reid. *A Life in Ragtime: A Biography of James Reese Europe.* New York: Oxford University Press, 1995.

Baer, Hans H. *The Black Spiritual Movement: A Religious Response to Racism.* Knoxville: University of Tennessee Press, 2001.

Bains, Parkash Kaur. "The New Orleans Race Riot of 1900." MA thesis, Louisiana State University, 1970.

Bakhtin, Mikhail. *The Dialogic Imagination.* Edited by Michael Holquist. Translated by Caryl Emerson and Michael Holquist. Austin: University of Texas Press, 1988.

_____. *Problems of Dostoevsky's Poetics.* Edited and translated by Caryl Emerson. Minneapolis: University of Minnesota Press, 1984.

_____. *Rabelais and His World.* Translated by Helen Iswolsky. Bloomington: University of Indiana Press, 1984.

_____. *Speech Genres and Other Late Essays.* Austin: University of Texas Press, 1986.

Baraka, Amiri (LeRoi Jones). *Blues People.* New York: William Morrow, 1963.

Barbarin, Paul, and Clint Bolin. "All Gone Now." *The Second Line*, Winter 1972, 21–22.

Barker, Danny. *Buddy Bolden and the Last Days of Storyville.* Edited by Alyn Shipton. London and New York: Continuum, 1998.

_____. *A Life in Jazz.* Edited by Alyn Shipton. New York: Oxford University Press, 1986.

Barlow, William. *Looking Up at Down: The Emergence of Blues Culture.* Philadelphia: Temple University Press, 1989.

Baron, Robert. "Amalgams and Mosaics, Syncretisms and Reinterpretations: Reading Herskovits and Contemporary Creolists for Metaphors of Creolization." *Journal of American Folklore* 116, no. 459 (Winter 2003): 88–115.

Baron, Robert, and Ana C. Cara. "Introduction: Creolization and Folklore—Cultural Creativity in Process." *Journal of American Folklore* 116, no. 459 (Winter 2003): 4–8.

Barrell, Alan. "The Baquets—Some Concluding Notes." *Footnote* 18, no. 2 (December/January 1987): 4–14.

Barrett, James R., and David Roediger. "How White People Became White." In *Race and Races: Cases and Resources for a Diverse America*, edited by Juan F. Perea, Richard Delgado, Angela P. Harris, and Stephanie M. Wildman. St. Paul: West, 2000.

Bastin, Bruce. *Red River Blues: The Blues Tradition in the Southeast*. Urbana: University of Illinois Press, 1986.

Bechet, Sidney. *Treat It Gentle*. New York: Da Capo, 1960.

Bell, Caryn Cossé. *Revolution, Romanticism, and the Afro-Creole Protest Tradition in Louisiana, 1718–1868*. Baton Rouge: Louisiana State University Press, 1997.

Benfey, Christopher. *Degas in New Orleans: Encounters in the Creole World of Kate Chopin and George Washington Cable*. Berkeley: University of California Press, 1997.

Bennett, James B. "Catholics, Creoles, and the Redefinition of Race in New Orleans." In *Race, Nation, and Religion in the Americas*, edited by Henry Goldschmidt and Elizabeth McAlister. New York: Oxford University Press, 2004.

———. *Religion and the Rise of Jim Crow in New Orleans*. Princeton, NJ: Princeton University Press, 2005.

Bergreen, Laurence. *Louis Armstrong: An Extravagant Life*. New York: Broadway, 1997.

Berlin, Edward A. *King of Ragtime: Scott Joplin and His Era*. New York: Oxford University Press, 1994.

———. *Ragtime: A Musical and Cultural History*. Berkeley: University of California Press, 1980.

———. "Ragtime and Improvised Piano: Another View." *Journal of Jazz Studies* 4, no. 2 (Spring/Summer 1977): 4–10.

Berlin, Ira. "From Creole to African: Atlantic Creoles and the Origin of African-American Society in Mainland North America." In *How Did American Slavery Begin?* edited by Edward Countryman, 19–63. Boston: Bedford/St. Martin's, 1999.

Berrett, Joshua, ed. *The Louis Armstrong Companion: Eight Decades of Commentary*. New York: Schirmer, 1999.

Berry, Jason. "African Cultural Memory in New Orleans Music." *Black Music Research Journal* 8, no. 1 (1988): 3–12.

———. *The Spirit of Black Hawk*. Jackson: University Press of Mississippi, 1995.

Berry, Jason, Jonathan Foose, and Tad Jones. *Up from the Cradle of Jazz: New Orleans Music since World War II*. Athens: University of Georgia Press, 1986.

Bethell, Tom. *George Lewis: A Jazzman from New Orleans*. Berkeley: University of California Press, 1977.

Bhabha, Homi K. *The Location of Culture*. New York: Routledge, 1994.

Bigard, Barney. *With Louis and the Duke*. Edited by Barry Martyn. New York: Oxford University Press, 1980.

Blassingame, John W. *Black New Orleans, 1860–1880*. Chicago: University of Chicago Press, 1973.

_____. *The Slave Community*. Rev. and enl. ed. New York: Oxford University Press, 1979.

Blesh, Rudy, and Harriet Janis. *They All Played Ragtime*. New York: Alfred A. Knopf, 1950.

Bontemps, Arna, and Jack Conroy. *Anyplace But Here*. Columbia: University of Missouri Press, 1966.

Borders, Florence E. "Researching Creole and Cajun Musics in New Orleans." *Black Music Research Journal* 8, no. 1 (1988), 15–31.

Borneman, Ernest. "The Roots of Jazz." In *Jazz*, edited by Nat Hentoff and Albert J. McCarthy, 1–20. New York: Da Capo, 1982.

Boulard, Garry. "Blacks, Italians, and the Making of New Orleans Jazz." *Journal of Ethnic Studies* 16, no. 1 (Spring 1988): 52–66.

Brasseaux, Carl A. "Creoles of Color in Louisiana's Bayou Country, 1766–1877." In *Creoles of Color of the Gulf South*, edited by James H. Dormon, 67–86. Knoxville: University of Tennessee Press, 1986.

Brearly, H. C. "Ba-ad Nigger." In *Mother Wit from the Laughing Barrel*, edited by Alan Dundes. Jackson: University Press of Mississippi, 1990.

Brothers, Thomas. *Louis Armstrong's New Orleans*. New York: W. W. Norton, 2006.

Brunn, H. O. *The Story of the Original Dixieland Jazz Band*. New York: Da Capo, 1977.

Buerkle, Jack V., and Danny Barker. *Bourbon Street Black: The New Orleans Black Jazzman*. New York: Oxford University Press, 1973.

Cable, George Washington. "The Dance in Place Congo and Creole Slave Songs." In *The Social Implications of Early Negro Music in the United States*, edited by Bernard Katz. New York: Arno and New York Times, 1969.

Campanella, Richard. *Geographies of New Orleans: Urban Fabrics before the Storm*. Lafayette: Center for Louisiana Studies, 2006.

Cangelosi, Robert J., Jr. "West End." *New Orleans Preservation in Print*, September 1984, 6–13.

Caponi, Gena Dagel. "Introduction: The Case for an African American Aesthetic." In *Signifyin(g), Sanctifyin', and Slam Dunking*, edited by Gena Dagel Caponi, 1–41. Amherst: University of Massachusetts Press, 1999.

Carew, Roy J. "Glimpses of the Past." *The Second Line* 9, no. 7/8 (July-August 1958): 1–4, available at www.doctorjazz.co.uk/glimpse.html.

_____. "Reflections on the Early Days of Jazz in the Crescent City." *Jazz Music* (England), July-August 1954, 3–25.

Carter, William. *Preservation Hall*. New York: W. W. Norton, 1991.

Chamberlain, Charles. "The Goodson Sisters: Women Pianists and the Function of Gender in the Jazz Age." *Jazz Archivist* 15 (2001): 3–6.

Charles, Hypolite. "Hypolite Charles Interview," by Austin Sonnier Jr. *The Second Line* 35 (Spring 1983): 27–31.

Chernoff, John Miller. *African Rhythm and African Sensibility*. Chicago: University of Chicago Press, 1979.

Chilton, John. *Sidney Bechet: The Wizard of Jazz*. New York: Oxford University Press, 1987.

Chireau, Yvonne P. *Black Magic: Religion and the African American Conjuring Tradition*. Berkeley: University of California Press, 2003.

Cockrell, Dale. *Demons of Disorder: Early Blackface Minstrels and Their World*. New York: Cambridge University Press, 1997.

Cogswell, Michael. *Louis Armstrong: The Offstage Story of Satchmo*. Portland, OR: Collectors, 2003.

Collier, James Lincoln. *Jazz: The American Theme Song*. New York: Oxford University Press, 1993.

———. *Louis Armstrong: An American Genius*. New York: Oxford University Press, 1983.

Collins, Lee. *Oh, Didn't He Ramble*. As told to Mary Collins and edited by Frank J. Gillis and John W. Miner. Urbana: University of Illinois Press, 1974.

Collins, R[alph]. *New Orleans Jazz: A Revised History*. New York: Vantage, 1996.

Cone, James H. *The Spirituals and the Blues*. Maryknoll, NY: Orbis, 1991.

Cook, Nicholas. "Making Music Together, or Improvisation and Its Others." *The Source: Challenging Jazz Criticism* 1 (Spring 2004): 5–25.

Crawford, Richard. "Mainstreams and Backwaters in American Psalmody." Booklet accompanying CD *Make a Joyful Noise* (see discography).

Crouch, Stanley. *Always in Pursuit: Fresh American Perspectives, 1995–1997*. New York: Pantheon, 1998.

Curtis, Susan. *Dancing to a Black Man's Tune: A Life of Scott Joplin*. Columbia: University of Missouri Press, 1994.

DaMatta, Roberto. *Carnivals, Rogues, and Heroes*. Notre Dame, IN: University of Notre Dame Press, 1991.

"Dance Hall Feud Ends in Death of Two Rivals." *New Orleans Daily Picayune*, March 25, 1913, 1, 6.

"Dance Halls Wide Open." *New Orleans Item*, November 16, 1902, 2.

Darensbourg, Joe. *Telling It Like It Is*. Edited by Peter Vacher. London: Macmillan, 1987.

Davis, F. James. *Who Is Black? One Nation's Definition*. University Park: Pennsylvania State University Press, 1991.

DeMicheal, Don. Jacket notes to *The Genius of Louis Armstrong*, vol. 1, *1923–1933*, Columbia LP G 30416.

Dethloff, Henry C., and Robert R. Jones. "Race Relations in Louisiana, 1877–98." In *African Americans and the Emergence of Segregation, 1865–1900*, edited by Donald G. Nieman. New York: Garland, 1994.

DeVeaux, Scott. *The Birth of Bebop: A Social and Musical History*. Berkeley: University of California Press, 1997.

_____. "Constructing the Jazz Tradition: Jazz Historiography." *Black American Literature Forum* 25, no. 3 (Fall 1991): 525–60.

Dixon, Richard R. "Milneburg Joys." *Roosevelt Review*, October 1962, 9–20.

Dodds, Baby, as told to Larry Gara. *The Baby Dodds Story*. Baton Rouge: Louisiana State University Press, 1992.

Dodge, Roger Pryor. "Consider the Critics." In *Jazzmen*, edited by Frederic Ramsey Jr. and Charles Edward Smith. New York: Harcourt Brace, 1939.

Domínguez, Virginia R. *White by Definition: Social Classification in Creole Louisiana*. New Brunswick, NJ: Rutgers University Press, 1986.

Donaldson, Gary A. "A Window on Slave Culture: Dances at Congo Square in New Orleans, 1800–1862." *Journal of Negro History* 69, no. 2 (Spring 1984): 63–72.

Douglass, Frederick. *My Bondage and My Freedom*. New York: Dover, 1969.

_____. *The Oxford Frederick Douglass Reader*. Edited by William L. Andrews. New York: Oxford University Press, 1996.

DuBois, Laurent. *Avengers of the New World: The Story of the Haitian Revolution*. Cambridge, MA: Harvard University Press, 2004.

DuBois, W. E. B. *The Souls of Black Folk*. New York: Dover, 1994.

Dunbar-Nelson, Alice Moore. "People of Color in Louisiana." In *Creole: The History and Legacy of Louisiana's Free People of Color*, edited by Sybil Kein, 3–41. Baton Rouge: Louisiana State University Press, 2000.

Early, Gerald. *Tuxedo Junction: Essays on American Culture*. Hopewell, NJ: Ecco, 1989.

Edwards, Brent Hayes. "Louis Armstrong and the Syntax of Scat." *Critical Inquiry* 28 (Spring 2002): 618–49.

Edwards, Richard Henry. *Popular Amusements*. New York: Arno, 1976.

Ellison, Ralph. *Invisible Man*. New York: Vintage, 1952.

_____. *Shadow and Act*. New York: Vintage, 1972.

Epstein, Dena J. *Sinful Tunes and Spirituals: Black Folk Music to the Civil War*. Urbana: University of Illinois Press, 1977.

_____. "A White Origin for the Black Spiritual? An Invalid Theory and How It Grew." *American Music* 1, no. 2 (Summer 1983): 53–59.

Erenberg, Lewis. *Swingin' the Dream*. Chicago: University of Chicago Press, 1998.

Evans, David. *Big Road Blues: Tradition and Creativity in the Folk Blues*. New York: Da Capo, 1987.

Evans, Nicholas M. *Writing Jazz: Race, Nationalism, and Modern Culture in the 1920s*. New York: Garland, 2000.

Fabre, Michel. "New Orleans Creole Expatriates in France: Romance and Reality." In *Creole: The History and Legacy of Louisiana's Free People of Color*, edited by Sybil Kein, 179–207. Baton Rouge: Louisiana State University Press, 2000.

Feibelman, Julian B. "A Social and Economic Study of the New Orleans Jewish Community." PhD diss., University of Pennsylvania, 1941.

Ferrante, Joan, and Prince Brown Jr. "Classifying People by Race." In *The Social Construction of Race and Ethnicity in the United States*, edited by Joan Ferrante and Prince Brown Jr., 109–19. New York: Longman, 1998.

Fiehrer, Thomas. "From Quadrille to Stomp: The Creole Origins of Jazz." *Popular Music* 10, no. 1 (1991): 21–38.

Fischer, Roger. "The Post–Civil War Segregation Struggle." In *The Past as Prelude: New Orleans 1718–1968*, edited by Hodding Carter, William Ransom Hogan, John W. Lawrence, and Betty Werlein Carter, 288–304. New Orleans: Tulane University Press, 1968.

Fishkin, Shelley Fisher. "Interrogating 'Whiteness,' Complicating 'Blackness': Remapping American Culture." *American Quarterly* 47, no. 3 (September 1995): 428–66.

Floyd, Samuel A. "African Roots of Jazz." In *The Oxford Companion to Jazz*, edited by Bill Kirchner, 7–16. New York: Oxford University Press, 2005.

———. "Ring Shout! Black Music, Black Literary Theory, and Black Historical Studies." *Black Music Research Journal* 11 (1991): 265–87.

Fontenot, Kevin. "Times Ain't Like They Used to Be: Rabbit Brown, New Orleans Songster." *Jazz Archivist* 13 (1998–99): 1–5.

Foster, George "Pops," as told to Tom Stoddard. *Pops Foster: The Autobiography of a New Orleans Jazzman.* Berkeley: University of California Press, 1971.

Foucault, Michel. "Of Other Spaces." Translated by Jay Miskowiec. http://foucault.info/documents/heteroTopia/foucault.heteroTopia.en.html.

Franklin, Benjamin. *A Benjamin Franklin Reader.* Edited by Nathan G. Goodman. New York: Thomas Y. Crowell, 1945.

Fremaux, Leon J. *Leon Fremaux's New Orleans Characters.* Edited by Patrick Geary. Gretna, LA: Pelican, 1987.

Gabbard, Krin. "Actor and Musician: Louis Armstrong and His Films." In *The Louis Armstrong Companion*, edited by Joshua Berrett, 201–36. New York: Schirmer, 1999.

Gambino, Richard. *Vendetta.* Garden City, NY: Doubleday, 1977.

Gates, Henry Louis. *The Signifying Monkey.* New York: Oxford University Press, 1988.

Gehman, Mary. "Visible Means of Support: Businesses, Professions, and Trades of Free People of Color." In *Creole: The History and Legacy of Louisiana's Free People of Color*, edited by Sybil Kein, 208–22. Baton Rouge: Louisiana State University Press, 2000.

George, Jeanne. "Jazz Was 'Beat Out' from a 'Spasm Band.'" *Clarion Herald* (New Orleans), October 1, 1964.

Giddins, Gary. *Satchmo.* New York: Doubleday, 1988.

———. *Visions of Jazz.* New York: Oxford University Press, 1998.

Gilkes, Cheryl Townsend. "'Together and in Harness': Women's Traditions in the Sanctified Church." In *Black Women in America: Social Science Perspectives*, edited by Micheline R. Malson et al., 223–44. Chicago: University of Chicago Press, 1988.

Gillespie, Dizzy. *To Be or Not to Bop: Memoirs.* New York: Da Capo, 1985.

Gilroy, Paul. *The Black Atlantic.* Cambridge, MA: Harvard University Press, 1993.

_____. *Small Acts: Thoughts on the Politics of Black Cultures*. London: Serpent's Tail, 1993.

Gioia, Ted. *The History of Jazz*. New York: Oxford University Press, 1997.

Goffin, Robert. "'Big Eye' Louis Nelson." In *Selections from the Gutter: Jazz Portraits from 'The Jazz Record,'* edited by Art Hodes and Chadwick Hansen, 126–29. Berkeley: University of California Press, 1977.

Gossett, Thomas F. *Race: The History of an Idea*. New York: Schocken, 1963.

Guglielmo, Jennifer. "Introduction: White Lies, Dark Truth." In *Are Italians White?* edited by Jennifer Guglielmo and Salvatore Salerno, 1–14. New York: Routledge, 2005.

Guglielmo, Thomas. "'No Color Barrier': Italians, Race, and Power in the United States." In *Are Italians White?* edited by Jennifer Guglielmo and Salvatore Salerno, 29–43. New York: Routledge, 2005.

Guillory, Monique. "Under One Roof: The Sins and Sanctity of New Orleans Quadroon Balls." In *Race Consciousness: African-American Studies for the New Century*, edited by Judith Jackson Fossett and Jeffrey A. Tucker, 67–92. New York: New York University Press, 1997.

Gushee, Lawrence. "How the Creole Band Came to Be." *Black Music Research Journal* 8, no. 1 (1988), 83–99.

_____. "The Nineteenth-Century Origins of Jazz." In *Jazz: A Century of Change*, edited by Lewis Porter. New York: Schirmer, 1997.

Hadlock, Richard. *Jazz Masters of the Twenties*. New York: Macmillan-Collier, 1965.

Hair, William Ivy. *Carnival of Fury: Robert Charles and the New Orleans Race Riots of 1900*. Baton Rouge: Louisiana State University Press, 1976.

Hall, Gwendolyn Midlo. *Africans in Colonial Louisiana: The Development of Afro-Creole Culture in the Eighteenth Century*. Baton Rouge: Louisiana State University Press, 1992.

_____. "The Formation of Afro-Creole Culture." In *Creole New Orleans: Race and Americanization*, edited by Arnold R. Hirsch and Joseph Logsdon, 58–87. Baton Rouge: Louisiana State University Press, 1992.

Hanchard, Michael. "Afro-Modernity: Temporality, Politics, and the African Diaspora." In *Alternative Modernities*, edited by Dilip Parameshwar Gaonkar, 272–98. Durham, NC: Duke University Press, 2001.

Haney López, Ian F. "The Mean Streets of Social Race." In *The Social Construction of Race and Ethnicity in the United States*, edited by Joan Ferrante and Prince Brown Jr., 161–76. New York: Longman, 1998.

_____. *White by Law: The Legal Construction of Race*. New York: New York University Press, 1996.

Harlan, Louis R. "Segregation in New Orleans Public Schools during Reconstruction." In *Reconstruction: An Anthology of Revisionist Writings*, edited by Kenneth M. Stampp and Leon F. Litwack. Baton Rouge: Louisiana State University Press, 1969.

Harris, Cheryl I. "The Story of *Plessy v. Ferguson*: The Death and Resurrection of Racial Formalism." In *Constitutional Law Stories*, edited by Michael C. Dorf. New York: Foundation, 2004.

Harris, Rex. *Jazz*. Harmondsworth, U.K.: Pelican, 1952.

Harvey, Paul. *Redeeming the South: Religious Cultures and Racial Identities among Southern Baptists, 1865–1925*. Chapel Hill: University of North Carolina Press, 1997.

Haskins, James. *The Creoles of Color of New Orleans*. New York: Thomas Y. Crowell, 1975.

Hazen, Margaret Hindle, and Robert M. Hazen. *The Music Men: An Illustrated History of Brass Bands in America, 1800–1920*. Washington, DC: Smithsonian Institution Press, 1987.

Hazzard-Gordon, Katrina. *Jookin': The Rise of Social Dance Formations in African-American Culture*. Philadelphia: Temple University Press, 1990.

Hearn, Lafcadio. *Inventing New Orleans: Writings of Lafcadio Hearn*. Edited with an introduction by S. Frederick Starr. Jackson: University Press of Mississippi, 2001.

———. *Lafcadio Hearn's America*. Edited by Simon J. Bronner. Lexington: University of Kentucky Press, 2002.

———. *Two Years in the French West Indies*. New York: Interlink, 2001.

Hersch, Charles. *Democratic Artworks: Politics and the Arts from Trilling to Dylan*. Albany: State University of New York Press, 1998.

Herskovits, Melville. *The Myth of the Negro Past*. Boston: Beacon, 1958.

Hetherington, Kevin. *The Badlands of Modernity: Heterotopia and Social Ordering*. London: Routledge, 1997.

Higgenbotham, Evelyn Brooks. *Righteous Discontent: The Women's Movement in the Black Baptist Church, 1880–1920*. Cambridge, MA: Harvard University Press, 1993.

Hill, Donald R., Maureen Warner-Lewis, John Cowley, and Lise Winer. Booklet accompanying the CD *Peter Was a Fisherman: The 1939 Field Recordings of Melville and Frances Herskovits*, vol. 1. Rounder CD 1114, 1998.

Hirsch, Arnold R. Introduction to *Creole New Orleans: Race and Americanization*, edited by Arnold R. Hirsch and Joseph Logsdon, 3–11. Baton Rouge: Louisiana State University Press, 1992.

Hobson, Barbara. "Prostitution." In *Encyclopedia of American Social History*, edited by Mary Kupiec Cayton, Elliott J. Gorn, and Peter W. Williams, 3:2157–65. New York: Scribner, 1993.

Hodes, Art, and Chadwick Hansen, eds. *Selections from the Gutter*. Berkeley: University of California Press, 1977.

Hoffman, Frederick L. "Race Amalgamation, August 1896." In *Plessy v. Ferguson: A Brief History with Documents*, edited by Brook Thomas, 76–100. Boston: Bedford, 1997.

Holt, Grace Sims. "Stylin' Outta the Black Pulpit." In *Signifyin(g), Sanctifyin', and Slam Dunking*, edited by Gena Dagel Caponi. Amherst: University of Massachusetts Press, 1999.

Huber, Leonard V. *New Orleans: A Pictorial History*. New York: Bonanza, 1980.

Hunt, Alfred N. *Haiti's Influence on Antebellum America*. Baton Rouge: Louisiana State University Press, 1988.

Huntington, Samuel P. *Who Are We? The Challenges to America's National Identity*. New York: Simon and Schuster, 2004.

Hurston, Zora Neale. *The Sanctified Church*. Berkeley, CA: Turtle Island, 1981.

Jackson, Joy. *New Orleans in the Gilded Age*. Baton Rouge: Louisiana State University Press, 1969.

Jacobs, Claude F., and Andrew J. Kaslow. *The Spiritual Churches of New Orleans: Origins, Beliefs, and Rituals of an African-American Religion*. Knoxville: University of Tennessee Press, 2001.

Jasen, David A., and Gene Jones. *Black Bottom Stomp: Eight Masters of Ragtime and Early Jazz*. New York: Routledge, 2002.

―――. *Spreadin' Rhythm Around: Black Popular Songwriters, 1880–1930*. New York: Schirmer, 1998.

"Jass and Jassism." *New Orleans Times-Picayune*, June 20, 1918, 4.

Jenkins, Willard. "Wynton Bites Back: Addresses His Critics." In *Jazz: A Century of Change*, edited by Lewis Porter. New York: Schirmer, 1997.

Johnson, Bruce. "Jazz as Cultural Practice." In *The Cambridge Companion to Jazz*, edited by Mervyn Cooke and David Horn, 96–113. New York: Cambridge University Press, 2002.

Johnson, James Weldon. *The Books of American Negro Spirituals*. New York: Da Capo, 1969.

Johnson, Jerah. "Jim Crow Laws of the 1890s and the Origins of New Orleans Jazz: Correction of an Error." *Popular Music* 19, no. 2 (2000): 243–51.

―――. "New Orleans's Congo Square: An Urban Setting for Early Afro-American Culture Formation." *Louisiana History* 32 (Spring 1991): 117–57.

Jones, Max. *Talking Jazz*. New York: W. W. Norton, 1988.

Jones, Max, and John Chilton. *Louis: The Louis Armstrong Story, 1900–1971*. New York: Da Capo, 1971.

Joyner, David. "The Ragtime Controversy." In *America's Musical Pulse: Popular Music in Twentieth-Century Society*, edited by Kenneth J. Bindas, 239–48. Westport, CT: Praeger, 1992.

"Keep the Dance Halls Closed" (editorial). *New Orleans Daily Picayune*, March 28, 1913, 8.

Keepnews, Orrin, and Bill Grauer Jr. *A Pictorial History of Jazz*. New York: Crown, 1955.

Kein, Sybil. "The Use of Louisiana Creole in Southern Literature." In *Creole: The History and Legacy of Louisiana's Free People of Color*, edited by Sybil Kein. Baton Rouge: Louisiana State University Press, 2000.

Kelley, Robin D. G. *Race Rebels: Culture, Politics, and the Black Working Class*. New York: Free Press, 1994.

Kennedy, Rick. *Jelly Roll, Bix, and Hoagy: Gennett Studios and the Birth of Recorded Jazz*. Indianapolis: Indiana University Press, 1999.

Kenney, William Howland. *Chicago Jazz: A Cultural History, 1904–1930*. New York: Oxford University Press, 1993.

_____. *Jazz on the River*. Chicago: University of Chicago Press, 2005.

Kernfeld, Barry, ed. *New Grove Encyclopedia of Jazz*. New York: St. Martin's, 1994.

_____. *What to Listen For in Jazz*. New Haven, CT: Yale University Press, 1995.

Kinzer, Charles E. "The Tios of New Orleans and Their Pedagogical Influence on the Early Jazz Clarinet Style." *Black Music Research Journal* 16, no. 2 (Autumn 1996): 279–302.

Kmen, Henry A. "The Joys of Milneburg." *New Orleans* 3, no. 8 (May 1969): 16–19, 46–47. In WRHA vertical file, "Milneburg."

_____. *Music in New Orleans: The Formative Years, 1791–1841*. Baton Rouge: Louisiana State University Press, 1966.

_____. "The Roots of Jazz and the Dance in Place Congo: A Re-appraisal." *Anuario Interamericano de Investigación Musical* 8 (1972): 5–16.

Knight, Franklin W. *The Caribbean: The Genesis of a Fragmented Nationalism*. 2nd ed. New York: Oxford University Press, 1990.

Knight, Franklin W., and Kenneth Bilby. "Music in Africa and the Caribbean." In *Africana Studies*, 3rd ed., edited by Mario Azavedo, 258–84. Durham, NC: Carolina Academic Press, 2005.

Knowles, Richard H. *Fallen Heroes: A History of New Orleans Brass Bands*. New Orleans: Jazzology, 1996.

Koenig, Karl. "Four Country Brass Bands." *The Second Line* 36 (Fall 1984): 13–23.

_____. *Jazz Map of New Orleans*. Running Springs, CA: Basin Street, 1983.

_____. "Magnolia Plantation: History and Music." *The Second Line* 35 (Spring 1982): 28–38.

_____. "The Plantation Belt: Brass Bands and Musicians; Part 1, Professor James B. Humphrey." *The Second Line* 33 (Fall 1981): 24–40.

_____. "Professor James B. Humphrey, Part 2." *The Second Line* 34 (Winter 1982): 15–19.

_____. "Sites of Jazz in New Orleans." *New Orleans Preservation in Print*, March-April 1985 4–9.

_____. *Under the Influence: The Four Hornsmen of Early New Orleans Jazz*. Running Springs, CA: Basin Street Press, 1994.

Koster, Rick. *Louisiana Music*. New York: Da Capo, 2002.

Kousser, J. Morgan. "Before *Plessy*, before *Brown*: The Development of the Law of Racial Integration in Louisiana and Kansas." In *Toward a Usable Past: Liberty under State Constitutions*, edited by Paul Finkelman and Stephen E. Gottlieb. Athens: University of Georgia Press, 1991.

Kramer, Karl. "Jelly Roll in Chicago, 1927." *The Second Line* 11, no. 1/2 (January-February 1961): 1–7, 23–27; *The Second Line* 12, no. 3/4 (March-April 1961): 19–22.

Latrobe, Benjamin Henry Boneval. *Impressions Respecting New Orleans*. Edited by Samuel Wilson Jr. New York: Columbia University Press, 1951.

Lefebvre, Henri. *The Production of Space*. Cambridge, MA: Blackwell, 1991.

Leonard, Neil. *Jazz and the White Americans: The Acceptance of a New Art Form.* Chicago: University of Chicago Press, 1970.

Levin, Floyd. *Classic Jazz.* Berkeley: University of California Press, 2000.

Levine, Lawrence W. *Black Culture and Black Consciousness.* New York: Oxford University Press, 1977.

———. "The Folklore of Industrial Society: Popular Culture and Its Audiences." *American Historical Review* 97, no. 5 (December 1992): 1369–99.

———. *The Unpredictable Past.* New York: Oxford University Press, 1993.

Lewis, John, with Michael D'Orso. *Walking with the Wind: A Memoir of the Movement.* New York: Harcourt Brace, 1998.

Leymarie, Isabelle. *Cuban Fire: The Story of Salsa and Latin Jazz.* London: Continuum, 2002.

Lincoln, C. Eric, and Lawrence H. Mamiya. *The Black Church in the African American Experience.* Durham, NC: Duke University Press, 1990.

Litwack, Leon F. *Been in the Storm So Long.* New York: Random House, 1989.

———. *Trouble in Mind: Black Southerners in the Age of Jim Crow.* New York: Vintage, 1998.

Lo Cascio, Claudio. "Nick La Rocca Story." www.odjb.com/NickLa RoccaStory.htm.

Logsdon, Joseph, and Caryn Cossé Bell. "The Americanization of Black New Orleans, 1850–1900." In *Creole New Orleans: Race and Americanization,* edited by Arnold R. Hirsch and Joseph Logsdon, 201–61. Baton Rouge: Louisiana State University Press, 1992.

Lomax, Alan. *Mister Jelly Roll.* New York: Grove, 1950.

———. "Selections from the 1949 New Orleans Jazz Interviews Recorded by Alan Lomax." Booklet accompanying Morton, *Complete Library of Congress Recordings* (see discography).

———. "Unrecorded Interview Material and Research Notes by Alan Lomax, 1938–1946." Booklet accompanying Morton, *Complete Library of Congress Recordings* (see discography).

Long, Alecia P. *The Great Southern Babylon: Sex, Race, and Respectability in New Orleans, 1865–1920.* Baton Rouge: Louisiana State University Press, 2004.

Long, Richard A. "Louis Armstrong and African-American Culture." In *Louis Armstrong: A Cultural Legacy,* edited by Marc H. Miller, 67–93. Seattle: Queens Museum of Art and University of Washington Press, 1994.

Longstreet, Stephen. *Sportin' House: A History of the New Orleans Sinners and the Birth of Jazz.* Los Angeles: Sherbourne, 1965.

Lovejoy, Paul E. "The African Diaspora: Revisionist Interpretations of Ethnicity, Culture, and Religion under Slavery." *Studies in the World History of Slavery, Abolition, and Emancipation* 2, no. 1 (1997).

Mackey, Nathaniel. "Other: From Noun to Verb." In *The Jazz Cadence of American Culture,* edited by Robert G. O'Meally, 513–32. New York: Columbia University Press, 1998.

Mahar, William J. *Behind the Burnt Cork Mask: Early Blackface Minstrelsy and Antebellum American Popular Culture*. Urbana: University of Illinois Press, 1999.

Malone, Bobbie S. "Rabbi Max Heller, Zionism, and the 'Negro Question': New Orleans, 1891–1911." In *The Quiet Voices: Southern Rabbis and Black Civil Rights, 1880s to 1890s*, edited by Mark K. Bauman and Berkly Kalin, 21–38. Tuscaloosa: University of Alabama Press, 1997.

Malone, Jacqui. *Steppin' on the Blues: The Visible Rhythms of African American Dance*. Urbana: University of Illinois Press, 1996.

Manuel, Peter, with Kenneth Bilby and Michael Largey. *Caribbean Currents: Caribbean Music from Rumba to Reggae*. Rev. and exp. ed. Philadelphia: Temple University Press, 2006.

Marquis, Donald M. *In Search of Buddy Bolden: First Man of Jazz*. Baton Rouge: Louisiana State University Press, 1978.

———. "Lincoln Park, Johnson Park, and Buddy Bolden." *The Second Line*, Fall 1976, 27–28.

Marsalis, Wynton, and Herbie Hancock. "Soul, Craft, and Cultural Hierarchy." In *Keeping Time: Readings in Jazz History*, edited by Robert Walser, 339–50. New York: Oxford University Press, 1999.

Martyn, Barry, ed. *The End of the Beginning*. New Orleans: Jazzology, 1998.

Maultsby, Portia K. "Africanisms in African-American Music." In *Africanisms in American Culture*, edited by Joseph E. Holloway, 185–210. Bloomington: Indiana University Press, 1990.

McBee, Randy D. *Dance Hall Days: Intimacy and Leisure among Working-Class Immigrants in the United States*. New York: New York University Press, 2000.

Medley, Keith Weldon. *We as Freemen: Plessy v. Ferguson*. Gretna, LA: Pelican, 2003.

Menand, Louis. *The Metaphysical Club*. New York: Farrar, Straus and Giroux, 2001.

Merrick, Caroline Elizabeth. *Old Times in Dixie Land: A Southern Matron's Memories*. Chapel Hill: University of North Carolina Press, 1997. Available at docsouth.unc.edu/merrick/merrick.html.

Mezzrow, Mezz. *Really the Blues*. New York: Random House, 1946.

Miller, David Michael. "Jazz and R&B Landmarks of Downtown New Orleans." webpages.charter.net/davidmmiller/neworleans.htm.

Miller, Marc H. "Louis Armstrong: A Cultural Legacy." In *Louis Armstrong: A Cultural Legacy*, edited by Marc H. Miller, 17–66. Seattle: Queens Museum of Art and University of Washington Press, 1994.

Mitchell, Reid. *All on a Mardi Gras Day: Episodes in the History of New Orleans Carnival*. Cambridge, MA: Harvard University Press, 1995.

Monson, Ingrid. "The Problem with White Hipness: Race, Gender, and Cultural Conceptions in Jazz Historical Discourse." *Journal of the American Musicological Society* 48 (1995): 396–422.

———. *Saying Something: Jazz Improvisation and Interaction*. Chicago: University of Chicago Press, 1996.

Morath, Max. "Ragtime Then and Now." In *The Oxford Companion to Jazz*, edited by Bill Kirchner, 29–38. New York: Oxford University Press, 2005.

Morgan, Thomas L., and William Barlow. *From Cakewalks to Concert Halls: An Illustrated History of African American Popular Music from 1895 to 1930*. Washington, DC: Elliott and Clark, 1992.

Morganstern, Dan. Booklet accompanying Louis Armstrong, *The Complete RCA Victor Recordings*. 4 CD set, BMG 09026-68682-2, 1997.

Morris, Ronald L. *Wait until Dark: Jazz and the Underworld, 1880–1940*. Bowling Green, OH: Bowling Green University Popular Press, 1980.

Morson, Gary Saul, and Caryl Emerson. *Mikhail Bakhtin: Creation of a Prosaics*. Stanford, CA: Stanford University Press, 1990.

Morton, Jelly Roll. "Jelly Roll Says He Was the First to Play Jazz." *Down Beat* 5, no. 9 (September 1938): 4. Available at www.doctorjazz.co.uk/page10bc.html.

Morton, Jelly Roll, and Alan Lomax. "Library of Congress Narrative." Transcribed and annotated by Michael Hill, Roger Richard, and Mike Medding. www.doctorjazz.co.uk/locspeech1.html.

Mugnier, George François. *Louisiana Images*. Edited by John R. Kemp and Linda Orr King. Baton Rouge: Louisiana State University Press, 1975.

———. *New Orleans and Bayou Country*. Edited by Lester Burbank Bridham. Barre, MA: Barre, 1972.

Mulira, Jesse Gaston. "The Case of Voodoo in New Orleans." In *Africanisms in American Culture*, edited by Joseph E. Holloway, 34–68. Bloomington: Indiana University Press, 1990.

Murphy, John P. "Jazz Improvisation: The Joy of Influence." *The Black Perspective in Music* 18, no. 1/2 (1990): 7–19.

Murray, Albert. *The Omni-Americans*. New York: Vintage, 1983.

———. *Stomping the Blues*. New York: Vintage, 1976.

Nanry, Charles, with Edward Berger. *The Jazz Text*. New York: Van Nostrand Reinhold, 1979.

Narvaez, Peter. "The Influences of Hispanic Music Cultures on African-American Blues Musicians." *Black Music Research Journal* 14, no. 2 (Autumn 1994): 203–24.

Nasaw, David. *Going Out: The Rise and Fall of Public Amusements*. Cambridge, MA: Harvard University Press, 1993.

Needham, Maureen, ed. *I See America Dancing*. Urbana: University of Illinois Press, 2002.

Newberger, Eli H. "The Transition from Ragtime to Improvised Piano." *Journal of Jazz Studies* 3, no. 2 (Spring 1976): 3–18.

Ogren, Kathy J. "Debating with Beethoven: Understanding the Fear of Early Jazz." In *America's Musical Pulse: Popular Music in Twentieth-Century Society*, edited by Kenneth J. Bindas, 249–56. Westport, CT: Praeger, 1992.

———. "Nightlife." In *Encyclopedia of American Social History*, vol. 3, edited by Mary Kupiec Cayton, Elliott J. Gorn, and Peter W. Williams. New York: Scribner, 1993.

Oliver, Paul. *Songsters and Saints*. New York: Cambridge University Press, 1984.

Olsen, Otto H., ed. *The Thin Disguise: Turning Points in Negro History; Plessy v. Ferguson, a Documentary Presentation, 1864–1896*. New York: Humanities, 1967.

O'Meally, Robert G. "Checking Our Balances: Louis Armstrong, Ralph Ellison, and Betty Boop." In *Uptown Conversation: The New Jazz Studies*, edited by Robert G. O'Meally, Brent Hayes Edwards, and Farah Jasmine Griffin, 278–96. New York: Columbia University Press, 2004.

Orsi, Robert A. "Parades, Holidays, and Public Rituals." In *Encyclopedia of American Social History*, vol. 3, edited by Mary Kupiec Cayton, Elliott J. Gorn, and Peter W. Williams. New York: Scribner, 1993.

Ostransky, Leroy. *The Anatomy of Jazz*. Seattle: University of Washington Press, 1960.

———. *Jazz City*. Englewood Cliffs, NJ: Prentice-Hall, 1978.

Palmer, Robert. *Deep Blues*. New York: Viking, 1981.

Panetta, Vincent J. "'For Godsake Stop!' Improvised Music in the Streets of New Orleans." *Musical Quarterly* 84, no. 1 (Spring 2000): 5–29.

Parenti, Tony, as told to Roy Morser. "Early Years in New Orleans." *The Second Line* 2, no. 9 (October 1951): 1, 6, 8, 14–15, 17; *The Second Line* 2, no. 10 (November 1951): 7, 9, 15; *The Second Line* 2, no. 11 (December 1951): 5, 7, 14–15, 17.

Pastras, Phil. *Dead Man Blues: Jelly Roll Morton Way Out West*. Berkeley: University of California Press, 2001.

Peretti, Burton W. *The Creation of Jazz*. Urbana: University of Illinois Press, 1992.

Piersen, William D. "African-American Festive Style." In *Signifyin(g), Sanctifyin', and Slam Dunking: A Reader in African American Expressive Culture*, edited by Gena Dagel Caponi, 417–33. Amherst: University of Massachusetts Press, 1999.

———. "A Resistance Too Civilized to Notice." In *Signifyin(g), Sanctifyin', and Slam Dunking: A Reader in African American Expressive Culture*, edited by Gena Dagel Caponi, 348–70. Amherst: University of Massachusetts Press, 1999.

Pitts, Walter F. *Old Ship of Zion: The Afro-Baptist Ritual in the African Diaspora*. New York: Oxford University Press, 1993.

Porter, Eric. *What Is This Thing Called Jazz? African American Musicians as Artists, Critics, and Activists*. Berkeley: University of California Press, 2002.

Pratt, Ray. *Rhythm and Resistance*. Washington, DC: Smithsonian Institution Press, 1990.

Provenzano, John A. "Jazz Music of the Gay '90s." *Jazz Record*, September 1945, 11, 16.

Public Dance Hall Commission. *Public Dance Halls Investigation and Ordinance*. Cleveland: Public Dance Hall Commission, 1911.

Radano, Ronald. *Lying Up a Nation: Race and Black Music*. Chicago: University of Chicago Press, 2003.

Raeburn, Bruce Boyd. "Confessions of a New Orleans Jazz Archivist." In *Reflections on American Music*, edited by James R. Heintze and Michael Saffle, 300–312. Hillsdale, New York: Pendragon, 2000.

———. "Early New Orleans Jazz in Theaters." *Louisiana History* 43 (Winter 2002): 41–52.

———. "Ethnic Diversity and New Orleans Jazz." Paper presented at the Popular Culture Association/American Culture Association Conference, New Orleans, April 18, 2003.

———. "Jazz and the Italian Connection." *Jazz Archivist* 6, no. 1 (May 1991): 1–6.

———. "King Oliver, Jelly Roll Morton, and Sidney Bechet: Ménage à Trois, New Orleans Style." In *The Oxford Companion to Jazz*, edited by Bill Kirchner, 88–101. New York: Oxford University Press, 2005.

———. "Louis and Women." *Gambit Weekly*, September 7, 2004. Available at www.bestofneworleans.com/dispatch/2004-09-07/news_feat.html.

———. "Stars of David and Sons of Sicily: Constellations beyond the Canon in Early New Orleans Jazz." Paper presented at Toronto 2000: Musical Intersections, Toronto, November 3, 2000.

———. "Submerging Ethnicity: Creole of Color Jazz Musicians of Italian Heritage." Paper presented at the Creole Studies Conference, New Orleans, October 23–25, 2003.

Ramsey, Frederic, Jr. "Vet Tells Story of the Original Creole Orchestra." *Down Beat*, December 5, 1940.

Ramsey, Frederic, Jr., and Charles Edward Smith, eds. *Jazzmen*. New York: Harcourt Brace, 1939.

Ramsey, Guthrie P., Jr. *Race Music: Black Cultures from Bebop to Hip-Hop*. Berkeley: University of California Press, 2003.

Rankin, David C. "The Forgotten People: Free People of Color in New Orleans, 1850–1870." PhD diss., Johns Hopkins University, 1976.

Reed, Teresa. *The Holy Profane: Religion in Black Popular Music*. Lexington: University Press of Kentucky, 2003.

Regis, Helen A. "Blackness and the Politics of Memory in the New Orleans Second Line." *American Ethnologist* 28, no. 4 (2001): 752–77.

———. "Second Lines, Minstrelsy, and the Contested Landscapes of New Orleans Afro-Creole Festivals." *Cultural Anthropology* 14, no. 4 (1999): 472–504.

Reich, Howard, and William Gaines. *Jelly's Blues: The Life, Music, and Redemption of Jelly Roll Morton*. New York: Da Capo, 2003.

Roach, Joseph. *Cities of the Dead: Circum-Atlantic Performance*. New York: Columbia University Press, 1996.

Roberts, John Storm. *Black Music of Two Worlds*. New York: Praeger, 1972.

———. *The Latin Tinge: The Influence of Latin American Music on the United States*. 2nd ed. New York: Oxford University Press, 1999.

Roberts, John W. *From Trickster to Badman: The Black Folk Hero in Slavery and Freedom*. Philadelphia: University of Pennsylvania Press, 1989.

Roediger, David R. *Colored White: Transcending the Racial Past.* Berkeley: University of California Press, 2002.

Romanowski, William D. *Pop Culture Wars: Religion and the Role of Entertainment in American Life.* Downers Grove, IL: InterVarsity Press, 1996.

Rorabaugh, W. J. "Alcohol and Alcoholism." In *Encyclopedia of American Social History*, vol. 3, edited by Mary Kupiec Cayton, Elliott J. Gorn, and Peter W. Williams, 2135–42. New York: Scribner, 1993.

Rose, Al. *I Remember Jazz.* Baton Rouge: Louisiana State University Press, 1987.

———. *Storyville, New Orleans.* University: University of Alabama Press, 1974.

Runyon, Randolph Paul. "Popular Music before 1950." In *Encyclopedia of American Social History*, vol. 3, edited by Mary Kupiec Cayton, Elliott J. Gorn, and Peter W. Williams, 1787–94. New York: Scribner, 1993.

Russell, Ross. *Jazz Styles in Kansas City and the Southwest.* Berkeley: University of California Press, 1971.

Russell, William (Bill). *New Orleans Style.* Edited by Barry Martyn and Mike Hazeldine. New Orleans: Jazzology, 1994.

———. *"Oh, Mister Jelly": A Jelly Roll Morton Scrapbook.* Copenhagen: JazzMedia ApS, 1999.

Russell, William, and Stephen W. Smith. "New Orleans Music." In *Jazzmen*, edited by Frederic Ramsey Jr. and Charles Edward Smith, 7–37. New York: Harcourt Brace, 1939.

Ryan, Mary P. *Civic Wars: Democracy and Public Life in the American City during the Nineteenth Century.* Berkeley: University of California Press, 1997.

Sancton, Tom. *Song for My Fathers: A New Orleans Story in Black and White.* New York: Other, 2006.

Sanders, Cheryl J. *Saints in Exile: The Holiness-Pentecostal Experience in African American Religion and Culture.* New York: Oxford University Press, 1996.

Saxon, Lyle, Edward Dreyer, and Robert Tallant. *Gumbo Ya-Ya: A Collection of Louisiana Folk Tales.* Gretna, LA: Pelican, 1991.

Scarpaci, Vincenza. "Walking the Color Line: Italian Immigrants in Louisiana, 1880–1910." In *Are Italians White?* edited by Jennifer Guglielmo and Salvatore Salerno, 60–76. New York: Routledge, 2005.

Schafer, William J., with Richard B. Allen. *Brass Bands and New Orleans Jazz.* Baton Rouge: Louisiana State University Press, 1977.

———. "Breaking into 'High Society': Musical Metamorphoses in Early Jazz." *Journal of Jazz Studies* 2, no. 2 (June 1975): 53–60.

Schafer, William J., and Johannes Riedl. *The Art of Ragtime: Form and Meaning of an Original Black American Art.* New York: Da Capo, 1977.

Schuller, Gunther. *Early Jazz: Its Roots and Musical Development.* New York: Oxford University Press, 1968.

Scruggs, Otey M. "Economic and Racial Components of Jim Crow." In *Key Issues in the Afro-American Experience*, vol. 2, edited by Nathan I. Huggins, Martin Kilson, and Daniel M. Fox, 70–87. New York: Harcourt Brace Jovanovich, 1971.

Sellman, James Clyde. "Louis Armstrong." In *Africana: The Encyclopedia of the African and African American Experience*, edited by Kwame Anthony Appiah and Henry Louis Gates Jr., 125–27. New York: Perseus-Civitas, 1999.

Senter, Caroline. "Creole Poets on the Verge of a Nation." In *Creole: The History and Legacy of Louisiana's Free People of Color*, edited by Sybil Kein, 276–94. Baton Rouge: Louisiana State University Press, 2000.

Shapiro, Nat, and Nat Hentoff, eds. *Hear Me Talkin' to Ya*. New York: Dover, 1955.

Smith, Charles Edward. "White New Orleans." In *Jazzmen*, edited by Frederic Ramsey Jr. and Charles Edward Smith, 39–58. New York: Harcourt Brace, 1939.

Sobel, Mechal. *Trabelin' On: The Slave Journey to an Afro-Baptist Faith*. Westport, CT: Greenwood, 1979.

Soderberg, Ronny. "All about Baby." *The Second Line* 2, no. 2 (February 1951): 7–8.

Sollors, Werner. "National Identity and Ethnic Diversity: 'Of Plymouth Rock and Jamestown and Ellis Island'; or Ethnic Literature and Some Redefinitions of 'America.'" In *History and Memory in African-American Culture*, edited by Geneviève Fabre and Robert O'Meally, 92–121. New York: Oxford University Press, 1994.

Somers, Dale A. "Black and White in New Orleans: A Study in Urban Race Relations, 1865–1900." *Journal of Southern History* 40, no. 1 (February 1974): 19–42.

———. *The Rise of Sports in New Orleans, 1850–1900*. Baton Rouge: Louisiana State University Press, 1972.

Sotiropoulos, Karen. *Staging Race: Black Performers in Turn of the Century America*. Cambridge, MA: Harvard University Press, 2006.

Souchon, Edmond. "King Oliver: A Very Personal Memoir." In *Reading Jazz*, edited by Robert Gottlieb, 339–46. New York: Pantheon, 1996.

Southern, Eileen. *The Music of Black Americans*. 2nd ed. New York: W. W. Norton, 1983.

———. *Readings in Black American Music*. 2nd ed. New York: W. W. Norton, 1983.

Spencer, John Michael. *Blues and Evil*. Knoxville: University of Tennessee Press, 1993.

Starr, Larry, and Christopher Waterman. *American Popular Music*. New York: Oxford University Press, 2003.

St. Cyr, Johnny. "Jazz as I Remember It: Part 1, Early Days." *Jazz Journal* 19, no. 9 (September 1966): 6–10.

———. "Jazz as I Remember It: Part 2, Storyville Days." *Jazz Journal* 19, no. 10 (October 1966): 22–24.

Stearns, Marshall W. *The Story of Jazz*. New York: Oxford University Press, 1956.

Stearns, Marshall W., and Jean Stearns. *Jazz Dance: The Story of American Vernacular Dance*. New York: Schirmer, 1964.

Stewart, Jack. "Cuban Influences on New Orleans Music." *Jazz Archivist* 13 (1998–99): 14–23.

_____. "The Original Dixieland Jazz Band's Place in the Development of Jazz." *Jazz Archivist* 6 (May 1991): 7–8.

_____. "The Strangest Bedfellows: Nick La Rocca and Jelly Roll Morton." *Jazz Archivist* 15 (2001): 23–31.

Stoddard, Tom. *Jazz on the Barbary Coast*. Berkeley, CA: Heyday, 1998.

Stokes, Martin. "Introduction: Ethnicity, Identity, and Music." In *Ethnicity, Identity, and Music*, edited by Martin Stokes. New York: Berg, 1994.

Stolorow, Robert D., and George E. Atwood. *Contexts of Being: The Intersubjective Foundations of Psychological Life*. Hillsdale, NJ: Analytic, 1992.

Stuckey, Sterling. *Slave Culture: Nationalist Theory and the Foundations of Black America*. New York: Oxford University Press, 1987.

Sudhalter, Richard M. *Lost Chords: White Musicians and Their Contribution to Jazz, 1915–1945*. New York: Oxford University Press, 1999.

Sumner, William Graham. *What Social Classes Owe to Each Other*. Caldwell, ID: Caxton, 1986.

Swanson, Betsy. "The History of Bucktown, U.S.A." www.stphilipneri.org/teacher/pontchartrain/content.php?type=1&id=437.

Synan, Vinson. *The Holiness-Pentecostal Tradition*. Grand Rapids, MI: Eerdmans, 1971.

Szwed, John. *Crossovers: Essays on Race, Music, and American Culture*. Philadelphia: University of Pennsylvania Press, 2005.

Szwed, John, with Roger D. Abrahams. "After the Myth: Studying Afro-American Cultural Patterns in the Plantation Literature." In John Szwed, *Crossovers: Essays on Race, Music, and American Culture*, 91–110. Philadelphia: University of Pennsylvania Press, 2005.

Szwed, John, and Morton Marks. "The Afro-American Transformation of European Set Dances and Dance Suites." *Dance Research Journal* 20, no. 1 (Summer 1988): 29–36.

Taylor, Jeff. "The Early Origins of Jazz." In *The Oxford Companion to Jazz*, edited by Bill Kirchner, 39–52. New York: Oxford University Press, 2005.

Thomas, Brook, ed. *Plessy v. Ferguson: A Brief History with Documents*. Boston: Bedford, 1997.

Thompson, Robert Farris. "An Aesthetic of the Cool." In *Signifyin(g), Sanctifyin', and Slam Dunking: A Reader in African American Expressive Culture*, edited by Gena Dagel Caponi, 72–86. Amherst: University of Massachusetts Press, 1999.

Thompson, Shirley E. "'Ah Toucoutou, ye conin vous': History and Memory in Creole New Orleans." *American Quarterly* 53, no. 2 (June 2001): 232–66.

_____. "The Passing of a People: Creoles of Color in Mid-Nineteenth Century New Orleans." PhD diss., Harvard University, 2001.

Titon, Jeff Todd. *Early Downhome Blues*. Urbana: University of Illinois Press, 1977.

Tomlinson, Gary. "Cultural Dialogics and Jazz: A White Historian Signifies." In *Disciplining Music: Musicology and Its Canons*, edited by Katherine Bergeron and Philip V. Bohlman. Chicago: University of Chicago Press, 1992.

Touchet, Leo, Vernel Bagneris, and Ellis L. Marsalis Jr. *Rejoice When You Die: New Orleans Jazz Funerals*. Baton Rouge: Louisiana State University Press, 1998.

Tregle, Joseph G., Jr. "Creoles and Americans." In *Creole New Orleans*, edited by Arnold R. Hirsch and Joseph Logsdon, 131–85. Baton Rouge: Louisiana State University Press, 1992.

Tucker, Sherrie. *Swing Shift: "All-Girl" Bands of the 1940s*. Durham, NC: Duke University Press, 2000.

Turner, Frederick. *Remembering Song: Encounters with the New Orleans Jazz Tradition*. New York: Viking, 1982.

Turner, Victor. *The Ritual Process*. New York: Aldine de Gruyter, 1969.

Unterbrink, Mary. *Jazz Women at the Keyboard*. Jefferson, NC: McFarland, 1983.

Van der Merwe, Peter. *Origins of the Popular Style: The Antecedents of Twentieth-Century Popular Music*. New York: Oxford University Press, 1989.

Veneciano, Jorge Daniel. "Louis Armstrong, Bricolage, and the Aesthetics of Swing." In *Uptown Conversation: The New Jazz Studies*, edited by Robert G. O'Meally, Brent Hayes Edwards, and Farah Jasmine Griffin, 256–77. New York: Columbia University Press, 2004.

Von Hornbostel, E. M. "African Negro Music." *Africa* 1, no. 1 (1928): 30–62.

Wagner, Ann. *Adversaries of Dance*. Urbana: University of Illinois Press, 1997.

Wald, Gayle. *Crossing the Line: Racial Passing in Twentieth-Century U.S. Literature and Culture*. Durham, NC: Duke University Press, 2000.

Walker, Daniel. "Cultures of Control/Cultures of Resistance: Slave Society in Nineteenth Century New Orleans and Havana." PhD diss., University of Houston, 2000.

———. *No More, No More: Slavery and Cultural Resistance in Havana and New Orleans*. Minneapolis: University of Minnesota, 2004.

Walker, Wyatt T. *"Somebody's Calling My Name": Black Sacred Music and Social Change*. Valley Forge, PA: Judson, 1979.

Walser, Robert. "'Out of Notes': Signification, Interpretation, and the Problem of Miles Davis." In *Jazz among the Discourses*, edited by Krin Gabbard, 165–88. Durham, NC: Duke University Press, 1995.

Wang, Richard. "Researching the New Orleans–Chicago Jazz Connection: Tools and Methods." *Black Music Research Journal* 8, no. 1 (1988): 101–12.

Ward, Alan, with Richard B. Allen. "Hot Tuxedos: The Story of Oscar Celestin." *Footnote* 18, no. 5 (June/July 1987).

Ward, Geoffrey C., and Ken Burns. *Jazz: A History of America's Music*. New York: Alfred A. Knopf, 2000.

Waterman, Richard Alan. "African Influence on the Music of the Americas." In *Mother Wit from the Laughing Barrel*, edited by Alan Dundes, 81–94. Jackson: University Press of Mississippi, 1990.

Whalum, Wendell P. "Black Hymnody." In *Readings in African American Church Music and Worship*, edited by James Abbington, 167–84. Chicago: GIA, 2001.

White, Shane, and Graham White. "Listening to Southern Slavery." In *Hearing History: A Reader*, edited by Mark M. Smith, 247–66. Athens: University of Georgia Press, 2004.

_____. *The Sounds of Slavery: Discovering African American History through Songs, Sermons, and Speech*. Boston: Beacon, 2005.

_____. *Stylin': African American Expressive Culture from Its Beginnings to the Zoot Suit*. Ithaca, NY: Cornell University Press, 1998.

Wilgus, D. K. "The Negro-White Spiritual." In *Mother Wit from the Laughing Barrel*, edited by Alan Dundes, 67–80. Jackson: University Press of Mississippi, 1990.

Wilkinson, Christopher. *Jazz on the Road: Don Albert's Musical Life*. Berkeley: University of California Press, 2001.

Williams, Martin. *Jazz Masters of New Orleans*. New York: Da Capo, 1978.

Williams, Raymond. *Marxism and Literature*. New York: Oxford University Press, 1977.

Williamson, Joel. *New People: Miscegenation and Mulattoes in the United States*. New York: Free Press, 1980.

Wilson, Olly. "Black Music as an Art Form." *Black Music Research Journal* 3 (1983): 1–22.

_____. "The Heterogeneous Sound Ideal in African-American Music." In *Signifyin(g), Sanctifyin', and Slam Dunking*, edited by Gena Dagel Caponi, 157–71. Amherst: University of Massachusetts Press, 1999.

_____. "The Significance of the Relationship between Afro-American Music and West African Music." *Black Perspective in Music* 2, no. 1 (Spring 1974): 3–11.

Winston, Donald E. "News Reporting of Jazz Music from 1890–1927." MA thesis, University of Oklahoma, 1966.

Wonk, Dalt. "Sons of Contessa Entellina." *Dixie Newspaper New Orleans*, 1983. Available at http://members.tripod.com/womanola/articles.html.

Woodward, C. Vann. "The Case of the Louisiana Traveler." In *Quarrels That Have Shaped the Constitution*, rev. and exp. ed., edited by John A. Garraty. New York: Harper and Row, 1967.

_____. *The Strange Career of Jim Crow*. 2nd rev. ed. New York: Oxford University Press, 1966.

Wright, Richard. *Black Boy*. New York: Harper and Row, 1966.

Discography and Videography

Armstrong, Louis

"After You've Gone" (vocal take). November 26, 1929. *Louis Armstrong*, vol. 5, *Louis in New York*. CBS CD 466965 2.

"Cornet Chop Suey." February 22, 1926. *Louis Armstrong V.S.O.P.*, vols. 1/2. CBS 88001.

"I'll Be Glad When You're Dead, You Rascal You." April 28, 1931. *Louis Armstrong*, vol. 7, *You're Drivin' Me Crazy*. Columbia CD CK 48828.

"Just a Gigolo." March 9, 1931. *Louis Armstrong*, vol. 7, *You're Drivin' Me Crazy*. Columbia CD CK 48828.

"Little Joe." April 28, 1931. *Louis Armstrong*, vol. 7, *You're Drivin' Me Crazy*. Columbia CD CK 48828.

Louis Armstrong and His Orchestra, 1942–1965. Video (VHS). JCVC 102. Rahway, NJ: Jazz Classics, 1986.

"Potato Head Blues." May 11, 1927. *Louis Armstrong V.S.O.P.*, vols. 1/2. CBS 88001.

"(What Did I Do to Be So) Black and Blue." July 22, 1929. *Louis Armstrong*, vol. 5, *Louis in New York*. CBS CD 466965 2.

"When You're Smiling" (vocal take). September 11, 1929. *Louis Armstrong*, vol. 5, *Louis in New York*. CBS CD 466965 2.

"You're Drivin' Me Crazy." December 23, 1930. *Louis Armstrong*, vol. 7, *You're Drivin' Me Crazy*. Columbia CD CK 48828.

"You're Next." February 22, 1926. *Louis Armstrong V.S.O.P.*, vols. 1/2. CBS 88001.

Brown, Joe Washington, and Austin Coleman

"Run Old Jeremiah." 1934. *Afro-American Spirituals, Work Songs, and Ballads.* Library of Congress Archive of Folk Song, AFS L3. (Included with White and White, *Sounds of Slavery*.)

Brunies, Albert, and His Orchestra

"Maple Leaf Rag." September 25, 1925. *New Orleans in New Orleans.* Jazz Archives CD 68, 157992.

Davis, Miles, Featuring Sonny Rollins

"Bluing." 1951. *Dig.* Prestige OJCCD-005-2.

Dodds, Baby

"Maryland, My Maryland." August 3, 1944. *Baby Dodds.* American Music AMCD-17.
"Talking: Brass Bands." May 1945. *Baby Dodds.* American Music AMCD-17.
"Tiger Rag." July 31, 1944. *Baby Dodds.* American Music AMCD-17.

Morton, Ferdinand "Jelly Roll"

"Aaron Harris Blues." 1938. *The Complete Library of Congress Recordings.* Rounder CD 1888.
"Dead Man Blues." September 21, 1926. *The Jelly Roll Morton Centennial: His Complete Victor Recordings.* RCA/Bluebird/BMG 2361-2-RB.
"Make Me a Pallet on the Floor." 1938. *The Complete Library of Congress Recordings.* Rounder CD 1888.
"Maple Leaf Rag." 1938. *The Complete Library of Congress Recordings.* Rounder CD 1888.
"Miserere." 1938. *The Complete Library of Congress Recordings.* Rounder CD 1888.
"The Murder Ballad." 1938. *The Complete Library of Congress Recordings.* Rounder CD 1888.
"New Orleans Blues." 1938. *The Complete Library of Congress Recordings.* Rounder CD 1888.
"[The] Stars and Stripes Forever." 1938. *The Complete Library of Congress Recordings.* Rounder CD 1888.
"Winin' Boy Blues." 1938. *The Complete Library of Congress Recordings.* Rounder CD 1888.

Oliver, Joseph "King"

"High Society Rag." June 22, 1923. *King Oliver 1923-1930.* CDS/Louisiana Red Hot Records RP2CD 607.

Original Dixieland Jazz Band

"Bluin' the Blues." December 30, 1920. *The 75th Anniversary*. Bluebird CD 61098-2.
"Tiger Rag." March 25, 1918. *The 75th Anniversary*. Bluebird CD 61098-2.

United States Marine Band

"Maple Leaf Rag." 1906. *The Bicentennial Collection: Celebrating the 200th Anniversary of "The President's Own" United States Marine Band*. United States Marine Band.

Various Artists

Make a Joyful Noise. 1978. New World Records 80255-2.
Ragtime to Jazz 1, 1912–1919. 1997. Timeless Records CBC 1-035 Jazz.

Williams, Henry

"What a Friend We Have in Jesus." 1939. *Peter Was a Fisherman: The 1939 Field Recordings of Melville and Frances Herskovits*, vol. 1. Rounder CD 1114.

Index